# BATTLE OF INK AND ICE

# BATTLE *of* INK *and* ICE

## A Sensational Story of News Barons, North Pole Explorers, and the Making of Modern Media

### DARRELL HARTMAN

VIKING

*To Dana*

It made them great! By heavens! it made them heroic; and it made them pathetic, too . . .

JOSEPH CONRAD, *LORD JIM*

# CONTENTS

PROLOGUE THE GREAT GOAL | 1

PART ONE ADVENTURES IN JOURNALISM | 9

PART TWO BONES IN THE WHITE NORTH | 45

PART THREE FIT TO PRINT | 115

PART FOUR ANTIHEROES | 217

PART FIVE YEARNING TO BELIEVE | 307

EPILOGUE NEWSPAPER OF RECORD | 325

ACKNOWLEDGMENTS | 329

A NOTE ON SOURCES | 333

BIBLIOGRAPHY | 359

IMAGE CREDITS | 369

INDEX | 371

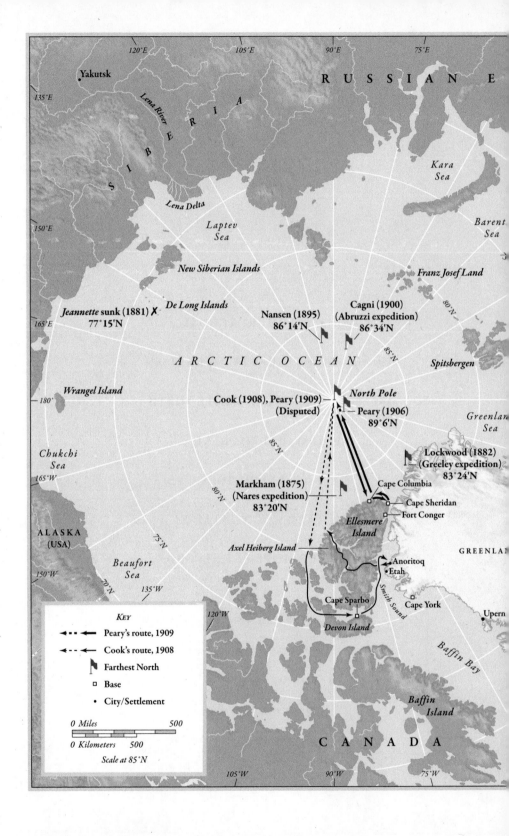

120°E · 105°E · 90°E · 75°E

135°E

Yakutsk

*Lena River*

S I B E R I A

R U S S I A N   E

*Kara*
*Sea*

150°E

*Lena Delta*

*Laptev*
*Sea*

*Barent*
*Sea*

*New Siberian Islands*

*Franz Josef Land*

*De Long Islands*

**Jeannette** sunk (1881) ✕
77°15'N

165°E

**Nansen (1895)**
**86°14'N**

**Cagni (1900)**
**(Abruzzi expedition)**
**86°34'N**

80°N

A R C T I C   O C E A N

*Spitsbergen*

85°N

**Cook (1908), Peary (1909)**
**(Disputed)**

*North Pole*

**Peary (1906)**
**89°6'N**

*Greenlan*
*Sea*

180°

*Wrangel Island*

85°N

**Lockwood (1882)**
**(Greeley expedition)**
**83°24'N**

*Chukchi*
*Sea*

165°W

80°N

**Markham (1875)**
**(Nares expedition)**
**83°20'N**

Cape Columbia

□ Cape Sheridan
□—Fort Conger

*Ellesmere*
*Island*

A L A S K A
(USA)

75°N

*Beaufort*
*Sea*

*Axel Heiberg Island*

GREENLAN

GREENLAN

150°W

70°N

135°W

120°W

Anoritoq
• Etah

Cape York

*Smith Sound*

Upern

**KEY**

◄ - - - ◄——— Peary's route, 1909

◄ - - - - - Cook's route, 1908

⚑ Farthest North

□ Base

• City/Settlement

Cape Sparbo □

*Devon Island*

*Baffin Bay*

*Baffin*
*Island*

0 Miles · 500

0 Kilometers · 500

*Scale at 85°N*

105°W · 90°W · 75°W

C A N A D A

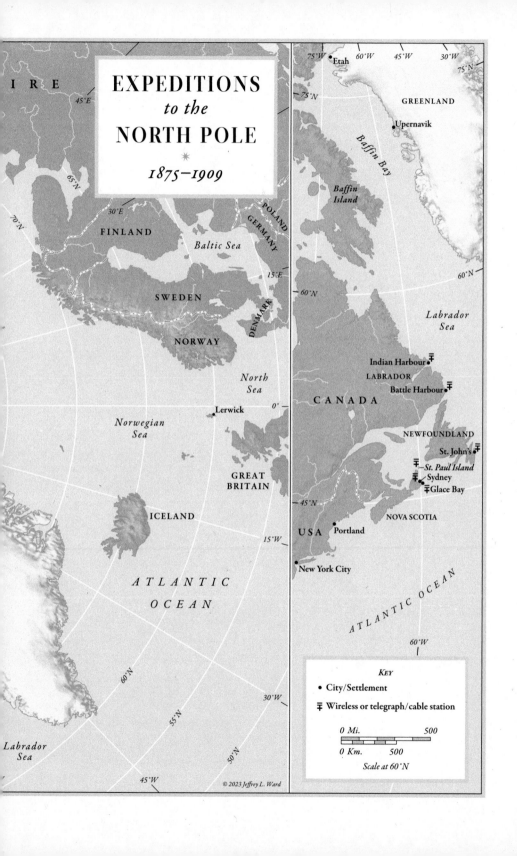

# EXPEDITIONS
## *to the*
# NORTH POLE

*1875–1909*

**KEY**

• City/Settlement

⟂ Wireless or telegraph/cable station

| 0 Mi. | 500 |
| 0 Km. | 500 |

*Scale at 60°N*

© 2023 Jeffrey L. Ward

# PROLOGUE

## *The Great Goal*

The steamer *Hans Egede* lay at anchor in Lerwick, the windblown capital of Scotland's Shetland Islands. Two men, a Danish mate and an American explorer, Frederick Cook, rowed ashore in a dinghy that morning and proceeded on foot through the town's jumble of narrow streets to the cable station, where Cook asked the operator to transmit several messages. The first was to his wife, Marie, in New York, his first direct communication with her in two years, confirming that he was alive and well. The second was to the International Polar Commission, in Brussels, and it contained the same startling announcement as the next message, which Cook cabled to James Gordon Bennett Jr., the Paris-based publisher of the powerful *New York Herald*:

REACHED NORTH POLE APRIL 21, 1908. DISCOVERED
LAND FAR NORTH. HAVE LEFT SEALED EXCLUSIVE
CABLE OF TWO THOUSAND WORDS FOR YOU WITH
DANISH CONSUL AT LERWICK FOR WHICH I EXPECT
THREE THOUSAND DOLLARS. I GO STEAMER HANS
EGEDE TO COPENHAGEN.

News of Cook's discovery had already traveled by word of mouth along the thinly populated coast of Greenland. The handful of missionaries, colonial officials, and others aboard the *Hans Egede*—which Cook, with no other way of getting back to America, had boarded at the insistence of his Danish hosts—had heard it, too. One of the ship's passengers, the inspector of North Greenland, had advised the explorer to publish his own account before speaking to the press, in order to avoid confusion. This had been the reason for the unscheduled stop at Lerwick.

James Gordon Bennett of the *Herald* wasted no time responding to the offer: "Cable Dr. Cooks 2000 words immediately."

The words raced along undersea cables and overland telegraph wires as the *Hans Egede* chugged south. Rough seas slowed the steamer down, and it was more than two days before Cook reached Skagen, at the northern edge of Denmark, where the commander of a Danish torpedo boat stationed there greeted the explorer on behalf of his government. A group of shivering Danish journalists came aboard as well and informed Cook that his account had been printed in the *Herald*. Denmark's major daily, the *Politiken*, had splashed the news of his discovery on its front page, they told him, and newspapers around the world had scrambled to do the same.

None, however, had celebrated quite as lustily as the *Herald*, which had devoted several pages to Cook's feat on September 2. Seven-column headlines screamed as though from a mountaintop: FIGHTING FAMINE AND ICE, THE COURAGEOUS EXPLORER REACHES THE GREAT GOAL. Geographers interviewed by the *Herald* predicted that the discovery would "mark an epoch in the history of the scientific world." The main feature, of course, was Cook's account itself, which told of his midwinter departure from the Greenland coast, some seven hundred miles from the North Pole, and narrated how he had traveled from terra firma onto the shifting sea ice, "beyond the range of all life," accompanied by two Inuit companions and two dozen hardy sled dogs. The route became smoother as the party advanced north, Cook wrote, and yet their swift progress brought little joy. "There was a depressing monotony of scene, and life had no pleasures, no spiritual recreation, nothing to relieve the steady physical drag and chronic fatigue."

Two months after leaving Greenland, and nine months after he'd departed from the United States, Cook wrote, his sextant readings showed the small party to be near its goal and then at it—that ultimate point where the world's meridians come together, there is nowhere farther north to go, and every time zone is a step away. According to Cook, his celebrations at the top of the world did not last long. He remained at the North Pole some thirty-six hours, dutifully recording astronomical observations and other details of his surroundings. A long, dangerous journey over crumbling ice lay ahead, and the place itself did not encourage lingering. "What a cheerless spot," he wrote in the *Herald*, "to have aroused the ambition of men for so many ages!"

AMBITIOUS MEN HAD INDEED VENTURED TO THE FAR NORTH FOR CENTURIES, pushing the limits of survival in a frozen world that was, both physically and conceptually, as distant from the place of human origins as could be imagined. Many of these explorers went there in search of the Northwest Passage, and with it a shorter trading route between Europe and Asia. This fruitless quest claimed hundreds if not thousands of human lives. The British Royal Navy's fantastically well-equipped 1845 Franklin expedition, whose 129 members all died in the High Arctic, was only the most notorious example.

By the end of the nineteenth century, the North Pole had replaced the Northwest Passage as the holy grail of Arctic exploring. Another important change had taken place as well: a certain realism had set in. Victorian explorers had dreamed of discovering something spectacular at the top of the world; now it was generally agreed that they would find nothing there but more drifting sea ice. The U.S. government had long ago stopped devoting blood and treasure to the so-called Arctic problem. The field had been ceded to entrepreneur-explorers like Frederick Cook and the private societies and wealthy individuals who backed them.

Even if some of the romance had gone out of it, exploring the Arctic was still rewarding. Discovering new territories and geographical features brought wealth and adulation, as did getting closer to the pole than anyone had before. Some explorers truly yearned to be in the Far North, and feats like these made it easier for them to raise the money to go back. The cooperation of the daily press was indispensable to the partly heroic, partly self-serving exploring enterprise. Newspapers were likelier than book publishers or magazines to pay for exclusive rights to a story in advance, and in an age before radio or television they were also the means by which an explorer's deeds were first conveyed to the public. Without the daily press, average Americans had no timely way of knowing what explorers were doing way up north, or what their so-called accomplishments really meant. What many readers urgently wanted to know was very simple: Was the expedition a failure or a triumph?

The press, for its part, had nearly as much to gain from these real-life Arctic dramas as explorers did. It was profitable to break big news of any kind, including news of geographical discovery. Newspapers were booming everywhere, and so was the competition for readers and all-important advertisers. Nowhere was this more the case than in New York, which was by 1909 the second-largest metropolis in the world after London and awash in newspapers. The owner-publishers of the city's biggest dailies pulled heavy strings and lived in royal splendor. They were ambassadors and kingmakers. William Randolph Hearst used his newspaper empire to upend national politics; Joseph Pulitzer's *World* had changed the way the American public thought and read. Bennett, the Paris-based owner and publisher of the *Herald*, was often called the most influential American abroad, and although his paper was not the force it had been a generation earlier, it still reached hundreds of thousands every day and pulled in a staggering $500,000 a year.

There was also *The New York Times*, whose performance over the previous decade had been most remarkable of all.

Its publisher, a comparatively unknown southerner named Adolph Ochs, had come to New York City in 1896, borrowed and sweet-talked his way into provisional ownership of the failing *Times*, and improbably rebuilt it into a force to be reckoned with. Hearst's and Pulitzer's sensational "yellow journals" had been considered the future of journalism at the time, but by turning the *Times* into a profitable paragon of respectability,

Ochs had proven the doubters wrong. Though the paper had flourished quietly under him at first, its growing readership and influence could no longer be ignored—especially not by the *Herald*. The famous rivalry between Pulitzer and Hearst, which had cooled by 1909, is one of the most discussed episodes in the history of journalism. But Ochs and Bennett's overlooked battle for New York City's "quality" readership would also have important consequences. That contest was well under way by 1909, especially when it came to areas of special interest for the city's educated middle- and upper-middle-class readers. Each paper saw the other as its chief rival in foreign news, science, technology—including the emerging fields of aviation and automobiles—and exploration.

The *Herald* had excelled at covering these topics for decades, and its exploration exploits were the stuff of newsroom legend. Bennett had famously sent the correspondent Henry Morton Stanley to Africa in 1871 in search of David Livingstone, a landmark moment in the history of journalism. He had also sponsored or cosponsored a handful of other major exploring ventures, including earlier efforts to reach the Northwest Passage and the North Pole. Though Bennett had scaled down the paper's involvement in exploring by the early twentieth century, the *Herald* continued to prioritize polar matters and had published exclusive accounts by both Cook and his better-known rival, Robert Peary.

The *Times* had dared to challenge this imposing legacy only recently, by investing in Peary's latest North Pole expedition. Peary was a navy engineer and veteran Arctic explorer with several important geographical discoveries to his name. He had secured financial backing from some of New York City's richest men and the priceless endorsement of President Theodore Roosevelt. He'd recorded a journey to within 203 statute miles, or 32 latitude minutes, of the North Pole in 1906, wresting the international "Farthest North" from the previous, Italian record holders. Despite his advancing age—he was fifty-two when his expedition sailed from New York on July 7, 1908—Peary was still considered America's best hope for attaining the pole. Whether he succeeded or failed, he was contractually obligated to give the *Times* the story of his attempt. When Cook's telegram arrived from Lerwick, Peary had not been heard from in almost a year, and no one within reach of a telegraph station knew whether he had reached the pole, and if so, when. He was presumed to be on his way back from Greenland but had not yet been heard from. Within the week, he would be.

Cook's situation was far different from Peary's. Though admired by most of his fellow explorers, he lacked the older navy man's financial and political connections. He had left a year earlier than Peary, with limited equipment and zero fanfare, and his failure to send news for nearly two years had led friends and family to worry that he had died in the Arctic. Cook's cables from Lerwick had taken the world by surprise, with veteran explorers hailing his low-profile, low-budget expedition as an "extraordinary feat" and a "miracle." The story he told was a scoop of generational significance, and the *Herald* let everyone know that it was its property. The paper boasted in all capitals of its "EXCLUSIVE ACCOUNT" and threatened to prosecute any publisher that violated its copyright, noting that "strenuous efforts" had already been made to do just that.

But other newspapers would do worse to Cook's account than steal it. They would contest the supposedly straightforward tale of his Arctic journey, generating nearly four straight months of headlines about the so-called North Pole Controversy. The journalist Lincoln Steffens later called it the "story of the century." The argument over the American discovery of the North Pole did, in fact, rage throughout most of the twentieth century and remains on a low simmer today. The newspapers that fueled this argument often obscured as much as they clarified, and in doing so revealed a lot about themselves—especially the *Times* and the *Herald*, which stood to win or lose the most from the debate. That debate and its aftermath would do more to reshuffle the hierarchy of American corporate media than is generally appreciated. Complicating the matter further, the presumed end of the argument in December 1909 was, in hindsight, only the latest plot twist. The story was in fact still riddled with unexposed lies and half-truths that it would take decades to untangle.

Cook was on his way to Copenhagen when the *Herald* broke his story on September 2, 1909. That preliminary telling had only whetted the public's appetite for more. The Danes who boarded the *Hans Egede* at Skagen told Cook that "Fleet Street"—London's newspaper district—"had moved to Copenhagen," he later recalled, and that reporters there were clamoring to interview him. Amid the heap of terse cablegrams awaiting Cook was an expensively verbose one from Bennett. "I never paid three thousand dollars more cheerfully than for the splendid dispatch which told of your triumph," the *Herald* owner purred. He requested photographs and a "full detailed story" of Cook's journey for the *Herald* and asked the explorer to name his price. The publisher was on familiar ground here. If any newspaperman knew how to get the most out of an exploration scoop, it was James Gordon Bennett.

# PART ONE

# ADVENTURES IN JOURNALISM

# CHAPTER ONE

James Gordon Bennett Jr. came into the world on May 10, 1841. Before he'd even learned to walk, the New York *Sun* was insinuating that he was a bastard child. Given the recent reports of his mother's flirting at an upscale beach resort, the paper speculated, it certainly was possible. Bennett's father responded to this insult by successfully suing *The Sun* for libel. The fine was a paltry $250.

James Gordon Bennett Sr. was accustomed to clashes like this one. During this bare-knuckled era of the New York City press, he was the most hated publisher in town. But his rabble-rousing *New York Herald* was the most popular daily sheet in the city if not the nation. Bennett, a Scottish immigrant, had launched it in 1835, after years of ink-stained toiling for other publishers. His first week in business, he published a stock report based on simple inquiries he'd made a few blocks away on Wall Street. The resulting "money article" was the first feature of its kind, and also novel for the fact that Bennett had no ulterior motive for printing it. He held no stocks, owed no favors, and refused to let entanglements of any kind derail his agenda. He was proudly, thornily independent, and while other sheets relied on the backing of political or business cronies and edited themselves accordingly, Bennett set out to be the first modern publisher to live or die by his readers. His big idea was to give the public what it craved, achieve unprecedented circulation, and ride the resulting profits beyond the grasp of powerful merchants and politicians. It seems like a conventional business plan now, but it was a radical departure from the norm back then, and Bennett's fierce adherence to it made him an object of almost universal scorn among elite New Yorkers.

Unfortunately for them, elite scorn only seemed to energize him. The original *Herald* office was a downtown cellar, Bennett's desk a piece of board laid across upright flour barrels. Bennett did all the work himself at first—the reporting, the bookkeeping, even the deliveries—and his iconoclastic daily sheet sold immediately. He railed against the "Wall Street Holy Alliance," earning battalions of new readers (and enemies) when he ventured to publish lists of recent bankruptcies. He invented the society column, which he used to mock fancy soirees to which he had not been invited. He made mincemeat of polite social conventions like the Victorian taboo against referring to female undergarments by name: "Petticoats—petticoats—petticoats—there, you fastidious fools, vent your mawkishness on that!" Uncowed by organized religion, Bennett insulted Protestants and Catholics alike, describing the pope as "a decrepit, licentious, stupid, Italian blockhead." But his unsparing opinions could also be more perceptive and precise than that. "The whole of his power as a writer," an editor who later worked for him reflected, "consists in his detection of the evil in things that are good, and of the falsehood in things that are true, and of the ridiculous in things that are important."

Editorially, Bennett kept the *Herald* grounded in the imperfect here and now. "I never wish to be a day in advance of the people," he declared. While Horace Greeley's *New-York Tribune* campaigned for temperance, women's rights, labor unions, utopian communities, vegetarianism, and abolition, Bennett dismissed its progressive notions as elitist claptrap, and Greeley himself as a "miserable dried vegetable." Personal attacks on rival editors were very much in demand and a common feature of the era's penny papers. Bennett, a master of this form of combat, sometimes got as well as he gave, especially from *The Sun*, which stated that his "only chance of dying an upright man will be that of hanging perpendicularly upon a rope." When verbal assaults weren't enough, Bennett's enemies resorted to beating him up in broad daylight. He always got the last word, by sardonically writing up each thrashing in the next day's paper.

Bennett's trollish antics attracted attention, but his innovations in the gathering and presentation of news had much greater lasting value. Though he was hardly the first publisher to be drawn to tales of sex and violence, he used new methods to pursue them. His sensational treatment of one of the most notorious news stories of the decade, the ax murder of a fashionable young prostitute named Helen Jewett, produced what is widely considered the first interview published in an American newspaper. Once he could afford it, Bennett hired reporters to do more of the legwork for him, and he sent them places other publishers didn't: to churches, where they recorded Sunday sermons; to steamship landings, where they interrogated returning travelers. Bennett hired a handful of foreign correspondents while in London for the coronation of Queen Victoria in 1838, making the *Herald* the first American newspaper to employ a European press corps. Its foreign news was in a league of its own after this, and even more so once Bennett began chartering pilot boats so that his reporters could intercept arriving ships in New York Harbor. *Herald* newsmen jumped aboard steamers while they were in quarantine, and the resulting stories appeared before passengers had even disembarked. As Greeley would later say of Bennett, "He was the first journalist who went to meet the news halfway."

Bennett sped up the delivery of news on land as well. When Cunard launched the first regular transatlantic steamship service in 1840, between Liverpool and Boston, he arranged for a special train so that his correspondents' letters could get to him faster. The rail network now linking northeastern cities created distribution opportunities, and he began putting stacks of the *Herald* on the early trains so that customers in Albany and Philadelphia could read it over breakfast.

While rival publishers had families and other interests, Bennett's life was the *Herald*. He worked sixteen-hour days and never drank excessively, smoked, or gambled. He attributed the success of the *Herald* to his avoidance of these vices, which left him more time and energy for his paper. A provocateur on the page, Bennett was sober and restrained in person and rarely kept female company. His looks were not his forte. He was tall and spindly, with a lazy eye; one of his many well-bred detractors, Philip Hone, privately described him as "an ill-looking, squinting man," and Bennett himself was under no illusions that he was handsome or charming. He practically boasted that the one and only time he'd tried to patronize a brothel, the working girls had been so put off by him that they'd thrown him out.

Bennett did finally fall in love, though, in 1840. He shared a description of his paramour with fifteen thousand *Herald* readers: "Her figure is most magnificent—her head, neck and bust, of the purest classical contour. There [is] a quiet and finish in her sweet looks, her graceful movements, which we have never seen surpassed in London, Paris or Washington." The apple of his eye—and the future mother of James Gordon Bennett Jr.— was a young music teacher from Dublin named Henrietta Crean. Three months later, Bennett Sr. cheekily announced their engagement in the *Herald*: NEW MOVEMENT IN CIVILIZATION.

His enemies set out to ruin their romance. Honeymooning that summer, the newlyweds were snubbed and harassed at the fashionable upstate resorts of Niagara and Saratoga, and the Manhattan hotel where they had secured a romantic suite was pressured (unsuccessfully) to cancel their booking. Rival publishers had closed ranks against Bennett by this point, refusing to do business with newsdealers who sold the *Herald* and theater managers who advertised in it, and reformist campaigners had persuaded clubs and libraries to stop carrying it. Luckily for Bennett, enough people stood by the *Herald* for the paper to survive this coordinated suppression effort.

Confident about the future of the *Herald*, Bennett expanded it to six columns and installed a new and improved printing press. He cemented his advantages in other ways, too, adding reporters, a business manager, and the profession's first circulation manager. The *Herald* further entrenched itself in the national scene, producing scoops at key junctures of the Mexican-American War and the California gold rush. News of such events traveled much faster after the telegraph system was established in 1844. Noting that it "totally annihilated what there was left" of the old geographical limits on news gathering, Bennett committed more fully to the new technology than his competitors. His primary rival, *The Sun*, still occasionally used carrier pigeons.

The *Herald* did its part to shrink the rest of the world as well. It was the favored American paper abroad and the only one available (even if many days behind) in major European and Latin American cities. By the late 1840s, the antagonism between Bennett and the rest of the New York press had cooled enough for the *Herald* to join a consortium of six city dailies, including *The Sun* and the *Tribune*, in securing lower telegraph rates for its members. The same group shared the cost of a steam-powered press boat, somewhat leveling the playing field in the ongoing race for ships' news. Out of this loose alliance emerged the Associated Press, which in its early incarnation gave the New York City dailies even more of an advantage in the gathering of foreign news.

Though Bennett had scaled back the more gratuitous provocations of his bachelor days, his slashing pen still occasionally drove men to violence. One autumn Saturday morning in 1850, a group of roustabouts accosted him on lower Broadway and assaulted him in full view of a horrified Henrietta Bennett and two indifferent police officers. The ringleader of this "gang of rowdies and ruffians," Bennett informed readers the next morning, was a Tammany Hall candidate for district attorney whose campaign the *Herald* had helped sink. Bennett predicted the attack would "become the subject of criminal investigation"—perhaps, he taunted, the first to be taken up by the prosecutor he'd just helped to elect. But while Bennett pined for justice, his wife yearned for escape. The life of an embattled social pariah was not for her. The Bennetts had two children of schooling age now, Jamie and Jeannette. Shortly after this latest beating, she moved with both of them to Europe.

# CHAPTER TWO

The Bennetts did not divorce; they just agreed to live apart, which enabled Henrietta to enjoy first-class life abroad. She toured France, Italy, Switzerland, and England with the children and visited her extended family in Ireland. The education of her son she outsourced to a string of private tutors, none of whom managed to instill any discipline. When not traveling with his mother and sister, young Jamie Bennett lived in a well-staffed house in Paris. His favorite pastime was playing with toy yachts in the Tuileries garden ponds.

As an adolescent, Jamie started spending part of the year in New York, where his father tried to interest him in the *Herald*. Bennett had referred to his son as *le jeune rédacteur*, "the young editor," since he was a toddler, and he now had a desk installed for him next to his own. More often than not, the desk sat empty. "Young Bennett," as the *Herald* staff took to calling him, was too busy introducing himself to New York society. As an only son, he could be expected to inherit Bennett Sr.'s huge fortune. Hostesses thus took an interest in him, despite his father's dubious social standing and his own tendency to raise absolute hell when drunk.

Young Bennett was more interested in having fun than in newspapering. Later, he would be credited for introducing America to polo and lacrosse and for helping to make the sport of shooting fashionable. Already as a teenager, though, he had a commanding—if reckless—way with horses and sailboats. He became, at sixteen, the youngest member ever admitted to the hyperexclusive New York Yacht Club. It was around this time, in 1858, that Jamie Bennett's audacity earned him his first taste of adverse publicity. His father's seventy-seven-ton sloop, *Rebecca*, won a race around Long Island, only to have it emerge that the skipper had taken an illegal shortcut. The *Rebecca* was promptly stripped of victory honors, a turn of events that a newer addition to the ranks of *Herald* antagonists, the seven-year-old *New-York Times*, decided to have some fun with:

> If our neighbor is going into sports of this kind he must learn to play fair. It is very difficult, we know, to teach an old dog new tricks; but BENNETT must make the effort if he expects to sail his yacht. Get up another race, old fellow,—and be honest, if possible. . . . The essence of all sporting is straightforward and honorable dealing. Men who cheat in the sports of gentlemen are ruled out. Poor BENNETT must look out for himself or he will be chucked overboard.

But the "old dog" had not even been on board. It was young Bennett who had ordered the change of course, a risky maneuver through a rough patch of water called Plum Gut. He had neglected to read the race rules, even though they had been published beforehand—in the *Herald*, no less. Bennett Sr. was not pleased. Nor did his son soon live down the incident. It earned him the mocking nickname Plum Gut Bennett.

BENNETT JR. MOVED TO NEW YORK SEMIPERMANENTLY AROUND 1860, after attending the elite École Polytechnique in Paris. His native country was coming apart at the seams, and his father was toeing his most dangerous line to date. As the abolition and secession movements gained steam, Bennett Sr. continued to pen fiery editorials in defense of the slaveholding South. Few people acquainted with the goading *Herald* owner could have claimed to be surprised. He had for years resorted to racial slurs to insult his rivals and referred disparagingly to the *Times* as "a daily abolition journal." But now his contrarianism was starting to look uncomfortably like treason. One day, a package from an anonymous sender arrived at the *Herald* offices, tied with green ribbon and labeled "For Mr. Bennett Only." Miraculously, a sticky lid prevented the black-powder bomb inside from blowing up in his face. Tellingly, Bennett chose not to make a news story of this incident. But it was not until the first shots of the Civil War were fired at Fort Sumter, South Carolina, bringing an angry mob of New Yorkers down on the *Herald* building, that he finally toned down his rhetoric. Fearing for his life, Bennett hastily hung an American flag out the window. From that day until the war's end, he kept a battery of rifles stored behind the wood paneling of his office—and a gag on excessively inflammatory editorials.

With war declared, Jamie offered up his new two-masted yacht, the *Henrietta*, to the Union cause. For better or worse, his father arranged for the schooner to come with its nineteen-year-old owner attached, and Jamie was present for the uncontested seizure of several Florida forts and cities. One night, a curious thing happened. Outside Port Royal, South Carolina, he nodded off while on watch and was awakened by a hooting owl just in time to prevent the *Henrietta* from running aground. The incident sparked a lifelong obsession with owls. The silver-spoon volunteer was soon sent back to New York by his commanding officer, and the elegant *Henrietta* was consigned to packet service.

Bennett Sr. mobilized in his own way during the Civil War, dispatching more than forty correspondents across the country to write about it. The *Herald* was hardly the only newspaper to send reporters to the front, but it poured more energy and resources into the effort than the competition. While other papers, most notably the abolitionist *Tribune*, treated the war as a moral struggle, Bennett simply approached it as one of the century's great news stories. He pioneered the use of engraved maps for illustrating troop movements, despite the painstaking difficulty of reproducing these illustrations on newsprint. He instructed his newly established southern bureau to pore over regional newspapers and generate a tally of rebel armed forces; the resulting list, when published, was so accurate and comprehensive that the Confederate war command arrested several clerks at its Richmond headquarters, on the assumption they had leaked secret documents. Outmatched New York papers lazily dismissed the scoop as just more evidence that the *Herald* had gotten too cozy with the enemy.

Bennett's views of the war seemed to change by the week, and not until later in the conflict did they align with those of Abraham Lincoln. The U.S. president privately sought Bennett's support, and eventually he got it. In gratitude, Lincoln offered him the French ambassadorship. It was among the most coveted positions in politics—famously held by Benjamin Franklin, the nation's original newspaper genius—and it would have allowed Bennett to reunite with his family. But he turned the posting down, on the grounds that it would prevent him from effectively managing the *Herald*.

There was more of it to run than ever after the war. Revenue from the year ending in May 1865, the month after the South surrendered, surpassed $1 million—as much as that of the next five competitors combined—and its daily circulation remained the nation's highest. Bennett had climbed to the top and stayed there, a contemporary observer noted, "in spite of the active opposition of almost every organized body in the country, and the fixed disapproval of every public-spirited human being who has lived in the United States since he began his career."

In the meantime, newspapers had become an indispensable tool of local and national culture. "Having once had daily papers, we can never again do without them; so perfectly does this great invention accord with the genius of modern life," the august *North American Review* determined that year. The press was in this respect like the railroad that was beginning to spiderweb the continent and that would by 1869 connect East Coast to West. Nowhere was its power more concentrated than in Park Row, at the northern edge of what is now the Financial District and the throbbing center of New York City's English-language press. The great newspaper buildings stood side by side there, and the clattering of their cellar presses traveled up to newsrooms where men sat writing in longhand, their shouts of "copyboy!" piercing the clouds of pipe and cigar smoke.

As ripe as the moment seemed for Bennett Jr. to join his father's paper, his desk sat empty awhile longer. The life of a moneyed young rapscallion still appealed to him, and he preferred the Union Club to the grind of the newsroom. One brandy-soaked evening there in the fall of 1866, a handful of wealthy members resolved to organize the world's first transatlantic yacht race. To up the ante, they would set sail in frigid December. Young Bennett was one of three owners to enter the contest and the only one to accompany his vessel. He hired a seasoned captain—one Sam Samuels—to handle most of the actual sailing duties. The journey was deemed so perilous that even Captain Samuels, a thirty-year veteran of the seas, barely managed to hire enough able hands.

The crossing proved to be the adventure the newspapers had cracked it up to be, a battering by heavy seas and numbing cold. All things considered, Bennett's party—a Union Club wit named Larry Jerome, the *Herald* correspondent Stephen Fiske, and a pair of Yacht Club umpires—kept comfortable enough belowdecks, feasting on oysters in a wood-paneled dining cabin that Bennett had draped with tiger-skin rugs. Outside these snug quarters, though, the elements did their worst. "For days the yacht was running between walls of water, as through a tunnel," Fiske wrote afterward. A monster wave smashed their lifeboat to bits. The *Henrietta* endured squalls and gales, including one so violent that Captain Samuels was forced to heave to for eighteen hours. The second half of the journey proved calmer, and when a local pilot came aboard to guide them through the English Channel, Bennett and company were stunned to learn that they were leading. *Henrietta* arrived at the Isle of Wight on Christmas Day, its thirteen-day, twenty-two-hour crossing having set a new record for sailing vessels. Queen Victoria and the hard-to-impress London newspapers tipped their caps at this daring feat. Plum Gut Bennett had not just restored lost face. He'd made spectacular news for the *Herald*.

YOUNG BENNETT GOT MORE SERIOUS ABOUT NEWSPAPER WORK AFTER THE transatlantic yacht race. Rather than nursing hangovers at home and frittering away afternoons at the Union Club, he regularly showed up at the office, where he was delivered every morning by a liveried coachman. At twenty-five, he was something of a disquieting presence in the newsroom. "He was tall and straight-backed, with an air of authority few of his fellow newspaper editors could manage," a *Herald* writer recalled years later. "His face was long and bony, with a firm jaw, rather suspicious and chilly blue eyes, an imposing nose, and a large tawny mustache."

His father put him in charge of a gossipy new journal, the *Evening Telegram*, and in the spring of 1867 the *Herald* began listing Bennett Sr. as "Editor and Proprietor" and Bennett Jr. as "Manager." Its founder, now white-haired and in his seventies, began overseeing more of the business by private telegraph from home or from his country estate in Fort Washington, ten miles north of Park Row. Though Bennett Jr.'s accelerated apprenticeship worked well at times, he also found himself chafing under remote supervision. One evening, probably after a boozy dinner at Delmonico's, he ordered a last-minute alteration to the masthead: "James Gordon Bennett, *Jr.*, Editor in Chief and Publisher." His eagle-eyed father ordered the presses stopped at once and the change reversed. To his son he thundered, "I have no mind to retire until I'm damned good and ready!"

That moment was not long in coming. Young Bennett formally took over on January 1, 1868, thereby joining an elect circle of editorial chieftains on Park Row. There was the intellectually omnivorous Charles Anderson Dana, who'd recently assumed leadership of *The Sun*. There was the crusading "Uncle Horace" Greeley of the *Tribune*, another old *Herald* nemesis. There was William Cullen Bryant, the poet, whose cultural influence loomed larger than that of his small-circulation *Evening Post*. And there was the talented Henry Jarvis Raymond, a Greeley protégé and cofounder of the highly respected *New-York Times*. These men were towering cultural and political figures, Greeley especially, but young Bennett was uncowed. He was far wealthier than any of them and occupied the most palatial building on Park Row. And the daily *Herald* still sold better than their papers did.

One of young Bennett's first steps as editor and publisher was to double the paper's news budget. For starters, he wanted to print more about Europe. Now that an undersea cable ran between Ireland and Newfoundland, important news from abroad arrived almost instantaneously, rather than by ship ten days after the fact. The cost of using this new technology was steep, but that simply gave the cash-rich *Herald* an opportunity to go where others couldn't—spending, for example, a staggering $7,000 to secure a transcript of a speech outlining the peace terms of the Austro-Prussian War.

Bennett cared little for good writing personally but competed for journalistic talent out of a desire to keep the *Herald* on top. Just as he was taking over the paper, he met with two aspiring *Herald* contributors who would shortly become household names. One was a drawling humorist and former Mississippi River pilot named Samuel Clemens. He was just back from Europe and the Near East, travels he had described in a series of satirical accounts for a San Francisco newspaper. The successful pieces had left their author, who wrote under the name Mark Twain, craving a wider audience and a bigger paycheck. Bennett furnished both, contracting with Twain to file uncensored weekly dispatches from Washington, D.C. ("I may abuse & ridicule anybody & *every* body I please," Twain gloated to a friend.) As promising as this arrangement seemed for the *Herald*, it was nothing compared with the deal that Bennett struck with another up-and-coming correspondent a few weeks later.

His name was Henry Morton Stanley.

# CHAPTER THREE

Whether Bennett or Stanley came up with the idea to go looking for Dr. David Livingstone is disputed, but what can be said is that Bennett was at least well aware, by 1869, of the public's growing interest in the Scottish explorer and missionary's whereabouts. Livingstone had gone missing since entering the African interior three years earlier with the intention of locating the Nile's source, one of geography's great remaining puzzles. The British explorers Richard Francis Burton and John Hanning Speke had undertaken a punishing search for this great fountainhead a decade earlier, only to emerge with vastly divergent theories. The day before they were scheduled to debate the matter publicly, Speke died of a self-inflicted gunshot wound while hunting partridge. His death was suspected of being a suicide, a mystery upon a mystery that only added to the dark aura surrounding the Nile question.

Livingstone's disappearance was not just newsworthy for the usual reasons, because he was no ordinary explorer. He was also a doctor and a man of faith whose vision for Africa, considered progressive at the time, had struck a powerful chord in the Anglo-American public. He had compared the Zambezi River to the Mississippi and appealed to the British government to expand trade and infrastructure throughout the continent so that Christianized Africans might learn and prosper alongside sympathetic white colonials. This grand plan for Africa garnered wide support, in part because it promised to end the Arab-run slave trade, and Livingstone enjoyed towering moral status among humanitarians on both sides of the Atlantic. When a letter from him finally made its way back to civilization in 1869, revealing that he was running short on supplies and men, public anxiety mounted even further. Bennett would play that anxiety the way a master violinist plays sheet music.

Stanley had given the demanding young publisher good reason to entrust him with an undertaking as massive as finding Livingstone. The Welsh-born journalist had first made a name for himself by reporting on the U.S. Army's campaign to protect white settlers from dispossessed Great Plains tribes. Bennett had then attached him to a British military campaign in Abyssinia, or present-day Ethiopia, and Stanley had succeeded beyond his wildest imaginings. Granted, he'd been lucky: the cable between Alexandria and Malta snapped right after Stanley's report of the British victory traveled over it, making the *Herald* the only source of news of the event for a week. But by beating all the London correspondents to the wires, he'd also shown himself to be immensely resourceful and hardworking. While abroad, he'd become intrigued by the strange case of Livingstone and begun making inquiries.

Sometime in 1869, Stanley later claimed, Bennett summoned him to a hotel suite in Paris and outlined his plan for the scoop of the century. The goal of the *Herald*, Bennett lectured, was to "publish whatever news will be interesting to the world, at no matter what cost." Staying ahead of the other papers for a day or two was well enough, but what if the *Herald* were to generate a news story that was so big, and so exclusive, it would have the world's press eating out of its hand for months? He proposed a special expedition in search of Livingstone, to be paid for by him and led by Stanley. No government or scientific institution would be involved. Bennett wasn't bothered by the cost or the difficulty of the mission or the fact that it was unprecedented in journalism. All that mattered, he told his reporter, was that it succeed: "Find Livingstone!"

Rather than send Stanley immediately, though, Bennett decided that it would be better for the *Herald* to discover Livingstone around two years later, after public interest had subsided and begun to rise again. He also correctly judged that the paper's only serious potential competitors, the British government and the Royal Geographical Society, were not about to launch relief expeditions of their own. Stanley worried that the delay would increase the chances that Livingstone died or reappeared before he could go looking for him, but Bennett's word was final. Stanley unhappily embarked on a meandering journey to India by way of Crimea, the Middle East, and Persia.

When he arrived at Zanzibar, off the coast of present-day Tanzania, in January 1871, still nothing had been heard from Livingstone. Stanley enlisted twenty armed soldiers and dozens of porters for his expedition, hiring more than a hundred men in total. He bought more than eight tons of supplies with *Herald* money, including relief supplies for Livingstone and piles of cloth, beads, wire, and other goods to trade with local chieftains in exchange for safe passage. Only moderately worried by rumors of tribal warfare and tales of the notoriously malarial Makata swamp, he departed in late March.

"LIVINGSTONE SAFE," A *HERALD* HEADLINE ANNOUNCED ON MAY 2, 1872.

Word of Stanley's success reached the coast more than a year after his departure. It was the first anyone had heard of Livingstone in three years, and the simple, amazing fact that Bennett's "special" had rescued the missing explorer in the heart of Africa spread as far and wide as any piece of news ever had.

Stanley lingered on the coast for nearly two months, recuperating and organizing an additional delivery of supplies for Livingstone. When his mailed dispatches reached the *Herald*'s London office in early July, selections were immediately cabled to New York, where they occupied two full pages of the next day's edition. Stanley's triumph was hailed not only as a great achievement but as a fantastically compelling travel yarn. "Nothing more heroic and more ludicrous . . . has been carried out and described in the history of modern adventure," the London *Daily News* exclaimed. The American press lobbed up even heftier superlatives, often with a blast of patriotism. "It is another lesson to John Bull of the capabilities of American pluck and enterprise," the *New Haven Courier* reckoned. Bennett packed his columns with glowing testimonials like these, positioning the *Herald* as the widely acknowledged champion of "a vigorous press system native to America, and America only."

Livingstone had chosen to stay in the interior to resume his search for the Nile's source. At Stanley's request, he had written a letter to Bennett personally, thanking the *Herald* publisher for launching the relief mission and providing exclusive details of his latest movements in the Central African watershed. Bennett published the letter before Stanley's dispatches, both to ensure that he received due credit and to fortify the *Herald* against charges of fabrication or self-aggrandizement. Here was no lowly journalist, after all, but the "lion-hearted missionary" himself, addressing the *Herald*. Livingstone affirmed to the world that he had been in duress—"dying on my feet . . . a mere 'ruckle' of bones," and nearly a beggar—before the "good Samaritan" Henry Stanley had come to his rescue with food, medicine, and other essentials.

When it was reprinted in the London press, the letter helped to underscore the true enormity of the *Herald*'s achievement. "Africa is a very wide target, but Mr. Stanley hit the bull's-eye at once," *The Times* allowed. *The Telegraph* went so far as to scold would-be detractors in advance, cautioning that the many honors awaiting Stanley in London and Paris were "far too well merited to be mixed with envy." In New York, the *Herald* published Stanley's riveting full account of his travel later that summer. He'd made a nearly thousand-mile journey through plain, forest, marsh, and jungle, endured the ravages of smallpox and dysentery, and faced down threats of desertion and even mutiny. He'd survived belligerent locals, impassable routes, and crocodiles and haggled endlessly over *honga*, the ritual payments designed to guarantee unmolested passage through each chieftain's territory. The blasé *Times* of London likened *honga* to a customs tariff; the *Herald* called it "blackmail."

Stanley had heard rumors of a white man with a long gray beard at Ujiji, an Arab trading post on Lake Tanganyika. Though his task was in some respects only halfway finished, the reporter's arrival there would be remembered for decades afterward as the journey's climactic moment. It was November now, more than eight months since Stanley had left the coast. His two white companions, both of them sailors he'd met in Zanzibar, had been incapacitated by illness and left behind. Now the vast inland sea of Lake Tanganyika stretched out before him, "bounded westward by an appalling and black-blue range of mountains, and stretching north and south without bounds." Stanley rode into town atop a donkey, his guards firing guns into the air, as astonished villagers dashed out to greet them. Ahead of him, on the veranda of a prominent house, a group of respectable-looking Arab traders stood gathered around an old white man. Stanley dismounted, stepped forward, and—if his *Herald* reporting is to be believed—delivered a famous greeting that would outlive both of them: "Dr. Livingstone, I presume?"

IT WAS—AND STILL IS—TYPICAL FOR REPORTERS TO CONCEAL THE MAKings of a scoop from rivals, and sometimes even to intentionally mislead other journalists. Because there were no hard-and-fast rules when it came to scoring a "beat," as scoops were called then, journalists often pushed the boundaries of fair play. One common method of securing priority was to bribe a telegraph operator. Another was to have the operator cable long passages from the Bible or some other lengthy text, thereby tying up the line and forcing rival correspondents to miss their next edition's deadline.

None of these shenanigans were required to preserve the *Herald*'s latest scoop, for the simple reason that there was no competition. Stanley and Bennett hadn't just broken the news of Livingstone's discovery; they had created it. And with one of the main subjects now unreachable and the other spoken for as a salaried *Herald* "special," it was just about impossible for other newspapers to get near the story.

The minute they tried, Bennett beat them back. Apparently out of courtesy, his European bureau chief allowed a reporter from the London *Telegraph* to speak with Stanley in Marseilles and then on the train back to Paris. Stanley gladly unburdened himself, sharing previously unpublished details of his journey and criticizing the British consul at Zanzibar for his indifference to Livingstone. When these conversations appeared as interviews in *The Telegraph*, Bennett had a message delivered to Stanley at his Paris hotel: "STOP TALKING." He also threatened to fire his London editor, T. P. O'Connor, for mailing Stanley's dispatches to New York rather than cabling them. O'Connor's decision saved the *Herald* around $8,000, four times his annual salary, but also delayed publication of the full exclusive too long for Bennett's liking.

Deprived of news of the *Herald* expedition, the London press began picking at it. Belittling of this sort came naturally to the Victorian British establishment, which did not yet have a popular press to contend with and generally looked down on American newspapers. *The Times* of London took care to note that whereas Livingstone traveled in the name of progress and science, Stanley had merely retraced the great explorer's footsteps in "the way of business," and insinuated that the *Herald* was hiding something. In early July 1872, with Stanley still in Africa, multiple London papers advanced rumors that he had stolen or forged Livingstone's documents. Having died in the field, his two white companions were unavailable to weigh in. "The general opinion," Stanley lamented in his diary, "is that I am a fraud."

The facts would later show that he had achieved a genuine feat of exploration. After meeting in Ujiji, Stanley and Livingstone had paddled up the coast of Lake Tanganyika and confirmed that the Rusizi River flowed into this inland water body and not out of it, effectively establishing the course of the river's watershed. The fruits of this four-week excursion made Stanley an obvious candidate for the Royal Geographical Society's Victoria Medal, awarded annually for the best feat of exploration, and yet the society's secretary, Clements Markham, withheld the honor. His stated reason was that Stanley had neglected to take regular longitude and latitude readings with sextant and chronometer and simply recorded the number of hours traveled on particular compass bearings. Markham's quibbling was swiftly judged to be a petty display of jealousy and class prejudice, though, and was effectively squelched by Queen Victoria's decision to honor Stanley.

Even so, doubts persisted. (It would be two years before a Royal Geographical Society expedition confirmed Stanley's claim.) During a lecture in Brighton, England, scientists in the audience disrupted Stanley's talk "to cross-examine, to badger, bully and bait the young correspondent of the *Herald* about his barometers and hygrometers and other 'ometers,'" according to the *Herald*. Meanwhile, in New York, *The Sun* enlisted a handwriting expert and a former traveling companion of Stanley's to argue that its Park Row rival was perpetrating an "enormous fraud." Testimonials from Livingstone's friends and relatives, and no less an authority than the British foreign secretary, eventually put an end to these accusations, and Bennett declared the argument over—or as close to over as one could hope for. "It would be a superhuman work to take every single doubter up," he wrote in the *Herald*, displaying some of his father's cynicism, "for such is the perversity of a man of this class who finds himself in the wrong that he would doubt his own existence sooner than the fact of his staring you in the face should be proved to him."

Stanley's book, *How I Found Livingstone*, sold out within a week of its publication in America. Unfortunately for him, his patron had by now come to resent him. Having originally encouraged his star "special" to take a victory lap, Bennett had now heard that Stanley's fees for his American lecture tour would surpass the cost of the expedition and blamed him for hogging the credit. It was an early example of the mistrust and pettiness that would eventually cost Bennett many a talented *Herald* employee—and an unfair view of the situation. Stanley's fierce sense of ambition was, after all, a major reason Bennett had assigned him to Livingstone in the first place, and Stanley had moreover gone to great lengths to ensure that his employer received due acknowledgment. Bennett, meanwhile, had initially failed to advance the promised expedition funds to Zanzibar, nearly sinking the whole enterprise with his negligence.

No one dared to make these arguments, which probably would have been lost on Bennett anyway. He gave Stanley a frosty reception when the two men met at the *Herald* offices in New York that fall and dismissed him after just ten minutes. Several weeks later, Stanley gave the first of four planned talks in New York City. According to Joseph Clarke, a reporter who'd spent months defending him in the *Herald*, Stanley made this first talk solemn and geographically precise "to prove he was truthful and not the villain the *Sun* was painting him." Whatever Stanley had been thinking, the lecture flopped. According to the *Herald*, all its correspondent proved that evening was his incompetence at the lectern. "Mr. Stanley's elocution is bad," wrote the paper's theater critic, George Seilhamer, who lamented that his *Herald* colleague had not shown "half the courage before an average civilized audience that he showed in the wilds of Africa." The harsh verdict of the *Herald*, which was popular among many of the readers who might have been inclined to hear Stanley speak, effectively ended his lecture tour before it began. Advance tickets to his third talk sold poorly, and the rest of his engagements were canceled.

This had been Bennett's plan all along. He'd made it known to his chosen reviewer that he wanted Stanley's performance panned. Stanley's story had served its purpose for the paper, and it was time to knock him off his pedestal and move on. By the time the *Herald* was referring to its own correspondent as "intolerably dull," Bennett had left for Paris.

# CHAPTER FOUR

### September 3, 1909

P hilip Gibbs, special correspondent for the London *Daily Chronicle*, smoked alone at a café in Copenhagen. The thirty-two-year-old reporter had arrived by steamer earlier that afternoon, a day later than the rest of the London press—he'd been on vacation in the English countryside—and already his mission of securing an interview with Frederick Cook faced two major obstacles. All of Copenhagen wanted to meet the famous explorer, and all of Copenhagen seemed to have a better idea than Gibbs did of where to find him.

Gibbs peered uncomprehendingly at the Danish newspaper in his hands. Its front page seemed to contain just one word that he could make sense of—"Cook"—and it was everywhere. Thankfully, his waiter spoke English. The whole city would be coming out to cheer Dr. Cook, the waiter enthused. The *Hans Egede* had been expected in Copenhagen that day, he explained, but now the evening papers were reporting that there were fog delays. Cook would arrive in the morning.

Gibbs relaxed a little. But he had plenty of other things to worry about—the fact that he knew next to nothing about the Arctic, for example. He might have been mulling this problem when he discerned heads inside the café turning. A striking young woman with bronze skin and regal cheekbones had entered, draped in white fox fur and accompanied by one of the tallest men Gibbs had ever seen. The waiter sidled over to fill Gibbs in. "That's Mrs. Rasmussen," he explained—the wife of the Danish explorer Knud Rasmussen, who was known to be a friend of Cook's and who had helped to provide the sled dogs for his expedition.

Gibbs rose and introduced himself to Dagmar Rasmussen and her companion. She was indeed the wife of Knud Rasmussen, she said in halting English, and her tall friend with unruly hair introduced himself as Peter Freuchen. Gibbs told the two Danes that he was hoping to meet Cook. They laughed and told him they'd been scheming to do the same. The president of the Danish Greenland Company, which owned and operated the *Hans Egede*, was a friend; he was currently several hours north of Copenhagen, arranging a pilot launch to bring select guests out to meet the famous explorer. Given the fog, though, it was almost certain that the visiting excursion had been called off, and so Rasmussen and Freuchen had stayed in Copenhagen. Why not go to Elsinore now, just in case?, Gibbs asked. The last train of the day had left, they told him. Why not hire a taxi? Dagmar Rasmussen chuckled at the reporter's enthusiasm. Automobiles, she explained, were not allowed to travel outside Copenhagen after dark.

Gibbs persisted, summoning the waiter and asking him to bring in a taxi driver from the street outside. One duly appeared, hat in hand. How much would the fine be, Gibbs asked, if the police flagged his vehicle down after dark? He was prepared to charge a small fortune to *The Daily Chronicle*. The driver named a fee, fines included, that he considered reasonable. Fully caught up in the spirit of adventure now, Rasmussen and Freuchen agreed to come along after dinner.

It was a long, cold drive to Elsinore. Around midnight, they reached a hotel where the shipping executive was making final arrangements for the boat journey, which had merely been delayed. The friend informed the Danes that Cook's arrival was a national event, and too significant for the Danish Greenland Company to be handing out casual favors, not even to the wife of the great Knud Rasmussen. But a foreign journalist—that was a different story. Gibbs was pleased to learn that he would be permitted to board the *Hans Egede*.

It was still dark when he boarded the launch with a small group that included two or three Danish reporters. The first dawn light appeared as the pilot boat steamed out, revealing the *Hans Egede* draped in festive bunting. Fur-clad seamen leaned along its railing, watching them approach. Gibbs, feeling self-conscious in his city overcoat and felt hat, leaped from the launch's gunwale onto a rope ladder and climbed up on deck.

There he found himself face to face with two white men, one of whom he recognized at once. The explorer's sturdy build and calm, engaging presence impressed him.

"Dr. Cook, I believe?"

Still reeling from his good fortune, Gibbs congratulated him. A smiling Cook led the handful of reporters into the dining room, where they sat down for breakfast amid Danish missionaries. Instinctively, the *Daily Chronicle* correspondent began sizing up his subject. Though he was a trained physician, Cook had the thick, worn hands of a laborer and a pear-sized nose. Most captivating of all were his blue eyes, which transfixed his interlocutors but also had a vaguely faraway quality to them. Cook certainly seemed willing to talk, Gibbs noted, but so far he'd spoken of his journey only in generalities. Hungry for details, he was relieved when the explorer ushered his guests into his private cabin after breakfast.

As the only journalist in the room who spoke native English, Gibbs led the questioning. He did not attempt to hide his ignorance of the Arctic, but Cook's responses to what he considered basic questions surprised him. He had brought along all the scientific instruments typically used for Arctic navigation, Cook said, and he knew how to use them. But he'd left his equipment and original travel diary in Greenland, in the care of an American sportsman there who had agreed to bring them back to New York for him. Gibbs pressed the American on how he intended to prove he'd been to the pole, but the whole line of questioning seemed to annoy him. Cook, his blue eyes gleaming, angrily pointed out that the press had taken other returning explorers at their word. "Why don't you believe me?"

The question of proofs was dropped, and Cook went back to describing his journey in the broad strokes of a fireside storyteller. Gibbs listened politely and took notes as a seed of doubt flowered within him. "By intuition, rather than evidence, by some quick instinct of facial expression, by some sensibility to mental and moral dishonesty," he later wrote, "I was convinced, absolutely, at the end of an hour, that this man had not been to the North Pole, but was attempting to bluff the world."

# CHAPTER FIVE

## September 4, 1909

The morning sky was bright, the water glimmering like diamonds, as thousands crowded the harbor in Copenhagen to greet Frederick Cook. The veteran British journalist W. T. Stead, who'd come to town on behalf of the Hearst news service, declared it "a capital day for outdoor photography." Amateur and professional photographers jostled for space along the pier; sailboats, rowboats, tugboats, and motorboats bobbed in the water. A surprising number of American flags had been sourced on short notice—little ones waving everywhere, a big one rippling atop a flagpole. When the *Hans Egede* came into view, the Stars and Stripes was flying from its mizzenmast.

A symphony of cheers, steam whistles, and brass-band music arose at the sight of it. The pleasure boats gave right-of-way to a steam pinnace bearing Christian, the crown prince, and a delegation of Arctic enthusiasts from the Royal Danish Geographical Society. The welcoming committee—which included two foreigners, Stead and Maurice Egan, the U.S. minister to Copenhagen—boarded the *Hans Egede* and met Cook, then whisked him ashore, where the mass of well-wishers could finally get a look at him.

With his overgrown hair and mustache, shabby brown suit, and moccasins, Cook looked very much the returning Arctic traveler. He wore a soft sailor's cap, which he raised repeatedly for the cheering quayside crowd that now pressed in from all sides. Men came forward to pump his hand and clap him on the shoulder. An ecstatic woman thrust a bouquet of roses at him. "His blue eyes seemed at first a little dazed at the sight of the morning multitude," noted Stead, who watched the chaos with rising alarm. The crown prince had slipped away by this point, taking his security guards with him, and the handful of remaining policemen appeared powerless to contain the mass of humanity now surging forward. Cook merely smiled dumbly and wobbled on his sea legs.

Flinging his arms around Cook's midsection, Stead hurled himself backwards against the throng. The throng pushed back, with some trying to sweep Cook off his feet and up onto thousands of grasping hands. Stead, Egan, a second reporter, and a lone policeman repelled them, creating a four-man phalanx around Cook that was able to cut through the crowd. Stead, ever the journalist, barked questions into Cook's ear as they jostled forward, and took mental notes on the explorer's physique. "From the grip around his waist I learned that he is well set-up, not spare but solid, with no superfluous flesh," he later wrote.

Finally, Cook and his improvised security detail reached the safety of the government's Meteorological Department headquarters. Egan's silk hat had been crushed in the fray, and Cook earnestly promised to buy him a new one. His own cap was gone, his bouquet was shredded, and one of his torn-off shirt cuffs had become someone's souvenir. Egan, rattled, sought to lighten the mood. Wouldn't it have been something, he quipped, for Cook to have survived two years in the Arctic wilds, only to die violently upon returning to civilization, so called?

The crowd continued to roar outside. At the urging of his handlers, Cook ascended to the balcony and briefly addressed them—"My friends, I have had too hard a time getting here to make a speech. I can only say that I consider it an honor to be able to put my foot first on Danish soil!"—and was then swept into a taxi and brought to the nearby Hotel Phoenix. A barber and the king's own tailor awaited him there—and a dentist, to repair the teeth Cook had broken in the Far North while gnawing on frozen walrus hide.

Egan escorted the cleaned-up explorer to the American legation for lunch with select American and British journalists and the inquisitive Russian ambassador, whose questioning Cook handled with straightforward good humor. Earlier that morning, the correspondent for *The Times* of London confessed, his "nervous manner and disheveled aspect had not prepossessed me." In these more settled environs, Cook struck the reporter as an "upright and honest man."

That afternoon, Egan brought Cook to meet privately with King Frederick VIII and then with Prince Valdemar, the king's brother. An exhausted Cook returned to the Hotel Phoenix at six o'clock, hoping to get an hour's rest before attending a banquet that the mayor of Copenhagen had organized for him at city hall, but the sixty or so international reporters at the hotel wouldn't hear of it. Cook's two-thousand-word *Herald* narrative, published two days earlier, had generated as many questions as it had answered. Some of the extraordinary figures in it demanded clarifying, and for all the talking Cook had done that day, he had yet to address the press corps. The journalists demanded an interview. The irrepressible Stead coaxed Cook into an empty banquet room and kicked off the questioning.

"So, Doctor, you've been to the North Pole?"

Cook unburied his head from his hands. "I think so."

Stead persisted: Had he put his foot right on it?

Not quite, Cook explained. "I got to where there wasn't any longitude," he said. Stead paused. In that case, would it be fair to say that he had been within shooting range of the pole? Yes, Cook answered. Dozens of pencils scratched away.

Cook claimed to have advanced fifteen miles a day during the final dash to the pole. This was an astonishing rate, and the first detail from his *Herald* article to be challenged by the assembled newsmen. Cook replied that he had traveled lighter than all other expeditions and used the finest dogs available at Cape York, and that he had found smooth ice and abundant game for much of the way. He had traveled through Axel Heiberg

Land, he added, a region recently demystified by the Norwegian explorer Otto Sverdrup—and west of the areas favored by most explorers, including the eminent Robert Peary. Cook also cleared up several of the confusing figures that had appeared in his original *Herald* article. Thanks to a transmission error, the -83 degrees Fahrenheit temperatures he'd endured had mistakenly appeared as an incredible -83 degrees Celsius, and his claim about exploring thirty thousand square miles had been misconstrued. This was a rough figure, arrived at by simple triangulation, based on the fifteen miles that Cook could see to either side of him as he marched. He had not actually covered that much ground.

The calm, easygoing manner in which Cook put such doubts to rest was noted by everyone in the room. "He smiled indulgently now and again as if he pitied our incredulity, but never once did he decline to answer questions, and they were put to him baldly and directly," the London *Daily News* reported. Cook praised Etukishuk and Ahwelah, the two young Inuit who'd accompanied him all the way to the pole, for their hunting skills and courage, and obligingly spelled out their names. These native companions were ignorant of Western scientific methods, Cook cautioned, and could verify his polar claim only "in a general way." But their story of the journey was already known to Knud Rasmussen, who would no doubt vouch for it.

Cook explained that he had carried state-of-the-art thermometers, barometers, sextants, compasses, chronometers, and pedometers, these last for measuring the number of miles traveled. Though he admitted that his navigational training had been informal, he certainly knew how to use the required instruments, he said, and had recorded his progress diligently on the drifting sea ice.

Because this was the North Pole, his documentation of that progress would be critical. The site under discussion was not a fixed point of land like the South Pole, which the British explorer Ernest Shackleton had very nearly attained less than a year before. It would be impossible for a subsequent explorer to validate Cook's polar claim simply by following in his footsteps. The pole itself was a notional place on shifting sea ice. Cook could leave no footsteps, and any record left on the ice was guaranteed to be swept away by swirling currents. As the Parisian journal *Le Temps* pointed out, the question of whether one had been there belonged to the "domain of metaphysics."

"Only a few observations so far have been figured out," Cook admitted. He repeated what he had said to Gibbs that morning: "I have brought back just exactly the sort of records and proofs that every Arctic explorer brings back." Strictly speaking, though, this was not true. Based on what he'd said earlier, his original diaries and scientific gear were still in Greenland, rendering any swift verification of his claim impossible. Gibbs, who'd raced back to his hotel room to write up his interview and skipped the press conference, was not there to point out the discrepancy.

Cook said that he had planted an American flag on moving ice within a reasonable distance of 90°N, taken a photograph, then packed the flag up, dug a hole in the ice, and buried a tin canister with a smaller flag balled up inside it. The assembled reporters found this symbolic gesture oddly satisfying, and it was widely reported in the next day's papers. So too were the details of Cook's arduous journey back to civilization. The spring breakup had blocked his return, forcing his three-man team to survive a second Arctic winter on their own. Cook described to the spellbound press corps how they had spent the coldest and darkest months huddled together in a snow cavity at Cape Sparbo, out of rifle ammunition and on the brink of starvation, and resorted to hunting musk oxen with rope nooses. Cook also said that he had discovered "a great unknown land" between the 84th and the 85th parallels, but that diminishing food supplies had prevented him from exploring it.

The one-hour interview—"the first hunk of real meat thrown to a ravening world," as one American correspondent described it—finally gave the world's press something it could sink its teeth into without risk of violating the *Herald*'s copyright. It also endeared Cook to the journalists in Copenhagen. The newsmen swarmed him after the interview, subjecting him to more handshakes and congratulations. Some of the Danish reporters even asked for his autograph.

ANNOYED BY THE SKEPTICISM OF THE LONDON NEWSPAPERS, BENNETT had asked Cook to craft a written rebuttal for the *Herald*. This Cook did not do, but the press conference at the Hotel Phoenix apparently satisfied Bennett on this front, because he didn't ask again.

Among those not fully convinced by the "Great Interview," as one American correspondent dubbed it, was the Australian physicist Louis Bernacchi, a member of the British National Antarctic Expedition of 1901–4. In letters to the London *Times* and the London *Daily Chronicle*, Bernacchi wondered how Cook could have determined where he was, given the navigationally challenging conditions he described, and worried that the purple prose of his *Herald* dispatches revealed him to be "somewhat of a sentimentalist." Bernacchi offered the contrasting example of his former co-expeditioner, Ernest Shackleton, who had just achieved a remarkable first ascent of Antarctica's Mount Erebus and marched to within ninety-seven miles of the South Pole. As Bernacchi pointed out, the precise and detailed account Shackleton had cabled the press from New Zealand "enabled the reader to follow him step by step."

> We travelled south along meridian 168 over a varying surface, high sastrugi ridges and mounds of snow, alternating with soft snow. The ponies often sank to their bellies. . . . On Nov. 26 we reached the Discovery expedition's southernmost latitude. The surface was now extremely soft, with large undulations. The ponies were attacked by snow-blindness. . . . We made a depot in latitude 82deg. 45min., longitude 170deg. On Nov. 30 the pony "Quan" was shot.

Cook's narrative, on the other hand, was hazy and impressionistic, especially when describing the explorer nearing his goal:

> Thus, day after day, the weary legs were spread over big distances. The incidents and the positions were recorded, but the adventure

was promptly forgotten in the mental bleach of the next day's effort. . . . When the sun was low the eye ran over the moving plains of color to dancing horizons. The mirages turned things topsy turvy. Inverted mountains and queer objects ever rose and fell in shrouds of mystery, but all of this was due to the atmospheric magic of the midnight sun. Slowly but surely we neared the turning point. Good astronomical observations were daily produced to fix the advancing stages.

Cook's romantic writing style didn't necessarily discredit his *Herald* narrative, Bernacchi wrote. It simply shifted the burden of evidence onto his "begrimed original daily diary," which would presumably receive expert verification as soon as possible. Bernacchi was not the only one puzzled by Cook's failure to bring "indispensable evidence of his alleged discoveries" with him to Europe. Though it was, as Cook said, customary for returning explorers to be taken at their word, the *Daily Mail* tartly noted that it was also traditional for them to scrupulously safeguard their travel records, "which usually are an explorer's most prized possessions." Cook had inexplicably left his in the Arctic.

ON SEPTEMBER 5, COOK MET WITH REPRESENTATIVES FROM THE UNIversity of Copenhagen, Denmark's most prestigious institute of higher learning. Its rector magnificus, Professor Carl Torp, and chief astronomer, Professor Elis Strömgren, subjected Cook to "an exhaustive series of mathematical and technical and natural and scientific questions," Torp told the *Daily Mail.* Both scholars declared themselves satisfied with his responses. Professor Strömgren's endorsement was considered the more significant, given the presumed importance of Cook's astronomical data in proving he'd been at the pole. Encouraged by the results of this two-hour examination, the Royal Danish Geographical Society decided to award the explorer a gold medal. Torp also announced that the university would give Cook an honorary degree of philosophy, pending King Frederick's approval.

Approval was granted the next day, after Cook dined at Charlotten-lund Palace as the monarch's guest of honor. The explorer reciprocated this act of national faith by promising the University of Copenhagen the first examination of his proofs, thereby extending the role Denmark would play in one of the world's great polar discoveries. He informed the *Herald* that he had pledged his "facts, figures and instruments" to a committee of the university's top experts and would "decline to engage in a controversy" until the Danish panel had reviewed his proofs and rendered judgment. All other details would be withheld, he added, until the publication of his book. It appeared that there was nothing for skeptics to do but wait.

Meanwhile, the feting of Frederick Cook continued. Backslappers and autograph seekers confronted him at every turn, and hundreds of onlook-ers gathered in the pouring rain just to get a glimpse of him. By day, Cook took refuge from the crowds inside the American legation, which occu-pied part of an old palace in central Copenhagen. Hundreds of telegrams, cablegrams, and letters had by now piled up in his hotel suite, including many urgent inquiries from the press. William Randolph Hearst's *Cosmo-politan* was ready to negotiate for a series on Cook's "epoch-making achievement." *Hampton's* offered an unprecedented $100,000 for the com-bined newspaper and magazine rights. Because Cook had sold only a two-thousand-word summary of his journey to the *Herald*, other American newspapers were now bidding for the rest of it, with the Hearst news syndicate promising to double the next-highest offer. Egan considered Hearst and *Hampton's* disreputable and advised against dealing with either one. In any case, Cook seemed partial to the *Herald*. It was championing him already, and its reputation among explorers was unmatched. Declin-ing Hearst's offer, he sold his exclusive newspaper rights to Bennett for $25,000.

On September 6, Cook attended yet another lavish dinner in his honor—the third in as many days. The venue this time was the Tivoli Casino, gilded centerpiece of the city's Tivoli Gardens and amusement park. The organizer was *Politiken*, the leading Danish newspaper, and more than the usual number of journalists attended. Cook sat garlanded in pink roses at the main banquet table, looking as complacent and comfortable as ever—"as if he had been crowned with roses all his life," Stead wrote.

As the familiar round of congratulatory toasts began, excited whispering swept through the room—a rumor of more fantastic news from the Arctic. A messenger entered and handed Cook a telegram. The guest of honor stood, and every reporter present craned forward to hear him read it aloud: "Stars and Stripes Nailed to the Pole. Peary." Not one but *two* Americans had reached the North Pole.

AFTER SO MANY YEARS OF FAILED ATTEMPTS, THE NEWS WAS ALMOST TOO improbable to be believed. The Danish news agency receiving Peary's message had, in fact, immediately wired back to London to confirm that it was not a hoax. For one thing, the note's wording seemed suspect. Many doubted that a respected navy man like Peary would describe a worldly achievement in such crassly jingoistic terms. Cook and other insiders knew better. "Stars and Stripes nailed to the pole" was exactly how Peary would phrase it.

Robert Peary was one of the thorniest characters in the history of exploration. Other polar adventurers were motivated at least in part by scientific curiosity, or a romantic temperament, or an eccentric love of life in the Arctic. Peary was driven purely by his desire to win the pole, and his determination to succeed could make him very unpleasant to deal with. He bristled at the merest whiff of competition, and was merciless when crossed. He'd spent twenty-three of his best years exploring and preparing to explore the Arctic, efforts that had cost him eight toes and many long months away from his wife and children. Peary's "Arctic work," as he called it, had brought him prominence, most recently for his attainment of a Farthest North in 1906. For this latest expedition, he had set off in 1908 in his custom-built icebreaker, the *Roosevelt*, in what had been billed as his final attempt to reach the pole.

Whereas Cook's message from Lerwick had surprised everyone, Peary's telegram from Labrador did not have quite the same effect. Given his financial advantages and track record, he had been considered America's best hope for attaining the pole, and his success had to some extent been expected. Still, it was a coincidence of historic proportions that America had won not once, but twice. Never had news of a great exploring triumph compounded so dramatically. The public celebrations momentarily subsumed all discussion of a rivalry or impending dispute between Cook and Peary, for their remarkable twin achievement had given everyone so many other things to talk about.

Hundreds of influential Americans were asked to comment on this extraordinary turn of events, whether they knew anything about the Arctic or not. What did the American discovery of the pole portend for science, trade, international relations, and even the arts? The answer was unclear, but the universally shared opinion was that surely it meant something good. Even the least enthusiastic observers were relieved to know that the race to the North Pole was over. Joseph Cannon, the Speaker of the U.S. House of Representatives, was among those who welcomed the opportunity for the exploring world to move on. The best thing that could be said about the discovery of the pole, in his opinion, was that it would end many years of needless expense and suffering. "It will stop further waste of lives and treasure in a quest that has engaged the attention of the explorers of two worlds for centuries," he told the *Herald*. "And that means a great deal."

PART TWO

# BONES IN THE WHITE NORTH

# CHAPTER SIX

The North Pole had beckoned for decades, but before the race to the pole there was the quest for the Northwest Passage, a more pragmatic endeavor. Generations of European explorers—British ones in particular—went off in search of this fabled sea link, threading their way through the Canadian-Alaskan Arctic's maze of ice barricades and cul-de-sacs in hopes of discovering a shortcut to the Far East.

Assuming it was reliably free from ice at least part of the year, a northwest passage had the potential to reshape international commerce and empire. Its prospective value was a major reason that kings and sea captains prioritized Arctic over Antarctic exploring for many decades. By the middle of the nineteenth century, though, it was clear that their optimism had been misplaced: the ice did not clear out of the North American Arctic completely or consistently enough for international business purposes. Still, some hope persisted, and there was glory to be had for any group that managed to climb over the world's shoulders during a summer of favorable ice conditions. There were also coastlines and islands to be mapped, botanical and mineralogical discoveries to be made, new whaling grounds to be opened, and all manner of inspiring tales to be recorded for a cheering public.

Great Britain's Royal Navy had these benefits in mind when it embarked on a remarkable era of Arctic exploration in 1818. The capstone of this heroic period came in 1845, when Sir John Franklin, a fifty-nine-year-old veteran of Arctic travel, went off in search of the Northwest Passage. The doomed Franklin expedition embodied all the majesty and might of the British Empire; its 129 officers and men were the cream of the Royal Navy, and its two stout vessels, *Erebus* and *Terror*, boasted the latest in shipbuilding technology, including screw propellers, which had never been used in the Arctic before. Franklin's ships carried enough supplies to last three years, including 136,000 pounds of flour and more than 1,000 pounds of raisins. The many tons of meat it carried were preserved by means of a groundbreaking new tinning method. Also aboard were enough pens, ink, and paper for a metropolitan newsroom; a hundred Bibles; two organs; and crates of fine crockery, engraved silverware, and other weighty luxuries reserved for use by the officers. Never had a nation committed itself so entirely to an Arctic venture. The Admiralty was so confident of success that for once it did not draw up a search-and-rescue plan.

*Erebus* and *Terror* sailed for Greenland in the summer of 1845 and were never heard from again. It took three years for the prospect of unimaginable disaster to register with the Admiralty. Once it did, dozens of relief expeditions sailed—in hope first of finding survivors and later of finding the tiniest bit of information about what had happened. The shock and mystery of the Franklin tragedy struck a nerve within the Victorian public, affecting millions who had never previously given a second thought to the Arctic—including Charles Dickens, who coauthored a play about the expedition with the pioneering detective novelist Wilkie Collins.

For ten years, relief expeditions sent by the Royal Navy and others learned next to nothing of Franklin's fate and much about the hostile geography of the High Arctic. The most notable achievement of this period belonged to Captain Robert McClure, who sailed east from the Bering Strait, above Alaska, to within sixty miles of known waterways on the Atlantic side of the Canadian Arctic. With Barrow Strait visible ahead, McClure could legitimately claim that he had discovered the Northwest Passage. Before he could attempt to navigate this last leg, wind and ice forced his ship, the *Investigator*, into winter quarters, where it remained frozen in for nearly three full years. Unable to break free, McClure and his men endured the ordeals of scurvy, -60 degrees Fahrenheit temperatures, and hunger so intense that they could not sleep. By the time they were rescued by a Royal Navy search party, most of them were walking corpses and some had gone completely mad.

McClure returned to England in 1854 a battered hero. His "discovery" of the Northwest Passage had cost him three men, a ship, and very nearly everything. It had required some very lucky breaks, and even then, he had failed to punch all the way through. Parliament duly awarded McClure and his men £10,000 for their achievement and swore off further dealings with the Northwest Passage. The British government also gave up looking for Franklin, but his widow, the popular and well-connected Lady Jane Franklin, continued to organize relief efforts. Five years after McClure's return, one funded by her and led by the Irish explorer Francis Leopold McClintock made the first (and ultimately only) discovery of a written record that had been left by the Franklin party. It stated that Franklin had died of unspecified causes during the expedition's second year and that the vessels had been abandoned after becoming locked in ice. McClintock followed a trail of bones and discarded items on King William Island, southwest of Lancaster Sound, and surmised that Franklin's 105 remaining men had straggled south over the barrens in a desperate bid for survival. The unavoidable conclusion was that every last man had died, the majority of them after suffering terribly.

Though McClintock's tragic findings surprised hardly anyone, they undammed a great reservoir of public sorrow. Mournful tributes poured out across Great Britain and beyond. The poet Alfred Tennyson expressed the nation's grief in lines composed for Franklin's cenotaph at Westminster Abbey: "Not here! the white North has thy bones; and thou, / Heroic sailor-soul, / Art passing on thine happier voyage now / Toward no earthly pole."

BY THE 1860S, THEN, TWO OF THE MOST PRESSING ARCTIC MYSTERIES— the Northwest Passage and the fate of the Franklin expedition—had more or less been solved. A new and more international era of polar exploration

now began as the withdrawal of the Royal Navy opened the frozen field
to countries like Italy, Germany, and Austro-Hungary. The British retreat
also made additional room for the United States, which had come down
with its own case of polar mania during the Franklin searches. A charismatic Philadelphia physician and explorer named Elisha Kent Kane was
largely responsible for this trend. His popular books and sold-out lectures
depicted the Far North as a wonderland in which ships emerged ghostlike
from the fog and strange creatures such as the "sea-unicorn" (narwhal)
and walruses ("grim-looking monsters, reminding me of the stage hob-
goblins, something venerable and semi-Egyptian withal") frolicked on ice
floes. Kane's bestselling *Arctic Explorations* turned him into a cultural
superstar, and his premature death by disease in 1857, at the age of thirty-
seven, was mourned nationwide.

One of Kane's many readers was Charles Francis Hall, a Cincinnati
printer and journalist who fashioned himself into an Arctic explorer with
the zeal of a midlife convert. Hall, an eccentric loner, took the unusual
step of picking up Inuit language and survival skills, and during the Civil
War he became the first white man to explore the Arctic with only non-
white companions. The Inuit he traveled with liked, respected, and generally worked well with him. They also considered exploration for its own
sake pointless and foolhardy. Hall went about it with religious fervor, and
his timing was good, for the U.S. government was finally in a position to
support him. Not only was the Civil War over, but thanks to America's
recent $7.2 million purchase of Alaska from Russia parts of the Arctic
Circle were now within the national domain. The United States was eye-
ing southern geographical expansion as well. According to *The Atlantic
Monthly* in 1870, however, the building of a massive Central American
interocean canal excited the public less than the prospect of discovering
the North Pole.

Hall set out for the "crowning jewel of the Arctic dome" in 1871 aboard
the 387-ton *Polaris*, a converted navy steam tug. Poor discipline plagued the
expedition from the beginning. The sailing master plucked freely from the
supply of alcohol, and the chief scientist treated Hall with a disrespect that
bordered on insubordination. A year and a half later, a sealer off the coast

of Labrador rescued nineteen shivering *Polaris* castaways. The bedraggled party of white men and Inuit families had become separated from the vessel during a gale and spent the previous six months on a floe, drifting south from Smith Sound and subsisting on seal and polar bear. The castaways also reported that Hall was dead.

The *Polaris* had reached a point farther north than any ship in history while under his uncertain command. Ocean currents had then forced it south again and into winter quarters on northern Ellesmere Island. Hall had set out from there on a short overland reconnaissance mission and returned, apparently in good health and confident he'd found a viable overland route to the pole. Then he'd fallen sick and begun vomiting. Delirious, Hall had raved that his shipmates were plotting against him. He'd recovered, then relapsed, then died. His companions had wrapped his body in an American flag and buried him two feet underground, as deep as the permafrost allowed.

The *Herald* took the lead in reporting these shocking findings, including the rumor that one of Hall's own officers had poisoned him. When the U.S. Navy dispatched the *Juniata* and *Tigress* to search for the missing ship and men—two of whom were prime suspects in the alleged murder— Bennett put a correspondent aboard both vessels. Neither one of the ships located the *Polaris* or its survivors, but the *Herald* ran full-page accounts of their efforts anyway. "Looking abroad on the immense fields of ice, glittering in the rays of the sun, and the thousands of huge, craggy icebergs as they sulkily floated out into Baffin's Bay, one became awed by the dreadful majesty of the elements, and wondered how it would be possible to avoid being crushed to atoms between the unshapely masses that floated above and beneath the surface of the water," the correspondent Martin Maher reported, in the first example of Arctic writing intended for immediate newspaper publication.

The hero of his story was a young lieutenant named George Washington De Long who coolly navigated a steam launch through treacherous Melville Bay before pack ice and dwindling coal supplies forced him back. "Our expedition was well managed, proving that the commander was a skillful and courageous officer, and worthy of honorable mention on the

record of Arctic heroes," Maher wrote. Later that month, after a British
whaler rescued the missing *Polaris* men and brought them to Dundee,
Scotland, the *Herald* complained that the survivors had "shut up like an
oyster" on the subject of poisoning. For this it blamed the impending
naval inquiry, which eventually determined that Hall had died of "natural
causes." A century later, forensic examiners exhumed his corpse and concluded otherwise. Murder could not be proven, but large amounts of ar-
senic were detected in Hall's hair and fingernails.

Though it had worked to expose the full scale of the *Polaris* disaster,
the *Herald* urged the government to try again. The question of what lay at
the North Pole simply had to be answered, it argued: "So long as it remains a secret it will possess a charm wholly irresistible. It will continue
to arrest the attention of the scientific world and draw towards its magic
circle the bold, the brave and the adventurous who love truth for its own
sake." The *Herald* suggested that the navy outfit another expedition to
the North Pole immediately, under the command of George Washington
De Long.

# CHAPTER SEVEN

The smaller-circulation *New-York Times*, on the other hand, considered government-funded Arctic adventuring a waste of taxpayer money.

Dollars-and-cents conservatism was one of the twenty-year-old paper's hallmarks. The genteel *Times* was known for its comprehensive summaries of important meetings and conventions and for sensible editorials that walked a "middle line between the mental eccentricity of the *Tribune* and the moral eccentricity of the *Herald*," as Charles A. Dana of *The Sun* neatly put it. The *Times* claimed to be the voice of reason amid chaotic screaming. "We do not mean to write as if we were in a passion, unless that shall really be the case; and we shall make it a point to get into a passion as rarely as possible," the founding editor and co-owner, Henry Jarvis Raymond, had vowed early on. Since 1851, the *Times* had delivered on that promise, churning out great slabs of plain text and earnest Whig-Republican commentary. In contrast to the *Herald*, it was proudly prudish, boasting to prospective readers that "all objectionable news and advertisements [would be] rigidly excluded." Advertisements for anything sex related, including abortion medicines and books on venereal disease, were rejected on principle.

These traits endeared the *Times* to the city's conservative business class, and its steadily increasing profits delighted shareholders. Raymond had a dazzling mind, but he was also overextended and unfocused; the *New York Mirror* aptly described him as "a man of more ability than stability." Like Horace Greeley, he attempted to juggle journalism and politics. In 1867, he returned from a two-year term in the U.S. House of Representatives, intending to atone for his absences and zigzagging editorial stances. Two years later, though, he suffered a stroke and died. The *Times* obituary claimed that Raymond had gone out on his last evening for a "political consultation." In fact, he expired in the arms of his mistress.

Raymond's business partner, an understated banker named George Jones, hired a fiery Englishman named Louis Jennings as editor. Under him, the *Times* launched one of the most famous anticorruption campaigns in the history of journalism. Its target was Tammany Hall's chieftain, William "Boss" Tweed, who had gained a choke hold on the city treasury and removed the accounting books from public scrutiny in order to bilk taxpayers of more than $1 billion in today's money. New York City Democrats hesitated to attack the leader of their own political machine, while influential Republicans, fearing recrimination in the form of increased taxes, also did nothing. Nor was the supposedly independent press any braver. Because Tweed decided which papers got the lucrative business of publishing the city's legal notices, even opposition organs like the *Times* looked the other way.

Jennings broke with this tradition of complacency by penning a series of outraged editorials, and a whistleblower subsequently gave one of his reporters the so-called Tweed Ring's secret ledgers. When Tweed learned that the *Times* intended to expose him by publishing hard evidence of his crimes, he offered Jones, the publisher, $5 million to kill the story. Jones refused the bribe, and the *Times* went to press with its findings, distilling the almost mythical machinations of the Tweed Ring into a dollars-and-cents reality that was easily comprehensible to the average reader. The *Times* consolidated its damning discoveries into a four-page supplement, had it printed in English and German, and kept the presses running around the clock for a week in order to distribute more than 200,000 copies. For months, the paper's only real ally in the city press was the cartoonist

Thomas Nast, whose caricatures in *Harper's Weekly* cemented the image of Tweed with his hulking frame, beady eyes, and belly resembling a sack of ill-gotten gold. Rivals like the *Herald* dithered for months until public opinion forced them to come around, and even then never gave the *Times* due credit for its bravery. Though little of the stolen money was ever recovered, Tweed did eventually end up—and die—in jail.

The lasting circulation gains for the *Times* were minimal, but the reputation of the paper soared. Its Tweed Ring exposé helped to end the seediest era of municipal corruption in New York City history and—no small achievement—created a template for modern investigative journalism.

JAMES GORDON BENNETT SR. DIED IN 1872, A MONTH AFTER THE NEWS that Stanley had met Livingstone. The funeral was held on June 13, at Bennett's mansion at Fifth Avenue and Thirty-Eighth Street. Encomiums to the "father of the modern newspaper" poured in from across the nation, but in New York opinions about his legacy were more nuanced. The *Times* attempted to reconcile Bennett's amorality ("so cynical, so pulseless, so cold") with his "naturally witty, sarcastic and sensible" takes on world events and his undeniable genius for the trade. "He made the newspaper powerful, but he also made it odious," concluded Horace Greeley, whose *Tribune* had so often found itself at odds with the *Herald*. One thing that almost everyone could agree upon was that Bennett had liberated the press "from the domination of sects, parties, cliques, and of what is called society," as *The Sun* acknowledged. "Before him a really independent newspaper was unknown, and now there is a number of them, and they are increasing."

Newspapers of all types were increasing. There were forty-five hundred of them in America in 1870, three times as many as in Great Britain. One out of every three newspapers in the world was American. Anyone seeking to explain this phenomenon could point to the widespread adoption of kerosene lamps, which facilitated reading at all hours, and to advances in literacy, and the abundance of cheap paper made possible by America's large supply of cotton and timber. Urbanization, immigration, and the increasing efficiency of steam-run presses were all factors, too. But there was also something quintessentially American about this "universality of print," a visiting writer for the upscale *British Quarterly Review* noted. "America is the classic soil of newspapers; everybody is reading; literature is permeating everywhere; publicity is sought for every interest and every order." To be a member of this rapidly expanding nation was to have something to say—or sell. As formidable an individual as Bennett was, he also owed a good deal of his success to the time and place in which he flourished. Fortunes greater than his were concurrently being made in oil, steel, and railroads, and the Civil War had increased newspaper circulation nationwide. After the war, the potential for growth seemed larger still, especially in New York City, where new millionaires and immigrants flocked like geese. The city boasted no fewer than twenty-six daily and Sunday papers in 1870, and an average total daily circulation of 600,000.

A new generation had taken charge of the New York press by 1872. When Horace Greeley, the era's most famous newspaperman, died six months after Bennett, the changing of the guard was complete. A suave protégé of Greeley's named Whitelaw Reid subsequently secured a controlling interest in the *Tribune*, steered it more conservative, and made it an accessory to his political career. It would never again seriously compete with the *Herald*, which was now breaking circulation records in the wake of the Stanley-Livingstone scoop. Before then, Bennett Sr.'s paper had only achieved a daily readership of 100,000 during pivotal Civil War battles. Once Bennett Jr.'s great gamble in Central Africa paid off, six-figure circulation became the norm.

With his father gone, Bennett swiftly asserted himself around the office. He began by revoking the various little perks that had been granted to favored veterans and ordered them to stop calling him "Young Bennett." In deference to his position at the New York Yacht Club, all subordinates would henceforth refer to him as "the Commodore." Bennett also began refashioning the paper in his own image. The scalding humor of its early days evolved into cool irony, a sign of the Commodore's posh upbringing but also of changing times. As the personal journalism of the preceding era faded, even some old-timers had to admit that the idea of eminent editors spending whole paragraphs insulting one another felt provincial and passé.

Bennett expanded the *Herald* in ways that appealed to him personally. He made it the first newspaper to devote a section to New York City real estate, in which he invested, and indulged his interest in meteorology by creating an official weather bureau for the *Herald*—before the U.S. government had one. Under him, the *Herald* devoted more columns than it had before to regattas, equestrian events, the comings and goings of wealthy travelers. It wasn't just that Bennett enjoyed these topics; he knew that they also appealed to a new generation of actual and aspiring elites. The Gilded Age—Mark Twain's apt term for the era—was in full swing, and a new American aristocracy was being minted. The *Herald* spoke its language.

Another thing the *Herald* specialized in was foreign news. It was said that it spent more on transatlantic cable fees than all other American newspapers combined, and its European coverage rivaled that of the Parisian—and sometimes even the London—dailies. The *Herald* routinely dominated in the realm of domestic news as well. When General George Custer was trounced at Little Bighorn, it had the story four days before anyone else did.

SOMETIMES THE *HERALD* WAS SO FAR AHEAD WITH ITS NEWS THAT IT WAS accused of faking. On one famous occasion in 1874, this was actually the case. Under the headline A SHOCKING SABBATH CARNIVAL OF DEATH, it reported that dozens of animals had escaped from the Central Park Zoo and wrought carnage around the city. A *Herald* writer claimed to have seen an enraged rhinoceros gore its keeper, break out of its cage, and destroy a handful of other enclosures, releasing dozens of carnivorous beasts into the streets. A brown bear killed an old woman inside a church on West Fifty-Third Street; a lion attacked four young children, "mangling the delicate little things past all signs of recognition." The *Herald* reported that policemen were out firing at the animals with their revolvers and that hospitals were swiftly becoming overwhelmed.

New Yorkers panicked. Some shut themselves in, while others rushed out with hunting rifles. The city editor of the *Times* stormed over to police headquarters, demanding to know why the story had been withheld from every newspaper except the *Herald*. Like so many others, he'd failed to read to the end of the article. "Of course the entire story given above is a pure fabrication. Not one word of it is true," the *Herald* had finally admitted. It had, it claimed, simply desired to call attention to the absence of a formal evacuation plan in the event of a disaster like the one described. Though widely condemned, the stunt sold 150,000 papers.

Thanks to the Commodore's tyrannical management, the *Herald* was often more fun to read than it was to work for. Nonetheless, every ambitious reporter was eager to land a job there. The opportunities it offered for career advancement were unparalleled, especially for anyone who had a taste for travel and adventure. As one popular illustrated newspaper put it, there was "a *Herald* man in every nook and cranny of the Earth."

In the wake of the Stanley-Livingstone scoop, other papers tried to imitate the enterprising ways of the *Herald*, and journalism took on a globe-trotting, swashbuckling aura. The *Tribune*, for one, heartily approved of this trend: "The reporter of today is the adventurer who penetrates the desert and the jungle, the scholar who searches for relics of the forgotten past, the courier who bears the news of victory to courts and congresses across a wilderness and through hostile armies." In reality, very few journalists did any such thing. Only the Anglo-American press operated with enough independence to risk running afoul of governments, and only very rich publishers like Bennett could afford big-ticket ventures. London's *Daily Telegraph* swiftly emerged as the main rival of the *Herald* in this respect. In 1873, it dispatched a British Museum scholar named George Smith to Assyria (present-day Iraq) in search of historical records of events described in the Bible. Though Smith hoped to collect thousands of cuneiform tablets, the *Telegraph* was only really interested in the discovery of a single lost shard: a three-inch-by-three-inch fragment that completed the ancient story of Noah's flood. Incredibly, Smith found the fragment just one week after breaking ground at the ruins of ancient Nineveh, near Mosul.

His sensational discovery inspired the *Telegraph* to try for something bigger. In 1874, upon receiving news of David Livingstone's death in Africa, it approached Henry Stanley about taking up the late explorer's search for the Nile's source. The owner of the *Telegraph*, Edward Levy-Lawson, agreed to contribute £6,000—nearly ten times what Bennett had spent on finding Livingstone—if the *Herald* would match that figure and share the newspaper rights to the story. The Commodore sent a one-word response: "Yes." But he agreed to the shared enterprise grudgingly, mainly to avoid losing out if Stanley succeeded. Bennett's exploration interests had migrated elsewhere by this point—northward.

# CHAPTER EIGHT

With the U.S. Navy unwilling to fund a North Pole expedition, Bennett began scouring the Scottish shipyards for a suitable vessel that he could outfit himself. It was during the early stages of this search that he received a letter from George Washington De Long, reminding Bennett that his navigation of ice-choked Melville Bay in search of the *Polaris* had received "flattering commendations at the hands of your paper." De Long proposed that if Bennett was in fact thinking about funding a North Pole attempt, he should be the man to lead it. The two Arctic enthusiasts—De Long, twenty-nine, and Bennett, thirty-three—met in New York early in 1874, but an economic recession halted immediate further discussions. By the time they next met, a year later, Bennett had already committed to a private expedition to the Northwest Passage led by the British Merchant Navy captain Allen Young, a veteran of the Franklin searches.

Young's *Pandora* sailed in the shadow of the Royal Navy's long-awaited return to Arctic exploring. Captain George Nares departed with two vessels for the North Pole that year, at the helm of the most celebrated British polar venture since Franklin's. Unable to send a correspondent along with Nares, Bennett paid £5,000 for the privilege of having his new favorite "special," Januarius MacGahan, go with Young. Melville Bay was surprisingly clear of ice during the summer of 1875, allowing *Pandora* to sail deep into the Canadian Arctic archipelago before the usual obstacle blocked its progress. "Ice, nothing but ice," MacGahan wrote, "and the higher we get, the better view we obtain, the more formidable becomes the prospect." Rather than risk a winter frozen in, Young sensibly returned to Great Britain. His experience showed again just how diabolically difficult it was to penetrate the Northwest Passage and gave explorers yet another reason to shift their attentions to the North Pole, if only because the challenge of getting there had yet to be fully proven.

By early 1876, Bennett had settled on De Long as the man to lead the *Herald*'s North Pole expedition. Confident that it could depart later that year—using his own refitted yacht, the *Dauntless*, if necessary—Bennett told MacGahan to prepare to join it. "If you succeed you will eclipse Stanley, Livingstone and any former explorers whether African or Polar," he urged. But MacGahan considered the emerging news of Turkish atrocities in Bulgaria a more important story and asked to be sent there instead. When Bennett refused, he quit the *Herald* and signed with the London *Daily News*. His reporting on the atrocities and the subsequent Russo-Turkish War made him a national hero in Bulgaria, where there are streets named after him to this day. MacGahan died of typhoid in 1878 in Istanbul, three days short of his thirty-fourth birthday. The *Pandora* expedition was his first and last trip to the Arctic.

De Long failed to find a ship that winter, and Bennett decided against refitting his own yacht. The *Herald* expedition lost another year. The delay enabled both men to ponder the lessons learned by Nares, who achieved a new Farthest North, added significantly to knowledge of the regions along Smith Sound, and further legitimized British (and ultimately Canadian) possession of great swaths of the Arctic. To his countrymen and his navy superiors, though, the Nares expedition had been a failure. A deadly outbreak of scurvy had forced him to return a year earlier than expected, and his sledging parties had gotten no closer than four hundred miles from the pole.

Disheartened by these results, the Royal Navy shifted its exploring focus to the Southern Hemisphere. Its latest retreat from the Arctic created an opening for De Long and Bennett, but the two Americans were unable to act on their polar ambitions immediately. Several obstacles would bar the way, including fallout from a society scandal involving Bennett that would have permanent consequences for the *Herald* and its investments in northern adventures.

# CHAPTER NINE

Bennett's reputation for drunken antics was by now firmly established in New York City, and stories of the bizarre things he got up to while in his cups were often told.

He was known to send his four-in-hand coach careening around Central Park after dark—on at least one occasion, stark naked. He had been seen circling his block atop a high-wheeled bicycle, with his butler stationed outside and pouring him a fresh brandy each time he pedaled past. He'd once shot up his own chandelier with a pistol in the middle of a dinner party.

Bennett was obnoxious and entitled—few would have argued otherwise. But he also suffered from a total inability to hold his liquor. As one early biographer put it, "Two glasses of champagne would completely destroy his equilibrium." It was thanks to pure dumb luck that he never ran anyone over in his carriage while under the influence. He did once overturn, throwing himself and a young debutante named Jennie Jerome from their seats. Fortunately, the future mother of Winston Churchill escaped serious injury.

While Bennett faced no serious consequences for his misbehavior, sometimes at least the joke was on him. He once took a swing at another patron inside a crowded upscale bar, unaware the man was a famous prizefighter, and was instantly knocked out cold. One evening a fire brigade arrived outside Delmonico's to put out a nearby blaze; Bennett lurched out onto the sidewalk in his evening clothes and began barking out directions to the professionals, until they blasted him with their fire hose. The cold light of day usually brought him to his senses—and reaching for his checkbook. The morning after that particular incident, the Commodore bought new rubber coats for the firefighters.

Victorian mores prevented Bennett from seeking casual sex within his own social sphere, but singers, dancers, and actresses were considered fairer game, and he pursued them. Even the period's naughtier newspapers generally considered such subjects off-limits, and details of his sex life are nonexistent, but the cozy arrangement he had with the powerful New York law firm of Howe & Hummel speaks volumes. The legal code of the time allowed women to sue for damages when a man reneged on a vow to marry, something less-than-honorable suitors often did after they'd talked a woman into sleeping with them. Howe & Hummel specialized in bringing (or threatening to bring) breach-of-promise suits, as they were called, regardless of whether they were righting a grievous wrong or simply abetting blackmail. Abe Hummel, the junior partner in charge of civil cases, was said to represent every theater manager in the country, and an incoming piece of mail with his name on it was enough to send even the most cavalier swordsman into a panic. Bennett likely knew the joke that for any swell who enjoyed New York City to its fullest, the only two certainties in life were death and dealings with Abe Hummel. But the Commodore also went out of his way to ensure that his relationship with the notorious firm would be a friendly one, allowing Hummel, a lover of horse racing, to file dispatches to the *Herald* from Saratoga and to contribute self-promoting essays on various legal subjects. Hummel reciprocated by offering Bennett special protection from the one thing that usually kept high-flying cads like him in check.

Bennett did, however, periodically court women of elevated social status. According to a contemporary gossip columnist, he'd already been engaged twice by the age of thirty-four, once to the daughter of a former Massachusetts governor and "once to a well-known Cuban society belle."

By 1876, he was pledged again, and this one appeared to be serious. Caroline May was a friend of his sister, Jeannette. Popular, blond, and pretty, she came from a respected Baltimore family of distinguished military ancestry. Bennett showered Caroline May with Tiffany jewelry and paid $20,000 to have her bridal trousseau sent over from Paris. They made plans to spend the honeymoon there in high style, following a small wedding ceremony in New York City. By the end of 1876, though, relations between Bennett and the Mays had begun to sour. The groom-to-be fought with his future mother-in-law over the bridal gown, and even threatened to exclude the family from the wedding.

On January 1, 1877, Caroline May hosted a daytime gathering at her family's Manhattan town house, in observance of an old Knickerbocker tradition that called for well-bred young women to open their doors to well-bred young men on New Year's Day and ply them with cake, wine, and whiskey punch. The tradition had degenerated in recent years into an excuse for the men to drunkenly roam the streets of Manhattan, and naturally Bennett participated. When he reeled into his fiancée's drawing room that afternoon and toward the punch tray, nervous glances followed him every step of the way.

Exactly what happened next would be debated by society gossips long afterward. Some said he approached the fireplace and urinated into the flames. Others said that he relieved himself into the grand piano. Whichever it was, the drawing room descended into shrieking chaos. The legs of several ladies present went out from under them. Caroline's kinsmen seized Bennett and frog-marched him out the front door.

When friends came to visit him the next day, Bennett could tell from their furrowed brows that he had well and truly crossed a line this time. The Mays were incensed. Caroline's brother Fred, a burly twenty-six-year-old known for his weight-lifting abilities, was said to be out looking for him. One day later, Bennett ventured to the Union Club for lunch, and a hush fell over the room when he entered. A friend said that Bennett "seemed much annoyed at the watchful glances" being directed at him and left. Outside, Fred May was waiting for him. As Bennett stiffly approached, smoking a cigarette, May pulled a small whip from inside his overcoat and began thrashing him with it. Some of the clubmen who'd been eagerly watching from the windows rushed out to break up the fight. May walked away unscathed. Bennett, his nose gushing blood, was sent home in a cab to get stitches.

Fred May's older brother, William, approved of Bennett's beating. "He ought to have been cowhided long ago," he told *The Sun*. Unlike the mysterious incident that had precipitated it, the confrontation outside the Union Club was vividly described in the press. But Bennett was not about to let the embarrassing affair end here, for reasons one of his friends explained to the *Tribune*: he "remembered, and always with bitter wrath, the blows received by the elder Bennett and the fact that he had never retaliated." Bennett challenged Fred May to a duel. A week later, the two men gathered their pistols, seconds, a referee, and a surgeon, and met in a brushy backwater on the Maryland-Delaware border called Slaughter's Gap. For some reason, they agreed to use May's poorly functioning old pistols. He fired first and missed, and then Bennett's weapon jammed. The referee decided that he was thus entitled to another shot, this time at his leisure and using one of his own exquisitely crafted firearms. Bennett, the fresh scar on his nose swollen from the cold, stood there gazing icily across the field at Fred May. Then he fired into the air, and both parties packed up and went home.

One of the biggest society scandals of the Gilded Age had ended with a single exchange of shots, if it could be called that, and no one harmed. In his private train car back to New York, Bennett grilled his friends on whether he'd resolved things honorably. They convinced him that he had, but the doors of New York society remained closed to him. Given that dueling was illegal in both Maryland and Delaware, he also faced possible indictment.

Later that January, Bennett held one last conference with his editors. He told them to keep the light in his office burning every night, as a reminder to anyone who walked by that he was watching. Then he quietly boarded a steamship for France. He never lived in America again.

# CHAPTER TEN

Bennett's ignoble flight from the United States marked the end of an era for the *Herald*. He would henceforth manage the paper from abroad, an unorthodox arrangement that gave other publishers a whole new reason to look askance at him. His unseemly feud with the Mays made headlines nationwide; *The Boston Globe* quipped that he had given "all the newspapers in the country, except his own, something to talk about." Millions of Americans probably chuckled at this latest tale out of New York City, with its ever-expanding population of boorish nouveaux riches—including in Tennessee, where eighteen-year-old Adolph Ochs was striving to make an honorable name for himself.

The New York City publisher who would eventually compete with James Gordon Bennett possessed neither his rival's privileged upbringing nor his rebellious streak. Ochs was born on March 12, 1858, in Cincinnati, the son of two Bavarian Jewish immigrants. His affectionate and well-educated father, Julius, served the Union during the Civil War, more usefully as a traveling salesman than as a combatant. After the war, Julius Ochs (born Ochsenhorn) failed as a merchant and in most of his other business pursuits, placing great financial strain upon his family. He later became a justice of the peace in Knoxville, Tennessee, which provided a small income and earned him the respect of the community. But because he refused to take bribes or play politics, the job paid less than he needed to support his wife and children and provided no opportunity for career advancement. Adolph's mother, Bertha, who'd immigrated to Natchez, Mississippi, as a teenager, ran the cash-strapped Ochs household with an iron will. A staunch Confederate, she was also at odds with her husband ideologically.

Young Adolph, their oldest son, thus learned the art of domestic diplomacy early, and the memory of his father's financial humiliation would always weigh on him. When he was eleven, he got a job delivering newspapers for the *Knoxville Chronicle*, sometimes rising as early as 3:00 a.m. to fold his bundle, complete his paper route, and be at school by the time classes began at 7:00. Adolph's younger brothers, George and Milton, did the same, and shared their meager weekly earnings with the family.

After short and dispiriting stints in the grocery and drugstore trades, Adolph began rising through the lower ranks at the *Knoxville Chronicle*, ascending from office boy to printer's "devil" (or assistant) to journeyman printer. He quit school at age fourteen to work there full time and continued to impress his superiors. When he took a job in Louisville, Kentucky, three years later, the head compositor who was about to lose him saluted Adolph as "a necessity, hard to part with." Adolph received a first-class education in typography at Henry Watterson's Louisville *Courier-Journal*. When his progress at that nationally respected paper stalled after six months, he came home and got a job in the composing room of another Knoxville paper.

Julius was working as an insurance broker now, and as Adolph began to settle in at the *Knoxville Tribune*, his father's business fortunes took their latest turn for the worse. To satisfy his creditors, Julius auctioned off the family's possessions and moved the Ochses into a rented house. He also sank into a pit of self-loathing. "I have often wished for death and a great boon it would be to me and a relief to my family," he wrote.

Adolph took it upon himself to end their penury. He was inspired by the example of the late Horace Greeley, who had not only been a celebrated writer and thinker but also escaped childhood poverty by way of the newspaper trade. Adolph had caught the eye of the editor and the business manager of the *Knoxville Tribune*, and when the older men approached him to be the advertising solicitor of a newspaper they were establishing in Chattanooga, he traveled south with them. Chattanooga was a promising city in which to set up shop. Outsiders like Adolph Ochs made up the vast majority of its residents, and he felt more at home there than in many of the other postwar southern towns he had visited. There was less anti-Semitism and factionalism in Chattanooga than in Knoxville, for example, and more room for new ideas and business ventures.

The *Chattanooga Daily Dispatch* failed after a year, dashing Adolph's hopes for a swift change of fortune. But its creditors appointed him receiver, and he impressed them by scraping together every cent the paper owed. Sensing an opportunity, Adolph also used its idle presses to produce Chattanooga's first city directory. The door knocking he did while collecting listings made him known to nearly every banker and business owner in town, and the profits enabled him to send $2 a week to his family.

Adolph Ochs had the classic traits of an upstanding self-made American. "Honest, zealous, reliable and trustworthy," an editor at the *Knoxville Chronicle* had called him. But he also had a few tricks up his sleeve. He grew a mustache to make himself look older and owned a handsome leather checkbook that he flashed whenever he asked creditors for an extra day to "audit"—that is, temporarily fill—his bank account. Whether they suspected anything or not, they always granted the extension.

Having begun to prove himself a worthy credit risk, Ochs put himself on the path to newspaper ownership. He acquired a half interest in the struggling *Chattanooga Daily Times* for $1,500, borrowing $250 from a relative in order to make the down payment. In July 1878, he persuaded his anxious and doubting father to sign the ownership papers on his behalf; at twenty, he was legally too young to do so himself.

Crucially, Ochs reserved the right to buy the remaining half interest within two years. He then set out to build his fortune, undaunted by the fact that he was beginning with a mere $12.50 in operating funds. He was a businessman—more of a businessman than a journalist. Though he'd proven himself capable in many other aspects of the trade, his brief service as a junior reporter had been unremarkable. Many years later, the trade magazine *Printers' Ink* suggested in a profile of Ochs that any number of professional fields "might readily have been distinguished by his personality." But newspapering was the one that he landed in, and the one in which he would make his mark.

# CHAPTER ELEVEN

George Washington De Long did not find a ship during the winter of 1876–77. The bad ones from the Scottish whaling fleet were not worth fixing, and the good ones were not for sale. He had the hot market for whalebone—an essential component of corsets, hoopskirts, and umbrellas—to thank for that.

Restless to proceed one way or another, Bennett traveled that spring from his new home in Paris to the medieval German town of Gotha to meet with Dr. August Petermann, the world's leading Arctic scholar. Of special interest to both men was the theory of an open polar sea. It was pretty much universally agreed that a ring of ice encircled the planet's upper regions. Some experts, though, believed that beyond this frozen barrier temperatures actually got *warmer* as one approached the pole. Supporters of this theory put much faith in recent studies of the Kuroshio, or "Black Stream," a warm current that swept from the Far East up to Alaska, and posited that it warmed points north of there much as the Gulf Stream did in the British Isles and western Europe. A widely read article in *Putnam's* hypothesized that winter temperatures at the North Pole were similar to those of Milwaukee or Buffalo. Petermann more or less agreed. "I should not be surprised if Esquimaux were found right under the Pole," he told the *Herald.*

Unfortunately, the theory of the open sea was poppycock. It owed some of its appeal—too much, probably—to a work of popular fiction: Jules Verne's 1865 novel *The Adventures of Captain Hatteras*, a tale of a Franklin-esque explorer who discovers giant jellyfish, new species of sea-birds, and a smoking volcano at the top of the world. It was true that the American explorers Elisha Kent Kane and Isaac Israel Hayes had earlier claimed to have glimpsed the unfrozen Arctic Ocean, but Charles Francis Hall had shown Kane's "sea" to be a mere strait of about fifteen miles wide. The recent experience of the Nares expedition, which had pushed farthest north of all, suggested that far from teeming with whales and waterfowl, the North Pole was "rather a desert," as the London *Daily News* drily put it.

*The New-York Times* dismissed the open-sea theorists as delusional. "This mirage is a thing that always seems just beyond the reach of the explorers. They see signs of it; they see itself; they smell it in the air, and can almost touch it; whereupon they usually come away from it, leaving it as before to exasperate the minds and purposes of the gentlemen of England (and other places) who live at home at ease." Among the most influential of those gentlemen was August Petermann, who'd never been north of Scotland and could be remarkably blasé about the risks involved in testing his armchair theories. "Perhaps I am wrong, but the way to show that is to give me the evidence," he said.

Bennett shared Petermann's optimism regarding the North Pole and came out of their three-hour meeting convinced that everyone else had been going about the problem wrong. Both men agreed that the Smith Sound approach favored by the British and Americans was overrated and that the untried route through the Bering Strait would offer smoother sailing. Bennett was so energized by the conversation that he told De Long he was considering outfitting a second ship and personally leading his own expedition up the east coast of Greenland. He instructed him to look into the possibility of using hot-air balloons for reconnaissance and lifting sledges over rough terrain. De Long dismissed balloons as impractical, and Bennett's enthusiasm for leading a parallel expedition soon faded. But when a suitable ship—none other than Young's 240-ton *Pandora*—finally came on the market, the Commodore hastened to England to close the deal personally.

*Pandora* was renamed *Jeannette* on July 4, 1878, in honor of Bennett's sister. The Commodore hosted the christening at Le Havre, in France, and said characteristically little during the toasting rounds. Lengthier remarks were provided by Henry Stanley, now the world's most famous living explorer. Thanks to him, the outstanding geographical questions about Central Africa's major lakes and river systems had been answered. His reports would shape the future of the region for years to come, laying the groundwork for commercial, colonial, missionary, and military decisions that would decide the fates of untold millions of Africans. Stanley's legacy would not prove to be an entirely positive one, to put it mildly, and even now, around the high point of his career, he was a controversial figure. Violent clashes with indigenous Africans, including his own porters, had become a recurrent feature of his travels, and Stanley's casual descriptions thereof a hallmark of his writing. Even his supporters struggled to defend the frank, even boastful way he talked about using deadly force. "I do not see how these fights could have been avoided, although possibly I would not, if I had been in his place, have given as much prominence to them in my letters to the *Herald*," Petermann commented.

Having received Stanley and Bennett's blessing, the *Jeannette* sailed from Le Havre for San Francisco that July. De Long decided at the last minute to oversee this six-month, eighteen-thousand-mile stage of the journey personally, after Emma De Long proposed that she and their seven-year-old daughter, Sylvie, come along. Her audacious proposition both pleased Bennett and made him wistful. "Well, your wife must think a great deal of you to take that long journey," he told De Long, with feeling. "No woman would ever do that for me."

EVEN THOUGH THE *JEANNETTE* HAD SURVIVED THREE ARCTIC VOYAGES already, the shipwrights at the U.S. Navy shipyard at Mare Island, California, took additional measures to fortify it against the ice, adding so many pounds of thick oak and pine bracing that the *Herald* was soon claiming that no vessel had ever been so thoroughly armored against the Arctic elements. De Long, however, carefully avoided tempting fate. "I don't want to go off through the big part of the horn and come back through the little one," he told a *Herald* reporter.

De Long busied himself with preparations, securing an elite group of officers that included Lieutenant Charles Chipp, his capable second-in-command aboard *Little Juniata*, and George Melville, a chief engineer with Arctic experience. Also mixed in among the thirty-one-man crew and officer corps was the *Herald* correspondent Jerome Collins, whose status within the expedition hierarchy was unclear. A bit of a polymath, Collins had been the man responsible for creating Bennett's pioneering weather bureau. He would be writing about the *Herald*'s North Pole expedition while also serving as its chief scientist.

De Long considered it important to have an escort vessel, which would enable him to save coal and establish winter quarters farther north. But when he asked the navy for a man-of-war to accompany the *Jeannette* as far as the Aleutian Islands, he was rebuffed. Bennett's response to this setback was not comforting. "If you should happen to meet with disaster, the nice old gentleman [Secretary of the Navy Richard Thompson] will be held responsible," he blithely assured De Long.

The planning that De Long had so capably overseen now entered a dangerous phase, because Bennett's attention started wandering just as it was needed most. Aware that he had canceled his trip to San Francisco for the send-off, the Navy Department had begun to deprioritize the expedition. De Long tactfully suggested to Bennett that this was why he had been refused the escort vessel. "I cannot help feeling that the impression gained ground that you did not care much about the expedition anyhow, and that there was no use bothering about it," he ventured.

In fact, Bennett had simply found a new aspect of the expedition to care about: the prospect of creating a Stanley-Livingstone sensation. While De Long prepared to risk life and limb for the original mission of attaining the North Pole, Bennett secretly advanced a conflicting plan. The summer before, a Swedish expedition led by Nils Adolf Erik Nordenskiöld had sailed from Gothenburg to Siberia, intending to navigate the Northeast Passage through to Japan. Bennett, dreaming of a scenario in which the beleaguered Norseman was rescued by the *Jeannette*, persuaded the Russian government to delay its nascent relief plans. In order to stoke enthusiasm for its rescue operation, the *Herald* began playing up the dangers facing Nordenskiöld's *Vega*, which was widely believed to have spent the winter comfortably frozen in. De Long either missed or ignored these sensationalized reports and was thus shocked to receive sailing orders to proceed to the pole only after he'd spent precious summer weeks in search of Nordenskiöld. He begged Bennett to get the navy to reconsider, unaware that the navy had altered the original plan at Bennett's urging.

The sluggish schooner that De Long chartered to escort the *Jeannette* across the Bering Strait was a week late for their planned rendezvous at St. Michael, Alaska. When De Long finally met with Chukchi natives on the Siberian side of the strait, they could not say whether Nordenskiöld had come through. He had, and would be hailed as the discoverer of the Northeast Passage in Yokohama several days later.

De Long, who had no way of knowing this, sent back word that he would continue to seek news of Nordenskiöld before steaming north. The *Jeannette* spent the winter of 1879–80 "safe at anchor in some cove of Wrangell Land [*sic*] where the frozen sea could not crush her"—or so the hopeful *Herald* speculated. Actually, the expedition's whereabouts and status were unknown.

# CHAPTER TWELVE

S till nothing had been heard of the *Jeannette* by the fall of 1880. Bennett's columns bulged with tales of Arctic travel anyway, because the *Herald* correspondent William Henry Gilder returned from three years in the Canadian Arctic with the U.S. Army lieutenant Frederick Schwatka. While the *Jeannette* sat on blocks at Mare Island, Schwatka's five-man party had set out from the northwest shore of Hudson Bay accompanied by twelve Inuit. The expedition reached King William Island, achieving by native dogsled what Young had failed to do with the *Pandora*, and discovered old clothing, skeletal remains, and other relics of the Franklin expedition that had eluded McClintock twenty years earlier. Natives uncontacted by previous search parties told Schwatka a story of bedraggled white men hauling a lifeboat overland, their bodies withered and their mouths "dry and hard and black." But no documents had been salvaged, and the Franklin expedition's camps and caches had evidently all washed away. Gilder, in his *Herald* write-up, peremptorily declared an end to thirty years of Franklin searching.

In hindsight, Schwatka's more noteworthy achievement was the journey itself. Amounting to 3,251 statute miles, it was the longest dogsled trip ever completed by white men. The party covered territory that was largely unexplored by Westerners, braving January temperatures that averaged

-69 degrees Fahrenheit and plunged as low as -101. Schwatka didn't just survive these frigid extremes; he thrived in them, and his wholesale embrace of native travel methods would be imitated by Robert Peary. As Gilder wrote in the *Herald*, "The Esquimau dog will do more work and with less food than any other draught animal existing." The problem was that if not managed properly, dogs would also ransack an expedition's food supplies, chew through their leather traces and run away, attack each other, and otherwise wreak havoc. Only the Inuit really knew how to handle them, and yet most previous explorers, including Hall, had been too arrogant to entrust nonwhites with anything as important as driving dogs. By setting such prejudices aside, Schwatka was able to make steady progress in even the worst snow and ice conditions.

Schwatka's party subsisted almost entirely on reindeer, musk oxen, seals, and walrus killed along the way. Though Gilder admitted that the native diet took some getting used to, he found himself and the other initiates "so well fortified against the cold by the quantities of fat we had eaten that we did not mind it." Relying on fresh game meat enabled them to travel for a year on one month's provisions, and also helped to prevent the scurvy that had ravaged the Nares expedition a few years earlier.

Gilder dwelled on practical considerations like these, but his *Herald* dispatches also had the flavor of an exotic travelogue. He wrote of tattooed Inuit women, and of mixing seal oil with the grassy contents of a reindeer's stomach to make an edible delicacy that "looks like ice cream." Explorers had described the minutiae of Arctic travel in books before, but never at such length in a newspaper. The *Herald* devoted more space to Gilder's dispatches than it would to the assassination of President Garfield a year later. For all its merits, though, the expedition would amount to a historical footnote. America—and James Gordon Bennett—had far more riding on the *Jeannette*.

NO FEWER THAN FIVE GOVERNMENT VESSELS SEARCHED FOR THE *JEANnette* during the summer of 1881, two of which were dispatched for the express purpose of finding it. One was the USS *Alliance*, which steamed northeast toward Spitsbergen, where De Long had predicted he would emerge if carried up and over the pole by drifting floes. The other was the USS *Rodgers*, which set out to retrace De Long's outbound route through the Bering Strait. Bennett, hedging his bets, put correspondents aboard both relief ships. None of the five search parties encountered the merest sign of the *Jeannette*, though, and by the time most returned, it had been more than two years since it had been seen or heard from.

International offers of assistance came flowing in. The Royal Geographical Society drew up plans for a relief effort; the Hudson's Bay Company prepared to mobilize dozens of its far-flung agents in Arctic Canada. In Copenhagen, the Danish captain of Nordenskiöld's *Vega* began raising funds to save the American expedition that had unnecessarily gone looking for his own two years earlier. This rush to cast a wide net ended shortly after it began. Just before Christmas, a message arrived from the governor of Yakutsk, the easternmost Russian outpost in Siberia, bearing long-awaited news of the *Jeannette*: "The poor fellows have lost everything."

De Long's ship had been crushed in the ice and sunk in June, more than six months earlier. So reported the engineer George Melville, who'd led twelve survivors to a Siberian native village in September. His written plea for help had traveled fifteen hundred miles by messenger sled to Yakutsk and then been relayed another thousand miles by sled to Irkutsk, capital of eastern Siberia and the terminus of the czar's telegraph line. The *Herald* devoted nearly three pages, or one-fourth of its December 21, 1881, edition, to the news of the disaster, which was far from over. De Long and eighteen other men were unaccounted for, and thought to be dead or dying.

Melville's report also indicated that the *Jeannette* had gotten nowhere near the pole and made no significant geographical discoveries. "Her apparent direct route was traversed by Nordenskiöld in his voyage from Hammerfest to Behring [*sic*] Strait, and the little that is worth knowing about the waters to the north of that part of Siberia we know already," the *Times* coldly noted. The *Herald* simply emphasized the search for survivors. Having launched an aborted attempt to rescue the rest of De Long's party in the Lena delta, Melville was now on his way to Yakutsk to secure additional resources and try again, this time with the full cooperation of the American and Russian governments.

Bennett immediately wired money for relief supplies and medical care for the survivors in Irkutsk. He also dispatched a Paris-based correspondent, John P. Jackson, to interview them. Melville's men (and the two from De Long's party who'd joined them) had undergone a serious physical and psychological ordeal, with the boatswain Jack Cole in the worst shape of all. Jackson's arrival convinced the addled young seaman that he was back in New York City; he returned from a supervised stroll around Irkutsk reporting that he'd attempted to drop by the *Herald* office but failed to find it.

Jackson got most of his story of the disaster from Lieutenant John Danenhower, the lone officer in the group, who'd lost the use of both eyes after an inflammatory condition had gone untreated. From behind his blindfold, Danenhower told of how the *Jeannette* had become trapped in ice soon after entering uncharted territory north of Alaska, then drifted erratically with the windblown floes, "at times gyrating in almost perfect circles." Rather than ease up as the men had hoped, the eight-foot-thick plates of ice held firm all summer, forcing them to endure a second Arctic winter at its mercy. The ice's death grip tightened in the spring, causing the weakened sides of the *Jeannette* to give in "like a broken basket," Danenhower said. As frigid water poured into the hold, the men unloaded their supplies, camped on the ice, and watched the *Jeannette* go under.

The thirty-three castaways hauled three boats and a total of fifteen thousand pounds of gear southward across the ice. Only two-thirds of the men were fit enough to move this enormous load, and at times they shuttled twenty-six miles back and forth in order to advance just two miles over the jagged and breaking ice. The party finally came upon an unknown island in late July, seven weeks after leaving the *Jeannette*. De Long named it Bennett Island and spent a week there recuperating, exploring, and hunting birds. They spent most of the next month navigating the floes by sail and oar; then as they neared the coast, the ice diminished and the boats began running aground on muddy shoals. The party was by now divided nearly evenly across three boats: a cutter, captained by De Long;

a second cutter, captained by Lieutenant Chipp; and a whaleboat commanded by Melville, with assistance from the impaired Danenhower. Fifty miles from shore, the boats separated during an overnight gale. The occupants of Melville's boat were luckiest: they discovered a patch of water that was deep enough for them to row into what Melville later described as a "desolate maze of shoal, swamps, and muddy islands." Rather than getting bogged down in a cul-de-sac, they found a river that flowed south into Siberia, where they were rescued and taken in by native Yakuts. Word reached them in late October that two members of De Long's party, William Nindemann and Louis Noros, had gone ahead to seek help for the captain and ten starving others. Chipp's cutter was presumed to have swamped, and all aboard to have drowned.

Jackson posted his articles for the *Herald*, including an exciting account of his own twenty-five-hundred-mile sleigh journey through Russia's "vast uncultured annex," and then set off to meet with Melville's search party in the Lena delta.

MEANWHILE, THE *HERALD* CORRESPONDENT ASSIGNED TO THE *RODGERS* had his own Arctic disaster to relate. The ablest of the government's relief vessels was assumed to have wintered somewhere west of the Bering Strait and launched searches for the *Jeannette* by dogsled. In fact, the ship's charred remains now rode the waves. A fire had broken out in the forehold late that fall and quickly spread, snapping the anchor line as officers and crew hastened to salvage precious stores. They had last seen the *Rodgers* drifting away in the current, smoking like a funeral pyre.

Luckily for the castaways, native Chukchis on St. Lawrence Bay lodged and fed them that winter—with the exception of William Henry Gilder. The *Herald* correspondent set off by dogsled for Irkutsk to inform the navy and the *Herald* of what had happened. Mileage-wise, the journey was the equivalent of traveling from Chicago to San Francisco—through waist-deep snow and winds so cold that Gilder spent large portions of the trip facing backward. His guide was an exiled Russian trader whom the locals had urged him not to trust; Gilder spoke no Russian, and the Inuit dialect he had learned while in Arctic Canada with Schwatka was incomprehensible to Siberians. Somehow, though, it all worked out. Three months after leaving his shipmates, Gilder reached a Russian station from which he was able to forward his messages to Yakutsk.

Near the Lena delta, he learned that the *Jeannette* had sunk and that Melville was nearby, and detoured north in hopes of meeting him. At a station on the Kolyma River, another of northeastern Siberia's Arctic Ocean feeders, Gilder came across a packet of mail that was bound for Irkutsk and addressed to the secretary of the U.S. Navy. He persuaded the Cossack stationmaster to let him open it. Inside he found Melville's official report of the search he'd made for De Long that winter.

Melville had spotted tent poles poking out of a snowbank and then the bodies nearby, after nearly tripping over De Long's half-buried arm. The captain and the last eight men had resorted in the end to eating boot leather, and had been so desperate for warmth that they had put their feet directly into the campfire. One last potential source of heat, however, had gone unused. De Long had refused to burn the records of the expedition, including the personal diary stored in his coat pocket. Melville informed the navy that he had recovered these precious documents and would deliver them personally to Washington. But he had copied out the last month of De Long's diary entries and included them with the report, and it was to these October entries that Gilder turned next.

De Long and his sodden men had waded ashore after landing in the vast shoals of the Lena delta, unsure of where Melville's and Chipp's boats had ended up. The mazelike river system that confronted them was like the end of a fraying rope, with strands flaring out in all directions, and the error-ridden map De Long carried soon proved useless. The castaways slept in abandoned hunting shelters, curled up in holes in the riverbank, or lay out entirely exposed. They ate reindeer for a while after their pemmican rations ran out, but then began to freeze and starve. Hoping to distract themselves from hunger, they consumed one-ounce rations of alcohol. A seaman who'd lost nine toes to frostbite died. De Long, worried that most of the group could not go on, sent the seamen Nindemann and Noros ahead to find help.

Deprived of its two strongest members, the main party languished. When their tea ran out, they resorted to boiling handfuls of Arctic willow. The second man to die was Alexei, an Inuit hunter who'd come aboard in Alaska and whose death ended any remaining hope of securing fresh meat. The weakening survivors prayed for rescue and built signal fires. The wind stopped them in their tracks, and some nights they were too exhausted even to collect firewood. De Long's record keeping shriveled. "Everybody pretty weak. Slept or rested today, and then managed to get enough wood in before dark. Read part of divine service. Suffering on our feet. No foot-gear," he wrote. One week later: "Boyd and Goertz died during the night. Mr. Collins dying." It was his last entry.

De Long's sad chronicle left Gilder speechless before the puzzled Cossack stationmaster. "For the first time in my life," he wrote, "I found it impossible to restrain my emotion before strangers, and buried my face in my hands for ten or fifteen minutes."

THEN GILDER WROTE UP EVERYTHING HE'D JUST LEARNED FOR THE *HERALD*. These were "very questionable liberties" to have taken with sealed government correspondence, Melville later argued, and the resulting articles were published right as the chief engineer's confidential report reached the navy, rendering it mostly redundant. But the dubious way in which Gilder had gotten his information did not raise undue widespread concern, especially in view of the fact that his employer had funded the expedition.

The actions of the other two *Herald* correspondents involved in the *Jeannette* disaster would prove to be more controversial. While Melville searched for Chipp's party, and Gilder proceeded south to Irkutsk, Jackson located the cairn tomb in which the engineer had buried De Long and his companions, removed some of the bodies, and searched them for documents. Before reburying them, Jackson permitted an illustrator who was traveling with him to sketch the corpses.

What Jackson had hoped to find was the diary of Jerome Collins, the expedition's *Herald* correspondent and chief scientist. He'd learned in Irkutsk that Collins had fallen out with De Long and recorded his many grievances against the commander, possibly in order for the *Herald* to make them public. Emma De Long later complained of Jackson's "desecration" to Bennett, and the grisly sketches were never published. But the well-connected brothers of Jerome Collins were so alarmed by rumors of their deceased sibling's mistreatment by De Long that they lobbied for an investigation. They got one, in part because Jackson's sensational reporting from Irkutsk had put additional pressure on the navy to determine who, if anyone, was to blame for the deadly catastrophe.

The *Herald* covered the ensuing weeks-long naval investigation closely, devoting at least a column to each session. The navy board ultimately found that all officers and crew had behaved honorably under trying circumstances. It turned out that Collins had been arrested for insubordination after refusing to take part in mandatory outdoor exercise and that many of his shipmates considered him lazy and incompetent. The *Times* drew a broad conclusion from the Collins affair, declaring it had been "a mistake to introduce civilians into the ship's company." Perhaps the mistake had simply been to bring a journalist along, for many of the qualities that made Collins useful in the newsroom rendered him an irritating liability in the Arctic.

Jackson, too, was found to have erred. Once Melville was back in America and able to defend his actions, the harsh treatment he'd been subjected to in the *Herald* (and by Jackson's main source, Danenhower) came to be viewed as misplaced. The pro-navy investigators found that Bennett's attempt to combine *Herald* business with serious exploring had backfired in another respect as well. Without mentioning him by name, it noted that the expedition's many early delays, including De Long's pointless search for Nordenskiöld, had "placed the commander at a great disadvantage on his meeting with the pack ice."

Hoping to put the matter to bed, Secretary of the Navy William Chandler hailed De Long and his dead companions as "martyrs in the cause of science." The expedition had in fact added to the Arctic map with its discovery of Henrietta, Jeannette, and Bennett Islands—part of an uninhabited group that would later be named the De Long Archipelago—and its fate ended serious discussion of an open polar sea. The navy went to the enormous trouble of retrieving the bodies that Melville had found and buried. Following a twelve-thousand-mile funeral journey, the caskets were delivered to New York in February 1884 amid an outpouring of patriotic sentiment, and De Long and his fellow servicemen lay in state at the Brooklyn Navy Yard. By this time, even the *Times* was lauding De Long as "the pride of the whole nation" and dismissing the complaints of the Collinses as "an attempt to cast dishonor on the noble dead." The congressional hearings that had for a time been expected to come down hard on the navy instead concluded that the expedition had been conducted properly.

Emma De Long, whose efforts to secure her late husband's legacy put her in regular contact with James Gordon Bennett, ventured to point out that the *Herald* reporters Collins and Jackson were to blame for their shared troubles. "All the annoyance to you . . . and intense suffering to me has come through your own people," she wrote to him. Bennett seems to have agreed with this assessment, albeit after profiting from the headlines his reporters generated.

He was never called upon to testify or to make a formal statement, nor did he attend the funeral ceremonies in New York. His ill-fated North Pole expedition had allegedly cost him $340,000. How he felt about it all can only be guessed at. According to a magazine profile of him written thirty years later, the *Jeannette* disaster "was one of the greatest disappointments of Bennett's life." He never organized anything like it again.

# CHAPTER THIRTEEN

For most of human history, news traveled only as quickly as a person could. The electric telegraph changed all that, sending information pulsing along at hundreds of miles per minute, exponentially faster than a horse or steam engine. Eastern American cities began to make use of this remarkable new invention in the mid-1840s, and before long the emerging communications network touched nearly every corner of national life. But few industries were as thoroughly affected by the telegraph as journalism. Information was the profession's stock-in-trade and a commodity whose value hinged on the speed of its delivery. As one astounded newsman said of the telegraph, "It gives you the news before the circumstances have had time to alter. The press is enabled to lay it fresh before the reader like a steak hot from the gridiron, instead of being cooled and rendered flavorless by a slow journey from a distant kitchen."

Europe remained a "distant kitchen" for two decades more, until the laying of the first workable transatlantic cable in 1866. Both the *Herald* and the *Tribune* claimed to have been on one end of the first recorded exchange; what mattered more, of course, was that a new era of international telecommunications had dawned. Foreign news that had previously required at least ten days to be delivered now arrived in minutes. It could run in the next day's paper, if not that same day's evening edition.

Only if it was deemed important, though. High cable rates generally prevented all but the most pressing items from flashing across the news-wires. The only exception to this rule was at the *Herald*. Where other big papers filled columns with cable dispatches, Bennett's filled whole pages, making it America's most comprehensive source of foreign news. It was said that the *Herald* spent as much on cable tolls as all other American newspapers combined. It could afford to, of course. It was the most profit-able newspaper in the world. And for Bennett, no price was too high to pay for a foreign scoop, whether the news originated in a spired capital or a vine-choked wilderness.

The only other newspaper that enjoyed such global reach was the re-vered *Times* of London. But while the so-called Great Thunderer was con-sidered the semiofficial voice of the British Empire, the *Herald* operated more independently, and Bennett worked the cables with profitability more than the public interest in mind. If handled correctly, his far-flung scoops could be very good for business. Big news from abroad usually landed in a sequence of splashes and ripples, first as a cabled summary and then, several weeks later, as a letter or series of letters. Once published, each dispatch left a froth of speculation and commentary in its wake. Ben-nett expertly used cable bulletins to tease an incoming *Herald* exclusive, printing terse reports from the likes of Stanley, Gilder, and other corre-spondents to create a mix of anticipation and debate that only the *Herald*'s full, proprietary narrative could satisfy. The next installment of the narrative might bring it to a satisfying conclusion—or inflame debate even more.

Bennett sent ostentatiously long-winded personal messages over the wires whenever he felt like it. More often, though, he kept his communi-cations as short and direct—that is, as cheap—as possible. Everyone did. For the price of a 250-word message to France, a second-class traveler could go there by ocean liner. Sending a 40-word cable from New York to Paris cost a staggering $10, whereas a letter traveling that same route cost 14 cents.

And this was before 1882, when cable rates doubled. The man respon-sible for the price hike was the financier Jay Gould, who had effectively cornered the American telecommunications market by using his vast railroad holdings and their associated rights-of-way to take over Western Union, handler of 80 percent of the nation's telegraph traffic. Gould had done this by launching one telegraph company and then another, decrying Western Union as a monopoly, and then secretly acquiring more and more of it as his incursions caused share prices to drop. Western Union tried to buy Gould out, only to discover that he owned a controlling interest. He then made Western Union into even more of a monopoly than it had been before.

Having decimated the American competition, Gould now moved to do the same internationally, using his control of the domestic network as leverage over the transatlantic cable companies. There were three of these at the time, each controlled by French or British capital and each running cables from Ireland to Atlantic Canada and then south by means of a different American-owned extension line. Gould, who controlled all three extensions, canceled the existing contracts and forced the cable companies to partner with Western Union. Then he doubled rates to fifty cents a word.

Next he began laying new transatlantic cables, positioning himself for total dominance of the wires. Though Gould cloaked his machinations in patriotic language, pointing to the need for an American-owned transatlantic cable, most onlookers saw it as just another of the predatory moves that had made him the era's most hated figure. The *Herald* called Gould's profit-sharing deal with the European cable firms "the most gigantic system of organized robbery in existence in any civilized country." To the *Times*, the success of his consolidation scheme would mean nothing less than "the transmission of intelligence throughout this country, and between the country and Europe, coming under the control of a money grabber who was universally believed to be without heart, conscience, or shame." The Fourth Amendment protected the confidentiality of the postal system, but not of the wires. The "Mephistopheles of Wall Street," as Gould was known, already wielded enormous influence over politicians, the stock market, and the Associated Press, which depended on favorable telegraph rates from Western Union. If every stock update and breaking news item were to pass under Gould's devilish all-seeing eye, the

*Times* warned, he would become "the autocrat of America as truly as Alexander is the autocrat of Russia."

Luckily for these critics, Gould's manipulations aroused the interest of a formidable rival named J. W. Mackay. Known as the "Bonanza King" for the spectacular success of his Nevada mines, the Irish American silver baron was eager to try his luck in the topsy-turvy telecommunications market, in part because Gould's exorbitant cable rates had become a source of annoyance to him and his wife, Louise, a fixture of the American expat scene in Paris. In 1883, Mackay invested $500,000 in the independent Postal Telegraph Company and immediately began expanding its service westward to Pittsburgh, Detroit, St. Paul, and St. Louis. He announced a new transatlantic venture a few months later, with cables to be laid as soon as possible. His collaborator in the $6 million enterprise was James Gordon Bennett Jr.

Breaking his personal rule against investing in non-*Herald* business ventures, Bennett took a 25 percent share in Mackay's Commercial Cable Company. Mackay held 70 percent, and a handful of small stockholders claimed the rest. Siemens, then based in London, was hired to manufacture more than six thousand miles of inch-thick cable—wrapped in a protective sheath of steel, to protect against the breakages that continued to cost earlier-generation cable outfits dearly. The firm's purpose-built steamer, the *Mackay-Bennett*, finished laying the first cable in June 1884 as scheduled. When a second, faster one went into service on Christmas Eve, traders inside the New York Stock Exchange were delighted to find that questions to their London counterparts sent via the Commercial Cable Company were received and answered in just six minutes.

Business-minded Americans appreciated that the new firm's capitalization had been done honestly, whereas Gould and his cronies had "watered" (intentionally overvalued) their stock to the detriment of small investors and charged exorbitant rates to keep the soggy enterprise afloat. Rather than join the cable pool's price-fixing scheme, Mackay-Bennett, as it was informally known, charged 20 percent less for service.

The Gould pool, bleeding customers, had no choice but to cut its rates, and a years-long war of words ensued as both sides dug in. Bennett was sued for libel by one of Gould's key allies, Cyrus Field, and forced to pay £5,000 in damages. In 1888, frustrated that his wealthy rivals had refused to bend, Gould abandoned his posture of watchful silence and publicly slammed Bennett for his history of "debauches and scandals." The newspapers, including Bennett's, gleefully reprinted Gould's outburst. "The proprietor of the Herald lost his reputation long before Mr. Gould was ever heard of," the *Herald* quipped. For once, the public overwhelmingly sided with James Gordon Bennett. Several months later, when twenty-five cents a word became the universal cable rate, the truce was deemed a victory for both consumers and the Commercial Cable Company. It was a win that the Commodore needed desperately, for the *Herald* had been losing ground to a disruptive rival of its own: Joseph Pulitzer.

# CHAPTER FOURTEEN

Joseph Pulitzer's first two years at *The World* have often been described as the birth of modern journalism. Even if many of his splashier innovations came later, the brash and crusading style he brought to New York City transformed the field immediately.

Pulitzer, a Hungarian Jew, had arrived penniless in America during the Civil War at the age of seventeen and fought with a German-speaking unit of the Union army. After the war, he joined the heavily intertwined political and newspaper scenes in St. Louis, where he merged a pair of failing papers into the vibrant *St. Louis Post-Dispatch*. Atop this foundation—part middle European, part midwestern—one of journalism's great legacies was built. Having established himself in St. Louis, Pulitzer arrived in New York in 1883 and bought the failing *World*. The seller was none other than Jay Gould, who had acquired the money-losing sheet as part of a railroad deal.

Pulitzer swiftly reinvented the paper for a whole new reader. One of his own slogans got it right: *The World* was "Spicy, Pithy, Pictorial." It addressed a vast stratum of the public that previous newspaper owners had considered too poor, uneducated, or otherwise irrelevant to be worthwhile, including immigrants whose first language was not English. *The World* reflected a city in which the old economic and cultural boundaries were dissolving. It spoke to the women who'd begun working in greater numbers as stenographers, typists, cashiers, and telegraph operators, if not also as editors and writers, and to the many thousands of New Yorkers who had risen from recent poverty to become small-business owners and office workers. Many of these newly middle-class readers found the legacy newspapers boring, condescending, politically irrelevant, prohibitively expensive, or otherwise inaccessible. The eager-to-please, two-cent *World* came to their rescue.

Its reporters wrote in plainer, simpler English than their counterparts elsewhere and were notoriously pushy in pursuit of interviews. Underlying Pulitzer's populism was an idealistic strain; while other New York City publishers had gotten cynical, he believed that newspapers could change the world for the better. He recognized the new mass culture emerging in America, and the depth of its frustration with the corruption and inequality of the Gilded Age, and he understood the power of a popular call to action as perhaps only a child of nineteenth-century European revolutionary movements could.

More than other papers, *The World* reported on how the poor lived. It exposed social ills such as unsafe tenement conditions and poisoned milk in immigrant neighborhoods, then built advocacy campaigns around these issues. It literally saved thousands of lives, in ways that went beyond the traditional Christmas charity drives and other feel-good initiatives favored by other newspapers—although it participated in those, too.

Critics complained that for every noble cause *The World* espoused, it printed dozens of lurid accounts of murder, suicide, and adultery. It also specialized in the "sob story," an urban genre that dwelled at length on the misfortunes of unknown individuals, usually poor immigrants or children, for no loftier purpose than to make the reader shed a tear. *The World* didn't just tell these stories; it elevated them. Pulitzer called them the "literature of the millions" and argued that they created the mass readership he needed in order to advance the cause of democracy.

Bennett claimed to be unimpressed. As he tried to blunt Pulitzer's offensive with a series of ill-advised business moves, he dismissed the newcomer as a "poor, misguided, selfish vulgarian" and predicted that

Pulitzer's momentum would soon peter out. But *The World* only spun faster. It took less than five years to surpass the *Herald* in circulation, thereby becoming the nation's most read daily. Two years later, Bennett was forced to admit in an editorial that Pulitzer had "made success upon success against our prejudices." The most conspicuous of these successes was architectural. Completed in 1890, the 345-foot-tall new headquarters of *The World* was the tallest skyscraper in New York City. It towered over the nearby Herald Building and literally put *The Sun* in the shadows. Just as alarming, from the competition's point of view, was the fact that Pulitzer paid the $2 million for the land and building entirely in cash.

Those attached to the old norms of restraint and proportionality insisted that Pulitzer's news empire wasn't really built on news. But Pulitzer had changed the definition of news. It was no longer what a small group of people considered important. It was what the masses considered interesting.

# CHAPTER FIFTEEN

While conservative commentators disparaged Pulitzer's "slang-whang" approach to news gathering, most publishers had no choice but to imitate it. Soon *The World* was not the only paper ambushing public figures in railway stations and hotel lobbies and printing their unpremeditated comments without express permission.

The new and pushy breed of reporter was too much for some. "No privacy [is] sacred to these men, no subject too trivial," one disgruntled commentator noted. In fact, newspapers had been nosy and sometimes careless about interviewing for a long time, just more deferential when dealing with individuals of wealth and influence. *The World* helped put an end to that prejudice, and stretched other traditional boundaries of the trade as well. Its reporters lingered outside New York City courtrooms, sniffing around cases that would previously have gone unnoticed. While their sensationalized coverage prevented the occasional miscarriage of justice, it also subjected nuanced legal proceedings to the chaos of public opinion. *The Journalist* dubbed this novel phenomenon "trial by newspaper," and warned that if it were allowed to become the norm, "the liberty of the press may very frequently degenerate into license."

The New York City press got a chance to test that thesis barely a month later, when yet another sensational story blew in from the Arctic.

*

ONE OF THE AMERICAN RELIEF VESSELS THAT HAD GONE LOOKING FOR
the *Jeannette* in 1881 carried a twenty-seven-man party under the command of Lieutenant Adolphus Greely of the U.S. Army's Signal Corps.
Finding no sign of De Long, the army men had proceeded to Lady Franklin Bay, on the east coast of Ellesmere Island, and established a crude base
there called Fort Conger. The original plan had been for them to receive
annual reprovisioning from government ships, thereby enabling them to
make a new attempt to reach the North Pole each spring. But things had
not gone that way. Thanks to a combination of poor ice conditions and
army blundering, the promised resupply vessels had failed to get anywhere
near the explorers for two years straight, and the Greely expedition was
now widely assumed to be in trouble.

In June 1884, a navy relief vessel under the command of Admiral Winfield Schley discovered what remained of the party at Cape Sabine, a
wind-blasted promontory 250 miles south of Fort Conger. All but Greely
and six of his men had died, and the survivors were bone thin and haggard. Only two were capable of walking; one of those who'd been immo-
bilized (and who would die on the voyage home) had lost both feet to
frostbite and was found with a spoon lashed to his mangled fingers.

Less than two years after the full scale of the *Jeannette* fiasco had been
revealed, here was news of yet another American polar disaster. The Greely
party had at least accomplished more than De Long before coming to
grief. Lieutenant James Lockwood and Sergeant David Brainard had
sledged to 83°24', or 396 miles from the pole. Not only was this the first
time in three centuries that a non-British expedition had logged a Farthest
North, but the sledging party's survey—which found no sign of land
above Greenland, only miles and miles of semi-frozen sea—would aid
future attempts on the pole. Though it paid for its achievements dearly,
the Greely expedition also mapped a hundred miles of previously uncharted Greenland coastline and traveled deeper into Ellesmere Island
than any predecessor.

Greely received a hero's welcome when he arrived in Portsmouth, New

Hampshire, in August. Though too weak to address the crowds, he bowed in gratitude and thanked the press for its "universally kind" consideration. The nation's journalists had no reason to treat him otherwise. Whatever aspersions could be flung at his higher-ups, Greely and his men appeared to be model explorers. "In the latest story of Arctic exploration there are no episodes of human weakness and cowardice to break the force of its showing of human strength and courage," pronounced the editors at *Harper's Weekly*. "We ought all to be thankful that no such pettinesses have come to light to belittle the heroism of the latest arctic explorer, and that there is nothing to indicate that any such have been concealed to be brought to light hereafter."

Barely had the ink on the *Harper's* presses dried when a *New-York Times* reporter prowling the Brooklyn Navy Yard "picked a chance word from a sailor's lips," as a rival newsman later recalled. The word was a potent one: "cannibalism." Members of the relief crew stationed in Brooklyn were murmuring that some of the bodies recovered at Cape Sabine had been picked clean of flesh. They said that navy officers had draped them in blankets before having them carried aboard, then left the wrappings in place while the strangely featherweight corpses were transferred to iron caskets, the lids of which were riveted shut. The *Times* also learned that one of Greely's men had died of gunshot wounds at Cape Sabine, apparently as punishment for stealing food. Asked to address these sensational rumors, the navy officers either discounted them or said nothing. Schley declined to comment.

HORRORS OF CAPE SABINE was the next day's lead story in the *Times*, whose editors demanded further investigation. The story occupied front pages nationwide for more than a week as more unofficial evidence of ghoulish acts at Cape Sabine accumulated. An enterprising local newspaper arranged for the freshly buried body of Lieutenant Frederick Kislingbury, Greely's second-in-command, to be exhumed in Rochester, New York, and two medical examiners declared in a sworn statement that the flesh on the legs and torso had been "cut away with some sharp instrument." If the horrible implications of these findings were borne out, the *Times* prophesied, the Greely expedition would be remembered as "the most

dreadful and repulsive chapter in the long annals of Arctic exploration."
The navy and the army declined to comment. "You fellows thrive on ca-
lamity," the disgusted commandant of the Brooklyn Navy Yard told a
*Herald* reporter—off the record.

The *Herald* argued, rightly, that the *Times* stories were exaggerated.
None of Greely's men had been killed for the purposes of consumption.
Nor was it true, as the *Times* claimed, that the survivors had "for a long
time been subsisting principally on the bodies of their dead comrades."
The likeliest perpetrators of cannibalism were now dead themselves, and
any devouring of corpses had probably been minimal and done in secret.
Schley's final report, issued later that month, confirmed that six of the
bodies had been found mutilated—"with a view no doubt to use as shrimp
bait," he added, under pressure from army and navy brass. As for the exe-
cution of an expedition member, it was true that Greely had tried to
conceal this unsavory incident, but in the end much of the public agreed
with the government (and the *Herald*) that the punishment had been
justified under both martial law and the extremity of the circumstances.

The tales of cannibalism—plausible, but unconfirmed by any of the
survivors—would darken the memory of the expedition for generations to
come. They also contributed to the public distaste for risky Arctic ventures. "Let there be an end to this folly. . . . Not even when it is played
under favorable conditions is the game worth the candle," begged the
*Times*. President Chester Arthur declared that the Greely party's achievements "could not compensate for the loss of human life." Buried amid all
the suffering and death was a bitter irony. Though the Lady Franklin Bay
expedition succeeded in underappreciated ways, in a larger sense it
achieved precisely the opposite of what had been intended. Dispatched as
America's contribution to the International Polar Conference, an idealistic
enterprise designed to foster collaboration between Western powers in the
Arctic, the expedition had been riven by internal conflicts, including
Greely's ongoing feud with his French-born chief scientist, Dr. Octave
Pavy. The expedition was also supposed to help inaugurate a new era in
which scientists and hard-nosed explorers finally found common cause in
the Far North. Instead—in America, at least—it marked the last time for

a long time that they worked seriously together. Until and beyond 1909, science would be a secondary concern for most of the nation's polar explorers. They were focused on the trophy.

American polar expeditions would evolve in other ways as well over the next decades. With public confidence shaken by the army's and navy's tragic mishaps, the government exited the field. Expeditions from this point on would be privately organized, not to mention cheaper and leaner. Liberated from the military chain of command, their leaders would be more flexible and in some ways more innovative. Because the new model rendered explorers accountable to geographical societies and wealthy individuals, rather than to bureaucrats or elected officials, it also made them more entrepreneurial.

Newspapers embraced this shift, as well they might have. Entrepreneur-explorers were dependent upon publicity, which made them more willing collaborators. Meanwhile, for the press, there was a huge potential upside to the stories of their high-risk adventures. The unspoken reality was that a newspaper, unlike the government, could benefit from the success *or* the failure of an Arctic venture, provided the failure made for interesting reading.

No explorer capitalized on these new opportunities as effectively as Frederick Schwatka, who retired from the army in 1885 in order to write, lecture, and explore full time. He soon found an eager client in *The New-York Times*, which hired him to produce about a dozen articles on the Arctic. The pragmatic *Times* still considered the North Pole a waste of time—"the truth is, the only men who should be sent to the pole are those who ought not to return"—but it was curious about regions of greater commercial or scientific interest. Having established Schwatka as its resident exploring authority, the paper commissioned him in 1886 to travel to Alaska, the first time in its thirty-five-year history that the *Times* had bankrolled an expedition. A primary goal was to conduct geographical research of the Alaskan coast and the St. Elias range, as well as a cursory ethnographical study of northern Tlingit tribes. The paper also vowed that "if any industry, fur, fishery, mineral, oil otherwise, can be found that seems likely to pay in this region it will be placed before the public through

THE NEW-YORK TIMES." More spectacularly, Schwatka would also attempt to climb Mount St. Elias, which was then believed to be North America's highest peak.

Though he failed to reach the summit, Schwatka claimed to have gotten closer than any white man, and he made several contributions to the map of Alaska. Among these was a glacier, which he named after the geologist Louis Agassiz, and a river—later revealed to be more of a seasonal drainway for glacial snowmelt than a true waterway—which he named in honor of the *Times* publisher George Jones. Apart from the "great torment" of ever-present mosquitoes, Schwatka's expedition avoided casualties and even serious hardship. His dispatches painted an interesting and reasonably accurate portrait of the Alaskan wilds that would come to prominence a decade later during the Klondike gold rush. The *Times* made a regular feature of them for two months, often running the articles at half a page or more.

*The World* subsequently commissioned Schwatka to attempt the first winter crossing of the fifteen-year-old Yellowstone National Park. Reeling from the effects of altitude, he turned back. He died in 1892, aged forty-three, of an overdose of laudanum that might or might not have been intentional, and is largely forgotten today. But he was, for a period, the most famous American explorer for hire after Henry Stanley, and his career served as a useful case study for an ambitious young expeditioner named Robert Peary.

# CHAPTER SIXTEEN

Robert Edwin Peary was born in Cresson, Pennsylvania, in 1856, and lost his father to pneumonia before reaching the age of three. Unsure of how to raise a boy alone, his mother moved with him to her native state of Maine. She sheltered and pampered her only child, dressing young "Bert" in girl's clothing and making him wear a sunbonnet whenever he went outside. Mary Peary had her reasons for adopting this unusual approach to parenting. As Robert Peary's daughter, Marie, later wrote of her, "She tried her best to make her small son over into the gentle little girl whom she would have known so well how to handle."

Out of this cosseted upbringing, and the schoolyard beatings that resulted from it, emerged an athletic loner eager to prove himself to the world—and to his doting mother. In 1877, Peary graduated from Maine's Bowdoin College, a promising ascent from modest roots, and he was subsequently commissioned as a civil engineer in the U.S. Navy. His first taste of foreign adventure came in 1884, when he was sent from his home in Washington, D.C., to the Nicaraguan wilderness to help survey a proposed route for an interocean canal.

Though the tropics were his first training ground, Peary dreamed of making a name for himself in the Far North, if only because there was more glory to be had there. In 1886, he secured a summer leave of absence

from the navy and self-financed an attempted first crossing of the Greenland ice cap. Though he failed, Peary traveled farther inland than any
previous expedition had, and the experience made him hungrier to succeed. "Remember, mother, I *must* have fame," he wrote to Mary.

Upon his return, he was promoted to deputy chief engineer of the
Nicaraguan canal survey, making him the project's second-in-command.
Gearing up for a return to this important work, Peary visited a Washington outfitter to buy a sun helmet. A young black man named Matthew
Henson was working in the stockroom there. Struck by Henson's intelligence and work ethic, Peary asked him to come to Nicaragua as his valet.
"Keep my clothes and quarters clean. Must be honest with regular habits,"
he explained. Henson agreed, persuaded more by Peary's icy confidence
and the promise of adventure than by the job description.

Peary proved himself an effective leader in Central America, where
another (and ultimately more consequential) canal survey was under way
at the Isthmus of Panama. His achievements in Nicaragua brought him
his first gratifying taste of good publicity, when his name appeared in
news items in the *Times* and the *Herald*. "I shall be indispensable to the
Canal Company after this trip and can make my own terms. At the same
time I am making myself known, as you see by the *Herald*," he wrote to
his mother.

Peary chronicled his Nicaraguan work for the fourth issue (May 1889)
of *National Geographic*. The article, "Across Nicaragua with Transit and
Machéte," introduced the thirty-two-year-old naval engineer to members
of the newly formed National Geographic Society, and his marriage that
summer to Josephine Diebitsch, the daughter of a Smithsonian Institution professor, opened more doors to Washington scientific and exploring
circles. Peary began to study the North Pole and to believe that methods
like those Frederick Schwatka had employed in northern Canada—a small
party, mostly Inuit, using sled dogs and other native travel techniques—
offered the best chance of getting there.

Schwatka was not a serious contender for the pole, but Fridtjof Nansen
was. The twenty-nine-year-old Norwegian neuroscientist and champion
skier had achieved the first crossing of Greenland the year before Peary

made his *National Geographic* debut, triumphing where the American had failed two summers earlier. Peary considered this defeat "a serious blow" and a personal affront, even though Nansen had traveled unconventionally from east to west and on skis, and thus had succeeded very much on his own terms. It was not the last time that Peary's hypercompetitiveness would override his better judgment.

His second polar expedition, in 1891, was sponsored by the Philadelphia Academy of Natural Sciences and the American Geographical Society, with additional funding provided by *The Sun*. The seven-person party included Josephine Peary, the first white woman to travel in the polar regions, as well as the first black man to do so. The remarkable Matthew Henson was on his way to becoming an Arctic jack-of-all-trades—"cook, hunter, dog driver, housekeeper, and body-guard," as Peary later wrote. The expedition's surgeon and ethnologist was a twenty-six-year-old Brooklyn physician, Frederick Cook.

Like Peary, Cook (whose German ancestors were named Koch) had grown up fatherless and enthralled by Elisha Kent Kane's *Arctic Explorations*. Unlike Peary, he was one of five children, and had felt the "sting of poverty" as a boy in the Catskills hamlet of Hortonville, New York. He'd paid his way through medical school at New York University by making predawn milk deliveries in Brooklyn, but by the time he learned (from an ad placed in Bennett's *Evening Telegram*) that Peary was assembling a small team for his 1891 expedition, Cook was struggling. His first wife and daughter had died during childbirth, and his Brooklyn medical practice had attracted only three patients in six months, leaving him much free time for devouring books and articles about the Arctic. He longed to go there and to escape his profound grief and boredom.

Cook proved his worth while the exploring party was still at sea. The sealer hired to deposit them in western Greenland struck ice while Peary stood at the taffrail, causing its iron tiller to smash against his leg. Cook determined that both bones above the ankle were cleanly broken, placed Peary's leg in a splint, and ministered to him so tenderly that Josephine described him as "goodness itself" in her diary. Peary himself later saluted Cook's "professional skill, and unruffled patience and coolness in an emergency." Thanks to Cook's handiwork, his leg healed well enough for him to trek twelve hundred miles that winter and spring.

The one-year expedition's biggest accomplishment was to confirm the insularity of Greenland, albeit on grounds that would later prove to be inaccurate. Peary ended any remaining speculation that the great land-mass might extend all the way to the pole and established himself as America's new leading polar explorer. The only significant blemish was the death of a wealthy young Kentuckian named John Verhoeff who clashed with both Pearys, stormed off one day to explore a glacier on his own, and was never seen again. But he had undertaken a foolhardy venture against the commander's orders, and no one except Verhoeff's grieving family held Peary responsible for his death.

Now the siren call of celebrity truly beckoned. "I believe little Mother that it will be but a short time before you have a son more famous than Stanley," Peary wrote to Mary. But his own publications about the expedition proved less popular than Josephine's articles for the *Herald* about domestic life in the Arctic. She was an able writer, and the novelty of her experience boosted sales of her subsequent book, *My Arctic Journal*, the profits from which she gave to her husband's next expedition.

Frederick Cook would not be a part of it. Like everyone else except Josephine, he'd signed a contract in 1891 granting Peary the use of his personal diaries and the exclusive right to publish anything about the expedition. Peary refused to budge on these strict terms, effectively banning his most promising expedition member from sharing the results of his botanical and ethnographic field studies. A disappointed Cook declined to return to Greenland with Peary the next year, though the two men remained on cordial terms.

Josephine again joined her husband in 1893 and created a media sensation by giving birth to a daughter, Marie, in Arctic Greenland. This was another American first, and news of "the Snow Baby" (as Marie was known to the Inuit who came from miles away to view her) further endeared the Pearys to the reading public. Mother and infant traveled home in the summer of 1894, while Peary stayed on, aching to achieve something big.

But a grueling trek the next year accomplished little more than nullifying a possible route to the North Pole.

Desperate for a trophy, and with his return date nearing, Peary coerced some of the Cape York Inuit into leading him to their "iron mountain." Since the early nineteenth century, Western explorers had wondered where the natives of northern Greenland got the metal for their knives, arrowheads, harpoon tips, and other tools. The answer, as Peary found out, was an elephant-sized chunk of meteorite. He used his engineering acumen to raise two smaller fragments in the vicinity—weighing three tons and eight hundred pounds, respectively—and haul them onto the ship he'd hired to take him home.

Peary's retrieval of these treasures enabled him to frame an otherwise frustrating expedition as a success while fundraising for the next one. The Philadelphia Academy of Natural Sciences was rumored to be interested in sending him back to collect the "Cape York meteorite," whose discovery was hailed by experts as the answer to a long-standing Arctic mystery. For Peary, who would struggle over the next few years to secure the required naval leave for another major polar effort, there was a more important consequence. By bringing items of scientific and financial value back from the Arctic, he got the attention of private interests whose deep pockets and political connections would later be of great use to him.

As his navy superiors moved to constrain his extracurricular polar ventures, Peary realized that his exploring career might be permanently derailed unless he could persuade these powerful allies to intervene on his behalf. He had already demonstrated that getting what he wanted out of the Cape York Inuit was one of his great talents. Cultivating the support of influential white men would prove to be another.

# CHAPTER SEVENTEEN

By 1895, *The New-York Times* was no longer moving mountains. Daily circulation had sunk to below ten thousand, the lowest in the city. Though its exposure of the Tweed Ring was still considered one of the greatest journalistic exposés of all time, the paper's glory days seemed a distant memory.

Many factors had contributed to its decline, including turmoil within the national two-party political system. Staunchly Republican at its founding, the *Times* severed those roots in 1884 when it declined to endorse the party's scandal-plagued presidential nominee, James G. Blaine. This decision proved successful in one respect, for the paper's preferred candidate, Grover Cleveland, won the election, followed by a nonsequential second term, and it also showed the publisher, George Jones, to be a man of uncompromising principle. But the ensuing damage was significant. Siding with the anti-Blaine "mugwumps" caused many angry Republican readers and advertisers to abandon the *Times*, and earnings tumbled, especially after Jones moved the company into an expensive new building on Park Row.

When Jones died in 1891, none of his heirs were interested in running the ailing paper. To prevent it from falling into other hands, a group of *Times* editors led by Charles Miller formed a syndicate and cobbled together the funds to buy it. The reorganization left Miller, a balding scholar who'd once contemplated a career as a Latin teacher, in the unlikely position of majority shareholder and president of the New York Times Publishing Company. The shaky new regime lacked the working capital to make needed changes, and the paper's outlook worsened during the panic of 1893, which decimated ad sales.

Desperate to stay in business, Miller slashed the news budget and then accepted several unsecured loans from friends and allies of President Cleveland's. In return, the *Times* aggressively opposed the "free silver" movement that was sweeping east from Democratic strongholds in the agrarian West and South. This proposed currency disruption threatened to upend the national economy, and the probability that it would destroy the fortunes of New York City plutocrats was for many Americans an appealing selling point. Fear of the populist free-silver movement was a major reason that *Times* shareholders like the super-bankers J. P. Morgan, August Belmont, and Jacob Schiff were still funding the paper; if nothing else, its editorial page could at least be counted on to uphold the "goldbug" cause. But floating the *Times* was costing shareholders $1,000 a day, a loss they were not likely to tolerate much longer—certainly not beyond the 1896 presidential election, which was expected to decide the silver question.

People in the trade called the *Times* "the most picturesque old ruin among newspapers in America." Its demolition would spell personal ruin for Charles Miller, who'd sunk everything he owned into the paper. He'd downsized his family's housing, taken in lodgers, and come to rely on his wealthy mother-in-law to make ends meet. He had more than himself to blame for the Times Company's fate. By 1896, New York had become an especially rough-and-tumble place to run a newspaper. The pace of change and the piles of money being thrown around were unprecedented. Even the legendary *Sun* was struggling, and two smaller papers, the *Recorder* and the *Mercury*, were on the verge of collapse. While the fledgling *Recorder* had never really found its stride, the *Mercury* had once produced the nation's most popular Sunday edition.

Unlike these two other failing papers, the *Times* was a revered institution.

It didn't seem to matter. The Times Company's reorganization committee had approached every notable publisher in New York City and been advised at every turn that the paper was beyond saving.

WHILE *THE NEW-YORK TIMES* FALTERED, ADOLPH OCHS'S *CHATTANOOGA Times* flew. Remarkably for its time and place, it prospered without sensationalizing the news or aligning itself with friendly political or business interests. Though the paper generally sympathized with the "Conservative Democrats of the South," as Ochs put it, it was no partisan mouthpiece and functioned more as a civic organ than as a vessel for controversy or politicking. Ochs had both noble and self-serving reasons for orienting his paper this way, but there was also the simple fact that this approach suited his personality. He felt more comfortable, and not just more upwardly mobile, sharing common ground with respectable neighbors.

The one partisan stance adopted by the *Chattanooga Daily Times* wasn't really partisan at all: the paper was vociferously pro-Chattanooga. Ochs vowed to make it a platform for the "material, educational, and moral growth of our progressive city and its surrounding territory." Boosterism like this came naturally to Ochs, who loved few things more than arranging a feel-good spectacle and did so often. He organized flashy Fourth of July displays and a backslapping banquet aimed at fostering cooperation between industrialists of the American North and South. These well-regarded extravaganzas advanced his reputation locally. They also got Ochs acquainted with senators, congressmen, business leaders, and other men of statewide and even national influence.

With his help, Ochs's adopted hometown of Chattanooga chugged ahead. In 1878, the year he acquired its *Daily Times*, the city's population was twelve thousand; fifteen years later, it had swollen to thirty thousand. His successful newspaper provided jobs for grateful relatives. Adolph hired his father, Julius, as a bookkeeper, made his brother George a reporter, put a brother-in-law in charge of the paper's lucrative printing-for-hire operation, and would later install his professionally unsettled other brother, Milton, as its managing editor. He also used his new wealth to buy a twelve-room house in a gentrifying riverside neighborhood called Cameron Hill, then filled it with his siblings and extended family. When he married Effie Wise, the wryly humorous and book-loving daughter of a prominent Cincinnati rabbi, she joined the busy household. Adolph and Effie's first child to survive infancy, Iphigene, was born on September 19, 1892, sending her father into spasms of teary joy. She arrived at what appeared to be an epochal moment in his newspaper career. The year before, the annual profits of the *Chattanooga Times* had cleared $25,000 for the first time in its history. Two months after Iphigene was born, Adolph unveiled the impressive new headquarters he had built for it, for an eyebrow-raising $182,000.

The six-story Ochs Building was the tallest in Chattanooga. It was also a giant bluff. Adolph Ochs, the apparently self-assured Chattanooga businessman and civic leader, was on the brink of ruin. The reason for this was that he had bet too heavily on local real estate during the 1880s and the bursting of that investment bubble had left him ominously deep in debt. He was too traumatized by memories of his father's failures to add up the figures at this point, but losses from that frenzied period totaled nearly $500,000. The Ochs Building was the brave face he put on this misfortune. He had paid for almost all of it using borrowed money.

By 1895, though, his usual loan sources had run dry, and it was all Ochs could do to keep up with his many interest payments. Unwilling to declare personal bankruptcy as Julius (who died in 1888) had done, he resolved to dig himself out by way of the business he knew best. He began shopping for a newspaper. Brazenly, he turned his gaze toward New York City, the most sophisticated and competitive marketplace of all.

His first negotiations were for the enfeebled *Mercury*, but as soon as he learned of the plight facing the vaunted *Times*, his enthusiasm for the lowlier paper waned. The *Times* was simply too great an opportunity to pass up. Ochs had not expected to find himself bargaining for "the greatest, cleanest and most respected newspaper in New York!" Not only was the *Times* well known, but it also stood for many of the values that he cherished and strove to embody. Most metropolitan dailies wielded power; the *Times*, despite its recent experiment with editorial selling out, wielded moral authority. Ochs hankered to use it as "a text from which to preach application, integrity and earnestness to young men."

Beneath these pieties, though, burned another, less saintly vision of the future Ochs desired for himself, one that he had described to a cousin during his early ownership of the *Chattanooga Times*. "I see myself living in luxury, honored and respected by all; the mantle of fame and position rests on my shoulders; my parents, sisters and brothers around me sharing the fruits of my success."

Ochs worried that *The New-York Times* lay tantalizingly outside his reach. But he also understood that he was "at my best in adversity," as he told Effie, and later described his perilous financial situation as a blessing in disguise. Looking back on this defining moment of his life, Ochs believed that had he been less desperate, he never would have had the "supremacy of gall" to pursue the *Times*.

# CHAPTER EIGHTEEN

When Charles Miller, the overwhelmed editor and chief executive of the *Times*, learned in March 1896 that a little-known publisher from Chattanooga wanted to meet with him, he was skeptical that anything would come of it. But he agreed to receive Adolph Ochs anyway.

The thirty-eight-year-old man who arrived at Miller's home on West Fifty-Fifth Street had a formal bearing, downturned blue eyes, and an oversized head crowned with thick, dark hair. The two newspapermen sat down to talk in the drawing room. Miller had planned to meet briefly with Ochs and then treat himself to a night at the theater with his family. But when his wife, Frances, stepped in to tell him it was time to leave, he instructed her and the children to go ahead without him. When they returned home later that evening, and after they had gone to bed, Miller and Ochs were still talking.

Ochs was alternately described by those who knew him as ingratiating, insecure, eager for the validation of his business and social superiors, and comfortably self-contained. It often depended on whom he was speaking with and what about. Talking business was his forte, and some who'd done this with Ochs likened the experience to being hypnotized. But his proposal to Miller that evening was not just smooth talk. He had given serious thought to how he might rescue *The New-York Times* and had nearly two decades of highly useful experience to draw upon. Yes, the *Chattanooga Daily Times* was a small-town paper. But it was a profitable and respected small-town paper, and its political attitudes and restrained style clicked unusually well with its big-city counterpart.

New York City was not Chattanooga, though, and Ochs would have tougher men to persuade than Charles Miller. Energized by the newcomer's ideas, Miller arranged for him to meet Charles R. Flint, owner of a controlling share in the New York Times Publishing Company. Flint was a hard-nosed businessman—when the first Dow Jones Industrial Average was tabulated later that spring, his U.S. Rubber Company would be one of the twelve powerhouse listings included—and had doubts about entrusting the *Times* to a small-time publisher from Tennessee. With his usual perspicacity, Ochs had already set out to dispel them. He arrived bearing a signed letter from none other than Flint's friend Grover Cleveland, whom Ochs had met some years earlier at a political event in Chattanooga. The outgoing president's letter praised Ochs for his dedication to "the safety of our country as well as our party." He could, in other words, be counted on to defend the existing financial system.

This was music to Flint's ears, and he was suitably impressed by the rest of Ochs's pitch to make him an offer: invest a substantial amount in the *Times* and manage it back to solvency for an annual salary of $50,000. It was a staggering sum, twice the annual profits of his Chattanooga paper. But Ochs turned the offer down, for a reason that he would soon explain to the paper's owners in writing: "I am impelled by only one desire in these negotiations, and that is to secure permanent control of the New York Times." He needed "almost autocratic power" to ensure that his restructuring plan would succeed, and would not implement it unless he was given a clear path to ownership.

Flint sent Ochs to Spencer Trask, the banker and *Times* shareholder leading the reorganization committee. Trask liked the general terms of Ochs's proposal and explained that the next step was for him to convince the committee of his good standing in the newspaper business and beyond. Ochs had spent much of his career cultivating men of influence, and their endorsements came flying in. "A man of very high purposes, with a very clear conception of public rights and public wrongs, and of unquestioned private integrity," wrote Melville Stone, general manager of the Associated Press. A southern captain of industry saluted his "indomitable perseverance," and Abram Hewitt, ex-mayor of New York City, described Ochs as "straightforward, capable, and prompt" in business matters. Even the managing editor of *The Atlanta Constitution*, a free-silver supporter, commended his fellow newspaperman's "splendid executive ability. If anybody can make a success of the *Times*, Mr. Ochs can."

H. H. Kohlsaat, owner and publisher of *The Chicago Times-Herald*, attested that Ochs's *Chattanooga Times* had "fought valiantly for honest money." Ochs had met with Kohlsaat in Chicago recently, while there laying groundwork for future loans. Like many of the letter writers, Kohlsaat likely saw in him a fine embodiment of American energy and optimism. But as a trusted friend, he had also been privy to a rare moment of self-doubt from Ochs, who'd confessed to him that he feared he wasn't a big enough man for the job. Kohlsaat's advice: "Don't tell anybody, and they'll never find out."

NEGOTIATIONS WITH THE *TIMES* ADVANCED. BY EARLY APRIL, OCHS WAS coming to understand that he would need $75,000 to buy into the paper— a pretty good deal, all said, but still a lot of money. The higher-ups at the New York Times Company did not know that he had less than a cent to his name. To keep things that way, Ochs performed a big-city version of his old checkbook trick by having a friendly bank in Chattanooga deposit a five-figure sum into an account that he promised never to draw upon. With the bank, at least, he did not mince words about what he was up to: the reason he needed the money put there, he admitted, was so that "those people [at the *Times*] will think that I have it."

Ochs worried that he would be exposed and ridiculed, and return to Chattanooga humiliated and even poorer than before. But he also earnestly believed that he could get the *Times* back on track. Discussions with Miller and others had convinced him that the paper's only serious problems were managerial. "It has no system, method, order or organization. Every-thing seems to be neglected and everybody seems to come and go when they wish," he noted. There were too many printers on staff, the advertis-ing manager didn't know "the first principles" of acquiring new business, and Miller's salary was too high by half. If given a chance to remedy these and other self-evident problems, Ochs argued, he would have the *Times* making money again in no time.

His positive reception and the rush of endorsement letters had him envisioning the impossible. "I am succeeding beyond my wildest flights of imagination," he wrote to a cousin. His reorganization plan would create a new entity with no debts and abundant working capital, including a "princely salary" for him as manager. Assuming he made good on his promises, half of the paper's yearly profits would also soon be his. "The whole thing is so remarkable," he wrote, "I can scarce believe but that I am dreaming."

LATER THAT APRIL CAME A RUDE AWAKENING. OCHS LEARNED THAT Charles Flint had been quietly advancing a merger of the *Times* and the moribund *Recorder* and getting a majority of Times Company sharehold-ers behind him. Luckily for Ochs, two board members came out strongly against this consolidation plan. One was Miller, who would lose his job and very possibly his last chance at financial redemption if it went through. The other was Edward Cary, another veteran *Times* editor and share-holder, who informed Flint that he would "personally rather see the stock thrown away than so perverted."

When Flint proceeded to file incorporation paperwork for a new Times-Recorder company anyway, the editors secured enough board votes to send the existing Times Company into receivership. Legally bankrupt now, the *Times* fell under the temporary control of a court-appointed in-termediary, and Flint's merger went on hold. Warier now of those around him, Ochs got Flint and the new reorganization committee to support a revised plan. The Times Company would issue $500,000 in bonds to sat-isfy its creditors and generate the working capital that Miller's earlier restructuring had failed to secure. Ochs claimed $75,000 worth of these bonds, and with it 1,125 shares of *Times* stock. His agreement with the committee called for 3,876 additional shares to be put in escrow for him. If Ochs ran the *Times* profitably for three years in a row, they would be his, giving him a total of 5,001 shares and a controlling stake in the company.

Ochs would deal with the problem of procuring $75,000 later. For now, his priority was collecting shareholder signatures. Optimistic as usual, he expected this step to take a day or two, but it was now mid-June, and most businessmen who might otherwise meet on a Saturday morning were at their country estates or beach houses. Forced to relax, Ochs treated himself to a rare moment of leisure that weekend, donning a new bicycling uniform and pedaling a rented "wheel" through Central Park to visit a relative. "It was a delightful ride and the myriads of wheels with their lighted lamps and tinkling bells made quite a sight," he wrote to Effie.

On Monday, he secured the signatures of August Belmont, J. P. Morgan, Jacob Schiff, and the other most powerful shareholders. By 6:00 p.m., he had taken a staggering eighteen meetings. If New Yorkers could be bothered to start work before ten in the morning, he griped, he could have arranged more. Later that week, Ochs won over Henry B. Hyde, founder and president of the Equitable Life Assurance Society, a major holder of *Times* debt; a bank lawyer involved in the restructuring declared him a "magician" for getting the mighty Equitable to agree to the new plan so quickly. With all the key stakeholders now on board, the new *Times* bonds were disposed of easily. As he waited for a date to be set for the court-ordered sale, Ochs felt the competitive pull of the city's world-famous newspaper arena. "The big Sunday Herald, World and Journals [*sic*] with their tens of thousands of dollars [of] advertising [are] making me eager to enter the contest for the business," he wrote.

Following another week of court delays, a judge finally set a sale date of August 13. This was later than Ochs had hoped for, and stoked fears that a rival buyer would emerge at the last minute and pull the *Times* out from under him. He still struggled to believe that he was the paper's only serious bidder. "I have heard numerous stories of rich men who are just aching to throw a few hundred thousand dollars in a New York Times venture," he wrote to Effie. There were indications that the *Recorder* consolidation deal wasn't quite dead yet after all, and a Chicago railroad developer named Joseph Torrence had made his interest in the *Times* known. Torrence had "money to burn," Ochs worried, and was "said to be wanting the *Times* to out-Hearst Hearst"—that is, become the loudest and lewdest daily in New York City, a prospect that pained Ochs greatly.

None of these perceived threats materialized, and Ochs managed to secure the required $75,000, including a $25,000 loan from Hyde. When Spencer Trask bought the *Times* at auction uncontested on behalf of the new company, Ochs considered himself the "least excited" person in the room. Congratulatory letters and telegrams flooded in, the most effusive of them coming from his family. "God was with you and you won," his brother-in-law Harry Adler wrote from Chattanooga. "You have achieved a splendid victory, and I mean no flattery when I say there is no other man in the whole broad country who could have accomplished what you have, with no money."

Several days later, Ochs formally installed himself at the paper's offices at 41 Park Row. One of his first acts as publisher was to put his plans for the *Times* in print. Advised by Effie to avoid "pyrotechnics," he penned a brief notice reaffirming the paper's devotion to the causes of "sound money" and "the lowest tax consistent with good government." The *Times* would "give the news impartially, without fear or favor," he wrote, and serve as "a forum for the consideration of all questions of public importance, and to that end to invite intelligent discussion from all shades of opinion." The announcement on August 19, 1896, barely lit a candle, let alone a case of fireworks, and that suited Ochs's purposes just fine.

# PART THREE

# FIT TO PRINT

# CHAPTER NINETEEN

On April 8, 1895, Fridtjof Nansen reached 86°14' N, two hundred statute miles beyond the Farthest North that had been achieved thirteen years earlier by members of Greely's U.S. Army expedition. Though he fell short of the pole by two hundred miles, the feat solidified the Norwegian's status as the world's leading Arctic explorer—and one of its most innovative, for he'd gone about the task in a fundamentally different way from his predecessors.

Generations of explorers had fought against the polar drift. Nansen, inspired by the discovery of *Jeannette* wreckage on the coast of Greenland, a reminder of the great range of the polar region's gyrating currents, decided to use the drift to his advantage. He set out in a round-hulled ship, the *Fram*, that had been specifically designed to become trapped in the ice and float with it toward the pole. Maybe the semi-frozen sea would deposit him right at the pole, or very close to it; no one knew. But to Nansen, an amateur oceanographer, the experiment seemed worth trying. Treating the ice as something to be worked with, not battled, represented a stark departure from warlike exploring tradition and struck many Anglo-American observers as irresponsible, even insane. Adolphus Greely, for one, considered it an "illogical scheme of self-destruction."

The *Fram* departed Oslo (or Christiania, as it was known then) on

June 24, 1893, entered the pack ice off Siberia's northeastern coast later that summer, and was frozen in by October. After months of erratic circular progress, the ship began slowly and steadily drifting northwest. Slow and steady was no problem: Nansen had packed enough tinned food for him and his twelve-man crew to survive five years afloat and had gone to great lengths to ensure comfort aboard. Strings of electric lights, illuminated by wind-powered generators, kept the worst of the Arctic winter night at bay. The expedition suffered mainly from boredom as idle men bickered and various pastimes, including Nansen's idea of publishing a weekly ship's newspaper, failed to sustain their interest.

Though the *Fram* drifted nearly as far north as any other ship had ever been, Nansen eventually realized that the swirling Arctic currents would not take it to the pole and had, in fact, begun pulling the ship away from it. If he was going to get there, he would need to go on foot. He left the *Fram* in March 1895, leaving it in the hands of Captain Otto Sverdrup. Nansen took with him a skilled driver named Hjalmar Johansen, twenty-eight dogs, three sleds, three kayaks, and enough rations for a hundred days. Both men also brought skis, because Nansen had previously determined that an expert skier could advance as quickly as harnessed dogs, enabling him to pack more equipment onto the sleds without lowering his travel rate.

All explorers who'd previously achieved Farthest Norths had launched their overland journeys on terra firma; Nansen and Johansen began on the Arctic Sea's shattered plain of hummocks, ice hills, and open water. At the time, more was known about the surface of the moon than about this unmapped, unmoored wasteland. It made northern Greenland seem like a cakewalk, and Nansen and Johansen swiftly came to appreciate the savage difficulty of sledging across it. Around three hundred miles from the pole, the surface became even rougher, and the southerly drift of the ice more pronounced. The Norwegians had already achieved a Farthest North at this point, but Nansen insisted they go farther, adding fifty miles to their record over the next five days. Finally, on April 8, 1895, after determining that they had smashed the Greely expedition's previous record by more than three latitude degrees, they turned around.

Their real troubles began on the return journey. Mushy spring snow slowed their progress and exhausted the dogs. Nansen and Johansen killed the weakest of the animals and fed them to the others, using knives for the unsavory deed in order to save ammunition for hunting. Huge leads spidered out across the thawing ice, requiring them to use the kayaks. They traveled in an exasperating zigzag pattern and uncertainly, with Nansen struggling to compensate for the drift as he navigated toward partially unmapped Franz Josef Land. Both of their chronometers stopped working, rendering it impossible to determine longitude. After 146 days and six hundred miles on the ice, the two Norwegians reached a small island north of Franz Josef Land in August. They wintered there, sleeping away the long nights in a three-foot-deep hole, subsisting on walrus and polar bear, unsure of where they were, bored stiff, and yet unfailingly civil. Up until about midway through their intimate shared confinement, the two compatriots continued to address each other as Dr. Nansen and Mr. Johansen.

In the spring they paddled south. While they were taking bearings from atop an iceberg, the kayaks containing all their supplies broke free. Nansen swam out to retrieve them, nearly dying from this bone-numbing rescue effort, and three days later the kayaks were all but destroyed by a pack of walruses. The Norwegians brought their boats ashore, spent several days patching them, and were preparing to relaunch them when Nansen swore he heard dogs barking and strapped on his skis to investigate. A few hours later, he was astonished to find himself face to face with an Englishman named Frederick Jackson.

Jackson was in the second year of a planned three-year expedition to Franz Josef Land, a joint undertaking of the Royal Geographical Society and the London newspaper publisher Alfred Harmsworth. He had glimpsed a human figure through his telescope and guessed that Nansen was a crew member from Harmsworth's *Windward,* which had been expected to return with news and supplies that summer. Then he noticed the figure was using skis, and wondered if he might be a lost walrus hunter. Nansen's shaggy, grease-slicked hair and beard made him nearly unrecognizable, and months of crouching over a blubber-fueled Primus stove had blackened his face like a chimney sweep's. "The complexion was that of native Central Africa, excepting for one or two white spots in the neighbourhood of the eyes and mouth," Jackson recalled. But then it dawned on him.

Jackson asked, "Aren't you Nansen?"

"Yes, I am Nansen."

The dumbstruck Englishman took his hand and shook it over and over. Many had given the Norwegian up for dead.

The relief ship *Windward* took Nansen and Johansen home that summer and carried a long letter for Harmsworth in which Jackson described his extraordinary Arctic rendezvous. It was a dazzling tale, reminiscent of Stanley and Livingstone. Harmsworth promptly published it in the *Daily Mail*, the popular newspaper he'd launched only a few months earlier. The *Fram* arrived in Norway a week after the *Windward*, having drifted all the way from central Siberia to Spitsbergen. It was in nearly perfect condition, with all hands alive and healthy. Like Nansen, its crew had actually *gained* weight in the Arctic.

Nansen's scientific work gave subsequent explorers much to contemplate. His soundings suggested that there was nothing but ice-covered sea in the heart of the polar basin, which helped to convince Robert Peary that the "American route" through Smith Sound was the most viable path to the pole. Nansen's experience on the drifting polar ice also led him to devise a simple equation by which future explorers could, by measuring wind speeds, determine the rate at which it was pushing them off course and adjust direction accordingly. Peary appears to have ignored this finding.

Nansen represented a rare combination of ingenuity, athleticism, courage, and scholarship. A scientific man, he knew that other scientists would demand to know how *he'd* known where he'd been, and he carefully logged his sextant, theodolite, and compass readings in real time. His only serious navigational error came on the return journey, when he forgot to wind his chronometer. While this oversight brought him and Johansen much grief while on the ice, it never called their Farthest North into question.

Tarnishing a great polar achievement by failing to record it properly was literally the stuff of Nansen's nightmares. During the tensely inactive early months aboard the *Fram*, in the winter of 1893–94, the fear of failing to account for his travels had been so persistent that it haunted him in his sleep. In his diary, Nansen wrote,

> I had a strange dream last night. I had got home. I can still feel something of the trembling joy, mixed with fear, with which I neared land and the first telegraph station. I had carried out my plan; we had reached the North Pole on sledges, and then got down to Franz Josef Land. I had seen nothing but drift-ice; and when people asked what it was like up there, and how we knew we had been to the Pole, I had no answer to give; I had forgotten to take accurate observations, and now began to feel that this had been stupid of me.

Nansen returned from the Arctic in 1896 a national and international hero and would go on to distinguish himself as a scientist, diplomat, and humanitarian. He lent his wisdom and influence to other explorers and later let one of his biggest admirers, Roald Amundsen, use the *Fram* for a successful attempt to reach the South Pole. His Farthest North of 1895 did not last long; it was surpassed five years later by the Italian explorer Umberto Cagni. But Nansen felt no need to reclaim his title and never tried to reach the North Pole again.

MEANWHILE, PEARY'S YOUTHFUL AMBITION OF REACHING THE NORTH Pole had become an obsession. Dissatisfied with the results of his 1893–95 northern Greenland expedition, he planned to return immediately. But he failed to secure the necessary funding or long-term naval leave, and managed to make only summer visits to the Arctic in 1896 and 1897.

Because there was no use trying to travel very far within a single season, Peary focused on collecting Arctic trophies instead and returned from both summer tours with furs, skins, tusks, and other booty that he sold and distributed as gifts to wealthy benefactors. Far and away the biggest prize was the most enormous of the Cape York meteorite fragments he'd discovered in 1895, which was at that time the largest known meteorite in the world. At thirty-four tons, it had been too heavy for Peary to move before, but now he levered the massive treasure onto a makeshift track, rolled it onto his ship, and brought it home, completing a three-piece collection that he lent and would eventually sell to the American Museum of Natural History for $40,000. It is hard not to view his reputation-building "discovery" of the meteorite as a simple plundering, even if Peary argued that the Cape York natives preferred the metal objects he was now trading with them and therefore would not miss their traditional source of iron.

Peary also profited during these two years by delivering dead and live natives to the American Museum of Natural History. After his retrieval of Cape York Inuit cadavers in 1896, a curator at the museum (Dr. Franz Boas, later a famous anthropologist) requested a live sample for scientific study. Peary, probably assuming he would be rewarded sixfold, brought back half a dozen. Unsure of how to care for the four adult Inuit and two children, the museum housed them in its basement, where the grown-ups contracted pneumonia. By the following May, all four had died at Bellevue Hospital. One of the surviving children, Minik, was disconsolate over the loss of his father, Qisuk. Museum officials staged a fake funeral to keep him from discovering that Qisuk's body had already been dismembered and his bones bleached and reassembled into a skeleton for public display.

The other child, Usaakassak, returned home, but Minik remained in America with a white foster parent for ten difficult years. Peary ignored this scandal in the making until it was exposed in 1907 by *The World*. Josephine arranged for Minik's return to Cape York in 1909, and Peary gave him a rifle and other practical items to help with his reintegration, but it never took. At home in neither culture, Minik returned to America seven years later and died during the influenza epidemic of 1918 while working in a New Hampshire logging camp.

Peary's careless treatment of the indigenous people on whom he depended is one of the darkest stains on his record. At the time, though, such high-handedness aroused only minor criticism, and his exploring career moved forward. Peary helped it along by describing his pursuit of the pole in lavishly jingoistic terms during a time when America was increasingly hungry to prove itself on the world stage. Though all explorers plucked at patriotic sentiment, none harped on it as relentlessly as he did. He emphasized American glory when addressing lecture audiences, big-ticket donors, and the naval superiors who were constantly weighing his requests for extended leave—and he did it because it worked.

Did America, let alone the world, have anything tangible to gain from his success? Not really; the true value of reaching the North Pole was symbolic. Even most of the public now assumed there was nothing of spectacular interest to be found there. The polar regions were, rather, an exotic proving ground for individual and national mettle. This was certainly the basis of their appeal for Theodore Roosevelt, who championed "the strenuous life" as a way of asserting manliness amid rising prosperity and urban decadence and who spoke for many when he praised Peary as a living embodiment of America's "great fighting virtues."

By 1898, Peary's body of Arctic work had won him exploring medals from the American Geographical Society and the Royal Geographical Society. No less important, the trophies he'd collected for the American Museum of Natural History had earned him the patronage of Morris Jesup, the institution's wealthy president. Jesup contributed a hefty sum to Peary's next North Pole bid and persuaded the railroad mogul James J. Hill, the Chase National Bank president Henry Cannon, and other financial titans to do the same. Alfred Harmsworth joined the cause, too, by donating the *Windward*.

Peary understood that these bigwigs were less interested in the pole itself than in having their names associated with a great act of discovery. As he reminded would-be donors in a fundraising pitch, "The one thing we remember about Ferdinand of Spain is that he sent Columbus to his life work." He also warned his supporters that Otto Sverdrup was busy trying to claim the pole for Norway. This was not the case, but Peary simply could not accept that an explorer as formidable as Sverdrup would venture forth (in the *Fram*, no less) without competing for the ultimate Arctic prize.

The *Windward* penetrated Kane Basin as far as Princess Marie Bay in the summer of 1898, near the Norwegian expedition's base on Ellesmere

Island. Peary "had a short and not effusive meeting with Sverdrup," he wrote to Josephine, and left this tense encounter as convinced as ever that the race was on. Desperate to improve his position for a spring dash to the pole, he risked an eighteen-day journey to Greely's old hut at Fort Conger in late December, the worst possible time of year for such a journey. It was such an insane gamble that Henson ventured to suggest that they wait until spring, but Peary would not be dissuaded. The two of them sledged with Dr. Thomas Dedrick, four Inuit, and thirty-six dogs, in near-total darkness and temperatures that plunged as low as -60 degrees Fahrenheit, and reached the hut in early January. As the party warmed themselves inside, Peary detected what he later described as a "wooden" feeling in his lower legs. Henson pried off his commander's frozen sealskin boots with a knife, gingerly removed his rabbit-skin undershoes, and watched in horror as most of Peary's toes came off with them. Distraught, Henson asked Peary why he hadn't mentioned his frostbite earlier. "There's no time to pamper sick men on the trail," Peary muttered. "Besides, a few toes aren't much to give to achieve the Pole."

But he could not hope to get to the pole in this state. The competitive fire that drove Peary had burned him badly this time, and the march back to the *Windward* for surgery was excruciating. By the time Dedrick was finished with him, only two of Peary's toes remained. And yet he returned to Fort Conger in the fall, alternately hobbling and riding on a sled. He reached the previously uncharted top of Greenland in 1900, naming it Cape Morris Jesup. For all his perseverance, though, Peary had once again fallen short of success as he defined it. On May 6, 1901—his forty-fifth birthday—he was reunited at Cape Sabine with Josephine and Marie for the first time in nearly three years. They'd come north in a relief vessel chartered by his backers, who'd recently christened themselves the Peary Arctic Club; a second relief expedition led by the club's secretary, Herbert Bridgman, arrived in August. Bridgman had persuaded Frederick Cook to volunteer his services in the event a second doctor was needed—wisely, it turned out, for Peary had fallen out with Dedrick and refused to see him. Cook was shocked at the condition of his old traveling companion. "The first impression was of an iron man, wrecked in ambition, wrecked in physique, wrecked in hope. To the public he was on his way to reach the Pole, but to himself no such effort had been made. Peary was worried, anxious, discouraged as I have never seen him before," Cook wrote. He told Peary that his damaged feet would make it impossible for him to use skis or snowshoes and that he was "through as a traveler." Peary ignored this comment, Cook later said. We do not have Peary's version of the exchange, because he never mentioned it.

Josephine and Bridgman pleaded with Peary to come home. But he insisted on staying another winter, a decision that only made a grain of sense because he still had Henson with him. Peary's capable assistant spoke the language of the Cape York Inuit and thrived as a trusted go-between for them and the imperious man they called "Pearyarksuah," or "the Big Peary." Henson not only helped Peary manage the physical difficulties of that year's journey but also encouraged reluctant Inuit to come along after a deadly outbreak of dysentery ravaged their community that fall.

With the help of these unsung heroes, Peary set foot on the frozen polar sea for the first time in his life in 1902. He covered a mere 82 miles in sixteen days before turning back. Having fallen 137 geographical miles short of Cagni's Farthest North of two years before, he returned limping and demoralized—"a maimed old man," he wrote. He would later refer to the Cape Morris Jesup expedition, when he spoke of it at all, as "four lost years." Sverdrup had used *his* four years to map 2,000 miles of previously uncharted coastline and 50,000 square miles of northernmost North American territory. Peary's achievements paled in comparison.

Discouraged by his poor results and mangled feet, Peary's backers lost faith. Some members of the Peary Arctic Club proposed disbanding. Rather than abandon his dream of discovering the North Pole, though, Peary simply devised a new way of going about it.

# CHAPTER TWENTY

The turn of the twentieth century was an exhilarating and exhausting time to run a newspaper. This was especially the case in New York, the nation's news capital, which produced more daily reading material for more people than any other city in America. The rewards of success were greater in New York, the competition stiffer, and the roller-coaster ride (a new form of amusement, originating at Brooklyn's Coney Island) of technological and social change all the wilder. The city was a hub of manufacturing, philanthropy, and the arts, and it swelled with new immigrants. Its official population exploded on January 1, 1898, when the five boroughs merged, creating a megalopolis that was double the size of any other city in America and the world's second largest after London.

Publishers around the country had come to rely on New York City's wire services and daily journals for their national and foreign news, special features, and syndicated comic strips. Huge amounts of labor, imagination, and money went into producing these ephemera, and the public's appetite for them seemed insatiable. By 1900, 94 percent of American households read the newspaper, compared with just one in three during the era of Stanley and Livingstone. The busy professional bought his first paper of the day for the breakfast table, a second for his commute to work, and a third for perusal at his club or office. Men and women of all classes consumed them now and demanded far more for their pennies. "The people of today want something more than the mere news in their daily paper," the trade journal *Newspaperdom* explained. "The women and children are newspaper-readers, and there must be stories, and poems, and fashion articles, and correspondence, and illustrations, sermons, and biographies, and holiday specialties, and serials." The trade term for this smorgasbord of printed material was "stuff," and piles of it were served up every day. Ad-crammed "boom editions," produced in honor of city centennials and other tempting pretexts, were trending around the nation. *The World* celebrated ten years under Pulitzer by printing a hundred-page issue, mainly just to show it could. Eager to prove he was no slouch, Ochs arranged for thirty-seven exclusive photographs of Queen Victoria's Diamond Jubilee to run in the *Times*. The handsome halftone images made a splash, and the fact that they had been published less than two weeks after the event itself was considered close to miraculous.

Newspaper promotional schemes multiplied around the turn of the century. Bennett, who'd once mocked *The World* as "the Gift Enterprise," was now doling out prizes himself, including a free around-the-world trip to the reader whose presidential campaign predictions proved most accurate. Names and slogans of the big New York dailies were emblazoned onto streetcars, delivery wagons, and elevated trains. Newspaper agents peddled subscriptions door to door, bribed newsdealers for preferential placement, and gave away free copies to plump their circulation figures. Perhaps the most remarkable thing about the "new journalism" of this decade was its cheapness for the consumer. Advances in the industrial conversion of trees to paper had sent the price of newsprint tumbling, which was bad news for Canadian old-growth forests but a boon for readers. (Meanwhile, newsprint remained a huge expense for publishers, simply because they were using so much more of it.) The era's advertising boom led publishers to prioritize circulation numbers over newsstand margins, and was a major reason that cheap sheets like *The World* literally sold for less than the paper they were printed on. The newspapers of the

1890s were, in short, an affordable luxury. Poorer readers actually spent *more* time enjoying them thàn did educated members of the middle class, who also had expensive books and magazines at their disposal.

Print media *was* mass media. Radio did not exist yet, let alone television or the internet, and newspapers served a broader purpose than they do now. Hundreds of thousands of immigrants viewed *The World* as an educational tool that would help them adapt to city life and get ahead— but also as a form of cheap entertainment, especially on Sundays, when many Americans "would consider themselves defrauded if they did not have a bale of printed matter delivered at their doors almost equal in bulk to a family Bible," the British journalist W. T. Stead noted. Overstuffed Sunday editions proliferated in the 1890s, generating hefty profits for publishers in New York and elsewhere. Religious leaders complained, to no avail, that it was immoral to enjoy them on the Lord's Day. The people would have their Sunday papers; Pulitzer claimed that he commanded a larger Sunday audience than all the ministers in New York state combined.

Color ink first came to newsprint during the Gay Nineties, beginning with the *Sunday World* in 1893. It was a costly, frustrating process, and when Pulitzer's first attempts failed to boost circulation numbers, overworked department heads begged him to stop. Instead, he fired his Sunday editor and ordered his replacement, Morrill Goddard, to move the color-ink experiments from the fashion section to the funny pages. This had the desired effect of selling more papers, and also turned a comic strip starring a bucktoothed slum urchin in a yellow nightshirt into a popular phenomenon. The "Yellow Kid," as the character came to be called, was just one of the successful elements of the reinvigorated *Sunday World*. Goddard, one of the few *World* employees regularly praised by Pulitzer, specialized in pseudoscientific features with titles like "The Suicide of a Horse" and "Experimenting with an Electric Needle and an Ape's Brain." His Sunday edition also served up tearjerker advice columns and expanded crime features, and stretched illustrations of leggy chorus girls over an unprecedented seven columns. Every page waged a war against boredom. As *Collier's* noted in a series on the newspaper business fifteen years later,

Goddard's guiding principle was "economy of attention." It worked like a charm, sending circulation of the *Sunday World* beyond half a million.

BUT *THE WORLD* WAS NOT AS INVINCIBLE AS IT SEEMED. IN SEPTEMBER 1895, as Ochs was beginning his discussions with the New York *Mercury*, thirty-two-year-old William Randolph Hearst bought the lowly *New York Morning Journal* for $150,000. Strictly speaking, the money wasn't his; his mother, Phoebe, had inherited it from his late father, the mining baron George Hearst. But the younger Hearst's dependence on his mother's generosity, like his reputation for delinquency, made him dangerously easy to underestimate.

After being expelled from Harvard for neglect of studies in 1885, Hearst had gone home to San Francisco and persuaded his father to give him the *Examiner*, a Democratic organ that the elder Hearst had accepted as payment for a poker debt. "Willie" Hearst turned the old-fashioned paper into a West Coast example of the "new journalism" that was ascendant in New York. His rambunctiously populist *Examiner* sniffed out corruption everywhere, including in places where there was none, and announced its startling findings in all capitals. "Sob sisters" related tales of woe; reporters were dispatched to capture the last grizzly bear in California and bring it back for public display. Though he claimed to idolize the *Herald*, Hearst's primary model was clearly *The World*. His goal, one of his deputies later explained, was to produce "the gee-whiz emotion," and by 1890 the *Examiner* had not only matched the circulation of the *Chronicle*, its respected local rival, but also achieved something resembling statewide distribution.

None of this guaranteed that Hearst would succeed in New York, where the prevailing opinion was that he would burn through his family fortune (George Hearst died in 1891) and go home. Early impressions of the young Californian did little to challenge this assumption. Shaking his hand was said to be like pawing a dead fish, and Hearst's thin, bleating voice reminded the *World* columnist Irvin Cobb of "notes on a child's toy flute." Other successful newspaper owners clubbed around with powerful allies or worked themselves to nervous exhaustion. Hearst took in musical theater shows with his friends and hangers-on and threw late-night parties at which he abstained from drinking the expensive champagne he had paid for. New Yorkers didn't really know what to make of him.

While they gossiped about the purported West Coast wunderkind, Hearst pumped another $250,000 of his mother's money into the *Journal*. He expanded the paper to sixteen lively pages of sex, crime, scandal, humor, illustrations, and pro-union politics, and kept the price at one cent. Hearst's attack on *The World* was nothing if not direct. He took up residence in the belly of its famous building on Park Row, where he leased office space for the *Journal* on the eleventh floor, and proceeded to consume it like a tape-worm.

In early 1896, Hearst persuaded Pulitzer's entire Sunday staff to come work for the *Journal*. Pulitzer lured the defectors back the next day with higher salaries, then lost them for good to Hearst's counteroffer. This brazen raid got Hearst evicted from 53-63 Park Row. It also launched what *The World*'s business manager at the time, Don Seitz, described some thirty years later as "the most extraordinary dollar-matching contest in the history of American journalism." Pulitzer stormed back to New York from his vacation estate in Jekyll Island, Georgia, to hold an emergency meeting with Seitz, *The World*'s publisher, S. S. Carvalho, and other top lieutenants. After much heated argument, it was decided to lower the price of *The World* to a penny. By initiating what was sure to be a costly price war, Pulitzer acknowledged Hearst as a serious rival. Privately, he conceded that the *Journal* was "a wonderfully able & attractive and popular paper" that had begun to shake up the business as he himself had done twelve years earlier.

Pulitzer's price cut failed to produce the desired circulation gains. Enraged, he blamed Carvalho, who resigned and joined the *Journal*. Though Hearst was rapidly gaining ground, the truth was that both penny-paper chieftains were bleeding badly. By late 1896, Hearst was rumored to be losing $100,000 a month; *World* profits were down by 60 percent, and in his desperation to secure more readers, Pulitzer had begun descending a slippery slope of lowered standards.

Hearst, not Pulitzer, was now setting the pace of popular journalism in New York City. One of his keener insights was that superior comic strips were critical to the success of a cheap Sunday paper. Goddard's replacement at *The World*, a rising star named Arthur Brisbane, was producing four of its eight comics pages in color, the maximum enabled by the latest printing machinery. Hearst thought the *Journal* could do better. He ordered his all-purpose assistant and nightclubbing pal, a mechanically gifted former vaudeville actor named George Pancoast, to tinker with the paper's Hoe presses, even at risk of breaking them. The resourceful Pancoast succeeded in short order, allowing the *Journal* to tout its new offering—with signature lack of understatement—as "eight pages of iridescent polychromous effulgence that makes the rainbow look like a lead pipe."

The star of Hearst's new full-color supplement was none other than the "Yellow Kid." His latest raid on *The World* had landed him the strip's creator, Richard F. Outcault. With Outcault gone, Pulitzer simply hired another illustrator, George Luks, to continue producing the popular comic. Now both the warring penny papers had Yellow Kids. Noting this shared feature, the editor of the struggling *New York Press* coined a name for the disreputable practices of *The World* and the *Journal*, a scornful term that was intended to impugn both papers for the sickly prurience they brought to politics, polar exploring, and whatever else they touched. The catchy moniker, "yellow journalism," would easily outlive both Hearst and Pulitzer.

## CHAPTER TWENTY-ONE

It was during this unruly phase in the history of the American press that Adolph Ochs assumed provisional control of *The New York Times*. (One of his first acts as publisher was to remove the old-fashioned hyphen.) "I am going to make things hum here," he assured Effie in late August 1896. It was a daunting task, to say the least.

Morale was low, the machinery outdated, the operations muddled. Half of the nineteen thousand issues printed every day were returned to the printers unsold. One bright spot for Ochs, he told a friend, was that he "could not make any new mistake in the management of The Times, for I believe my predecessors made every mistake that it is possible to make." The office had just two telephones. Ochs bought more, as well as several typewriters, ignoring the protests of old-timers who preferred to write in longhand and disliked the constant rattling of the newfangled contraptions. As he worked on getting new presses installed, Ochs found immediate ways to improve the way the paper looked: larger type, roomier spacing, better ink and newsprint. A week after he'd taken charge, a trade publication likened his typographical adjustments to a "gleam of sunlight on a cloudy day."

Cautious by nature, Ochs arrived at most management decisions after due consideration and consultation. He sought the advice of lower-placed employees ignored by most publishers. He addressed even the humblest of these workers formally and by name, and impressed the compositors in particular with his deference and knowledge of their trade—thus softening the blow when he fired a handful of them. Ochs had resolved to cut his weekly payroll by $1,000 and knew from his teenage years as a printer in Tennessee that the mechanical departments at the *Times* were "ruinously overmanned." Rather than hire anyone new, he asked the existing staff to do better, starting with the editor Charles Miller, whose salary he cut in half. The Dartmouth-educated newspaper veteran and *Times* shareholder was now earning as much as a Hearst cartoonist and having to prove he was worth every cent of it.

Ochs could feel his methods working. "I can say without any conceit that every man in the office from the editor-in-chief to the janitor recognizes that I am capable of conducting this business, and they respect me accordingly," he wrote to a relative in Louisville that fall. Though he bragged to his family that he was "the czar of the establishment, monarch of all I survey from cellar to dome, and so recognized by all," Ochs was in fact intimidated by the intellects of men like Miller and only just beginning to prove himself to Times Company shareholders. His easiest and most productive discussions were with "Mr. Loewenthal"—the managing editor, Henry Loewenthal, forty-three, who'd been with the paper since the Jones era and before that with the *Tribune.* The somber Loewenthal shared Ochs's business sense and soon became a valued adviser; the two men often went from the office to dinner nearby, then walked the streets together after dark, discussing the paper's future. Unlike many others at the *Times*, Loewenthal and Ochs saw its dullness as a virtue. They agreed that if the paper expanded its financial coverage, for example, it could win back many of the merchants and other professionals it had lost during the "mugwump" rebellion and the subsequent decline of the Miller era. They launched a daily feature for wholesalers called "Buyers in Town" and a weekly half-page financial review. The *Times* also began printing lists of real estate sales and structure fires and expanded its legal coverage. None of these changes made it a livelier read, per se, but they did render it increasingly indispensable to business professionals.

What is remarkable, in hindsight, is how little competition Ochs faced in this niche—in America's financial capital, no less. *The Wall Street Journal* was at this time a fledgling four-page newsletter. The conservative *Tribune* might easily have beefed up its financial reporting, but its publisher, Whitelaw Reid, was either too stuck in his ways or too distracted by his own political career to see the opportunity. Competitors considered Ochs's embrace of straight, bland news to be "insane," the Associated Press's chairman, Melville Stone, later recalled, even as white-collar professionals began referring to the three-cent *Times* as their "Business Bible." Meanwhile, revenue from financial advertising grew. By spring, sixty of the ninety New York City banks required by law to publicize their quarterly statements were opting to do so in the *Times*.

It took Ochs all of three weeks to produce the first Sunday supplement in *Times* history. These illustrated magazines were a specialty of the despised yellows, but the tabloid-sized ancestor of *The New York Times Magazine* gave morally squeamish readers nothing to complain about. Its inaugural issue contained earnest considerations of British politics, needlework, "old-time telegraphers," "the war against disease," and the proliferation of golf clubs in New York City suburbs. In his ongoing quest for "quality" readers, Ochs also introduced a Saturday book review during his first months on the job. This section treated the publication of books as news, not as occasions for fiery debate; Ochs wanted the *Times* to be an impartial arbiter of ideas, and to this end he also took the unusual step of publishing reader letters that were both supportive and critical of the paper's views.

Ochs even briefly considered dropping the paper's vaunted editorial page, before deciding simply to make it more anodyne. The *Times* endorsed neither of the major parties' presidential candidates that fall; neither William McKinley, a business-friendly Republican from Ohio, nor William Jennings Bryan, the Democratic torchbearer of the free-silver movement. The *Times* announced that after examining all the angles, it had found a bright side to the populist Nebraskan's otherwise terrifying campaign. "Bryan, with his shallow mind, with his reckless and untiring tongue, is the best of all leaders to develop the total strength and full weakness of the silver cause," its editors concluded, and they prophesied that his electoral defeat would effectively end the movement. To the enormous relief of *Times* readers and shareholders, this prediction proved correct.

Now that the one topic the paper seemed to get worked up about had lost its urgency, Ochs continued softening the editorial voice of the *Times*. He was not one to ruffle feathers unnecessarily, and by maintaining a friendly—or, at worst, constructively critical—attitude toward the White House, regardless of which party occupied it, he believed the paper could eventually become the sort of national authority that *The Times* of London was in Great Britain. McKinley, a conservative whose Republicanism had been the main strike against him for the *Times*, was unlikely to test the limits of this broad-minded policy.

Ochs also insisted on shielding the newsroom from the paper's business dealings. For Times Company shareholders, this firewall took some getting used to. Many of them were in the habit of receiving friendly treatment from the *Times* and complained to Ochs whenever it printed something unfavorable to their personal or business interests. He reminded them that the independence of the newsroom was sacrosanct and, unless the offending item demonstrated a genuine lapse in judgment or opposed "the fixed policy of the paper," refused to intervene. Ochs also turned down a hefty contract for city advertising, despite assurances from Tammany Hall that no strings were attached, because he worried that the impartiality of the paper would be threatened anyway—if not in practice, then in the minds of readers. Of course, Ochs also understood the publicity value of such ethical conduct and made it known that the *Times* was rejecting shady offers. When the Board of Aldermen offered the paper $33,000 to print election-related public notices, its editorial page responded by scolding the city for wasting taxpayer money.

Now that he'd begun to clean up the *Times*, Ochs needed a catchy slogan for it. He'd already tried out a couple. "NO WOMAN IS EVER ASHAMED TO BE SEEN READING THE NEW YORK TIMES IN PUBLIC PLACES," blared ads on elevated train lines, and a similar-sounding endorsement from the Presbyterian luminary the Reverend Theodore Cuyler—"The New York Times does not soil the breakfast

cloth"—had been reprinted elsewhere. Ochs turned the search for a permanent motto into a promotional opportunity, challenging readers to
come up with a slogan of ten words or fewer and offering $100 for the
winner, only to reject all twenty thousand submissions. A favorite entry
("All the World's News, but Not a School for Scandal") was announced,
and a check duly sent to its author in New Haven, Connecticut, but Ochs
chose a similar, tidier slogan of his own invention: "All the News That's
Fit to Print." It first appeared on the front page, in the left "ear" (a box next
to the paper's nameplate), on February 10, 1897.

The timing of its unveiling was apt, for disgust with the yellow journals
had begun to coalesce into a moral crusade. The *Times* supported this
emergent campaign, albeit cautiously. Its editorial page blamed the excesses of "freak journalism" for various social ills and argued that the way
to suppress offenders like *The World* and the *Journal* was to turn the reading of them into "a social offense punishable with scorn and contempt."
But while Ochs admitted privately that "an organized revolt against the
sensational newspaper" would benefit the *Times*, he considered it unwise
to "manifest our interest" in the subject by creating a special department
to report on it.

The movement gained ground anyway. Boycotts were set in motion in
early 1897, at a meeting of the New York Ministers' Association that was
thoroughly reported on by the *Times*. Not since the early days of Bennett
Sr.'s *Herald* had New York's religious and cultural establishment mobilized this effectively against the penny press. But the moral guardians
would not get far. Events in Cuba were about to overtake their reform
campaign and help make the yellow journals more popular and powerful
than ever.

## CHAPTER TWENTY-TWO

B y 1897, Spain's decrepit New World empire was lurching toward a violent end less than half a day's boat journey from Florida, and the question of whether to support the Cuban insurrection was being debated across America.

The New York press was split. The *Herald* offered a nuanced view of the situation, while the *Tribune* urged caution and the *Times* argued for government intervention only as a last resort. The yellow journals, on the other hand, firmly believed that more should be done to help the insurrectionists and acted accordingly. Hearst even had one of his reporters break the seventeen-year-old daughter of a revolutionary leader out of a Havana jail. When Hearst put the "Cuban Girl Martyr" Evangelina Cisneros on the stage at Madison Square in a white satin gown to celebrate "the greatest journalistic coup of this age," New York City's police chief described the fifty-thousand-person crowd as the largest he'd ever seen. Though *The World* accused Hearst of creating "reckless war scares," its belligerence rivaled his, and its reporters worked so closely with rebel leaders that they were often mistaken for Cuban spies. Several weeks after the Cisneros affair, Pulitzer published true-to-life illustrations of starving Cubans so disturbing that he later issued a rare apology.

By early 1898, as warlike sentiment approached a boiling point, Hearst and Pulitzer were battling on a new front: the afternoon. The traditional reason to publish an afternoon or evening edition of a morning paper was to run late-breaking news items, or "extras." Pulitzer's recent success had highlighted another reason: stupendous profits. His *Evening World* was not just an updated edition of that morning's paper; it was, in many ways, an entirely different product, offering more sports, humor, crime, and scandal and less political news from Washington and abroad. The morning edition was a brisk cup of coffee; its evening counterpart was a frosted treat. It was also a huge moneymaker, not only because it was cheaper to produce, but also because men who bought evening papers at the end of the workday often brought them home to their wives, which made these cheap sheets an especially attractive venue for advertisers of household products. It was the evening yellows, more than the morning yellows, that spawned the checkout-aisle tabloids of later eras.

After two years of building up his morning and Sunday editions, Hearst finally turned his attention to the *Evening Journal*. From Pulitzer he stole Arthur Brisbane, who embarked on a familiar Hearst strategy: make it like *The World*, but yellower. Brisbane started on page 1, creating supersized (and often blatantly misleading) headlines that occupied half the page. One of his most famous innovations was to print crucial elements of the headline in a much smaller typeface so that what read as shocking news from a distance revealed itself to be mundane upon close examination, ideally after the paper had been purchased. For example, from the spring of 1898: "WAR will probably be DECLARED."

Brisbane, the self-proclaimed "yellowest journalist in the world," understood that readers did not mind being hoodwinked by "split heads" like these and in fact often found them amusing. His successful early experiments for Hearst would help turn him into a cynical guru of early twentieth-century mass media, widely quoted on subjects ranging from advertising ("Always remember that it is impossible to exaggerate the stupidity of the public") to sensationalism ("The people must have it—just as the Chinese take opium, the ignorant man takes whiskey, and the higher-class person takes a philosophical discussion"). By early 1898, his gleefully unchained *Evening Journal* was gaining steadily on *The Evening World*.

One reason for this was its constant clamoring for war in Cuba, which was becoming more of a powder keg every day. President McKinley ordered the 319-foot cruiser *Maine* to Havana in January, purportedly to protect American commercial interests in the wake of pro-Spanish riots. Several weeks later, a scandal involving the Spanish ambassador to the United States caused relations between the two countries to deteriorate even further. Writing to a friend in Havana two months prior, Enrique Dupuy de Lôme had described McKinley in pointedly unflattering terms. The damaging letter was fished out of a desk or wastebasket by an anonymous Cuban sympathizer, provided to the junta's press office in New York, and first offered to the *Herald*, whose editors asked for a day to authenticate it. The junta refused to wait and took its scoop to the *Journal*, which unhesitatingly published a facsimile of the letter under the headline WORST INSULT TO THE UNITED STATES IN ITS HISTORY. A diplomatic crisis ensued, only to be swallowed up by the explosion of the *Maine* six days later.

The critical question was whether the explosion, which killed 266 Americans, had originated inside or outside the vessel. *The World*, the *Herald*, and the *Journal* all sent divers from Florida to Havana, but Spanish authorities refused to let them descend. While the U.S. government investigated what it called an "accident," *The World* and the *Journal* treated the disaster as a Spanish act of war. (Subsequent investigations have all but proven that the explosion originated in the ship's own coal bunkers.) As vengeful cries of "Remember the *Maine*!" swept the nation, Hearst organized a congressional junket to Cuba for holdout legislators. It was during this call to arms that the combined morning and evening circulation of the *Journal* surpassed a million, matching Pulitzer's feat of a year before.

Pressure mounted on Washington to act. "The newspaper men cluster like bees about me," Secretary of the Navy John Davis Long wrote in his diary. Publicly, at least, McKinley resisted the furor. The president got most of his news not from the yellow journals but from lower-circulation newspapers favored by the East Coast business establishment, including the anti-interventionist *New York Times*. With his options narrowing, McKinley secured $50 million in Treasury funds for national defense. The allotment was described as a "peace appropriation" by the *Tribune* and a "pacific measure of great merit and potency" by the *Times*. The *Journal*'s interpretation would ultimately prove more accurate: FOR WAR! $50,000,000!

ONE REASON THE SPANISH-AMERICAN WAR HAS BEEN THOROUGHLY CHRONicled is that so many journalists collected firsthand impressions of it. Some five hundred American writers, photographers, and artists descended on Cuba. Inevitably, they sent back tales of heroism. Theodore Roosevelt became the most popular man in America after leading his Rough Riders (and Buffalo Soldiers from the all-black Ninth and Tenth cavalry regiments) to victory on San Juan Hill, and Admiral George Dewey was lionized for trouncing Spain's Pacific fleet at Manila Bay.

*The World* and the *Journal* continued furiously trying to outdo each other, and Brisbane later confessed that the front pages of both papers came to look "more and more like aggravated circus posters." Hearst was generally willing to take the fight one step further than Pulitzer was, provocatively christening the war "The *Journal*'s War" and traveling to Cuba as a pistol-toting correspondent for his own paper. But the *Herald* often showed up both the yellow giants with its reporting and scored many of the war's biggest scoops. Though *The World* was first to report the sinking of the *Maine*, the *Herald* got the full story first, after its Havana bureau chief, Walter Scott Meriwether, tied up the wires in Key West by transmitting the contents of a legal textbook so that his twelve-thousand-word dispatch could receive priority. The *Herald* also printed the most famous line of the war, which was delivered by Dewey in Manila as the flagship *Olympia* came under heavy shelling: "You may fire when ready, Gridley." It was a stirring example of American courage under fire, and it might have been lost to history had Bennett's correspondent Joseph Stickney not been there at Dewey's side to record it.

When the U.S. Navy destroyed the enemy's vaunted Caribbean fleet in Santiago Harbor that summer, Bennett happily paid $6,500 in cable fees for the first detailed account of the battle. That defeat (which was somewhat controversially credited to Admiral Winfield Schley, Adolphus Greely's old rescuer at Cape Sabine) effectively ended any remaining Spanish hopes of retaining Cuba, and after signing an armistice with the United States in mid-August, the colonizers gave it up—as well as Puerto Rico, the Philippines, and Guam, a 130,000-acre volcanic island with strategic proximity to China and Japan. These territorial gains ended a long tradition of American isolationism. Ignoring signs of impending trouble in the Philippines, McKinley's secretary of state (and former *Tribune* editor), John Hay, dubbed it a "splendid little war."

Another important truce was struck that August, when Pulitzer directed a deputy to "stop the unfriendly utterances between the *World* and the *Journal*." The war with Spain had been a mixed blessing for the yellow journals. On the one hand, it sold newspapers and attested to the enormous influence of the penny press. On the other, it stretched their budgets and production capacities close to the breaking point. The *Journal* had struggled to keep up with demand, despite owning the world's largest newspaper printing facility. It was said that the newsboys had made out better than publishers because, for all the papers the war sold, the cost of covering it was astronomical. The *Journal* blew through $3,000 a day, more than its newsstand sales could make up for. *The World*, *The Sun*, and the *Herald* spent heavily as well—up to $9,000 a month apiece simply to charter, fuel, and insure their press boats. A big paper might have as many as two dozen salaried correspondents in the field at once, racking up eye-watering telegraph and cable bills. Arthur Brisbane guessed that it would have taken the war just two years to "bankrupt the resources of every first-class newspaper in New York City." According to Don Seitz, *The World*'s business manager, the paper's profits had been "wiped out" by the time the Spanish stronghold of Santiago fell in mid-July, forcing Pulitzer to "call on his resources for working capital" for the first time in fifteen years of ownership.

Eager to get back to making money, Hearst and Pulitzer eased up on each other and slashed budgets that fall. His position now assured, Hearst turned to politics. Pulitzer, meanwhile, began trying to restore the dignity and credibility *The World* had sacrificed in order to keep up with the *Journal*. But raising his paper's standards without ruining it financially would be more difficult than he imagined. It wasn't just that sales lagged in peacetime. The Cuban crisis and the price war with Hearst had caused many ugly things to spill forth at *The World* and elsewhere. Among these was a troubling phenomenon that Pulitzer would refer to several years later as "fake news."

# CHAPTER TWENTY-THREE

Joseph Pulitzer once told his personal secretary that he had tried to get his editors and reporters to embrace one journalistic value above all others: "Accuracy, accuracy, accuracy, is the first, the most urgent, the most constant demand I have made of them." Strictly speaking, this might have been true of the famously demanding publisher. But Pulitzer also pressured his staff to produce interesting and eye-catching stories quickly. In the daily grind of the newsroom, something almost always had to give. Often, it was the accuracy. Color was simply easier to generate—especially if the writer was permitted to dream it up. According to the novelist Theodore Dreiser, who spent six months as an underemployed *World* reporter between 1894 and 1895, the editors there didn't just tolerate the casual injection of untruths into the news pages; they actively encouraged it. His city editor demanded "not merely 'accuracy, accuracy, accuracy,'" Dreiser wrote, "but a kind of flair for the ridiculous or the remarkable even though it had to be invented, so that the pages of the paper, and life itself, might not seem so dull."

Pulitzer was at least troubled by fake news; Hearst appeared to be indifferent to it. This might have been because Hearst lacked a conscience, as many of his early chroniclers believed, but maybe he was simply under fewer illusions about mass media. "The modern editor of the popular journal does not care for facts," Hearst once wrote privately. "The editor wants novelty. The editor has no objection to facts if they are also novel. But he would prefer a novelty that is not a fact to a fact that is not a novelty."

Fake news did not originate with Pulitzer's "new journalism." Long before he or Hearst came along, it had amassed a colorful and occasionally gravely harmful history. Popular accounts of fake news in nineteenth-century America tend to focus on a handful of famous hoaxes, the grand-daddy of which was the "Great Moon Hoax" of 1835, a six-part series in *The Sun* about the purported discovery of life on the moon. The great success of this oddly appealing story helped to establish *The Sun* as the city's leading penny paper until its eclipse by Bennett Sr.'s *Herald*. *The Sun* struck again in 1840, with a spectacular fictional account—written by a thirty-one-year-old Edgar Allan Poe—of a hot-air balloon crossing the Atlantic in three days. Bennett Jr.'s mean-spirited "Zoo Hoax" of 1874, which fooled many thousands despite its small-print admission that the story was hypothetical, belonged to the same tradition of creative fabrica-tion. The authors of these elaborate and entertaining lies described them as satire and professed to be surprised when they succeeded in fooling thousands. The publicity and sales they generated came at the expense of credibility, and serious publishers attempted them only rarely.

In the hot pot of late-1890s yellow journalism, however, a different type of fake news predominated. As standards of accuracy slipped during the Hearst-Pulitzer circulation wars, blatant falsehoods became a *regular* feature of *powerful* newspapers, and especially of their lowbrow evening editions. Thomas Edison complained about the innumerable articles "pur-porting to be interviews with me about wonderful inventions and discov-eries. . . . Scarcely a single one is authentic." It is possible that the literate urban masses didn't care if many of the deaths, divorces, crimes, and Spanish evils they read about in the papers were partly or wholly fabri-cated. According to an item in the trade journal *The Fourth Estate*, New York City newsboys in 1898 took to yelling, "Fake Extra! All the fakes! Exclusive fakes!" because it helped them to sell their bundles faster. This anecdote aside, it's also possible that readers simply didn't know any better. The education gap between New York City journalists and the newspaper-buying public at this time was significant; the top reporters and editors at the yellow journals were every bit as talented as their "quality" counterparts, and the artists were actually better.

Even more confusing was that sometimes the most sensational accounts from Cuba proved to be the truest. The venerable Vermont senator Redfield Proctor was shocked to find that when it came to the humanitarian crisis there, the yellows had largely gotten the story right. "I went to Cuba with a strong conviction that the picture had been overdrawn; that a few cases of starvation and suffering had inspired and stimulated the press correspondents, and that they had given free play to a strong, natural, and highly cultivated imagination," he told his Senate colleagues. In fact, he'd discovered the Spanish *reconcentrado* policy to be every bit as appalling as described. The revelation persuaded Proctor, a McKinley ally, to support American intervention, and the speech in which he announced his change of heart proved to be an important turning point on the path to war.

The problem was that accurate and important reporting appeared alongside all manner of tall tales, making it very difficult to tell the two apart. The Cuban crisis invited a perfect storm of fake news: it was near and pressing enough to be of interest, creating a demand for stories, but it was also a foreign affair, making it easy to embellish with impunity. Reporting on the Cuban insurgency, *The World* and the *Journal* took liberties that they probably would not have risked with a domestic conflict. They claimed that guerrillas were burning sugarcane fields using flaming snakes doused in kerosene, that they were carving cannons out of tree trunks and plotting to dynamite the enemy's morning coffee. These were the types of implausible "gee-whiz" stories that Hearst loved and that Pulitzer, who was more ambivalent, tolerated in his Sunday and evening editions. A *Journal* reporter who'd invented much of his paper's account of Dewey at Manila later justified his creative liberties on the grounds that they were so widespread: "It was a shameless bit of faking, but all the newspapers were doing it." The foreign correspondence of *The Sun* and the *Herald* was more reliable, but not entirely. Leading up to the war, the *Chicago Daily News* publisher, Victor Lawson, instructed his managing editor to open bureaus in Key West and Havana rather than buy news from any of the Big Four, "just because the New York papers do so much faking."

Rather than manufacture news from nothing, most unscrupulous journalists simply inflated the facts into something almost unrecognizable. According to the novelist Stephen Crane, who filed vivid dispatches for *The World*, Florida bureau chiefs were usually to blame. "If the news arrived at Key West as a mouse, it was often enough cabled north as an elephant," he wrote. The result, and not just in *The World*, was "a general mess of exaggeration and bombast." It was also strangely acceptable for a paper's morning edition to say one thing about Cuba and the evening edition to say the opposite, without any acknowledgment of the discrepancy. For editors to correct an error, let alone admit that they had made one, was virtually unknown, and unless someone rich and powerful had been demonstrably injured by their carelessness, they had no reason to fear legal consequences. The weak libel laws of the time, which tended to put the plaintiff under more scrutiny than the defendant, were a poor deterrent. Filing a libel suit required money and patience, and so most victims settled for a terse apology instead, even if it ended up buried in the offending paper's shipping news.

The most vigilant monitors of fake news were the very newspapers that traded in it most heavily. *The World* labored to expose a *Journal* "beat" as a "fake" a day or two later and vice versa, a form of rival tracking known as "running." The *Times* dismissed this competitive tail chasing as a huge waste of time and energy. Why subject yourself to a "series of conflicting and exciting emotions," it wondered aloud, when you could simply get your news from a reliable source twelve or twenty-four hours later? The *Times* proceeded on the assumption that these readers prioritized—or could be taught to prioritize—efficiency and truthfulness over speed. Perhaps this was naive. Lincoln Steffens, writing on the newspaper business for *Scribner's* in 1897, theorized that most people were as interested in the competition over scoops as they were in the scoops themselves, and rooted for rival papers the way they supported political parties or sports teams. "An exclusive story is supposed to cause talk, to suggest purchasing to the man who has it not, to mix up generally in discussion the paper and its 'beat,' and, best of all, perhaps, to instill in the reader interest and pride in 'his paper's' triumph," Steffens explained.

During the war with Spain, the American popular press came up with ways to deliver its dubious goods even faster and more frequently. The time-honored tool for this was the "extra"—a repackaging of the regular morning or evening edition that included important late-breaking news. In the past, these supplemental editions had been produced sparingly, but now they came out by the handful and on the slightest pretext, turning the old once-a-day or twice-a-day dispensation of the news into a nearly constant feed as the slide toward war accelerated. On its busiest days, the *Journal* produced more than forty editions.

In order to print news faster, Brisbane extended the office telegraph line into the composing room and created a placeholder called the "fudge box" that allowed late-breaking items to be hand set (or "fudged") into a page that had otherwise been prepared in advance for the presses. With efficiencies like this in place, the *Evening Journal* could begin printing a new edition just five minutes after the arrival of a hotly anticipated news item, which appeared in eye-catching red ink. These "Red Extras" were notorious for being misleading and gratuitous, but they brought news of the war to the streets in record time and sold like candy.

The Spanish-American War has been called the first international conflict that Americans followed in something resembling real time, and many readers found the effects of this self-refreshing news stream to be intoxicating. "Some people have become so addicted to the 'extra' habit that they buy every copy put forth from the presses of the *Journal* and *World*," *The Fourth Estate* observed in May 1898.

The dizzying pace of news that spring and summer did not outlast the war, but nor did things go back to what they had been before. The metabolism of the reading public had quickened irreversibly. "The newspaper which tells at four in the afternoon here what happened in London at eight o'clock the same night has become as much a matter of course as the thunder-storm, the rainbow, the X-ray or anything else that has ceased to seem marvelous," Brisbane wrote just after the war ended.

This great shrinkage of space and time had been made possible by steady advances in land-to-land communications. Just a year earlier, though, an Italian electrical engineer named Guglielmo Marconi had formed the first company devoted to the next frontier in communications: wireless. The long-term implications of his new technology were thought to be enormous; the more immediate hope was it would enable ships to communicate with stations onshore and with one another, stitching the world's oceans together as the wire and cable services had done with its landmasses. Around a decade later, in 1909, the tightening news cycle amplified both the drama and the confusion surrounding Cook's and Peary's dueling polar claims. Wireless, too, would play a role. Crucially, it would enable Peary to announce his success while Cook was still in Copenhagen. It would also allow him to remain in remote Labrador for nearly a week, plotting his next moves with allies back home while avoiding the questions of prying journalists.

Adolph Ochs, for one, was energized by the potential applications of Marconi wireless at the dawn of the twentieth century. But he was too busy fighting for survival to give the subject much thought. The war with Spain had made the difficult task of restoring the *Times* even harder.

# CHAPTER TWENTY-FOUR

Rather than compete for scoops on the battlefront, the *Times* saved money by relying on bland Associated Press reports for most of its war coverage. More troubling to Ochs than these news-gathering constraints was the paralyzing effect of the war on Wall Street. The belligerent cries to "Remember the *Maine!*" chilled investment activity, and the formal declaration of hostilities froze it. (The economic uncertainty also led many backers to renege on their commitments to the Peary expedition that left that summer.) Financial advertising, a critical source of revenue for the *Times*, dried up completely for six months, forcing Ochs to pitch New York City's dry-goods merchants and department stores even harder.

Desperate to secure their business, he offered more favorable terms than usual. He also claimed to sell twenty-five thousand newspapers a day. This was considerably fewer readers than the *Tribune*, *The Sun*, or the *Herald* claimed; even so, it was a gross overstatement. While the *Times* printed that many copies daily, nearly half of them went unsold, and only around ten thousand of them were bought by the Manhattan readers coveted by most advertisers. The true circulation of the *Times* was known only to an inner circle, and standardized independent auditing was unknown. Deceptively conflating the number of newspapers printed with the number of newspapers distributed was, moreover, a fairly common trade practice. Ochs likely calculated that his exaggerating would go unnoticed. Events would prove him sorely mistaken.

That summer, the powerhouse retailers being wooed by Ochs began receiving hand-printed circulars urging them not to be "fleeced" by the *Times* and its inflated circulation claims, and Bloomingdale's stopped placing paid notices. Ochs learned that the author of this alarming campaign was a former bookkeeper in the paper's circulation department named W. L. Woolnough who'd been fired months earlier to reduce overhead. Although the ex-clerk's actions reeked of personal grievance—he referred darkly to Ochs and the *Times* circulation manager, Louis Wiley, as "those Jews"—his charges commanded attention.

Ochs assured advertisers that Woolnough's purported whistleblowing was "an admixture of rascality and insanity." Privately, however, he and Wiley were worried enough to hire a private investigator, who discovered that members of the paper's mail and delivery departments had furnished some of the figures in the handbill and were prepared to sign affidavits if challenged. "Your troubles are only commencing," Woolnough warned Ochs. "You have no circulation and never will have one and advertisers will not keep on waisting [*sic*] their money."

OCHS MET WITH HIS ANTAGONIST IN HOPES OF PERSUADING HIM TO BACK down, but this attempt at diplomacy went nowhere. Let the *Times* try to sue him, Woolnough taunted. Then the numbers that actually mattered would be revealed, "and were it generally known that the Times circulation was so small, how long would it live?"

It was a legitimate question, under the circumstances. The paper had finished its first year under Ochs only $68,000 in the red, a major improvement. But its second year under him, which had just ended, had produced a slightly larger deficit—an increase in the wrong direction. With these troubling realities bearing down on him, Ochs unilaterally made one of the most important business decisions in the history of the *Times*. On October 10, 1898, he reduced the price of it from three cents to one.

An astonished Spencer Trask asked him to explain himself. "Does this mean such an increase in circulation and such financial prosperity that the Directors felt we could venture it—or the reverse?" In order to turn a profit, the famously boring *Times* would need to attract at least three times as many readers. Selling "a high-class newspaper at the lowest price," as Ochs now proposed to do, had never been done before.

Ochs promoted the newly affordable *Times* aggressively, giving it out for free to help spread the word and instructing newsdealers to do the same with unsold copies. He also positioned the price reduction as a public service for "educated, intelligent, refined" readers who "would prefer to read a newspaper not given over to vulgarity and madhouse methods." This explanation was not completely disingenuous, but nor was it the whole story. And yet for a century, the myth persisted that Ochs had risked the price cut for high-minded reasons. The 1898 advertising slump was downplayed in accounts of the paper's rise to glory, and until the publication of a comprehensive history of the Ochs-Sulzberger dynasty in 1999, Woolnough's harassment campaign went unmentioned.

Regardless of what made Ochs do it, reducing the price of the *Times* to a penny that fall turned out to be an extraordinarily smart decision. Angry newsdealers were pacified by an immediate uptick in sales, which rendered Woolnough's exposures irrelevant. Three days after the change was implemented, Ochs noted that the paper's printing facilities were "taxed to their utmost." He suspended publication of the Sunday supplement in order to keep up with demand and was soon boasting to advertisers that the paper's circulation was "greater than ever before in its history." The growth was largely traceable to affluent sections of New York City and its suburbs, confirming that even rich people enjoy a deal and suggesting that the new *Times* readers had all the education and purchasing power of the old ones. This was great news for the business department, even if it contradicted Ochs's claims that he was guiding the benighted poor away from the "vulgarity" of *The World* and the *Journal*.

By November, the mood at *Times* headquarters had brightened noticeably. "Everyone is happy around the office, and the signs of prosperity are already causing applications for increase of salary," Ochs reported. The

*Times* leapfrogged the *Tribune* in circulation almost overnight and by spring drew seventy-six thousand readers a day. Ochs kept this tally under wraps; the Woolnough scare had taught him to discuss such numbers in approximate terms, if at all. He emphasized the "quality" of the paper's growing readership over its quantity, and when industry auditors pressed him to be more specific, he suggested that they talk to newsdealers on the prosperous Upper West Side of Manhattan about how well the *Times* sold— knowing full well that in that particular neighborhood it sold very well.

Without resorting to exact numbers, Ochs continued to stretch the truth about the paper's reach. He told advertisers that he could "almost guarantee" them the largest Monday-to-Saturday readership in New York City, with the exception of *The World* and the *Journal*. The "almost" covered the glaring exception of the *Herald*, which still far outpaced the *Times*. Still, Ochs had reason to feel he was gaining on James Gordon Bennett. New revenues from his price reduction had more than offset the losses in per-copy sales, putting the *Times* in the black for the first time under his management. In the summer of 1899, less than a year after the price cut, the Times Company resumed paying shareholder dividends. A pleased Charles Flint wrote to Ochs, "The sensation of receiving money from the New York Times is an agreeable one."

So confident was Ochs that summer that he even made a play for Bennett's other New York City sheet, the forty-year-old *Evening Telegram*, which the Commodore had indicated he wanted to sell. Having recently borrowed an additional $150,000 in working capital from the Equitable, Ochs sent Charles Miller to Paris to negotiate for it. Bennett told Miller that he would sell Ochs the *Telegram* for $125,000, but on one condition: that the payment be made in *Times* stock. Ochs turned down Bennett's proposal, and all bidding for the *Evening Telegram* ended there. Bennett subsequently hired a new business manager for the *Telegram* and returned his unloved evening paper to profitability. Perhaps Ochs's show of interest led him to reconsider the value of what he had. Perhaps Bennett's startling counteroffer did the same for Ochs.

According to his contract with the Times Company, the controlling share that had been put in escrow for Ochs would be given to him once the paper profited for three years in a row. In the summer of 1900, Ochs tried to claim ownership two years ahead of schedule, on the grounds that the total earnings of the past thirty-six months exceeded the total losses. The reorganization committee rejected this creative reinterpretation of their agreement. Ochs must have been distraught by its decision, for he destroyed all correspondence in which he'd discussed the matter with Trask or his brother George, and instructed George to do the same. Rather than declare defeat, though, he spent a month lobbying the committee and then formally made his case again. On August 14, 1900, the committee voted 3–1 in his favor. Almost four years to the day after gaining a foothold at *The New York Times*, Adolph Ochs took control of it.

# CHAPTER TWENTY-FIVE

The rebounding *Times* remained a skeptical observer of polar ventures. Not so the *Herald*, which cut an exclusive deal with the Peary Arctic Club to publish photographs, sketches, and articles resulting from his 1898–1902 expedition. The arrangement guaranteed that if Peary reached the North Pole, the *Herald* would get his account of the expedition first. Bennett did not assign a monetary value to that prospective feat in advance. In the event that Peary succeeded, a *Herald* editor airily informed the Peary Arctic Club's secretary, Herbert Bridgman, "the question of remuneration shall be left to Mr. Bennett's liberality." In the end, Bennett's liberality was never tested, and Peary's "four lost years" furnished little of great value to the *Herald*.

Bennett was less disappointed by this outcome than he might once have been, for he had by now found a new way to scratch his itch for adventure: sponsoring high-profile automobiling, ballooning, and aviation events in France. The various "James Gordon Bennett Cups" generated less heartache and sunnier headlines than his old exploring gambits had, and while polar discovery remained a topic of personal interest, the feverish enthusiasm he'd shown while planning the voyage of the *Jeannette* twenty years earlier had never returned. Rather than organize his own

Arctic expeditions, Bennett now supported those he deemed most interesting or likely to succeed, and he still paid top dollar. When Salomon August Andrée made a widely publicized attempt to reach the North Pole by hydrogen balloon in 1897, Bennett offered the Swedish aeronaut $27,000 to let a *Herald* reporter accompany him. By declining the offer, Andrée unwittingly saved a journalist's life. He and his two companions died on an island east of Svalbard less than four months after liftoff.

Two years later, the *Herald* devoted nearly a full page to Frederick Cook's first newspaper account of the 1897–99 *Belgica* expedition, which made history as the first time that human beings wintered in Antarctica. Cook, who'd served as its surgeon and anthropologist, touted the Belgian-funded expedition's geographical discoveries in the *Herald*. But the medical experiments he undertook aboard the *Belgica* were arguably a more important outcome. The "polar anaemia" he described later came to be understood as "winter-over syndrome," and the cures that Cook devised for his morose, sun-deprived shipmates eventually helped with the development of treatments for seasonal affective disorder.

Though the *Herald* contributed less to polar exploring than it had before, it was still more active in this area than the rest of the New York City press. The *Tribune* lavished publicity on Peary, but stopped short of funding him. *The Sun* was losing influence in general. More than a decade had passed since the *Times* had dispatched Frederick Schwatka to Alaska, and it was in no hurry to send anyone into the northern wilds again. The *Journal*, with its notebook-toting "murder squads," was more interested in solving mysteries closer to home, and Pulitzer considered polar exploring one of the few subjects that *The World* should categorically decline to get involved in. His business manager, Don Seitz, later recalled that Pulitzer had authorized him to "do anything on behalf of the paper except hunt for the North Pole or back the invention of a flying machine, both ideas seeming chimerical to him."

When American publishers outside New York City decided to get entrepreneurial about polar exploring, the results could seem downright buffoonish. *The Chicago Record-Herald* and the Washington *Evening Star* underwrote the ex-journalist Walter Wellman's attempts to reach the North Pole by dirigible in 1906 and 1907, but these overhyped airborne expeditions failed miserably to achieve what had been promised. If anything, they reinforced the impression that when it came to participating in North Pole ventures, the only American newspaper that really had any idea what it was doing was the *Herald*.

## CHAPTER TWENTY-SIX

"Y ou can't hurt the *Herald*," Bennett had always said. This mantra rang truer than ever in the last two years of the nineteenth century, for the Hearst-Pulitzer price war had served his paper well. While the penny papers bled, the *Herald* earned more than a cent for every three-cent copy sold. It achieved record circulation in 1898, briefly surpassing 500,000, and did more business in 1899 than in any other year in its history. For all the excited talk of the yellows, America's most profitable daily was the sixty-four-year-old *Herald*. A more serious publisher would have reinvested this windfall into his newspaper. Bennett blew $625,000 on a boat.

When completed in 1901, his new super-yacht was hailed as the largest and most powerful private vessel ever produced by the famous shipyards of Scotland's river Clyde. The *Lysistrata* measured 314 feet from stem to stern and displaced more than two thousand tons. Powered by state-of-the-art twin engines, it could achieve an astonishing twenty-one knots. It was unmistakable from a distance—not just on account of its size, but also because its design (by the eminent G. L. Watson) was most unusual. Whereas most steam yachts of the period at least nodded to their elegant, wind-powered forebears, Bennett had dispensed with such romantic gesturing in favor of warlike utility. The *Lysistrata* possessed a stumpy single mast, which was used for signaling purposes only. One thick funnel protruded amidships, like a rudely extended finger. Its bow was dead straight, and its elongated stern made its proportions look weirdly unbalanced; the *Lysistrata* resembled a fast ocean liner or a navy scout more than a traditional pleasure vessel. The lone concession to classical design was its carved wooden figurehead, which depicted Bennett's mascot, an owl, with outstretched wings.

As strange and menacing as Bennett's yacht looked from afar, it was also awash in creature comforts. Many of the guest cabins in this "floating palace," as one trade publication called it, offered the luxury of attached dressing rooms and bathrooms, and the twenty-by-twenty-five-foot dining room was done up in decorous Grecian style. Bennett's guests feasted on Chesapeake crabs, plover eggs, and other delicacies imported from the earth's far corners, and were treated to massages, champagne, and a seemingly endless supply of custom-made Havana cigars. There was even a Turkish bath, although this feature was for Bennett's use only. Beneath the poop deck was a padded stall, over which hung an enameled sign that read, BOSSY. Within this cozy enclosure resided the yacht's most notorious amenity: the dairy cow kept aboard so that Bennett would never be without fresh milk or cream. There was even an electric fan to keep Bossy cool in warm climates.

Though Bennett most loved cruising the Mediterranean, his pampered wanderings took him as far afield as Venezuela and Havana, up the Nile and across the Indian Ocean, and as far east as Saigon. For additional comfort, he reserved a personal stateroom for himself on each of the boat's three decks. In calm seas he would sleep in the upper one, which had the most sunlight and a commanding view; in rough seas he retired to the lower one, which rocked less; if he was in a Goldilocks sort of mood, the middle stateroom would feel just right. Bennett, who turned fifty-nine in 1900 but still carried himself like a younger man, might also have had other reasons for regularly changing his sleeping quarters. It was said that he kept a different mistress in each one.

Everyone aboard the *Lysistrata*, from Bennett's aristocratic friends to the deckhands, submitted to the absolute authority of its owner. The Commodore referred to the hired captain as his "executive officer," as a reminder to all that he could take the wheel or change course whenever he felt like it. He never yielded to other vessels at sea, regardless of their size or weaponry, and the shrieks these dangerous games of chicken elicited from his guests pleased him visibly. This—Bennett's wacky mean streak— was the trade-off for all the luxury and splendor of sailing with him, and the well informed knew to weigh such invitations carefully. A trio of fashionable American women once came aboard in Monte Carlo for what had been billed as an elegant dinner in the harbor. The next thing they knew, they were steaming toward Egypt, with the "executive officer" refusing to reverse course until ordered to do so by the Commodore, who'd locked himself in his stateroom and did not respond to knocking. Mishaps like this occurred often.

The irony of it all was that Bennett imposed strict rules aboard. Apparently in a nod to British naval tradition, any man who set foot on the *Lysistrata* had to be clean shaven. And because Bennett did not like it when his guests stayed belowdecks, even in foul weather, he had their luggage inspected for playing cards before they sailed. If any decks were discovered, he rendered them useless by personally tearing up the aces.

BENNETT HAD A STANDARD WAY OF DECLINING PRESS INTERVIEWS. "I'D rather not take any of my own medicine, if you please," he would say. Tales of his extravagance and eccentricity spread anyway, and he eventually became known, as one former *Herald* writer put it, as "the most picturesque figure in the whole history of journalism."

He lived like royalty abroad. In addition to his two Parisian town houses on the Champs-Élysées, he owned an eighteen-hundred-acre estate in Versailles with a palace that had been built by Louis XIV. There was also a shooting estate in Scotland, at which Bennett regularly hosted King Carlos of Portugal and the monstrous King Leopold of Belgium. The Commodore's favorite property, though, was said to be his palm-shaded villa in Beaulieu-sur-Mer, a seaside village between Nice and Monte Carlo, where he kept a majestic rose garden, four private chefs, and the *Lysistrata* moored in the quiet bay.

Though he'd been an expatriate for more than twenty years, Bennett's personal American domain was no less imperial. In New York City, it included an East Twenty-First Street town house, where he stayed on his rare visits to the city, and his father's old mansion at 182nd Street, which no longer felt like the country getaway it had been and was now lent out to favored *Herald* executives as a weekend tennis-and-picnicking retreat. In Newport, Rhode Island, Bennett owned a large estate and an architecturally impressive country club, the Newport Casino. But his most prestigious property, and the perennial source of his enormous wealth and influence, was *The New York Herald*.

The sheen was still on the new Herald Building in 1900. Commissioned in 1891, less than a year after the unveiling of the World Building, and completed in 1894, Bennett's headquarters was physically different from Pulitzer's (which he considered an eyesore) in every possible way. Designed by the ultra-fashionable Stanford White, it was a Renaissance-inspired building of classical proportions and barely fifty feet tall. Its facade of beige masonry was adorned with graceful arcades, arches, and columns of polished granite, and a pair of massive clocks were inlaid high on the southern wall. Atop these stood a pair of mechanical bronze figures resembling burly pressmen—and nicknamed Stuff and Guff—who struck a resounding bell on the hour. Instead of gargoyles, the Herald Building featured bronze owl statues. Some two dozen of them perched at regular intervals along its cornice, and the electric lights they had for eyes blinked throughout the night. The idea for this spooky effect had been Bennett's, and the message was unmistakable: the all-seeing *Herald* never sleeps.

The boldest touch of all was the building's location. The *Herald* was now based where Broadway and Sixth Avenue intersected with Thirty-Fifth and Thirty-Sixth streets, a full three miles north of its old home on Newspaper Row. Bennett's uptown move did more than advertise his aloofness from the rest of the New York City press. It acknowledged and advanced the northward migration of Manhattan business and leisure activity. The *Herald* was now in the middle of a rapidly gentrifying district of theaters, hotels, and upscale department stores that bustled day and night, and the paper's headquarters was itself a popular attraction, not only for its European-flavored architecture, but also for its magnificent lofted pressroom, which occupied the basement and first floor. Every day, thousands of pedestrians stopped in front of arched plate-glass windows to watch the *Herald*'s awesome printing machinery at work. It was a scene of furious mechanical reproduction and yet bathed in eerie calm—the opposite of the popular image of newspaper making as a rattling, wheezing, ink-stained operation. Eight tank-sized presses sat directly on the building's stone foundation, barely vibrating; with only the upper bodies of the pressmen visible from the street above, the workers appeared to float between their stations. It seemed a minor miracle that the great ribbons of white paper never tore or snagged as they raced tautly off the cylinders. The *Herald* did most of its printing at night, under the glare of nearly two thousand electric lights; watching the orderly flurry of bright white newsprint caused some onlookers to see bright spots, as though gazing at a snowy landscape on a sunny day.

The Herald Building's interiors were tastefully opulent—the first-floor business office in particular, with its mosaic floors, columns of Italian marble, and furniture of matching white mahogany. A steep marble stairway led to a second-floor landing that gave onto the executive offices and editorial departments. These included Bennett's empty private chambers, the main conference room, and the telegraph room. The largest space on this floor, the newspaper's nerve center, was the open-format city room, where reporters wrote at desks that were placed side by side as in a schoolroom, facing a long table of copyreaders wielding blue pencils. Edited copy was sent to the compositors on the third floor by pneumatic tube, just one feature of a vast communications infrastructure that also included internal and external telephones, twenty telegraph machines, and more than two dozen speaking tubes.

Having fallen out with Stanford White, the architect, by the time the building was unveiled, Bennett did not attend the opening in 1894. Some commentators expressed hope that his gleaming new headquarters would encourage him to spend more time in New York, or take more of an active role in the national newspaper scene. It was not to be. The Commodore preferred life in Europe.

A DISAPPROVING THEODORE ROOSEVELT ONCE SAID OF BENNETT, "HE possesses one redeeming characteristic: He lives abroad." Given his personality and background, it is not hard to understand why. Life in Europe was more luxurious, and society there was more forgiving of his antics. The discreet French press ensured that the worst stories involving "Monsieur Gordon-Bennett," as he was mistakenly called in France, never saw the light of day. The tales that did were so colorful, and so abundant, that "Gordon Bennett!" later entered British English as an expression of shocked incredulity.

The Commodore had by the turn of the century become a celebrated figure of the Parisian boulevards, where he was often seen wearing his signature spats and bowler hat, walking his Pekingese dogs. The onset of late middle age (he turned sixty in 1901) had done little to mellow him. It was true that he'd given up coaching after returning home one night drunkenly at the reins, smashing his head into a stone arch at 104 Champs-Élysées, and fracturing his skull—an accident that nearly killed him. For the most part, though, Bennett continued to behave as he pleased. He was the archetypal Crazy Rich American, whose riches shielded him from the consequences of his craziness. Restaurant managers looked the other way when he smashed champagne bottles or sent nearby table settings crashing to the floor. He was the biggest buyer of wine in Paris and reliably paid for all the damage. Nor did his fellow diners necessarily even mind Bennett's rampages. Some of the more socially ambitious ones considered it a mark of distinction to have a meal ruined by him at a name-droppable place like Voisin or Maxim's.

Bennett's more lasting contribution to the beau monde was his European edition of the *Herald*. Launched in 1887, during a time when more Americans had begun traveling abroad for business and pleasure, the groundbreaking *Paris Herald* furnished these wealthy visitors with useful

English-language briefings on the latest in French art, fashion, and literature. "Le New York," as it was known among French newsdealers, was for a long time the only example of the American press that many Europeans had ever seen, and it was always an amusing read. Though it no doubt helped to foster international cultural exchange, the eight-page *Paris Herald* probably did more to promote tourism than world peace or the high arts. Bennett's New York editors privately denigrated it as his "Paris toy," and he did play with it in a way that he never ventured to do with his father's *Herald*. When friends complained to him that they struggled to read the newsprint, he ordered the ink changed to blue, and then green, and then other colors over the course of a week or two—more as a prank than as an earnest attempt to address the problem. He also let personal friendships dictate the paper's coverage of various royal courts and used its fashion and sports pages to shape popular taste to his liking. Even the restaurant reviews of *The Paris Herald* were a reflection of Bennett's tyrant whims, for any European establishment that failed to pay him due deference found itself ignored or condemned by it.

Unsurprisingly, *The Paris Herald* lost money. It was said that Bennett spent $100,000 a year keeping it afloat. It was also said that he considered it worth every penny.

# CHAPTER TWENTY-SEVEN

The 1900 Exposition Universelle in Paris was anticipated around the world as the spectacular launch of the new century. The Paris Expo, as it was generally known, would spread across 275 of the city's finest acres, luring tens of millions of international visitors over seven months, and represent an even grander celebration of human enterprise and industry than the previous edition of 1889, which had famously produced the Eiffel Tower. The encyclopedic scope of the undertaking, the mix of seriousness and spectacle, the breathable sense of optimism—all these qualities appealed to Adolph Ochs.

The *Times* was no longer a charity case in 1900, not by a long shot. By the end of that year, it was earning more from Monday-to-Saturday advertising than the mighty *World*. Ochs boasted on the eve of its fiftieth anniversary that the paper's finances were in better shape than ever before "in its eventful history." Annual net profits totaled $140,000 in 1901, and its average daily circulation of 102,000 that year represented an all-time high. Most miraculous of all was that the *Times*, the only morning paper in turn-of-the-century New York City that did not print illustrations, had gone about it all with utmost modesty and decorum. The general impression among shareholders, one of them later recalled, was that Ochs had "taken over a ship that was in serious trouble and, practically without changing the crew, had made it a great success." Many would-be investors tried to get their hands on New York Times Company stock, only to find that anyone who owned it wasn't selling.

Having restored the paper's foundations, Ochs now set to building on them. "I myself feel that the experimental stage has been passed, that [the paper's] future is no longer problematic," he wrote to his family in Tennessee. "The New York Herald of course shows how much is yet to be accomplished, but I believe I will hereafter make some rapid strides towards a favorable comparison." The *Herald* was rumored to net a million dollars a year. Ochs coveted its "monopoly" of classified advertising while also preparing to challenge it in another area that the *Herald* had long dominated: foreign news.

For years, the *Times* had achieved a lot with a little in this department by leaning heavily on its London correspondent, Harold Frederic, who wrote both trenchant cable dispatches for publication and highly useful private letters to the *Times* editor Charles Miller. While the *Herald* retained a robust network of international correspondents and stringers, and reportedly spent more on foreign news than all other American newspapers combined, the *Times* squeezed as much as possible out of a single overworked individual. It exhausted this resource in 1898, when Frederic dropped dead of heart disease at age forty-two. The last thing he ever wrote—"with great difficulty," his *Times* obituary noted—was his weekly cable letter. One is tempted to conclude the job killed him.

After Frederic's death, Ochs approached newspapers in Boston, Chicago, and St. Louis and humbly proposed splitting the cost and contributions of a shared London correspondent. (When it came to something this important, there was no question of relying on the wire services, as he had done in Cuba.) A year later, however, with the *Times* on much firmer financial ground, Ochs decided to indulge his international ambitions at the Paris Expo. He was reassured by the fact that the United States, feeling newly confident on the world stage after its military defeat of Spain, was spending more on its national showcase than any other country, giving potential *Times* subscribers and advertisers even more of a reason to travel over for the event.

Ochs rented fifteen hundred square feet on the Left Bank, in an annex of the American pavilion that had been set aside for publishers, and sent his brother George to Paris to work out the details of the exhibit. The plan was to print and distribute a daily international edition of the *Times* that would raise the paper's profile at home and abroad during the Expo, and perhaps even remain in production afterward. George began negotiating with European news agencies, soliciting advertising, and arranging for the delivery of technologically superior American printing machinery.

When its exhibit was unveiled that June, the *Times* officially joined one of the greatest shows on earth. Among the futuristic novelties on display were escalators, moving sidewalks, diesel engines, talking films, and a Ferris wheel. Guests at the Palais d'Optique were invited to view the moon using the largest telescope ever made. Two new Beaux Arts additions to the Parisian cityscape, the Grand Palais and the Petit Palais, housed impressive collections of Western art, and the Expo of 1900 would later be remembered as the high-water mark of the decorative style known as Art Nouveau. Eastern art traditions claimed overdue consideration, too, when a geisha turned actress named Madame Sadayakko became a surprise hit and beguiled the likes of André Gide, Isadora Duncan, Auguste Rodin, and an adolescent Pablo Picasso.

The Arctic regions received a smattering of attention at the Paris Expo as well. On the Left Bank of the Seine, where two rows of national pavilions enlivened the stately gray monotony of the Quai d'Orsay, the gabled Norwegian pavilion devoted most of its first-floor gallery to a model replica of the *Fram* and relics of Nansen's celebrated 1893–96 North Pole attempt. The colonial section included displays for Danish Greenland and Asiatic Russia, the latter of which introduced visitors to the new Trans-Siberian Railway. It was a work in progress at the time, but within two years this massive project would enable travelers to shuttle between Irkutsk and St. Petersburg in a mere eight days, as opposed to the six weeks it had taken the survivors of the *Jeannette* disaster.

From the colonial displays it was a short walk across the Seine to the Palace of Literature, Science, and Arts and its showcase of modern printing methods. The highlight of this exhibit was the Linotype machine, an intricate contraption that was roughly the size of an upright piano. One enthralled observer described it as "a machine marvelous in speed, approaching perfection in its quality of its products, and unsurpassed in the perfection and action of its diversified movements." Its workings did more than just please the eye. The Linotype had revolutionized newspaper production by making it possible for a single unruffled professional at a typewriter-style keyboard to perform the work that five or six cursing, sweating tradesmen had done before. It halved production costs for the *New-York Tribune* when it was introduced there in 1886. It also enabled last-minute additions and changes that had previously been impossible to implement, thereby extending the news day by several hours. In short, Linotype changed everything. For millions of men and women who did not work in the newspaper trade, the printers' exhibit at the 1900 Paris Expo was their first opportunity to see it in action.

Anyone wishing to witness the soup-to-nuts creation of a modern daily newspaper, though, had to walk over to the broad Esplanade des Invalides, where the *Times* had set up its small but state-of-the-art production facility. Here specialists from the paper's New York office coolly operated Linotypes and octuple presses capable of printing twenty-five thousand issues an hour. The *Times* churned out newspapers of ten to sixteen pages, each of which contained a mix of repurposed items from New York and fresher material published exclusively for the Expo edition. In an implied challenge to Bennett's *Paris Herald*, the *Times* boasted that its daily offering provided "fuller American cable news and more elaborately detailed American news than has ever before been published in any one newspaper in Europe." Tens of thousands of copies were given away inside the Expo every day, with additional copies sold at kiosks around Paris. The technologically inferior French journals swooned, with *L'Écho* declaring itself "amazed at the neatness, rapidity, and precision" of the operation. The French government considered it such an impressive display that it later awarded George Ochs the Legion of Honor for his role in organizing it.

Pleased with how his foreign experiment had turned out, Adolph debated whether to continue publishing the *Times* abroad. "I am seriously contemplating making it a permanent edition," he wrote to a Cincinnati news broker that August. The *Times* shareholder Spencer Trask offered to invest $10,000 in the "Paris Times," and George lobbied hard for it. In the end, though, Ochs decided against competing with James Gordon Bennett on French soil. But the successful showing of the *Times* in Paris broadened his horizons in ways that would soon reveal themselves. As one biographer noted, "Here was the point at which the man who had already emerged from provincialism into regionalism and then into nationalism first began to look attentively at the world beyond the boundaries of his own country."

# CHAPTER TWENTY-EIGHT

After his disappointing effort of 1898–1902, Robert Peary determined to try again. He visited a medical specialist in Philadelphia who partially restored his mutilated feet by drawing the remaining skin over the toe stubs, creating a sort of pad beneath them. The operation reduced but did not eliminate the pain of walking great distances, and Peary would limp for the rest of his life. But the surgical procedure restored the confidence of his backers, as did the moral support of President Theodore Roosevelt, who considered him an American hero and secured him three years of navy leave so that he could make another attempt for the pole. Doors Peary had momentarily thought closed reopened.

Peary now made the important decision to ditch Harmsworth's *Windward* in favor of a ship that could break through the ice-choked channels of Nares Strait, thereby sparing him the exhausting overland journey up the coast of Ellesmere Island. It would vastly improve his chances, he reasoned, to winter near land's end and then set off with fresh dogs in the spring just five hundred miles from the pole. Peary also revised his thinking about the dash to the pole itself. Whereas he had previously used a small party, traveling more or less together, he now envisioned a complex relay operation by which teams of white navigators and Inuit drivers would go ahead and perform the arduous work of breaking trail, building snow houses, and depositing supply caches, then turn back as they grew short on food, fuel, and strength. Each "division" would make daily "marches" of twelve to sixteen hours each. Like a conquering general, Peary would bring up the rear, sledging the path that had been cleared for him, sleeping in the prebuilt igloos, inspecting the supply line, and conserving energy for his eventual sprint to the pole. It was military-style planning, for Peary believed that the fiendishly challenging travel conditions demanded nothing less.

The more weight his sledges carried during this final dash, the slower they would go, and Peary carefully balanced the need for speed against the risk of starvation. He planned to consume two thirds of his food (pemmican, mostly) on the outward journey and one third of it on the return, when the dogs could pull lightened loads and be slaughtered and fed to each other—a brutally effective way of conserving food weight that he had used before. The so-called Peary system was aptly named: it was a highly disciplined and regimented product of long Arctic experience, and misleadingly promoted as something that was entirely of his own invention. In reality, it combined Schwatka's embrace of native methods with a team structure much like the one that Francis Leopold McClintock had adopted while searching for the Franklin expedition, only with dogs doing the hauling instead of men. But Peary, to his credit, learned from past mistakes, and his apparently small improvements made an enormous difference.

Energized by his descriptions of this next attempt on the pole, and newly confident that it would be his last, Peary's backers opened their wallets to him again. The Peary Arctic Club was still led by Morris Jesup, its most reliable donor, and overseen on a day-to-day basis by its secretary, Herbert Bridgman, the New York City businessman and exploration enthusiast. The club incorporated in 1904, as it prepared to fund the building of Peary's new ship from scratch. Construction began in Bucksport, Maine, later that year. The 184-foot steam schooner, named the *Roosevelt* in honor of Peary's most famous patron, was only the third vessel in the world (and the first in the Western Hemisphere) to be designed specifically for Arctic navigating. Its heavy bow framing and raked stem enabled it to smash through ice as thick as fifteen feet. The *Roosevelt* was, in short, a battering ram, a steam-powered expression of the slogan Peary had lifted from the ancient conqueror Hannibal: "I shall either find a way or make one."

The bill came to $100,000. The Peary Arctic Club paid for nearly all of the *Roosevelt*, with George Crocker, a director of the Southern Pacific Railroad, contributing $50,000 and Jesup providing $25,000. The rest of the costs were underwritten by smaller donors and by Peary himself, who nearly went bankrupt to ensure that the *Roosevelt* sailed in 1905. When it did, it provided the expected power advantage, but also took a pummeling from the ice that previous explorers had never dared to challenge. The frozen polar sea, which Peary stepped onto at Cape Sheridan, was no less punishing. Sledging across it that spring, he encountered a mile-wide channel of open water separating the fast ice (that is, ice clinging fast to land) from the trickier pack ice. Lacking boats, the party was forced to wait a week until temperatures dropped enough for this barrier to solidify. No sooner had they crossed "The Big Lead," as Peary called it, than a vicious snowstorm pinned them down for another week. Having concluded that the best he could hope for that year was a Farthest North, Peary pushed on with Henson, and returned after a total of sixty-four days on the sea ice bearing the news that they had reached 87°06′ N—32 nautical miles beyond Cagni's record and 174 nautical miles from the pole. Peary later reported that while surveying the northern edge of Axel Heiberg Land that summer, he spotted the "snow-clad summits of [a] distant land in the northwest." He named it Crocker Land, in honor of the patron who'd put $50,000 toward the *Roosevelt*.

It took every ounce of Captain Robert Bartlett's grit and seafaring skill to bring the battered icebreaker home in one piece. "The poor old Roosevelt, as well as ourselves, was ready for the insane asylum or the dump heap," he wrote. Peary's Farthest North, news of which arrived during the climax of William Randolph Hearst's tempestuous gubernatorial campaign, was only tepidly acknowledged by the New York City press. His book *Nearest the Pole* would sell only twenty-five hundred copies when it was published the following year. Peary had been so confident of reaching the pole that people had begun to wonder whether getting a few miles closer was actually worth celebrating. The truth was that Peary's victory-or-nothing attitude had begun to work against him. Whereas Frederick Cook, to cite one contrasting example, had intellectual curiosity and an evocative way with words, Peary seemed fully preoccupied with getting from A to B. The ins and outs of Inuit folkways and ice behavior seemed to appeal to him only to the extent that they helped him to achieve his goal. He was, in short, interested only in winning, and by 1906 the public had evidently decided that unless he won the pole, it wasn't that interested in him, either.

Luckily for Peary, the National Geographic Society was considerably more impressed with his latest achievement. On December 15, 1906, at a white-tie dinner at the Willard Hotel in Washington, D.C., it awarded him its prestigious Hubbard Medal.

Somewhat awkwardly, the other honoree that evening was Frederick Cook.

FOLLOWING THE *BELGICA* ADVENTURE OF 1897–99 AND HIS ALARMING 1901 meeting with Peary at Cape Sabine, Cook had gone from serving noteworthy expeditions to leading them. He had also gotten interested in Alaska, home of North America's tallest peak, and set out to become the first person to summit it.

On his first attempt on Mount McKinley, in 1903, Cook made the mistake of taking along a twenty-six-year-old writer named Robert Dunn. An experienced backwoods traveler, Dunn was secretly planning to write an unsparing series of articles about the McKinley expedition for *Outing* magazine. It was for this very reason, in fact, that Dunn's former boss, the famous journalist Lincoln Steffens, had recommended him for the expedition in the first place. "I had seen a good deal of arctic explorers, read their books, and heard their gossip, which revealed to me that no book in the field had told it all; they all left out the worst of the wranglings and depressions which were an essential part of the truth about human nature in such tests," Steffens later explained. "Dunn simply could not lie," Steffens added. He was just the man to write the world's first warts-and-all exploration narrative.

Dunn did not disappoint his mentor. His published journal (and the book it became, *The Shameless Diary of an Explorer*) detailed the constant bickering and blundering of Cook's McKinley expedition, and while Dunn admitted that much of the grumbling came from him, he also criticized his leader's "fearful combination of stubbornness and indecision" in the boggy, buggy Alaskan wilderness. There was not a mountaineer in the group, and as it became clear to all that McKinley (now called Denali) would be a much harder climb than expected, Cook's unfounded optimism began to wear on Dunn. Every great explorer's "insensitiveness" to reality enabled him to push on and ultimately achieve great things, the journalist mused in his diary. He believed that Cook wore these essential blinders but that he could be downright pathetic once they came off. "The Doctor determines on a move; he has the feat accomplished before starting. He will not hear of difficulties, and when his unreasonable dream of success turns out a nightmare, he is all meekness and dependence and asks your advice in a hopeless, demoralized way."

Dunn's attitude changed, however, once they began to ascend McKinley. Its icy slopes were so steep that the four-man climbing party had to cut steps with axes; they clung to the mountainside by their toes, shoulders numb under heavy packs, each one of them a single misstep away from certain death. Cook, the man with the fixed smile and "bovine face," did not for a moment express fear or doubt, and Dunn, who was suffering intensely from both, had to admit that his quietly encouraging words were a godsend when the going was at its toughest.

In late August, the party reached a ridge that Cook had hoped would lead to the summit, only to discover that it sloped three thousand feet down into a glacier instead. "Checkmated at 11,300 feet," Dunn concluded—with nearly half the mountain still to go, they turned back. Maybe, Dunn added, seasoned alpinists could succeed where they had failed.

✳

COOK HAD RETURNED TO MCKINLEY IN 1906. INSTEAD OF A GARRULOUS freelance journalist, he brought along Herschel Parker, a physics professor at Columbia University. He hired six men to come with him, including Fred Printz, the lead horse packer from his previous McKinley attempt, and Ed Barrill, a burly blacksmith from Hamilton, Montana, as Printz's assistant. Another new addition to the expedition was a forty-foot-long motorboat that spared man and beast weeks of grueling overland travel.

It was a brutal journey nonetheless, rife with muck and thick under-brush, and the endless crossings of raging glacial rivers spooked Parker, the physicist, in particular. By the end of July, the party had only managed to climb Mount Kliskon, a mere hill at thirty-nine hundred feet, and to discover a sawtooth granite massif, which they named the Tokosha Moun-tains. When Cook and his companions finally got an unobstructed view of fortresslike McKinley, they concluded that it could not be conquered from the south. Nor was there time to try another approach, for Cook was contractually obligated to return to the coast. A manufacturing heir from Philadelphia had given the expedition $10,000 on the condition that Cook take him big-game hunting in Alaska later that summer.

A downriver journey in the motorboat brought the party to Seldovia, on the Kenai Peninsula, where Professor Parker returned to New York and Cook learned that his wealthy benefactor would not be coming hunting after all. Eager to make the most of the remaining season, Cook motored back up the Susitna in late August with Barrill, the assistant horse packer. In a telegram to Herbert Bridgman, who was still his friend at that point, he explained that he intended to scout a summit route for the next year.

On October 2, Bridgman received a second telegram from Cook, this one reporting that he had "reached the summit of Mount McKinley by a new route in the north." He and Barrill had been climbing a northeastern ridge, Cook later explained, when a break in the weather convinced him that the top was within their grasp. The two men reached it the morning of their eighth day on the mountain, so weakened by the effects of altitude that they descended after just twenty minutes. "For danger, hardship, and maddening torture this essay of the great mid-Alaskan peak has been my worst experience. For hellish conditions and physical discomforts the north-pole chase is, compared with Mount McKinley, tame adventure," Cook wrote in the May 1907 edition of *Harper's*. Included in his sixteen-page magazine account was a long-range photo of Barrill standing on a snowy outcrop, which would later become one of the most controversial expedition images ever published. The caption read, "The flag on the summit of Mt. McKinley, 20,300 feet above sea-level."

## CHAPTER TWENTY-NINE

While explorers like Cook and Peary sought to demonstrate that no corner of the earth's surface was beyond man's grasp, Adolph Ochs took up a task that many had considered equally quixotic: proving that a modern metropolitan newspaper could earn a healthy profit from straight news. He had brought sound management to the *Times*, but he had also bet on a future in which information—not sensation, not entertainment, not influential opinionating—was at the heart of what the paper did. He'd bet that the competition undervalued unbiased financial and political intelligence and that the supposedly humdrum task of providing it could in fact be good business—especially in a financial capital like New York City, where the news of a railroad merger was, for thousands of readers, quite literally worth more than the savory details of a theater actress's breach-of-promise suit. As the twentieth century dawned, it was increasingly clear that these bets were paying off.

As one historian of the press has neatly put it, Ochs made the *Times* the narrator of the city's "most vital running story: money." Ochs, of course, framed it slightly differently. "We have practiced, as best we could, old journalism—the journalism that succeeds in small towns where the high standards of the profession are demanded and practiced by self-respecting men," he said. For those exhausted by the excesses of the yellow press, the rise of the *Times* was welcome news. So often in the past, the daily task of modeling civility and sound reasoning had fallen to small-circulation journals like the *Evening Post*. The *Times* under Ochs was shaping up to be far more influential, and the editor of the venerable *Post*, E. L. Godkin, openly praised the larger paper for its "decency, temperance, and moderation." These finer qualities of the *Times* not only served the ongoing search for truth, Godkin wrote, but also motivated "sensible and high-minded men" to brave the bloody arena of public life.

Prosperity accompanied success, and Ochs calculated in 1900 that he had earned half a million dollars from the *Times*. Because most of this new wealth resided in Times Company stock, which he protected at all costs, and his annual salary remained modest, Ochs continued to pay down his old Chattanooga debts using borrowed money. He no longer struggled to obtain personal loans from banks, and rich friends assured him that any additional working capital he might need for *The New York Times* was there for him if he wanted it. "There is something more than money, and you have got it," the department store magnate Louis Stern told him. Like more and more of the city's leading businessmen, he considered Ochs a sure bet.

Ochs's family's living situation had also improved by the turn of the century. After four changes of residence in three years, the Ochses now inhabited a spacious rental unit on Seventieth and Broadway. It was a new apartment in a new building, with the modern luxury of electric lighting and more privacy than their previous boarding arrangements. Ochs ate breakfast there in the morning, walked Iphigene to school, then rode the elevated train to the *Times* offices on Park Row. Most evenings, he came home for dinner and then went back downtown to oversee production of the next day's paper; if he stayed in, galleys of the editorial page were delivered to him by messenger. Only rarely did Ochs accept invitations to mingle with the "big men of New York," as he described them. He dared not distract himself from the *Times*, believing that it was "easier to earn than to keep" and that a newspaper owner needed to attend to his interests as closely in good times as in bad.

※

OCHS WAS BEGINNING TO VIEW JAMES GORDON BENNETT AS A PEER AND rival, which must have felt odd in at least one respect. While the *Herald* publisher owned more sprawling estates than he could keep track of, Ochs still did not feel financially secure enough to buy a country house.

Instead, he rented a large house in Atlantic City every summer for Effie and Iphigene, and for his mother and three sisters, all of whom came up for the season from Chattanooga. Iphigene would later characterize these long beach holidays as a defining ritual of a "remarkably united and devoted" family. Setting aside the discomfiting fact that many of the nicest hotels in Atlantic City excluded Jews, Adolph found these family getaways deeply gratifying. Though he could not swim and avoided the water, he spent hours on the beach with Iphigene, spoiling her with candy, ice cream, and pretzels. His mother, Bertha, organized five-course menus that combined heavy German and southern cooking, and the dinner table over which he presided buzzed with in-laws, cousins, and other friends and relatives who came and went throughout the summer.

Arriving on the five o'clock train every Saturday, Adolph was treated like a returning king. As ever, his most loyal subject was his mother. She once whispered to young Iphigene, "Your father is not human—he is divine!" The rest of the family more or less shared this view. George had wept with joy when his older brother bought the *Times*, likening him to "Washington after Yorktown, Wellington after Waterloo," and the recent flourishing of the *Times* had turned Adolph into even more of a provider and patriarch. Distant cousins held Uncle Adolph up to their children as an example of the fruits of hard work and responsibility. He was the presenter of sound advice and lavish wedding gifts, the connector who put in a good word, the benefactor who gave even his most hopeless kinsmen a chance to make good on a small loan or two. He could be domineering and sanctimonious, and his generosity often came with strings of moral obligation attached. But he had made the Ochses financially secure and proud, and for this all was forgiven.

Adolph told Bertha that his ability to inspire and help those closest to

him was a "source of great satisfaction." But overwork and the accumulat-
ing obligations of social and family life made him yearn to escape, if only
temporarily. "I am making myself believe that it is perhaps best that I now
get away for a few weeks, twice a year, from my surroundings," he wrote.
Five months later, in the summer of 1901, he treated himself to his first
European holiday.

APART FROM A BRIEF BUSINESS TRIP TO THE PARIS EXPO THE YEAR BEFORE,
it was his first time abroad. He traveled with five women: Effie; Iphigene;
Iphigene's Swiss governess, Christine; and Rita and Alice, relatives from
Effie's side of the family who were both around twenty years old. The
abundance of dance partners served Adolph well on the SS *Deutschland*:
during the six-day journey over, he quaffed champagne and twirled late
into the night.

The moment he landed in England, Iphigene recalled, her father became "an insatiable tourist." He whisked the traveling party off to castles,
museums, and battlefields in Germany, France, Belgium, and Switzerland, and relentlessly quizzed his daughter on what they had visited and
learned. He basked in the aristocratic aura of European grand hotels,
where he dined next to "lords and ladies." His cup overflowed, and for the
next seven years he would return almost every year for a refill.

On this first trip and subsequent ones, Ochs occasionally mixed business with pleasure. He did not use the *Times* to obtain special treatment,
apart from the occasional courtesy visit with a relevant commercial outfit.
In 1901, he learned so many useful things while touring a printing office
in Stuttgart that he predicted the experience would end up offsetting the
cost of the whole trip. Another revelation for Ochs during this first journey abroad was the surprising popularity of the *Times* in Europe. He had
expected to have to choose between one of the London dailies and Bennett's *Paris Herald* for English-language news, but the *Times* was in such
high demand that some newsstands sold nothing but two-week-old editions of it. This observation helped convince Ochs that he needed to build
on the gains he had made at the Paris Expo, even if he had already decided

against launching a European edition of the *Times*. Before sailing home in 1901, he met with the management of *The Times* of London and laid the groundwork for an important business deal. It came to fruition the following year, when *The New York Times* began supplying its London counterpart with special correspondence from America in exchange for special correspondence from Europe.

The pro-British inflection of *The New York Times* became even more pronounced following Ochs's 1902 agreement with *The Times* of London. Rivals spread unsubstantiated rumors of backroom London business deals as a means of questioning its patriotism, and in doing so doubled down on the conspiratorial thinking by which they sought to explain the rise of the *Times* at home. Did Hearst, Pulitzer, and other populist or left-wing critics of the *Times* genuinely believe that Ochs was in corrupt league—as opposed to general sympathy—with the ruling powers of Wall Street and Fleet Street? If so, they failed to make their case persuasively. Ochs was, in fact, serious about preserving the independence and impartiality of his paper. In 1904, he made an important personnel change at the *Times*, one that would help turn the low art of American journalism—with its history of personal prejudice, willful inaccuracy, and other enduring blemishes— into something resembling a science.

*The New York Herald* published this image on October 3, 1909, with the following caption: "The North Pole as it was photographed by Dr. Cook, its discoverer—probably the most remarkable picture ever taken." Pictured are Cook's Inuit traveling companions, Etukishuk and Ahwelah.

The September 2, 1909, *New York Herald* scoop about Frederick Cook's polar journey.

The well-funded Peary—shown here aboard his ship, the *Roosevelt*, in 1909—had long been considered a favorite in the international race to the North Pole.

Cook at Upernavik, Greenland, in 1909.

Cook in Copenhagen, at the press dinner where it was learned that the American explorer Robert Peary had apparently reached the North Pole, a year after Cook claimed to have been there and by a different route. "The almost simultaneous announcement . . . is surely the most astounding coincidence in all history," the *Herald* declared on September 7, 1909.

James Gordon Bennett Sr., publisher of *The New York Herald* and founding father of the modern newspaper, in a daguerreotype taken by Matthew Brady in 1851.

James Gordon Bennett Jr. inherited the *Herald* from his father in 1872 and—when not engaged in drunken debauchery—refashioned it for the Gilded Age. His Civil War service was brief and undistinguished.

Chief Engineer George Melville (*center*) and other survivors of the *Jeannette* disaster, in Yakutstk during the winter of 1881–1882.

*Herald* correspondent Henry M. Stanley, whose rescue of the British explorer David Livingstone in Central Africa in 1871–1872 was the story of the decade.

U.S. Navy Lieutenant George Washington De Long, commander of the 1879–1881 *Jeannette* expedition funded by James Gordon Bennett Jr.

U.S. Army Lieutenant Adolphus Greely. The 1881–1884 expedition under his command achieved a Farthest North but was overshadowed by the sensational news of how it had subsequently all gone wrong.

Josephine Peary accompanied her husband to northern Greenland in 1893 and there gave birth to their first child, Marie. Their so-called Snow Baby became an American press sensation.

Frederick Schwatka was one of the first Arctic explorers to adopt indigenous survival methods. He was also a pioneering explorer-for-hire who persuaded collaborating newspapers to publicize and pay for his exploits. Though largely forgotten today, he served as a useful model for both Frederick Cook and Robert Peary.

Robert Peary in Greenland, 1894.

Frustrated in his attempts to get near the North Pole, Peary secured other trophies to burnish his reputation and keep the donations coming. The most valuable of these was a 34-ton meteorite fragment, which he transported to New York in 1897 and later sold to the American Museum of Natural History.

The Norwegian explorer Fridtjof Nansen, an international superstar and for a time Peary's most formidable rival. After achieving a Farthest North in 1895, Nansen never tried for the North Pole again.

Morris K. Jesup, wealthy president of the American Museum of Natural History and the Peary Arctic Club.

The *Times* newsroom (or "city room") in 1895, a low point in the paper's history.

Adolph S. Ochs, probably in 1896, the year he acquired the floundering *New York Times*.

The frantic "yellow journalism" of Joseph Pulitzer (*top left*) and William Randolph Hearst (*top right*) was itself the subject of endless press commentary, including this 1898 *Puck* cover.

An undated portrait of legendary *Times* managing editor Carr Van Anda, hired by Ochs in 1904.

A powerful paper in the heart of a powerful city: the Herald Building, Herald Square, 1903.

State-of-the-art *Herald* printing presses.

Bennett's 314-foot yacht *Lysistrata*, which was described in its time as a "floating palace."

A middle-aged James Gordon Bennett Jr.

Adolph Ochs in 1911.

A 1920 photograph of the reporter Philip Gibbs, whose doubts about Cook's claim slowly gained traction during the fall of 1909—especially at *The New York Times*.

*Times* editor and executive William C. Reick, formerly of the *Herald*, who played a secretly important role in the North Pole controversy.

Frederick Cook in Alaska in 1906.

Peary expedition members attacking a pressure ridge.

President Theodore Roosevelt wishes Peary good luck before his departure for the North Pole in July 1908.

Dogsled teams at Cape Sheridan, Ellesmere Island, where Peary made winter camp and left the *Roosevelt* during his 1908–1909 polar attempt.

"The pole at last!" Peary's assistant Matthew Henson (*center*) and the native guides who accompanied them hundreds of miles onto the frozen sea ice: Egingwah, Ootah, Ooqueah, and Seeglo.

Peary's polar party, of April 7, 1909, minutes after the all-important victory photograph.

Peary with Captain Robert Bartlett (*right*) in Battle Harbour, Labrador, in 1909. His decision to leave Bartlett behind during the final dash to the pole was later questioned.

Secretary of the Peary Arctic Club Herbert L. Bridgman (*right*) with the Peary family. He effectively served as Peary's press agent.

Thomas Hubbard, president of the Peary Arctic Club. An eminent lawyer and businessman, Hubbard shared Peary's thirst for success. Also, his alma mater: Maine's Bowdoin College.

The African American polar explorer Matthew Henson, who served as Peary's assistant in the field for more than two decades and was called the world's best nonnative driver of Arctic sled dogs.

HUDSON-FULTON NUMBER

PUCK

BOOK ROYALTIES

LECTURE RECEIPTS

So did I —Peary

Etukishuk and Ahwelah, Cook's only companions during his hotly debated polar attempt of 1907–1909.

One of many thousands of press commentaries on the 1909 Cook-Peary feud.

Ed Barrill, Cook's only companion during his controversial Mt. McKinley (now Denali) climb of 1906.

The flag that Peary famously declared he'd "nailed to the pole" in 1909.

The only known photograph of August W. Loose (*left*) and George H. Dunkle, the conspirators who schemed both with and against Frederick Cook during the fall of 1909.

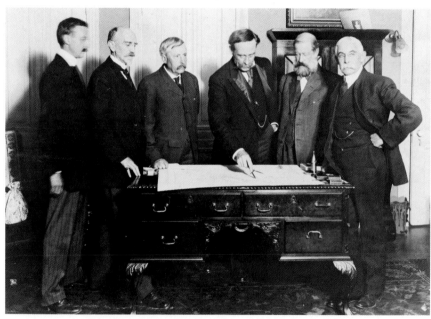

Peary with National Geographic Society brass, including the three men assigned to review the proofs of his 1908–1909 North Pole journey. *From left*: *National Geographic* editor Gilbert Grosvenor, Otto H. Tittmann, Society president Willis L. Moore, Robert Peary, Henry Gannett, and Rear Admiral Colby Chester.

# CHAPTER THIRTY

When Carr Van Anda joined *The New York Times* as managing editor on February 14, 1904, the temperature inside the office dropped a few degrees—or so it felt.

Van Anda, who replaced the veteran Henry Loewenthal, was a chilly newsroom presence, a formal man who wore rimless glasses and a stickpin through his impeccably starched collars. He was aloof and demanding, the sort of boss you wanted to approach only if you'd done your homework. Reporters lived in fear of his chastening glare, which lasered out from pale, bespectacled eyes. They called it "the death ray."

His high forehead had expanded upward, or so it seemed, in order to accommodate an oversized brain. Van Anda had impressed his teachers as a teenage math whiz in his home state of Ohio, and at forty—the age at which Ochs hired him—he studied physics, read Egyptian hieroglyphics, and could summon the batting averages of dozens of baseball players from memory. "V.A.," as he was known around the office, spent sixteen years at *The Sun* before becoming the formative newsroom chief of the modern *Times*. The most famous stories about him came a little later—the time he corrected an equation of Albert Einstein's, the time his identification of an ancient forgery forced the British Museum to revise its official biography of King Tutankhamen—but Van Anda's savant-like intelligence was picked up on almost immediately by his *Times* colleagues. "He scents buncombe and fraud miles away," one of them later wrote. He had the sort of skeptical mind that reflexively questioned the assumption that the *Titanic* was unsinkable, and the news sense to spring into action the moment the great ocean liner's radio went silent one fateful morning in 1912. Years before he scored the *Times* that famous scoop, Van Anda helped it to become the first American paper to print on-the-spot wireless news of a naval battle. The message—which came via *The Times* of London— announced Japan's important defeat of Russia at the Tsushima Strait off southwestern Japan, and Van Anda waited at the telegraph key until just before dawn to get it. He rushed the story to press after the city's other papers had all been put to bed, and even rode a delivery truck that morning to ensure that the forty thousand extra editions containing the scoop arrived safely at newsstands.

Ochs could not have hired a better man to execute his vision for the *Times*. It was not just that Van Anda was the best managing editor in the business. Like his boss, he relished the clean and dignified look of a "well-dressed" paper. In the words of one admirer, he "believed that managing a paper could be done as scientifically and intelligently as running a laboratory," and his omnivorous intellect matched the encyclopedic tendencies of the *Times*. So too did his predilection for facts and figures and his indifference to the stylish writing he'd encountered at *The Sun*. Whereas the stodgy *Tribune* decried the spread of "telephone mania," with its "constant 'helloing'" and "senseless chatter," the *Times* broadly embraced technological and scientific progress. Van Anda, who typically worked twelve-hour days, shared Ochs's enthusiasm for these subjects. He also understood them far better than Ochs did, enabling him to masterfully oversee the paper's expanding coverage of automobiles, aviation, and exploration.

Decades later, Ochs would bristle at all the credit given to Van Anda for the success of the *Times*. Displeased with a glowing 1933 biography of his superlative managing editor, Ochs contrived to have the niche book withdrawn by its publisher. He was at pains to remind the world that he had been the one to recognize and direct Van Anda's genius. "He never undertook a large operation without my knowledge and approval," Ochs later said. To his credit, Ochs also had the good sense not to interfere with the running of Van Anda's newsroom. If this meant that powerful friends like August Belmont and the lawyer Samuel Untermyer were occasionally disparaged in the *Times*, then so be it. Ochs wrote conciliatory letters when he had to and waited for petty feuds to burn themselves out. The retail mogul Nathan Straus stopped speaking to him for years, for example, after the *Times* reported on an embarrassing elevator mishap at Macy's. Ochs assumed that Straus and other thin-skinned supporters of the paper would eventually come around. Inevitably, they did.

Impartial, impersonal, comprehensive, authoritative: the *Times* during this first decade under Ochs was moving toward a modern ideal of journalism that did not yet have a name. Its newsroom was also at the forefront of a fundamental change in the way that editors and reporters collaborated. Reporters had traditionally been tasked with interpreting the news they gathered, even at the risk of misjudgment. But as daily metropolitan newspapers evolved into complicated operations, news editors like Van Anda increasingly demanded just the facts. They took it upon themselves to determine what those facts meant, and they headlined, ordered, amplified, and excised the reporter's work accordingly. The editor's loftier perspective and superior training qualified him for this responsibility, the thinking went, and the modern reader preferred his discreet framing to the blatantly opinionated journalism of years past. Some examples of that older, more personal style persisted, but only rarely in the serious daily newspapers—with the notable exception of *The Sun*. Van Anda was, moreover, notoriously resistant to crediting reporters by name. The *Times* under him granted bylines only in extraordinary circumstances—as in the case of Philip Gibbs, for example—as if to indicate that an exception were being made.

Newspapers around the country adapted to the emerging preference for information over opinion and to a quasi-scientific model of journalism in which educated readers were entrusted to decide for themselves how they felt about impartially presented facts. No paper did more to make this quiet revolution come about than the *Times*. Only after World War I did the new standard of journalism it embodied become entrenched enough to merit a name: objectivity.

The *Times* came to represent this celebrated journalistic ideal thanks in large part to the relationship between its farseeing owner and its formative newsroom chief. Ochs, the peacekeeper and institutionalist, found an ideal partner in Van Anda, the frosty investigator and scholar. It was not that Van Anda lacked for strong opinions, Ochs later recalled. He simply suppressed them while on the job. "It was most extraordinary, that feeling as intensely as he did towards many men and measures, there never was the slightest indication of his personal point of view in his presentation of the news concerning them," Ochs said. "Of course, it would not have been tolerated, but I often marveled [at] how he avoided having it unconsciously shown."

CARR VAN ANDA WAS ONE OF THE THREE ASSOCIATES OCHS CONSIDERED most responsible for the eventual preeminence of the *Times*. The other two were the editor Charles Miller and the business manager, Louis Wiley.

Ochs managed each of these three important deputies differently. Whereas Van Anda was largely left alone, the diminutive Wiley—who stood just four feet, seven inches tall—routinely took orders from Ochs. This was only natural, given Wiley's position. As Ochs's spokesperson and chief lieutenant, the sociable Wiley represented his publisher at professional and social functions. He excelled at shaking hands and making small talk and accepted regular invitations to preside over formal luncheons. Keenly aware that his popularity might make his boss jealous, and anticipating that he might be called upon one day to defend himself, Wiley kept a diary of all the times he'd made flattering reference to Ochs in interviews and speeches.

Wiley had joined the *Times* in 1896 as circulation manager, and his subsequent promotion to business manager put him one step below Ochs. But it was not just because Wiley was in the business department that Ochs felt comfortable telling him what to do. Wiley was a self-made schmoozer, and Jewish. He was a mini-Ochs. Miller and Van Anda, the paper's two top editors, were a different story. They were intellectually confident college graduates, belonged to upscale clubs that barred Jews, and made Ochs uncomfortably self-conscious about his origins.

Far from telling Miller what to write, Ochs made tentative suggestions. He had a habit of grinning whenever he weighed in so that he could, if necessary, "retreat on the pretext of not having meant it too seriously," Miller's deputy, Garet Garrett, wrote in his private diary. But while Ochs feared the intellectual condescension of these editors, he also impressed them with his decency and earnest curiosity. "None of us values his mental processes highly, and yet, he has a way [of] seeing always the other side that stimulates discussion, statement and restatement, and leaves a better product altogether than is approached in his absence," Garrett wrote. Edward Cary, Garrett's predecessor under Miller, praised Ochs as "a singularly complete representative American" who intuitively understood the average *Times* reader.

Ochs also had a talent for getting the best out of his employees. He took special care when hiring people, because he disliked firing them, and wooed the likes of Wiley and Van Anda by giving them the desirable option of acquiring *Times* shares—while also reserving the right to buy them back if his executives departed within five years. His goal was to instill feelings of loyalty and shared enterprise at all levels of the organization, and Ochs would later boast that he never once reduced a salary, even during the tribulations of World War I, when such voluntary protections cost him dearly. Like Bennett, he did not let his executives put their names on business cards, as a way of reminding them that the institution preceded the individual. Unlike Bennett, though, Ochs was a constant physical presence in the workplace, encouraging and evenhanded. He listened to the complaints of copyboys, politely insisted on neat work spaces, and routinely commended good work. Whether he was strolling through the *Times* office alone or showing it off to distinguished visitors, the pride he took in his newspaper was obvious—and contagious. His employees felt as though they were working not for "Mr. Ochs" but for a great entity, one that looked after its own like family—which made it very difficult for employees to leave the *Times* voluntarily. The "only decent way" to do so, Garrett quipped, was "to die and have a Times funeral."

Meanwhile, metropolitan journalism was maturing. Long dismissed as the refuge of drunks and rascals, or as a useful stepping-stone for those with business, literary, or political ambitions, it began to take on the aspect of a worthy career path. While Ochs quietly helped to professionalize the field, Joseph Pulitzer anointed himself this cause's leading advocate. In 1903, he committed $2 million to the endowment of a pioneering journalism school at Columbia University; though construction was delayed until his death, in 1911, and the first classes were not held until 1912, his magnanimous gesture sparked an earnest reevaluation of the field. In a widely reprinted essay, Pulitzer called for "a movement that will raise journalism to the rank of a learned profession, growing in the respect of the community as other professions far less important to the public interests have grown." To that end, his eventual gift to Columbia would also provide for so-called Pulitzer Prizes, to be awarded annually for excellence in journalism.

Newspapers had, of course, continued to evolve in the absence of formal training programs, and the best of them were now run as efficiently as any other modern enterprise. They had to be, given the vast increases in the scope and complexity of their operations. Running a viable metropolitan daily at the turn of the twentieth century was a far bigger undertaking than it had been a generation earlier. The enlarged scale of news gathering, printing, and distribution required huge cash reserves and disciplined management. There was little room anymore for the raffish, personality-driven journals of the past. The mainstream American press was entering a new phase, an era of consolidation and corporate structuring. It was arguably also getting blander, because the advertising-centric profit model that had liberated publishers from old constraints now made them newly averse to offending readers or important advertisers. More newspapers began shying away from potentially divisive editorializing; some of them now expressed no opinion at all, causing *Editor & Publisher* to complain in 1902 that "the discontinuing of editorials in newspapers makes journalism more of a business than a profession."

Ochs had contemplated just such a move six years earlier at the *Times*. The rationalized, organized new era of the press in which he flourished suited his temperament. His lack of editing or reporting experience led traditionalists to disparage Ochs as a lesser form of newsman, a canny businessman who happened to have ended up in their trade. Whatever truth there was in that, his talent as a publisher was indisputable. "Mr. Ochs is easily the first figure in the country in the business of making newspapers," *Printers' Ink* declared in 1907. His knack for envisioning and executing, departmentalizing and delegating, helped the *Times* to increase its circulation during these years with "machine-like regularity," the author of a contemporary journalism textbook noted. His personal aversion to making enemies allowed him to creep up on rivals without attracting undue attention. While showier publishers indulged in yachting, art collecting, political campaigning, and social climbing, Ochs focused diligently on the *Times* and continued to pour its earnings back into the company.

AS THE *TIMES* OUTGREW ITS PARK ROW OFFICES, OCHS FOLLOWED BENNETT'S lead and decided to move several miles north, to a location that was six blocks up from the *Herald* and smack in the geographical center of Manhattan. Longacre Square, as it was called, anchored an emerging entertainment district whose hotels, theaters, and late-night eating and drinking dens were drawing comparisons to London's Piccadilly Circus. There in the middle of it, beginning in 1905, sat the new Times Tower: a turreted, Renaissance-inspired shaft of white brick and terra-cotta that rose up from a five-story base of pink granite. The 476-foot, twenty-two-story Times Tower was one of the world's ten tallest buildings—a list that also included New York's Park Row Building, Philadelphia's City Hall, and several celebrated European cathedrals—and its freestanding placement allowed it to be seen from all sides, cementing its status as an instant landmark. City officials were easily persuaded to approve the renaming of Longacre Square. Henceforth—except in the *Herald*, which spitefully ignored the name change—the junction of Forty-second Street and Broadway would be known as Times Square.

What Ochs built below Times Square was no less impressive. Contractors blasted through nearly fifty-six feet of rock to dig the deepest foundation in city history. New York City's newly operational first subway line, which covered the nine miles between city hall and 145th Street, rumbled within earshot of the pressroom, and a station with subterranean commercial arcades served tides of passengers. The new rapid-transit system, whose Manhattan line was privately owned and operated by August Belmont, represented the latest leafing out of the city's commuter infrastructure. It fast-tracked the residential development of upper Manhattan and the Bronx, helped to bring once-remote towns into the urban fold, and further sidelined the old nexus of Park Row, city hall, and the Brooklyn Bridge.

The nocturnal bustle of Times Square, coupled with the nonstop operating of the subways that brought people there and back, went a long way toward establishing New York as "the city that never sleeps." Ochs would add to the international reputation of Times Square two years later, when he inaugurated the New Year's tradition of sending an illuminated globe down from the Times Tower's flagpole.

# CHAPTER THIRTY-ONE

The cost of building the Times Tower exceeded Ochs's original estimate by some $600,000. While loans from rich friends eventually saw him through, they also fueled more rumors that he was just a cutout for the Wall Street power brokers who actually ran the *Times*. The *Evening Journal* published anti-Semitic conspiracy theories to this effect, describing Ochs as "an oily little commercial gentleman" who was indirectly supported by "Rothschild backing." Stung by these hateful accusations, Ochs sued Hearst for libel—and won.

The *Evening Journal* made much of Ochs's real estate dealings with August Belmont, secularized son of one of the city's biggest Jewish bankers. Actually, though, his thorniest financial entanglement was with the Equitable Life Assurance Society. The Equitable's founder, Henry Hyde, had lent Ochs $25,000 on short notice in 1896, ensuring his acquisition of the *Times*. Having gained the trust and personal friendship of the Equitable director and munitions dealer Marcellus Hartley, Ochs had secured an additional $150,000 in working capital three years later, against his escrowed ownership stake of the Times Company. More recently, he'd borrowed around $1 million for the land and construction of the Times Tower, using the controlling share of the *Times* that he now owned outright as collateral.

This decision would come back to haunt Ochs in 1905, when the Equitable was swept up in one of the greatest financial scandals in U.S. history. Early that year, it came to light—in *The World* and elsewhere—that the company's officers had been treating its $400 million holdings as a personal investment fund and enriching themselves at the expense of shareholders. A trusted national firm that was known as the "Protector of the Widow and Orphan" had been gambling the life savings of everyday Americans on risky Wall Street ventures and distributing the spoils to its own executives. Amid deafening public outcry, the state of New York and the Equitable's board of directors launched twin investigations.

The *Times* was gentler in its condemnation of the Equitable than most other papers, and for a time went conspicuously easy on James Hazen Hyde, heir to the firm's late founder and its most flamboyantly corrupt officer of all. This preferential treatment ended only after Ochs quietly transferred the Equitable's six-figure mortgage on the Times Tower (and the Times Company shares he had secured it with) to Marcellus Dodge, grandson and heir to his late friend Marcellus Hartley. Ochs warned Dodge that Hearst in particular would decimate the reputation of the *Times* if the Equitable's leverage over the paper became public knowledge. Luckily for him, it didn't. Apart from Ochs, no one at the paper ever knew about it.

The *Times* continued to follow the Equitable story closely when the New York state legislature took up an industry-wide investigation that fall. Van Anda put the widening scandal on the front page no fewer than 115 times in 1905, roughly as often as *The World* did. But the manner in which each paper treated the controversy could hardly have been more different. *The World* condemned greed and cronyism and howled for executives to be arrested. The *Times* approached the story carefully, warning that an overreaction would cause "widespread injury of financial interests." Even after Ochs disposed of his secret conflict of interest, *Times* editorials spared investment bankers like Jacob Schiff, who'd corruptly sold the Equitable $50 million in stocks while also serving on its board, and questioned President Theodore Roosevelt's argument that such "crooked and objectionable practices" highlighted the need for tough federal oversight. The *Times* honored the facts of the matter, but never dug too far beneath them.

Rather than doing investigative reporting of its own, it largely scrutinized and corrected the hard-nosed work of *The World*. As news oriented as the paper was, this was standard practice there at the time, for the *Times* continued to resist the trend of expository journalism, with its absorbing chronicles of corporate and political wrongdoing. "Muckraking," as it came to be called, was the specialty of a new type of mass-market magazine. Aided by favorable federal postage rates, these periodicals were now flourishing under a largely ad-supported business model, attracting audiences vaster and more diverse than the "gentle readers" targeted by earlier generations of monthly magazines. Investigative journalism wasn't the only thing they published, but it was their bread and butter, and reporters were given generous amounts of time and money to produce it. Their blockbuster articles were enlivened by dramatic pen-and-ink illustrations and published serially over months, sometimes years; often, they were subsequently released in book form. More factual and comprehensive than the earlier crusading work of the yellow journals, these dramatic exposés were read nationwide and helped to rein in the trusts, pools, monopolies, combinations, syndicates, cartels, political machines, and other unscrupulous entities whose grip on power had for a long time appeared to be unbreakable.

Though it is remembered today as a great journalistic step forward, muckraking was a highly controversial subject at the time. *The Atlantic* complained of "moral overstrain," arguing that nonstop tales of rottenness made readers and malefactors alike "insensitive to criticism," and some responsible citizens noted that the so-called literature of exposure was better at tearing down institutions and bad actors than at proposing useful alternatives. Even the progressive Roosevelt did not intend it as a compliment when he coined the term "muck-rakes."

While other journals combed through the filth, the *Times* held its nose. Wiley, who often did press interviews on Ochs's behalf, once explained the paper's standoffish attitude this way: "The 'Times' is not a detective bureau or prosecuting attorney. It, however, is always glad to support the efforts of fearless public officials." To be fair, the *Times* had been playing this supporting role for a while now. For three decades, it had stepped back and let *The Sun* and the *Herald*, and more recently *The World* and the *Journal*, follow the fearless example of its Tweed Ring exposures. Now that New York–based progressive magazines like *McClure's* and *Munsey's* were at the vanguard of investigative journalism, Ochs found no new reason to rock the boat. His personal correspondence from this economically divided era suggests that the prospect of upheaval arising from inequality worried him more than inequality itself. Pulitzer once wrote that without a strong and independent press American democracy would devolve into "government of either money or the mob." If compelled to choose between these opposing forces, the *Times*, it is fair to say, would have favored money. Pulitzer's *World* probably would have thrown in with the mob.

Ironically—or appropriately, perhaps—the contemporary figure most often associated with mob rule during the first decade of the twentieth century was a New York City newspaperman. When William Randolph Hearst sought to ride his influence with the masses all the way to the White House, every non-Hearst newspaper in New York City, including the *Times*, would rise up in opposition. But the *Herald* would pay the highest price.

## CHAPTER THIRTY-TWO

Hearst's newspapers excelled at getting readers riled up, often in support of candidates and causes that appealed to the native-born working class. In his 1902 book *The Americanization of the World*, the English editor W. T. Stead described him as the embodiment of "government by journalism." By the turn of the century, though, Hearst also aspired to wield power the traditional way.

In 1902, he ran for and won a seat in the U.S. House of Representatives. He rarely occupied it, because he was busy managing the strongest of the nation's emerging news chains. By 1904, Hearst owned popular dailies in New York, San Francisco, Chicago, Boston, and Los Angeles. He mobilized this publicity machine in pursuit of high office, but the Democratic presidential nomination eluded him, and he lost the New York City mayoral election of 1905 by a hair.

By the time Hearst ran for governor of New York in 1906, his third campaign in three years, the political establishment was finally taking him seriously. Worried about Hearst's "enormous popularity among ignorant and unthinking people," President Theodore Roosevelt helped to persuade Charles Evans Hughes, vanquisher of the despised insurance trusts, to run against him. Though Hearst campaigned as a Democrat, New York City's Democratic press derided him as unfit for office, a hypocrite,

a demagogue, an evader of taxes, a self-seeker, and an inciter of mob violence. Some opponents described his platform as socialistic. The *Herald* went
further, calling it "organized hatred."

Bennett hadn't wielded the editorial hatchet this ferociously since his
cable war with Jay Gould. As in that feud, his animosity was personal:
Bennett bore Hearst none of the grudging respect that he had for Pulitzer
and considered his coverage of the Cuban conflict a disgrace to journalism. Hearst attempted to placate Bennett by sending a peace broker to
Paris and requesting to place $42,000 of campaign advertising in the
*Herald*. When these overtures were rejected, he berated "Cadet" Bennett
from the podium. Hearst coined demeaning nicknames for other New
York City publishers as well—Ochs was "the tame Ochs"—and he got
plenty from their newspapers in return, including the blame for the assassination of William McKinley five years earlier. The accusation that editorials published in Hearst's papers had inspired the killer to act was unfair
and yet also effective, in a wickedly Hearstian way—especially after Roosevelt himself embraced it within a week of Election Day. Hearst lost to
Hughes by a mere sixty thousand votes; his political career went downhill
from there, and he never held office again. His defeat was celebrated lustily by the *Herald*, which vowed to keep fighting candidate Hearst "if he
so much as dares to run for dog-catcher." But Hearst had already begun
preparing to deal the *Herald* a massive blow.

As relations between the two publishers soured, he'd probed a notorious *Herald* weak spot: the "personals," a lucrative mainstay of the paper's
classified advertising business. For a dollar a line, *Herald* readers could
address short, often coded messages to a single individual or thousands of
anonymous readers. Some of these listings were pleas for estranged family
members to return home, while others sought to recover precious lost
items. But men-about-town also used the personals to arrange encounters
with women:

- "34 St. car Saturday night, 12:10. Will tall blond young lady, got off
  Lexington and noticed young gentleman, write in confidence?"
- "Jolly sport desires acquaintance stylish, refined, affectionate, witty

lady, possessing beautiful figure, hair, teeth. Matrimony. Trips, dinners, pleasant possibilities."

The most suggestive listings, however, were for women seeking men:

- "Young lady, good figure, wants to pose for artists; references exchanged; positively no triflers."
- "Refined young woman desires immediate loan."
- "A woman finds paddling her own canoe dreary task, seeks manly pilot."

These were thinly veiled advertisements for paid sex. It was no great secret in press circles that Bennett was operating the newspaper equivalent of a red-light district; the personals owed their survival to an unspoken agreement among publishers to let them be, lest the *Herald* begin looking too closely at any of their own shady advertising traditions and general embarrassment ensue. And yet this mutual understanding—one of many peculiar accommodations constantly being struck by New York City's warring papers—was unlikely to protect Bennett indefinitely, especially as his grudge with Hearst worsened. The Commodore's own executives warned him that the personals would one day land the *Herald* in legal trouble. Naturally, he ignored them.

As the New York City press ganged up on him in 1906, Hearst assigned a team to investigate Bennett's personals. Reporters from the *American* (as the *Morning Journal* had since been renamed) rented mailboxes and used them to respond to dozens of coyly worded *Herald* notices. Just how Hearst's reporters pulled back the curtain on so many "massage parlors" and "cozy suites" without engaging in illicit acts themselves was never convincingly explained. In any case, the sordid reality of the personals came to light in a series of sensational *American* articles that June. Bennett was indicted that fall for sending obscene materials through the mail, after anti-vice reformers citing Hearst's findings filed a complaint with the U.S. attorney general. The indictment left Bennett cold with rage. "I shall never forget you in this matter," he wrote to Hearst from Europe. Candidate

Hearst read Bennett's message in front of five thousand cheering New Yorkers and declared, "I *hope* he will never forget me!"

Bennett, who pleaded guilty, was unable to avoid appearing in court the following spring. He arrived at the Criminal Branch of the U.S. Circuit Court in downtown Manhattan in April 1907, flanked by the *Herald* advertising executive who was his co-defendant and a pair of expensive lawyers. The presiding judge upbraided the *Herald* for being "a potent aid to local libertines, and a directory of local harlots," and fined Bennett and the Herald Corporation $30,000. A *Herald* employee stepped forward and presented the court with a handful of crisp $5,000 and $1,000 bills. Bennett departed wordlessly with his entourage, sped away in an automobile, and sailed for Europe—and ordered that Hearst's name never appear again in the *Herald*.

The fines were nothing compared with the loss of readership and profits. Not only did Bennett lose the personals as a source of revenue, but their exposure cost him readers who'd either ignored or been unaware of the racy section's true purpose. Family subscribers in particular abandoned the paper, many of them for the *Times*. The personals scandal also led to some soul-searching within the trade, which lacked any formal means of holding wrongdoers like Bennett accountable. "A dishonest lawyer can be disbarred, a physician can be punished for malpractice, a clergyman who does wrong can be deprived of his office, but there is no effectual way of holding up a newspaper to a high standard of honesty or deportment," *Life* magazine complained after the verdict. It had taken a vengeful Hearst, hardly an ideal arbiter, to bring the smutty personals to light. The rest of the New York press, with the notable exception of the *Times*, had conspicuously ignored the story.

The shaming of the *Herald* added fuel to an ongoing campaign to clean up newspapers, and not just of risqué material. Over the next few years, new professional standards emerged in New York and beyond. State legislatures strengthened libel laws, and newspapers established complaint departments. Prodded by the federal government, many also began rejecting advertisements for sketchy investment schemes, so-called miracle cures, and other dubious products and services. None of this affected the forward-looking *Times*, which already subjected its reporting and advertisers to careful scrutiny.

Amid the reshuffling, the *Herald* remained an outlier: a reliable but titillating source of news in which excellent reporting appeared alongside sleazy ads for "bust development" therapies. While many other big publishers modernized, James Gordon Bennett held out. He answered to no one, and especially not to scolds and watchdogs. But the *Herald* was paying a price for his high-handed ways.

# CHAPTER THIRTY-THREE

Even though Bennett visited New York for no more than two or three weeks a year, his office at the Herald Building was aired and dusted every morning. His inkwells were kept refreshed, his pencils sharpened, his ashtray polished. Each day's papers were delivered to his unused desk, and in cold weather a fire was lit in his fireplace. Anyone who didn't know any better would have thought that the boss had just stepped out for a moment. In fact, he was across the ocean.

The elaborate charade around Bennett's New York office was designed to create the impression that he was there in spirit and that he might, at a moment's notice, also descend in person. The Commodore had other ways of reminding his subordinates that he was watching from three thousand miles away, including the regular communications he received from hand-picked office spies. Bennett's "white mice," as he called them, kept him abreast of the latest power struggles, performance lapses, and other note-worthy updates from the New York headquarters, giving him an aura of all-knowing authority. Some *Herald* employees were so convinced of his omniscience that they swore he knew when the wastebaskets had been emptied.

Bennett stretched the era's telecommunications to their utmost in order to manage (or mismanage) the *Herald* from afar. He was said to be the largest individual user of the transatlantic cables, and being six hours ahead of New York time also helped. In Paris, he would rise early, scan the European morning papers over coffee, and cable last-minute instructions to his long-serving deputy, William C. Reick, as that day's American edition went to press.

His authority was total. "No newspaper in the world is more absolutely dominated by one man than the *Herald*," *The Fourth Estate* noted in 1903, and strict office protocols drove this fact home. Every commercial order, editorial memo, and other internal *Herald* document was signed "James Gordon Bennett," irrespective of who had actually drawn it up. The Commodore had a rule that he did not shake hands with anyone on his staff, and any correspondent wishing to meet with him had to make a formal request through his secretary. *Herald* reporters were often made to feel like personal assistants. Bennett asked them to interview owl experts for his own amusement and to look into the availability of premium Welsh coal for him before he went yachting.

In some respects, the *Herald* was on the cusp of modernity. It was headquartered in up-and-coming midtown Manhattan, made use of the latest printing and communications tools, and paid close attention to aviation, automobiles, and other exciting technological innovations of the new century. But Bennett oversaw its operations, when he could be bothered to, with all the whimsy and grandiosity of a fairy-tale monarch. He appeared to get with the times in 1900, when he belatedly incorporated the *Herald* and changed his official title to chairman of the Executive Committee of the Herald Corporation. In reality, little had changed. Each of his top executives owned a single share of stock in the reconstituted company; the other 994 were held by Bennett, who remained the emphatic last word on everything from major business decisions to minor typos.

When it wasn't buried in a glass of champagne, though, Bennett's nose for news remained sharp. "His random guess is usually more certain than the ordinary man's deliberate judgment," wrote James Creelman, who experienced the best and worst of that judgment as a *Herald* correspondent. Bennett's guesses were not always as random as they seemed. His royal

friends kept him informed of the latest palace intrigues, and a secret network of *Herald* stringers—ships' chandlers, lighthouse keepers, and other
monitors of the world's ocean highways—provided him with a steady flow
of maritime intelligence. The Commodore kept a notebook containing
the cable addresses of these informal contributors, but no record of their
services, making for chaotic scenes whenever they turned up at the Paris
or New York offices demanding payment. Bennett acted on their tips by
moving his full-time correspondents around the globe, like pieces on his
personal chessboard. He often took these steps without informing his
editors, who would then receive unexpected scoops from places as far-
flung as Japan, Australia, and Venezuela. It made for a less pleasant surprise when an editor would try to assign a correspondent to a pressing
story, only to discover that the Commodore had sent him elsewhere.

The base salaries Bennett paid were moderate, but he threw cash bo-
nuses around for outstanding work. He always knew who had done what.
A reporter might return to his desk to find one of Bennett's signature pale
blue envelopes with $50 in it, in appreciation of something he'd written
weeks earlier—or a terse note informing him he'd been demoted. Unlike
Pulitzer, who also knocked employees down the ladder often, Bennett
reduced their pay accordingly. The work of copy editors (then called copyreaders) was also monitored, with a story's path to publication carefully
tracked so that Bennett could levy fines on the individuals who'd allowed
unacceptable errors to slip through. The usual mistakes had to be avoided,
but so did the Commodore's long list of pet peeves. He objected to slangy
abbreviations—it was "telephone," never "phone"—and despised uncouth
Americanisms like "week-end" and "New Yorker." In his circles, "hunting" meant foxhunting only, and anyone who suggested otherwise in the
*Herald* could expect a talking-to. Bennett was least forgiving when it came
to his favorite sporting pastimes, and it was for this reason, according to
the *Herald* correspondent Ralph Paine, that "the thing most dreaded by a
'Herald' reporter was to be assigned to a news story which in any manner
pertained to yachts or yachting." Getting the tiniest sailing detail wrong
was grounds for a severe reprimand, or even firing.

There was "bigness as well as littleness about Bennett," as a correspondent who joined the *Herald* around 1903 noted. The bigness was in his spontaneous acts of generosity, his fearless opposition to the likes of Gould and Hearst, and the magisterial aloofness he maintained from the press. The littleness was most evident in his mistreatment of his employees. "His judgments are swift, severe, and as often as not inflicted upon the wrong person," a contemporary magazine profile noted. He fired people for inane reasons and was then at pains to demonstrate that he had never needed them to begin with. Having just sent his star drama critic packing, he once assigned crime reporters to write all of the next week's theater reviews. One of the most frequently retold Bennett stories was of the time he fired an editor in Paris, decided on his replacement, and asked the city editor, William Reick, to send the man over immediately. Reick begged him to choose someone else, arguing that the requested editor was indispensable to the New York office. Bennett then asked Reick to send him a list of all the *New York Herald* men he considered indispensable. Upon receiving it, Bennett cabled Reick: "Fire all these men. I want no indispensable men in my employ."

Bennett summoned employees to France so often, and on such short notice, that the weeklong transatlantic passage was known around the office as the "Atlantic shuttle." His reasons for sending for them were as likely to be trivial as serious. He once called over a rising star in the paper's advertising department in order to confirm office rumors that the young executive was getting fat. Reick, on the other hand, reported to Paris four or five times a year, often for important business discussions. These European trips could feel like a paid vacation: a comfortable ocean liner to Cherbourg, a stay in a good Parisian hotel, first-class wining and dining, all of it paid for by the Commodore. But all that free Pol Roger and *poulet cocotte* sat uneasily, for Bennett rarely explained in advance why he'd sent for anyone and was known to treat doomed employees to a grand last meal. Sometimes he was undecided about an underling's fate and simply wanted to see how the man defended himself before selecting a course of action. Other times he had changed his mind by the time the requested person arrived in Paris, or even forgotten that he'd sent for him.

Bennett treated even his most loyal employees harshly. The *Herald* editor Julius Chambers had turned down a job offer from Pulitzer and recently been rewarded for his handling of the Jay Gould feud when Bennett chewed him out for something he had not done. Feeling "very sore" about the Commodore's failure to apologize for his misguided tirade, Chambers went to work for Pulitzer. A similar fate befell the *Paris Herald* editor Samuel Chamberlain, a jolly reveler whose company Bennett enjoyed—until he didn't. A resentful Chamberlain returned to the United States, made himself indispensable to William Hearst, and became managing editor of the *New York Journal* around the turn of the century, where he worked alongside the city editor, Julius Chambers. Many of Bennett's competitors hired mistreated former *Herald* employees who knew his weaknesses. Unlike him, they managed to hold on to them.

Those who knew him best agreed that one glaring personal flaw of Bennett's loomed above the rest: his fundamental mistrust of others. "His official friendship was like a wax-taper—liable to be extinguished by the faintest breath or doubt or by intrusive external influence," Chambers wrote, after his own relationship with Bennett had been snuffed out. Beneath the Commodore's careless way with personnel, moreover, lay a consistent pattern: the quicker an employee proved himself to be exceptional, the swifter his comeuppance would be. To "go up like a rocket and come down like a stick" was an all-too-common trajectory at the *Herald*, wrote Stephen Bonsal, whose distinguished journalism career included an early stint there. Office veterans shrugged at the Commodore's self-defeating ways and said it was just how his brain worked.

One charitable interpretation was that Bennett kept everyone at arm's length in order to live up to the ideal that "an editor should be a man in a watch-tower, out of sound and out of reach," as James Creelman put it. "Friendships are to be regarded as traps for the editorial conscience. So Mr. Bennett is a lonely man in a crowd, a hermit in the midst of bustling life," Creelman posited. This strained defense ignores the fact that Bennett routinely put the *Herald* at the service of wealthy friends and kept a list of royals, fellow clubmen, and other pals who were under no circumstances to be given adverse publicity in the paper. Bennett's list of "untouchables" was extensive and, like his shorter list of unmentionables like

Hearst, subject to his ever-shifting moods. His faithful deputy, William Reick, privately complained of the difficulty of keeping track of who was on it. "How in hell," Reick once complained, "can I be expected to carry the names of all the members of the Union Club in my mind?"

The "lonely man" got lonelier in 1903, when two of his closest aides died in relatively quick succession. One was James Williams, the black man who'd served him since childhood and taken care of his Manhattan town house after Bennett uprooted to France. The other was Gardiner Howland, president of the Herald Corporation and the paper's former business manager. Howland was a New York City blue blood, seven years older than Bennett, a fellow member of the Union Club and New York Yacht Club, and probably the only employee the Commodore treated as something resembling a social equal. On May 9, 1903, Howland wrote to Bennett wishing him a happy sixty-second birthday, left the office with orders for the message to be wired to Paris at midnight, then suffered a fatal heart attack that evening. Bennett's mail that morning must have been discomfiting: birthday wishes from an old friend, alongside a note informing him the friend was dead.

Finding quality replacements for departed staffers was harder now than it had once been. For more than three decades, Bennett had sacked skilled newspapermen and simply replaced them with others who were eager to prove themselves at America's most storied daily. This revolving-door exchange had begun to show signs of breakdown by the early twentieth century, as top-notch talents like Stephen Bonsal, Ralph Paine, George Bronson Rea, and Ralph Blumenfeld left the *Herald*, often in disgust, and were replaced by reporters and editors who never achieved anything resembling their stature.

A crisis of confidence was taking shape inside the *Herald*. Where would the paper be ten or fifteen years from now? Though the heirless Commodore spoke vaguely of it becoming a "headless republic" after his death, the question of what happened next did not truly seem to interest him. He was not expanding his news operation, as Hearst and Ochs were; nor was he trying to build a long-standing personal legacy in journalism, like Pulitzer. Bennett the arch-hedonist seemed content to let it all be forgotten once he was dead and gone, and the real estate deal he'd cut for the Herald Building a decade earlier suggested that the paper's future was anything but foremost in his mind. Rather than buy the plot of land upon which it was built, which Bennett certainly could have afforded, he had simply taken out a thirty-year lease. When someone—according to Don Seitz, it was Pulitzer—asked him if the impermanence of this arrangement bothered him, he had replied, "When the *Herald*'s lease expires, I shall not be here to worry about it." In another version of the story, Bennett explained his decision slightly differently: "Thirty years from now, the Herald will be in Harlem and I'll be in Hell."

# CHAPTER THIRTY-FOUR

While Bennett's star was falling, Frederick Cook's was rising. After his claimed 1906 first ascent of Mount McKinley, the Explorers Club asked him to serve as its second president, succeeding Adolphus Greely, and the National Geographic Society named him guest of honor for its forthcoming annual dinner in Washington. The subsequent news of Peary's Farthest North put society leadership in a quandary: How to recognize America's preeminent polar explorer without offending Cook or making Peary feel like a runner-up? It solved the problem by having a new gold medal struck for Peary and arranging for Theodore Roosevelt to present him with the award in person. The charismatic commander in chief would be the star, with Peary shining brighter as a result. The December 15, 1906, event would also be the last time that Peary knowingly shared a room with Cook.

Cook was introduced to four hundred well-heeled diners that evening by Alexander Graham Bell, inventor of the telephone and one of the society's founders, as "one of the few Americans, if not the only American, who has explored both extremes of the world, the Arctic and the Antarctic regions." Cook began his tale of conquering McKinley by crediting Peary for advances in cold-weather equipment that had enabled him to achieve the snowy summit. Of all the polar explorers, he declared, Peary had "worked hardest to reduce the outfit to its utmost simplicity. Thus indirectly to Commander Peary should fall a part of the honor of scaling the arctic slopes of our greatest mountain." Cook was nearing the end of his story—"and so, with knees bent, and back bent, and chests laboring like bellows, we digged one foot after another over the big blocks of granite at the top"—when an upswell of cheers drowned him out. President Roosevelt had bustled into the room, eliciting a standing ovation.

Cook hastily wrapped up his speech and ceded the podium to Willis Moore, president of the society, who turned the stage over to the president of the United States. In his reedy voice, Roosevelt praised Robert Peary for his "courage and hardihood" and for being a model of manliness and self-sacrifice in decadent times:

> Civilized people usually live under conditions of life so easy that there is a certain tendency to atrophy of the hardier virtues. And it is a relief to pay signal honor to a man who by his achievements makes it evident that in some of the race, at least, there has been no loss of hardy virtue.

Roosevelt handed Peary the society's first-ever Hubbard Medal, to thunderous applause. In his acceptance speech, Peary cannily described his goal of reaching the North Pole and the president's own legacy project, the Panama Canal, as kindred enterprises:

> President Roosevelt, for nearly four centuries the world dreamed of the union of the Atlantic and the Pacific. You have planted the Stars and Stripes at Panama and insured the realization of that dream. For over three centuries the world has dreamed of solving the mystery of the North. Tonight the Stars and Stripes stand nearest to that mystery, pointing and beckoning. God willing, I hope that your administration may yet see those Stars and Stripes planted at the Pole itself. For between those great logical cosmic boundaries, Panama to the south and the North Pole to the north,

lies the heritage and the future of that giant whose destinies you guide today, the United States of America.

Discovering the North Pole, Peary said, was "the thing which it is intended that I should do, and the thing that I must do." For that reason, he announced, he would try again next year.

HE DIDN'T, THOUGH, BECAUSE THE *ROOSEVELT* WAS TOO BADLY DAMAGED for him to return to the Arctic in 1907. But on July 3, right around the time Peary would have departed, had he been able, Frederick Cook quietly sailed from Gloucester, Massachusetts, in a private yacht. His stated purpose was to guide its owner, a casino tycoon named John Bradley, on a big-game hunt in northern Greenland, but Bradley had also agreed in advance to support a polar attempt if conditions favored one. Arriving in Cape York, Cook quickly recognized that the crucial components were in place. As he later explained to the press, "The best natives and the best dogs were there within seven hundred miles of the pole."

After informing the 250 Inuit at Etah that "Pearyarksuah" would not be coming north that year, Cook secured their help in preparing sleds, dogs, clothing, food, and other necessities for his journey. Based on reports of abundant game herds to the west, he charted a course—across Smith Sound and Ellesmere Island to Axel Heiberg Land, then northward along Nansen Strait—that would allow him to subsist on fresh game meat as far as the 82nd parallel. Cook's optimistic assessment convinced Rudolph Franke, Bradley's German cook, to remain with him in Greenland. Bradley returned to the United States that October, bearing hunting trophies and messages from Cook to key supporters. "I have hit upon a new route to the North Pole and will stay to try it," he informed Herbert Bridgman, perhaps as a courtesy to Peary. He sent a nearly identical message to the Explorers Club.

There is no record of Peary's immediate reaction to this news; presumably, it was volcanic. But not until the following spring, as he prepared to launch his own delayed North Pole journey, did Peary explicitly criticize Cook's actions. He wrote a letter to the *Times* (which it would not print until more than a year later) in which he accused Cook of "appropriating" the dogs, manpower, and raw materials he'd planned to avail himself of at Etah. Peary also registered a similar protest with the International Polar Commission, in Brussels, to which he added a pointed request: "If Dr. Cook returns and claims to have reached the Pole, he should be compelled to prove it."

# CHAPTER THIRTY-FIVE

I f James Gordon Bennett was in fact grooming a successor at the *Herald*, it was the city editor, William Reick, who had developed a special feel for his erratic boss, the way some handlers do with animals.

Reick was a mustachioed, powerfully built man who had first caught Bennett's eye as the twenty-four-year-old author of a story about a mad dog that had bitten two children in Newark. He was still in his twenties when Bennett made him city editor of the *Herald*, one of the most prestigious jobs in the business. His skill at marshaling reporters had served him well over the years, and his expert handling of the Spanish-American War coverage had confirmed that he was born to run a newsroom. Reick also excelled at deciphering Bennett's most confounding moods and cable messages and at making the sorts of executive decisions generally avoided by those who feared the Commodore's wrath. He enjoyed unprecedented authority over what did and did not appear in the *Herald*. According to Don Seitz, Reick also became "closer to his employer than any other man who ever served him." When he turned down Hearst's persistent offers to come work for the *Journal*, Bennett gave him a parcel of valuable uptown real estate as a token of his appreciation. Unlike everyone else in the history of the *Herald*, Reick had shot up like a rocket and stayed aloft.

Reick's title of city editor did not do full justice to the importance of his role; other newspapers would have described him as their general manager. Bennett upended this congenial arrangement in 1903, after Gardiner Howland died, by making Reick president of the New York Herald Corporation. Though it looked like a promotion, it wasn't. Bennett had grown jealous of Reick's impressive wealth and social connections and removed him from the excitement and responsibility of the newsroom in order to punish him.

Reick, displeased, began talking with Ochs about joining the *Times* in late 1903. They reached a tentative agreement by which he would acquire a one-sixth interest in the New York Times Company and commit to securing a $500,000 loan for the *Times*, if needed. Van Anda was hired as city editor shortly after this written exchange, and the deal was never signed, but Reick and Ochs remained on good terms. They even completed a mutually agreeable transaction shortly afterward, when Reick sold Ochs his used Mercedes.

Then, in 1906, came the scandal of the personals. Bennett blamed Reick for his indictment, even though his top deputy had in fact warned him against continuing to publish the risqué notices. It was during this new chill in relations that Bennett issued Reick one of his inscrutable transatlantic travel invitations. Bring the family over to France, Bennett suggested, and show them a good time. Reick duly reserved rooms at a nice Parisian hotel and enjoyed several days of sightseeing with his wife and children. Having heard nothing from Bennett during this time, he went to the Commodore's private office on the Champs-Élysées, where he was told that Bennett was at his villa in Beaulieu-sur-Mer. Reick gathered his family, boarded a train to the Côte d'Azur, and waited to be summoned, but his messages went unacknowledged. Reick wrote one last time, this time in anger, demanding to know when Bennett would see him. Finally, Bennett responded: "Go on home, Reick. You won't see me. I never wanted to see you. I just wanted to show you that the *Herald* can get along just as well without you."

The gratuitous snub had Reick stewing for months. According to Albert Stevens Crockett, a *Herald* correspondent at the time, Reick "expressed himself bitterly with regard to the Commodore, and told me that some day he was going to give the latter a surprise." The surprise came early in 1907, when Reick informed Bennett that he was quitting the *Herald* for the *Times*. The fact that Ochs couldn't match the $30,000 a year that Bennett paid him did not bother him. "The chance to get even," Crockett recalled, "weighed quite as heavily with him as any thought of personal gain." Bennett's private secretary later called his humiliation of Reick the worst business mistake the Commodore ever made.

STUNNED BY REICK'S PERCEIVED BETRAYAL, BENNETT WENT BACK TO HIS old mistrustful ways. From this point onward, Crockett wrote, he "lived in a state of expectation that his hand was going to be bitten." Never again did he grant any *Herald* employee more than a modicum of authority or affection, and any decision that would have previously been made by Reick was now handled by an advisory council that did whatever Bennett told it to. Under the new rules, not even entry-level reporters could be hired or fired without his explicit approval.

Bennett's overreaction made it even easier for Reick to bring old *Herald* colleagues over to the *Times*, where a saner form of management prevailed. Ochs asked Reick to beef up the paper's foreign reporting in particular, and thus—perhaps unwittingly—gave him a perfect way to get back at his former employer. Reick wasted no time poaching the twenty-year *Herald* veteran Ernest Marshall, whose talents were being wasted in an unhappy co-editing arrangement at *The Paris Herald*. By hiring Marshall as its chief foreign correspondent, the *Times* made crystal clear its intention to challenge Bennett in the areas that mattered to him most.

The year of Reick's arrival was a notably experimental one for the *Times*. Ochs introduced color illustrations and even the first (and only) comic strip in the paper's history, *The Roosevelt Bears*. Both novelties were soon abandoned, but another innovation embraced by its newsroom that year, Marconi wireless, would prove to be more enduring. Ochs put Reick in charge of expanding the paper's use of the new technology, which the *Herald* had written off prematurely. Bennett had commissioned Marconi to transmit minute-by-minute updates of an America's Cup yacht race from a *Herald* press boat as far back as 1899, before realizing that wireless would eventually compete with his Commercial Cable Company and losing interest. Ochs, facing no such constraints, assigned Reick to oversee the installation of a wireless transmitter atop the Times Tower in 1907 and enter into a six-year contract with the Marconi Company.

The agreement allowed the *Times* to exchange messages with a newly constructed wireless station in Glace Bay, Nova Scotia, thereby gaining a potentially cheaper and faster alternative to land-based transmission and a significant competitive advantage in the reporting of news from sea. Thanks to a groundbreaking deal Reick struck with *The Times* of London, *The New York Times* on October 18, 1907, was on the receiving end of the first wireless press message ever sent between America and Europe. Though the airwaves in these pre-radio days were less reliable than undersea cables, participating in the world's first regular transatlantic wireless news service nevertheless had its benefits. With vessels able to transmit from sea, Bennett's famous fleet of press boats became increasingly obsolete, and the *Times* gained an important edge in maritime reporting, another traditional *Herald* strong suit. Bennett claimed to be unconcerned by these encroachments, but his subordinates knew otherwise. Shortly after Reick quit, he ordered a deputy to begin performing comparative readings of the *Times* and the *Herald* in order to determine all the ways in which the latter was losing ground.

The *Times* was also paying closer attention to aviation, automobiles, and exploring as Ochs and Van Anda fashioned it into a leading chronicler of the emerging international age of velocity. In 1908, Ochs took the remarkable step of organizing an around-the-world automobile race. The twenty-thousand-mile contest, which ludicrously proposed to send drivers across the wilds of Alaska and the frozen Bering Strait, was exactly the sort of promotional stunt that would have been anathema to the old *Times*. But with Ochs eager to sell more advertising to automobile manufacturers, it launched from Times Square that February, with one of the paper's own reporters crammed into the bucket seat of the lone American entry, a $4,000 runabout manufactured by the E. R. Thomas Motor Company of Buffalo. Nearly six months later, only two of the original six vehicles (the Thomas Flyer and a German Protos) crossed the finish line in Paris. Endless route changes, rescue tows, and vehicle overhauls made it difficult to determine what, if anything, the sensational race had demonstrated. It certainly proved less than the series of flights performed by Wilbur Wright in France later that summer, a watershed moment in the history of aviation.

The *Times* by 1908 had warmed to heavier-than-air flight, too. Its enthusiasm for technological and scientific news, and its willingness to invest in exclusive stories about these subjects, were both on the rise when Robert Peary came to New York City that spring to raise money for his latest North Pole attempt.

# CHAPTER THIRTY-SIX

A *New-York Tribune* headline on May 18, 1908, put the matter frankly: PEARY HERE FOR MONEY. He needed more of it than usual. The death in January of his biggest banker, Morris Jesup, had left a large hole in Peary's expedition budget, and he arrived in New York unsure anyone would fill it.

He would need another $35,000 in order to depart in July as planned. The friendly *Tribune* raised the "tantalizing and splendid possibility" that Peary would at last bring home the great prize and quoted him at length on why this particular expedition, his ninth, would succeed where the rest had failed. Several days later, Peary secured $10,000 from a Massachusetts paper manufacturer named Zenas Crane. The donation elicited a congratulatory telegram from President Roosevelt, giving the *Tribune* and other major newspapers a reason to treat Crane's contribution as front-page news. On May 24, the *Times* became the next "quality" daily to extend its promotional consideration, reporting that Peary had, over the years, sunk $80,000—"practically his entire personal fortune"—into Arctic exploring. The *Times* also quoted at length from the solicitation letter that Peary had been sending around, effectively repeating his pitch word for word to its 175,000 readers.

Fundraising appeals were not the only letters Peary was writing. He had by now begun complaining privately about Cook's attempt to "forestall" (that is, preempt) him. The *Tribune* had made subtle reference to this emerging dispute already, opining that "Peary is much better qualified than any other explorer now planning to attempt the task." The *Times*, though, appeared to be more divided in its loyalties. It had greeted Cook's surprise announcement the previous fall with measured approval, mainly on the grounds that Cook, "an expert in both Arctic and Antarctic exploration," had rejected the foolish trend of trying to achieve the North Pole by hot-air balloon or airship. The *Times* had also downplayed any discussion of a brewing rivalry: "That Cook has got the start of Peary does not count for so much. Peary will be in the race. But . . . Dr. Cook knows his business, and he has started in the right way." How Cook would finish was, at this point, still anyone's guess.

Citing recent votes of confidence he'd received from the *Tribune* and *The Sun*, Peary now sought to bring the *Times* more definitively into his camp:

> I beg to note that Dr. Cook has located himself at Etah, which has been my rendezvous and depot for years; that he has about him my Eskimos and my dogs, assembled at Etah with the expectation of meeting me there last summer; that he is appropriating to his own use the services of the Eskimo, whom I have trained in methods of protracted serious arctic sledge work, and is utilizing their intimate knowledge of the routes and game resources of the lands to the north, which they have gained under my lead and guidance.

It is unclear what *Times* editors thought about these accusations when Peary first made them. No part of the letter was published until September 1909, well after the *Times* had taken a financial interest in him.

Peary did not yet know that he would be in business with the *Times*, because he expected, as he had done before, to sell his newspaper rights to James Gordon Bennett. As he shuffled into the Herald Building one day in early July, the fifty-two-year-old explorer also was under the mistaken impression that his friend William Reick, who'd helped broker some of those previous agreements, still worked there. But a receptionist informed him that Reick was now employed by the *Times*, and when Peary asked to see Charles Lincoln, the city editor who'd also negotiated on behalf of the *Herald* for news of his 1905–6 expedition, he was told that Lincoln, too, had gone to the *Times*. Peary was granted a short meeting with the new city editor, who politely declined to commit the *Herald* to his expedition.

Peary received a warmer reception six blocks uptown at the *Times*, where he was met by Lincoln and introduced to Carr Van Anda. Reick and Ochs joined the meeting shortly afterward, and all four men gathered around Peary to hear of his North Pole plans. After an hour of contract negotiations, the *Times* agreed to advance his expedition $4,000 in exchange for exclusive newspaper rights, on the condition that the resulting syndication earnings were large enough to cover the investment. If the story of the expedition proved so devoid of interest that those earnings fell short of $4,000, Peary would repay the difference himself.

Ochs could hardly have done better. The *Times* appeared, in the time-honored tradition of exploring patronage, to have put money on the line in the name of science and love of country. In reality, all it had done was extend a low-risk loan. The *Herald* later derided the "leonine contract" of the *Times* as a miserly "game of 'heads I win, tails you lose'" and scoffed that it was "inconceivable that an American newspaper can be proud of such a document." But the deal that Peary cut with the *Times* before departing for the North Pole on July 8, 1908, was not as one-sided as the *Herald* claimed. It secured the explorer a powerful ally in the press, one whose support would prove to be far more important than he could have guessed.

PART FOUR

# ANTIHEROES

# CHAPTER THIRTY-SEVEN

## September 8, 1909

It looked like the first exploring investment that Ochs had ever made was going to pay off nicely. "I find all well, and the office in the greatest excitement about the marvelous and overwhelming good luck in regard to Peary," he wrote to Effie in Atlantic City. "We are the exclusive publishers of Peary's story, and only through us can newspapers get the rights to print it. Every newspaper in New York is in a panic about our *stupendous scoop* and they are moving heaven and earth and offering all kinds of money to us and our employees to get hold of the story. Nothing in American journalism equals *this* achievement of the N.Y.T."

Of course, Cook's prior discovery made the paper's scoop less "stupendous" than it might have been. It was for this reason, according to a 1921 history of the *Times*, that Ochs and the rest of management had received Cook's news from Lerwick with "a good deal of disappointment." Still, the *Times* ran the story of his discovery on its front page and indicated that many experts considered his claim credible. Members and officers of the National Geographic Society not only vouched for Cook's reputation, the *Times* reported, but also considered it "almost inconceivable that a man of any knowledge of the requirements of scientific proof should deliberately try to palm off a fake discovery on the world."

Philip Gibbs had taken a taxi from the Copenhagen harbor straight to his hotel to write up his troubling interview with Cook aboard the *Hans Egede* and had remained glued to his typewriter during the explorer's crowd-pleasing press conference later that day at the Hotel Phoenix. If his memoirs are to be believed, Gibbs left out many alarming details of the earlier encounter. He did not mention Cook's extreme touchiness under questioning or his strange behavior afterward. As the crown prince of Denmark's greeting party prepared to board the *Hans Egede* that morning, Cook "could hardly pull himself together," Gibbs later wrote, adding that he'd "never [seen] guilt and fear more clearly written on any human face."

But the article by Gibbs that ran on September 5 in the London *Daily Chronicle* and (by special arrangement) in *The New York Times* made no such claims. It was, rather, written in a tone of naive surprise, especially concerning the revelation that Cook had returned without his navigational instruments or travel diaries. "Surely he should have retained the strongest proofs of his claim so that it might be immediately established," Gibbs ventured. Otherwise, he mostly let Cook's responses to his "seemingly impertinent" questions speak for themselves. "Whether his answers feel satisfactory I will leave the readers to judge. They will have to stand the test of men of geographical science," Gibbs concluded. The *Times* ran his account on the front page, under the headline COOK UNDER FIRE STICKS TO STORY. Inside the paper, its editors decided that some confusion had probably arisen from Cook's attempts to lighten the mood aboard the *Hans Egede*, which they considered ill-advised. "Jocularity is dangerous just now. But as he has returned to civilization his more sober statements will doubtless follow," the *Times* editors predicted on September 5.

But the paper had reached an important turning point in its treatment of Cook's story. Thanks to Gibbs, the *Times* had located a thread of doubt in Copenhagen, and it would continue tugging at it.

PHILIP GIBBS, THIRTY-TWO, DESCRIBED HIMSELF AS A "PALE-FACED YOUNG man, with his third finger deeply stained by nicotine." A mid-career free-lance journalist, he'd learned his trade during the great Fleet Street shake-up initiated by Alfred Harmsworth, who'd modernized the popular daily press in London much as Joseph Pulitzer had done in New York. Gibbs admired the young Harmsworth—later known as Lord Northcliffe—for his radical reframing of news as "anything which had a touch of human interest for the great mass of folk." He also shared Harmsworth's prefer-ence for reporting that "avoided the obvious by seeing the human stuff on the sidewalk while some pompous pageant passed."

Several polar authorities in Great Britain, including Captain George Nares and the Australian physicist Louis Bernacchi, were already openly questioning Cook's claim. In Copenhagen, though, the only skeptic seemed to be Gibbs. His editor at the *Chronicle*, E. A. Perris, who was si-multaneously publishing Bernacchi's expert commentary, encouraged him to keep probing Cook's story, as did the reporter's newest collabora-tor, Peter Freuchen. The jovial young Dane had analyzed the American explorer's purported route, dates, number of sled dogs, food supplies, and travel distances, and decided that the math just didn't add up. Frustrated that local editors refused to publish his findings, Freuchen began helping Gibbs to pore through the Danish-language press and pursue new lines of questioning.

Gibbs's doubts overshadowed his reporting more and more each day, even as the veteran journalist W. T. Stead and others getting to know Cook in Copenhagen became increasingly convinced that the affable American was being honest. "We all liked Mr. Gibbs," recalled Maurice Egan, the U.S. minister in Copenhagen, "because he had such good man-ners in private life; but we all pitied him for being so entirely in the wrong." Gibbs noticed various small discrepancies between what Cook had told him aboard the *Hans Egede* and then said later that day at the Hotel Phoe-nix. The rest of the press appeared to be ignorant of these lapses, or else willing to attribute them to Cook's frenzied interrogation by reporters "who know no more about Arctic exploration than an Eskimo knows about aviation," as the *Herald* put it. Equally striking to Gibbs was how many explorers were willing to take Cook at his word. Granted, some had sounder reasons than others for doing so. One of the firmest believers was Roald Amundsen, who had wintered in the Antarctic with Cook eleven years earlier and emerged from that harrowing experience a lifelong admirer. The steely Norwegian had fully navigated the Northwest Passage since that time, earning a place among the world's top explorers, but he had not traveled with Cook again. He considered his old friend to be "upright, honorable, capable, and conscientious in the extreme."

Another respected Norwegian explorer, Otto Sverdrup, vouched for Cook's rate of travel and other contested details. A cynic might have noted that Sverdrup had plenty to gain by supporting Cook, given that the American kept crediting him for having revealed a splendid new route to the pole. Pressed by Gibbs, Sverdrup admitted that his belief in Cook was based on "nothing but his simple statement." Meanwhile, the Danish explorers whose ruling monarch, King Frederick, had all but openly declared his faith in Cook were finding it increasingly difficult to step out of line. When Andreas Hovgaard of the Royal Danish Geographical Society, former captain of Nordenskiöld's *Vega*, reminded guests at a royal banquet that the world was still awaiting many details of Cook's journey, the remark "cast rather a chill upon the company," Gibbs reported, and his otherwise gregarious toast to Cook that evening was met with stony silence.

Gibbs, whose reporting seemed to grow more critical of the Danish establishment each day, concluded that the University of Copenhagen had acted naively. When it was reported that Professor Strömgren had in fact reviewed some of Cook's original observations, Gibbs confronted the astronomer at his departmental offices to set the record straight. The report was false, Strömgren clarified; Cook had simply written out the results of his journey for him. "Until we can see his original observations we can prove nothing at all," he told Gibbs. As far as Strömgren knew, the original observations were not in Copenhagen.

Cook's unruffled demeanor had convinced the Copenhagen press corps of his honesty, especially during the "Great Interview" at the Hotel Phoenix. "The look on his face was calm and the sincere manner in which he answered awkward questions produced on all present a profound impression," the correspondent for *The Times* of London had written afterward. Gibbs believed that Scandinavia's leading experts and explorers (with the notable exception of Fridtjof Nansen, who reserved judgment) were essentially behaving no differently than these excitable polar amateurs, searching Cook's face for signs of truth or falsehood while leaving the facts of the matter unexamined. All of Copenhagen, he marveled in *The New York Times*, had come under the spell of a personality "so strange and so powerful that I believe if Cook claimed to have come from Mars there would be many people who would say, 'We believe him because he tells us so. Such a simple, honest man would not deceive us.'"

Another of Cook's most influential supporters was the anthropologist and explorer Knud Rasmussen, a leading authority on Greenland's Inuit. Rasmussen's faith in Cook was partly based on a friendly encounter he'd had with him at North Star Bay, south of Etah, before the American had set off for Axel Heiberg Land. Rasmussen believed that Cook possessed enough supplies and fit dogs to have gone to the pole and back. At Cape York the next summer, he'd confirmed that Etukishuk and Ahwelah had turned southward "only because they believed the goal was reached," though it was unclear whether Rasmussen had interviewed the two young Inuit personally or gotten their story secondhand. Gibbs cleared this matter up in early September. The same day he confronted Strömgren, Dagmar Rasmussen showed him a letter she'd just received from her husband in Greenland. Knud Rasmussen wrote that he had not spoken directly with Etukishuk or Ahwelah, and also disavowed—or at least qualified—his overall faith in Cook's story. Gibbs tore a sheet out of his reporter's notebook, had Freuchen copy these explosive passages out in pencil, and presented them for translation to Oscar Hansen, the *Daily Chronicle*'s Copenhagen correspondent. Anything having to do with Rasmussen's views was considered big news, and the Danish press had no choice but to run the story, momentarily creating an uproar.

That evening, September 7, Cook took the stage at the Odd Fellow

Palace, a rococo concert hall directly opposite the Hotel Phoenix. The crown prince of Denmark began the proceedings by awarding him the Royal Danish Geographical Society's gold medal. Cook, standing before a giant hanging map of the Arctic, waited five minutes for the applause to subside, then eased into the eagerly awaited narrative of his journey. Perturbed by the handful of naysayers, and perhaps also now by Peary's claim, the society's leadership had urged him to elaborate on his discovery of the pole. Instead, Cook devoted a mere two minutes to this portion of the journey and made only two newsworthy statements. One was a defense of his decision not to bring a white eyewitness to the pole, which he said would have made it "necessary to double the Eskimo force, but that would have meant dividing its efficiency by two." The other was Cook's announcement that he would, for the moment, withhold additional new details from the public. "There will be nothing further given of the story until you get it in consecutive form in the book," he announced.

Even Cook's biggest supporters had to admit that he won no converts that evening. "His great anxiety was to confine himself to what he had already said, and to say no more," Stead noted. Gibbs declared the performance a flop, writing that Cook's speech "proves conclusively that his claim to have reached the North Pole belongs to the realm of fairy tales." The Englishman was dangerously far out on a limb now. His press colleagues warned him that he was risking his career, or at the very least a libel suit. Barely had these warnings registered when Gibbs learned that two of his latest scoops were in trouble. *Le Matin*, the Parisian newspaper, had obtained a statement from Knud Rasmussen reaffirming his faith in Cook, and Dagmar Rasmussen, owner of the letter that said otherwise, was suddenly nowhere to be found. Strömgren, too, had recanted. Not only did the astronomer deny making comments about Cook's lack of evidence; he claimed never to have spoken with Gibbs in the first place.

In the space of a day or two, the skeptical reporter appeared to have slandered Denmark's top university and its most popular explorer. GIBBS THE LIAR, ran one Danish headline. C. M. Norman-Hansen, a Danish surgeon and Arctic disease specialist who'd befriended Cook aboard the *Hans Egede*, publicly challenged him to a duel. Stead gravely informed

Gibbs that he had destroyed his own career and tarnished the reputation of one of London's finest papers. A chilling telegram arrived from Perris, his editor at *The Daily Chronicle*: "Please explain."

After ransacking his newspaper-strewn hotel room for the transcription of Rasmussen's letter, Gibbs finally found the precious document crumpled up beneath his bed. He brought it to a Danish newspaper editor who identified the handwriting as Freuchen's and then listened to the *Daily Chronicle* correspondent Oscar Hansen swear that he had translated its contents for Gibbs. For the moment, this was as far as their defense could go. Dagmar Rasmussen still could not be located.

Strömgren, on the other hand, was easily tracked down at the observatory, but whether he would speak candidly with Gibbs was another matter. Gibbs enlisted Stead and two other journalists to come along as witnesses, and the astronomer reluctantly received them in his office. Asserting that a fellow journalist's professional honor was at stake, Stead persuaded him to answer the same questions Gibbs had asked him two days before. Gibbs resubmitted them one by one, extracting each "yes" or "no" from Strömgren as painfully as embedded shrapnel. He then obtained a written statement from him confirming that Cook had, to date, presented the University of Copenhagen with no scientific evidence of his claim. As the satisfied visitors stood to leave, Strömgren asked that none of what he'd said or sworn be published. This set off a renewed round of pleading from Stead and Gibbs, until the astronomer finally relented. Gibbs fled to file the story before his exasperating source changed his mind again. Examining the timeline afterward, Gibbs realized that Strömgren must have been under enormous pressure to withdraw his earlier statements. King Frederick had awarded Cook an honorary diploma from the nation's finest university, for an achievement the royal astronomer had subsequently admitted was unproven.

The presentation ceremony unfolded with austere gravitas on the afternoon of September 9. The entire faculty and student body filled the University of Copenhagen's Great Hall. Crown Prince Christian, Crown Princess Alexandrine, and Prince George and Princess Marie of Greece and Denmark seated themselves on the dais, opposite a bench full of robed professors. After praising Cook in a brief speech, Rector Torp turned to Cook and said, "Whether your scientific research will rank very highly or not, the faculty gives you this degree in recognition of your great achievements in exploration and the qualities you have shown therein." He then handed the American the diploma in its silk case. "I accept this degree with due appreciation of the honor done me. By it you have stamped my journey to the pole," Cook said. He repeated his promise that the University of Copenhagen would be the first institution to examine his records, and asked for its patience while these were prepared. "I do not want you to examine mere fragments, but want you to examine it all," he explained, and he announced that he would send a ship to Greenland as soon as possible so that Etukishuk and Ahwelah could be brought back for questioning by Knud Rasmussen. "I can say no more, I can do no more," Cook concluded. "I show you my hands." So stirring was this heartfelt speech that Gibbs later confessed to feeling a twinge of uncertainty: "At that moment, I was tempted to believe that Cook believed he had been to the North Pole."

The presentation of the diploma was Cook's last formal event in Copenhagen. He sailed for New York City the next day, via Norway, where he boarded the Scandinavian-American Line's *Oscar II*. Two days before, Gibbs had described the explorer in *The New York Times* as "the most remarkable, most amazing man I have ever met." Gibbs would never cross paths with him again, for after Cook's departure the *Chronicle* recalled him to London.

# CHAPTER THIRTY-EIGHT

Private jealousies and resentments had always simmered in the exploring world, as they do in any competitive arena, but never had one polar explorer accused another of outright fraud. To do so was to violate a long-standing code of honor and threatened the heroic aura surrounding men like Cook and Peary. If even one notable explorer lost that aura, all of them would suffer, for it would become harder for the rest of humanity to be inspired by their accounts of their exotic journeys, or to support the next one. Robert Peary would violate the time-honored tradition of taking explorers at their word in excruciatingly public fashion in September 1909. The act would haunt him for years to come.

It would also bring no end of headaches to Herbert Bridgman, secretary and de facto head of public relations for the Peary Arctic Club. When news of Peary's success was received on September 6, Bridgman was the man reporters went looking for. The sixty-five-year-old businessman kept in regular touch with Peary. He was an Arctic enthusiast, more conversant in the subject and more available for interviews than the other, busier members of the Peary Arctic Club. As co-owner and business manager of the Brooklyn *Standard-Union*, he was also a seasoned newspaperman and rarely made a misstep when addressing the press.

Bridgman had been vacationing in the Berkshires with his wife, Helen, when the long-awaited telegram from Peary arrived; it contained a single code word, "Sun," which meant that the pole had been reached and the *Roosevelt* was safe. Bridgman caught the first train to New York City, where he spoke with reporters at Grand Central Station. He was overjoyed to learn that Peary had finally achieved his life's goal, he told them, but not surprised. This was the indomitable Robert Peary, after all. Asked about Cook's tepidly disputed claim, Bridgman demurred: "It is unfortunate that a controversy over the real discovery of the pole should have arisen, but that is Commander Peary's own fight."

But America did not want a fight; it wanted a party. For the second time in a week, it had literally come out on top of the world. There was no thought of doubting Peary, whose word and abilities were considered unassailable. His claim would presumably also have the corroboration of whichever other explorers trained in the use of sextant and theodolite had been with him at the pole. Bridgman guessed that Peary had chosen the thirty-four-year-old Donald MacMillan or the twenty-three-year-old expedition photographer George Borup, or perhaps both of them.

The main topic of discussion now was the significance of America's remarkable twin achievement. Some argued that the discovery of the pole contributed meaningfully to human knowledge. "The observations of the one will doubtless complete those of the other, and science will be the richer by two contributions of inestimable value," *The Paris Herald* predicted. But Bennett's paper and other boosters were in fact on shaky ground here. Many scientists had a different take, especially once they learned that nearly all of Cook's and Peary's "observations" had been made for the limited purpose of navigating to the pole and back.

"It is a great event and the story of the conquest of the Pole will live in history; and yet not a vital human interest will be affected by it," the geographer Cyrus Adams predicted. The *Times* had become less critical of the race to the pole in recent years and had effectively joined it by backing Peary. But early in September 1909, during the five-day period when Cook's success had been reported but Peary's hadn't, the *Times* momentarily took up its old position. "In sober truth, the quest of the pole has none except sentimental attractions," its editors noted sourly, and it distracted too many "men whose energy and courage could be put to more profitable uses."

Peary's Arctic Ocean soundings, which were flawed and merely reinforced the prevailing wisdom that no significant northern lands remained to be discovered, still constituted the most important scientific work done during the American polar journeys of 1907–9. Well-informed observers understood that he and Cook had not ventured forth for scientific reasons. The acting supervisor of the U.S. Coast and Geodetic Survey told the *Herald* that September, "Pole hunting is a sportsman's job; the scientific value of the discovery is very slight." Nor did the sports editor of the New York *World* have any trouble identifying what it was all about. "The greatest sporting event in history is just ended with the finding of the North Pole," he wrote. Cook himself referred to the race to the pole as a "feat of brain and muscle," the sort of blood-quickening race that any man of vigor might want to join, and compared himself to "one who seeks preeminence in baseball, running tournaments, or any form of athletics or sport." Peary, for his part, had recruited the newest members of his team along similar lines. Borup, a former championship runner at Yale, had joined the expedition "as a sort of athletic enterprise," according to *The World*, and MacMillan worked as a fitness instructor.

If, for most Americans, the race to the pole was an international athletic contest, then its competitors inspired critical scrutiny in the way that famous athletes always do. The contrasting approaches of Cook and Peary were quickly noted: Cook had hitched a ride to Greenland in someone else's refitted schooner, while Peary had sailed in a powerful ship that had been built specifically to penetrate the frozen seas. Cook had gone quietly and undecided about his plans; Peary had made it widely known that he aimed to reach the pole and received a send-off from none other than the president of the United States. Cook had stepped onto the Arctic Ocean some 500 miles from the pole, at northern Axel Heiberg Land, but only after sledging 300 miles west from Greenland—a preliminary journey so grueling that he had sent Franke back with seven Inuit and instructions to recuperate at Anoritoq. He had then braved the sea ice with just one sledge and two companions, Etukishuk and Ahwelah. Peary had used the icebreaker *Roosevelt* to smash his way farther north, to Cape Sheridan, at the northern tip of Ellesmere Island, and had then sledged from Cape Columbia, 475 miles south of the pole. His expedition consisted of nineteen sledges, 133 dogs, eighteen Inuit guides, five white men, and the perennially underrated Henson.

The virtual consensus was that Cook, the underdog, had won a contest in which both Americans had competed honorably. But that predominant view lasted only a day or two. Now that Peary had claimed success, the *Times* reported that he had long disapproved of Cook's unannounced polar journey, and that prior to departing in 1908, he had accused Cook, in writing, of exploiting his yearlong travel delay by launching a "sub rosa"—that is, secretive—bid to snatch the pole out from under him. The reason Cook had found the Etah Inuit perfectly equipped and ready to travel over the sea ice, Peary maintained, was that these indispensable assistants had been spending the spring and early summer preparing to work for *him*.

The same day that the *Times* aired these grievances, two of Peary's latest telegrams from Indian Harbour were made public. One, intended for publication, read, "Cook's story should not be taken too seriously. The Eskimos who accompanied him say he went no distance north and not out of sight of land. Other men of the tribe corroborate their statement." (In response to these charges, Cook announced later that same day in Copenhagen that he would bring Etukishuk and Ahwelah back from Greenland for questioning.) A leaked private telegram to Josephine, Peary's wife, in Maine, was blunter: "Don't let Cook story worry you. Have him nailed."

Peary sent these messages along with news that the twenty-eight-year-old Ross Marvin, his personal assistant and chief scientist, had drowned on the sledge journey back to the *Roosevelt*. The explorer had failed to mention this tragedy in his first batch of telegrams, apparently for the purpose of securing untainted headlines. The public backlash to Peary's intentional oversight was swift. By implying that all was well, the *Herald* and others noted, he had caused unnecessary distress to Marvin's friends and loved ones, including the young explorer's widowed mother in upstate New York.

Dismayed by the negative response to Peary's messages, Bridgman tried to urge him to stop attacking Cook. With the *Roosevelt*—which did not have wireless—lying at anchor and communicating with Indian Harbour by means of rowboats, Peary either missed or ignored Bridgman's warning. The next day, he sent a fateful telegram to the *Herald* that read, in part, "Cook has simply handed the public [a] gold brick. He's not been at the pole April 21, 1908, or any other time."

Peary later claimed that he had not intended the message for publication. When it appeared on front pages everywhere, his dispute with Cook entered treacherous and uncharted territory. Four years later, sitting in front of a roaring fire at the Explorers Club, Peary confessed to an aspiring young explorer named Roy Chapman Andrews that it had been a grave mistake to fling fighting words at the newspapers. "I'd give anything if I hadn't sent those telegrams," he said.

PRIVATELY, ADOLPH OCHS WELCOMED PEARY'S ACCUSATION OF POLAR fraud. "There is now little doubt that Cook is a faker," he wrote to Effie on September 8, 1909. Like many at the *Times* and elsewhere, he assumed that Peary's forthcoming three-part newspaper series would show that he had been to the pole and Cook hadn't. Ochs was to be disappointed. If anything, Peary's narrative actually tilted the argument in Cook's favor.

His description of the North Pole as a lifeless plain of broken ice matched Cook's. Peary also reported that travel conditions improved after the 88th parallel and compared this previously untraveled stretch of snow-covered sea ice to a glacier—both of which Cook had done already. More important, Peary's narrative failed to meet the elevated standard of evidence to which his supporters were now holding Cook. The heavy refraction of sunlight near the pole rendered it especially difficult to take bearings there; the shifting ice and up-and-town topography of hummocks and pressure ridges made it hard to determine just how many miles one had advanced in a day. Complicating factors like these had been considered too esoteric for popular consumption in the past, but now they had real urgency. And yet Peary ignored them, just as Cook had.

In one respect, Peary's journey actually appeared to be the less credible of the two. Cook claimed to have advanced fifteen miles a day on average, a rate some experts had dismissed as impossible. But Peary reported in his *Times* series that he had covered nearly twenty-five miles a day. Rather than cast doubt upon the stories of both explorers, as it might conceivably have done, this revelation was treated as a validation of Cook's stated travel rate. "It seems to me that Cook is not losing, and that everything he has reported is practically substantiated by Peary," the explorer and American Geographical Society officer Frederick Dellenbaugh told the *Herald*. The distinguished ex-secretary of the Royal Geographical Society, Sir Clements Markham, said that while reading Peary's account, he'd "failed to find anything of scientific value which gave it precedence."

Peary's most stunning admission, though, was that he had brought no credible—which at the time meant white—eyewitness to the pole. MacMillan had turned back early, on account of frostbite, and Borup had retreated as well. The last expedition member capable of independently confirming Peary's whereabouts, Captain Robert Bartlett, had been sent back 133 nautical miles short of the pole, apparently due to lack of resources. Peary had completed the journey with four Inuit—Egingwah, Ootah, Ooqueah, and Seeglo—and Henson. The racial prejudices that undermined the contributions of all five of these participants are now clear, but at the time the men themselves were also written off as valid eyewitnesses on the legitimate grounds that they were untrained in the use of scientific instruments. One patch of uppermost Arctic Ocean ice looked like any other; if Peary said they had reached the pole—as opposed to some point 100 miles to the east, west, or south—they basically had to take his word for it.

Now the world was being asked to do the same. As a French newspaper quipped, the only proven fact of the matter was that "Dr. Cook arrived before Commander Peary at the telegraph office." A case that should have been decided by expert testimony and hard evidence now hinged on personal character and credibility. Peary had shown himself to be surprisingly deficient in both, even before new tales of his appalling conduct emerged in mid-September. It was known already that he had discovered Rudolph Franke suffering from scurvy and a leg injury at Etah, and that in the summer of 1908 he had sent Cook's ailing assistant home aboard a Newfoundland sealer that had come to Etah to resupply the *Roosevelt* with coal. Now it came to light that Peary had demanded trophies belonging to Cook, including fifty-three fox pelts, in exchange for his evacuation of Franke. "I felt very ill. I felt that my life depended upon my getting away, so I signed over the skins and walrus tusks and went aboard the Roosevelt," Franke told the *Herald*. The Peary Arctic Club had also subsequently billed John Bradley $100 for services rendered.

With Franke gone, Peary had installed the *Roosevelt*'s boatswain, John Murphy, in Cook's hut at nearby Anoritoq before steaming north again. C. M. Norman-Hansen, the Danish physician who'd befriended Cook in Greenland, now stated publicly that Peary had left a note which read, "This house belongs to Dr. Frederick A. Cook, but Dr. Cook is long ago dead and there is no use to search after him. Therefore I, Commander Robert E. Peary, install my boatswain in this deserted house." When Cook staggered back to Anoritoq in the spring of 1909, Norman-Hansen related, Murphy had at first refused to let him enter his own dwelling. Finally he had backed down, only for Cook to discover that the seaman supposedly charged with protecting his property from looters (as Peary later claimed) had spent the winter looting it himself, trading Cook's guns and provisions with local Inuit in exchange for valuable fox and bear skins. The sordid story first appeared in *Politiken* and was immediately picked up by the American press. Norman-Hansen claimed that Cook possessed a copy of the note in which Peary had declared him dead, but had honorably declined to make it public.

Even some of Peary's longtime admirers now condemned his behavior. "Commander Peary is a man of undaunted courage and of high attainments," one Arctic Club of America member told the *Herald*, "but in this matter his conduct has been somewhat like that of a child who has been deprived at the last of something on which it has set its heart." The *Times* reprinted Norman-Hansen's accusations, without comment, on September 13. On its editorial page that same day, it unironically hailed Peary's "discovery in the name of peace" by noting that he had planted the banner of an antiwar organization at the North Pole.

Meanwhile, Jo Peary and other well-wishers awaited her husband in Sydney, Nova Scotia, an industrial hub at the end of the eastern Canadian railway line. With Jo were their fifteen-year-old daughter, Marie, and five-year-old, Robert Jr. The welcoming party also included Herbert Bridgman and two more recent acquaintances, Elsa Barker and Henry Rood. Barker, a writer, hoped to secure Peary's latest success story for *Hampton's Magazine*; Rood, who worked at Harper & Brothers, was seeking book rights.

But with Cook en route to New York aboard the *Oscar II*, the *Roosevelt* inexplicably remained anchored more than four hundred nautical miles north of Sydney, at the cod-fishing village of Battle Harbour. A week had passed since Peary's first telegrams had come in from Labrador, leaving the world's press in tense limbo. Philip Gibbs had punched what amounted to a pinhole in Cook's story, then withdrew. Peary had threatened to rip it wide open, then provided no further details. Tired of waiting for him to come to them, the two dozen or so reporters who'd gathered in Sydney chartered a ship to Battle Harbour. Rood joined them, bearing a letter from Jo Peary begging her husband, as Bridgman had tried to do earlier, to stop attacking the "miserable creature" Cook. "If you only can keep still and not discuss this creature until you have had an opportunity to see what he and others have said, it would be far better," she pleaded. It was one of the most difficult things anyone had ever asked of him.

# CHAPTER THIRTY-NINE

## September 13, 1909

The Canadian cable ship *Tyrian* left North Sydney for Battle Harbour on the morning of September 13, 1909, carrying more than twenty representatives of the Boston, New York, and Canadian press. Captain Alexander Dickson would have taken more, but Roy Howard of the United Press wire service and Delt Edwards of *The New York Herald* persuaded him to weigh anchor before fifty more journalists arriving on the evening train from Montreal could come aboard. Howard and Edwards didn't want the competition, and there wouldn't have been anywhere for the newcomers to sleep anyway.

For three days the *Tyrian* faced headwinds and heavy seas. For most of the passengers, it was their first encounter with the dangerous charms of the Arctic. The correspondents were roused from their nightly poker games by the phosphorescent glow of the aurora borealis. "Green and red streaked the whole north sky, skipping from brilliant to a soft haze," Edwards of the *Herald* wrote. An old seaman on watch pointed ahead and told the doubting newsmen that he smelled an iceberg. "Within half an hour here came his iceberg, like a monster out of the evening mist," Edwards marveled. The newsmen learned that the most lethal of these were the "growlers" that barely broke the surface and that their route through the Strait of Belle Isle was littered with them.

The *Tyrian* approached Battle Harbour "with a forty-mile gale piling seas over the stern and with icebergs threatening the destruction of the vessel on every side," wrote Barton Currie of the New York *World*. As Captain Dickson and his pilot eased the steamer to a safe mooring in the darkness, the reporters huddled on the bridge, their knees "rattling like castanets." They awoke to the sight of granite fjord walls looming above them—as high as the Bunker Hill Monument, the Boston correspondents wagered—and reached the forty-house village of Battle Harbour later that morning. The *Roosevelt* lay behind a point of land, its raised American flag visible in the distance. Upon closer inspection, it reminded Edwards of a barbarian warship. "All up and down her rigging, from topmast to rail, skulls of walrus, seals and other animals stood out in gruesome white. The sides of the ship were streaked with oil and bore some scars of her battles with the ice," he wrote. The *Tyrian* hailed the *Roosevelt* with three whistle blasts and was treated to a chorus of barking Arctic pups in reply.

The tugboat *Douglas Thomas* had been chartered by six members of the Associated Press and arrived in a rain squall the day before. Now that both press boats were present, "reporters and photographers swept down upon the *Roosevelt* like so many boarding parties of pirates, swarming over the sides by ladders or ropes or anything handy," Currie wrote. Peary, wearing a bibbed blue flannel shirt and old trousers tucked into tall rubber boots, emerged from his cabin to pose for photographs on the quarterdeck. His eyes were pale blue and narrow, the untrimmed hair beneath his wide-brimmed soft hat a reddish gray. His mouth was unreadable, hidden as it was behind a thick mustache that tapered and frayed at the ends. His stubbled face looked smooth for a man of fifty-three, as though it had been scrubbed clean of wrinkles by the Arctic winds, but the muddle of crow's-feet around his small eyes gave his true age away. He stood six feet tall, with an erectness that seemed to add to it.

Peary puffed his chest out as he presented himself to the pencils and cameras of the press and knocked his heels together. The journalists had arrived determined to wrest secrets from this unloved man, but as he squared his broad shoulders against the mizzenmast and posed silently beneath the American flag, some of their professional resolve deserted them. "Every inch of him, every ounce of him was hard as Bessemer steel; his muscles danced and squirmed under his shirt as he moved and breathed," Currie noted. The journalists spontaneously belted out three cheers for Peary. "He bowed to this and smiled from ear to ear, showing every one of his big strong teeth," Currie reported.

Peary announced that he would give his first interview in an hour and returned to his cabin to read the letters that the press boats had delivered to him. The journalists used the delay to grill everyone they could find aboard the *Roosevelt*, but did not get far. Peary had ordered his men to say nothing about Cook or the North Pole. Currie wrote that Matthew Henson "seemed greatly reluctant to talk and manifested not the least emotion when he described his final dash to the Pole with Peary."

Donald MacMillan was more forthcoming. He cheerily discussed Arctic birdlife and all the interesting things he'd found in the months leading up to the polar journey. The *Roosevelt*'s attainment of Cape Sheridan, just 520 miles from the pole, had put several legendary exploration bases within easy sledging distance, and he had retrieved relics of the Greely expedition at Lady Franklin Bay. Among these was a handwritten note carried by Second Lieutenant Frederick Kislingbury that read, "May God be with you and return you safely to us." Kislingbury had starved to death at Cape Sabine; the note was from his eleven-year-old son. Reminders of Peary's ill-fated predecessors were not really what the journalists were after, though. They wanted news of the Cook-Peary feud, and they got it from the cabin boy Billy Pritchard.

Pritchard had been left by Peary at Anoritoq in 1908 with the *Roosevelt* boatswain, John Murphy, either to protect or to plunder Cook's stores. Both seamen had met Cook there when he'd returned in April, as had Harry Whitney, the New Haven big-game hunter who'd subsequently agreed to transport the explorer's instruments and documents back to the United States by steamer. Pritchard now told reporters that he had overheard Cook telling Whitney that he'd been to the pole. Cook had asked Whitney and Pritchard to keep this information to themselves so that he could be the first to share it. Whitney had come aboard the *Roosevelt* with Pritchard in August after the *Jeanie*, the schooner he'd hired to take him home, failed to arrive in Etah; he'd disembarked a week later, when the *Roosevelt* met the *Jeanie* at Saunders Island, off northwestern Greenland, and was now thought to be hunting musk oxen somewhere in that vicinity. Neither man had said anything to anyone on the *Roosevelt* about the conversation with Cook. Why Pritchard, who worked for Peary, had shown such unwavering devotion to his employer's rival was unclear.

Peary was unaware of his cabin boy's confession when he gave his interview later that morning in a dim and low-ceilinged fish-house loft in Battle Harbour. The journalists seated themselves as comfortably as they could on barrels, soft heaps of netting, and the bare floor. Their eyes were still adjusting to the light when Peary entered, flanked by Captains Dickson of the *Tyrian* and Bartlett of the *Roosevelt*. He began by lecturing the reporters about the basics of North Pole geography. He then lowered himself onto a crate and showed the teeth that Currie considered "almost wolfish in their set and grip." He would now take questions, Peary said.

The first question was about Cook. Peary's smile disappeared.

Had he seen any sign of Cook on the polar ice? "There was not the slightest impression of Cook or anyone else," Peary replied. According to Currie, "This was said with a vehemence that approached a snarl."

Would it be possible, another reporter asked, for Cook to have been at the pole the year before and left no sign of his presence? "Peary's jaws opened and shut with a snap," Currie wrote.

"Yes."

Peary held out a restraining arm. "Wait a moment. I said yes, but let me put it this way. Without reference to Cook, I will say that there are hundreds of routes outside of mine, any one of which could have been taken by a reputable explorer with a well equipped expedition"—not Cook, in other words—"and have left no trace which I would have noticed." Peary repeated his outright assertion that Cook had never been to the pole. As for proving his own claim, he explained that five sextant observations had been recorded while on the frozen Arctic Ocean: the first two by the now-dead professor Marvin, records of which Peary possessed; a third by

Bartlett, near the 88th parallel; and the fourth and fifth by Peary alone, including one he'd made five miles from the pole. Peary also announced that he would say no more about what he had found there "until other statements as to conditions at the Pole have been submitted"—the implication being that Cook would take note of anything he revealed and use it to bolster his own false claim. His own records, Peary added significantly, were with him but sealed within waterproof animal skins and would remain unopened until his return to the United States.

There was also the important question of why Peary had chosen Henson to accompany him beyond the 88th parallel and not Bartlett, a trained navigator who could have confirmed Peary's assertion that the pole had been reached. Asked in Sydney to shed some light on this decision of her husband's, Josephine had virtuously declared that "there is no color line in the Arctic." Aboard the *Roosevelt* that very morning, reporters had learned that Peary had, in fact, selected Henson against the racist objections of some of his white expedition members. But the explanation that Peary now gave for choosing Henson over Bartlett was a purely selfish one: "Because after a lifetime of effort, I dearly wanted the honor for myself." In other words, he'd brought only a black man and four Inuit to the pole in order to avoid sharing the glory with another white man. It was a startling admission, and his detractors would not forget it.

Asked about his extraordinary travel rates, Peary explained that his newly redesigned sledges featured slick steel runners and reduced the strain on his men and dogs by as much as 75 percent. He also said that an absence of wind had enabled the polar party to return on the same trail it had taken during the final dash, rather than waste time breaking a new one. Peary would say nothing about his alleged commandeering of Cook's hut at Anoritoq, except to deny that he had ever declared his rival dead in writing. He also declined to discuss his earlier conversations with Whitney. "I shall pay no attention to any fake stories or side issues which are only raised to detract from the main question," he said. "The issue is, has Cook been at the Pole?"

For the moment, at least, the question of whether Peary had been there was considered settled.

# CHAPTER FORTY

## September 20, 1909

The schools and businesses of Sydney stayed closed on this Monday, and thousands of the town's citizens draped their houses and boats in festive bunting and milled about the ferry wharf in their finest clothes. The *Roosevelt* was expected to arrive from Battle Harbour. Jo Peary, having accepted an offer to travel aboard the yacht of a local coal baron, prepared to meet her husband at sea. She dressed little Robert in a sailor's suit for the occasion and departed with him and Marie that morning.

They returned around midnight in tears, for there had been no sign of the *Roosevelt*. Peary had spent most of the day anchored seventy miles out from Sydney, using the cable station at St. Paul Island to deal with fallout from the disastrous press reports from Battle Harbour. The newspapers had treated the seaman Pritchard's revelation, that he'd heard Cook say he'd been to the pole, as a major plot twist. Rather than damage Cook, moreover, Peary's own interview at Battle Harbour had simply reinforced the general impression that he was a sore loser. Who was he to decide whether his rival had been to the pole, anyway? "He is a party in the suit, not one of the judges, and that being the case he would do well to imitate the dignity and gentlemanly courtesy of Dr. Cook," the *Herald* chided.

Peary's three-part account of his polar journey had run in the *Times*, and still he was losing the public-relations battle—badly. And so, rather than proceed to Sydney, he made the undersea cable northeast of Cape Breton Island pulse as he discussed next steps with Bridgman (who'd returned to New York from Sydney) and another key cohort, General Thomas Hubbard.

Bridgman had worked with Peary longer and had a better understanding of how the press functioned. But Hubbard, who'd succeeded Morris Jesup as president of the Peary Arctic Club, was about to become one of the explorer's most important allies. Hubbard, a Civil War veteran, had gained wealth and influence first as legal counsel and then as a director of railroads. At seventy, he was now retired as a lawyer, sat on the boards of more than half a dozen major corporations, and owned the small-circulation New York *Globe and Commercial Advertiser*. Like other wealthy New Yorkers of his age and station, the native Mainer enjoyed wood-paneled men's clubs and philanthropy; he was a long-serving trustee of Bowdoin College, his alma mater, and the institution's largest donor. He had met Peary at an alumni event in 1903, and the *Tribune* later claimed that his devotion to the explorer was "due largely to the fact that both were Bowdoin men." Hubbard had pumped $20,000 into the explorer's North Pole efforts since that first meeting. More recently, he'd seen the Peary Arctic Club through the fundraising crisis that had resulted when Morris Jesup's widow, Maria, resentful of all the stress Peary had caused her late husband in his dotage, contributed just $5,000 to the 1908–9 expedition.

Hubbard was drawn to Peary's cause by the man himself and his worthily patriotic enterprise, rather than by any personal enthusiasm for the Arctic. One of his first public comments following news of Peary's success had been to express "no doubt that the Pole will become government property." At the outset of the polar controversy, Hubbard had insisted, echoing Bridgman, that any dispute with Cook would be Peary's own to fight. Either this was a seasoned lawyer's attempt to play down the influence of the Peary Arctic Club, or Hubbard swiftly changed his mind, because when Peary cabled him from northeastern Canada, asking if they could meet in Maine "regarding the most destructive way of presenting and disseminating my evidence of [the] falsity of Cook's story," Hubbard readily agreed.

Of what did Peary's evidence consist? He would not elaborate when asked in Sydney, where an estimated fifteen thousand of the seventeen thousand local residents turned out to celebrate him. The town's mayor and the American consul squired him to the finest hotel in town, where Peary and his family were joined by a crowd of reporters and well-wishers. Peary's men made their way to the hotel shortly afterward, and some of the stony reticence they had shown at Battle Harbour softened amid the hoopla. In the case of Robert Bartlett, it nearly turned to mush. Pressed by Delt Edwards of the *Herald*, the salty Newfoundlander broke down and admitted that Peary's order to turn back less than 140 miles from the pole had left him shocked and devastated. "I—well, it was a bitter disappointment," he confessed. "I don't know; perhaps I cried a little. I guess perhaps I was just a little crazy then. I thought perhaps I could walk on the rest of the way alone. It seemed so near." Desperate to go on, Bartlett had woken up before the others that last morning and walked five miles alone before finally coming to his senses. He'd sledged back to the *Roosevelt* "in a daze," he said. Bartlett would later disavow these dramatic comments.

When had Peary first heard of Cook's feat, and how had this knowledge influenced his subsequent actions, including his inexplicable delay at Battle Harbour? These questions would be debated for decades afterward, but at the time they were just two of the many things that Peary refused to talk about. Matthew Henson was less tight-lipped. He told reporters that he had learned about Cook's claim a month earlier, from a letter that had been left for Peary at Etah by a Scottish whaling skipper who'd crossed paths with Cook in Greenland. Henson's immediate response to this news, he claimed, had been to laugh. He knew that Cook's prior Arctic sledging experience consisted of a single outing on the Greenland ice cap in 1892 and that he had never before tangled with the physical and navigational challenges of crossing the Arctic Ocean. Henson also claimed to know "every Esquimau of the Etah tribe" and considered Etukishuk and Ahwelah "mere inexperienced boys" in the field of polar travel. Etukishuk, the more seasoned of the two, had been on the ice with Henson and Peary once before, but never on the rougher sections found north of the 84th parallel.

Then Henson dropped a bombshell: He had met with both "boys" at Etah in August and grilled them about where they'd been with Cook. "After I had questioned them over and over again they confessed that they had not gone beyond the land ice," he revealed. If true, this meant that Cook had never gotten closer than four hundred miles from the pole. Asked by reporters in Sydney if he had discussed his discovery with Peary, Henson demurred. "Now, you'll have to see the boss about that," he said. When they did, Peary declined to comment. He gave them another piece of headline news instead: on the advice of Bridgman and Hubbard, he would be declining all honors and invitations "until the present controversy is settled by competent authority."

The following morning, Peary took the train to Portland, Maine, with his family, once again leaving Bartlett to steam south without him. But the *Roosevelt* was missing more than its commander by the time it eventually left Sydney. In the chaos of arrival, hundreds of souvenir seekers had scrambled aboard and made off with ditty bags, traveling furs, and cooking and eating utensils, as well as more precious items, including Borup's photography equipment and MacMillan's hand-annotated science textbooks. Fortunately, the most valuable objects were recovered after a public appeal was made for their return. Peary's records and instruments, which he'd kept on his person and under lock and key aboard the *Roosevelt*, remained untouched.

# CHAPTER FORTY-ONE

Frederick Cook beheld the New York City skyline for the first time in more than two years on September 20, 1909. As the *Oscar II* awaited quarantine processing near Fire Island, press tugs sidled up to it to query the famous explorer by megaphone. He shouted back the expected pleasantries, adding, "I would much prefer landing quickly and quietly without repetition of the scenes at Copenhagen! I hope I shall be left in peace with my family tomorrow night at least!"

It was not to be. Cook's ten-day absence from the public eye had, if anything, made hometown crowds even more excited to get a look at him. The *Herald* was publishing the serialized account of his polar journey on alternate days, splashing each new installment across all six of its front-page columns. Unlike the sedate *Times*, it was also printing photographs and asserting that Cook's narrative was "being followed with an intensity of interest greater than was ever inspired by the most fascinating of romances." It was also pouring cold water on everything Peary had to say about him.

Adding to the momentous sense of occasion, Cook's homecoming coincided with one of the largest civic events in New York City history. The Hudson-Fulton Celebration had been organized to commemorate both the three hundredth anniversary of the European discovery of the Hudson River and the one hundredth anniversary of the launch of the first commercial paddle steamer, invented by Robert Fulton. Preparations for the two-week festival were nearly complete when the *Oscar II* arrived in New York Harbor; soon every hotel in town would be fully booked, and some of the anticipated 1.5 million visitors were already trickling in. The *Herald* in particular delighted in pointing out that America's North Pole discoverer was returning just as its finest city was gearing up to honor Henry Hudson, that leading luminary of the age of sail. It was an auspicious coincidence, one that helped to place Cook's achievement within a grand tradition of Western exploring.

It also brought more people out to celebrate him, and more boats. Warships, merchant steamers, and other large and splendid vessels in town for the impending ceremonies crowded the waters around Brooklyn and Manhattan when Cook arrived. A tugboat carrying Cook's wife, Marie, and their two daughters—Ruth, ten, and Helen, four—chugged out to fetch the explorer early on the morning of September 21. He was granted half an hour with his family before being waved through quarantine and picked up by the paddle steamer the *Grand Republic*, which carried officers from the Arctic Club of America and the borough president of Brooklyn. Also aboard were 424 men and women who'd paid $2.50 apiece for the privilege of personally greeting the returning hero. They were intent on getting their money's worth, for no sooner had Cook stepped off the gangway than he was surfing atop the crowd—smiling at first, and then pleading to be put down. So dense was the crush of humanity that the *Grand Republic* began listing on its forward port side; hands grasped at Cook as he regained his footing, and those that did not find his palm yanked at his sleeves and coattails. "He got several slaps on the back which only an Arctic explorer could stand, but he took it all good naturedly," the *Herald* reported.

Once some of the din had subsided, Cook distributed copies of a press statement to reporters. His prepared comments struck a familiar chord: "As said upon several occasions, all the charges, accusations, and expressions of disbelief are based upon entire ignorance of the supplementary data which I possess." Scientists around the world were impatient to see that data, a journalist pointed out. "They must wait, then," Cook replied. Such formalities had never been treated with great urgency in the past, he noted, and in any case the Danish authorities had all but declared themselves satisfied already:

> The Danish Government and the University of Copenhagen, as well as the Danish Geographical Society, have on their report taken over the virtual guarantee for the sincerity and authenticity of my records. They have stood up for them, so to speak. They do not ask me to furnish any further proof or evidence of any kind, but, in justice to Denmark, it is my intention to place the first completed record of my polar journey at the disposal of the University of Copenhagen.

Rather than challenge this debatable version of events, the reporters asked Cook what he made of Peary's latest attacks. He declined to take the bait. "I prefer for the present to think that the statements attributed to him have been incorrectly reported," he said.

The *Grand Republic* chugged up the west side of Manhattan and then back down again, around the Battery, and up the East River, to a cacophony of factory whistles and roaring crowds. Construction workers waved from the cables of the half-finished Williamsburg Bridge; factory workers waved from the windows of riverside sugar refineries. The *Herald* called it the noisiest welcome the city had given since Admiral Dewey's victorious return from Manila.

The throng cheering Cook at Brooklyn's South Fifth Street pier swept aside the seven-soldier guard that had been arranged for him like twigs in a flood. Luckily, the hundred or so policemen on hand were more effective and cleared the way to the automobile awaiting Cook and his family. Down Bedford Avenue they rolled, at the head of a three-hundred-vehicle motorcade, past a blur of waving American flags and blasts of brass-band music. A perfectly arranged row of schoolchildren lined up along the street at one point and shouted in unison, "Howdy, Dr. Cook!" *The World* noted that for all his smiling, Cook remained remarkably "unemotional" amid the celebrating: "The crowds roared and stamped, whistles blew and horns honked, and several times the doctor was almost swept off his feet, but he showed no sign of great joy or pride. Behind his dancing blue eyes of shallow depth there lies either wonderful power of self-control or an innate insensibility to the ordinary emotions."

On Bushwick Avenue, a triumphal arch had been erected outside his former residence, and four doves were released as the motorcade passed beneath it. From this garlanded makeshift monument hung an oversized portrait of Cook and a message that had been spelled out in foot-high letters: WE BELIEVE IN YOU. He was delivered to the Bushwick Club, which was no refuge; its doors were open to all comers. At four o'clock, when Cook begged the organizers to cut the reception short, the lines stretched for five blocks in either direction. As he and Marie dined inside the Bushwick Club with some two dozen supporters that evening, a group of singers materialized outside and serenaded him. Cook went onto the balcony, smiled, and bowed to the thousands gathered below. He decided against making a speech, *The Sun* noted, "as he realized that it was a hopeless task to try to talk to that crowd." Someone invited the singers—there were seven hundred of them—inside to meet Cook. Having shaken hands for nearly fifteen hours straight by this point, he kept his arms behind his back and simply nodded at them.

The Cooks spent the night at the Waldorf Astoria, where the Arctic Club of America had booked them a suite in preparation for a celebratory dinner there the next evening. The following afternoon, before the banquet, Cook met reporters in a second-floor parlor at the hotel. The press reports from Battle Harbour and Sydney had seeded a whole new crop of questions, all of which Cook handled with perfect composure. According to *The World*, "There was no hesitation at any time and the answer was always complete enough to satisfy the audience."

He positively declined to discuss the data he would submit to Copenhagen. How confident was he in his astronomical readings, someone asked, given that he had never been personally responsible for making these observations on past expeditions? "Dr. Cook smiled broadly at this shot, but answered without a change of tone," *The World* reported. "I shall have to let the scientific investigators of my observations determine that," he said. As for the tale that Etukishuk and Ahwelah had apparently told Henson, about never having traveled beyond sight of land, Cook appeared untroubled by it. He had instructed his companions not to discuss their polar journey with Peary's men, he explained, and they had accordingly lied about where they'd been. The truth would all come out in due time; Cook assured the newsmen that the two Inuit would come to New York and "answer all questions."

Pressed again about his proof, Cook stood up and left the room. Minutes later he returned, cradling a heavily worn 173-page diary. He would not permit this precious document to be copied or even handled, but the reporters could see with their own eyes that he had covered every centimeter of every page with penmanship so tiny that it required a magnifying glass to read. Cook explained that he'd been forced to conserve paper while in the Arctic and that he had two more full notebooks just like this one. The diaries contained a total of around 100,000 words, all of them written by candlelight during the winter he'd spent denned in on Devon Island. He'd shown the notebooks to several Danes in southern Greenland, but claimed that no one had asked to see them in Copenhagen. He predicted that it would take two months to collate this vast material and his astronomical observations for expert review.

The work could not really begin in earnest, Cook added, until Harry Whitney returned from Greenland with the rest of his notes and his instruments. What was it about Whitney, someone asked, that had led Cook to entrust him with such precious items? "That is something I cannot talk about," Cook said. What he did explain was that he'd ruined his best sleds farther north and believed that his equipment would be safer aboard the *Jeanie* than trundling along the soft spring ice of Melville Bay.

Presumably Whitney was making his way south aboard the *Jeanie* now. Because he was the only white man unaffiliated with either explorer to have spoken with both Cook and Peary in the Arctic, it was hoped that he would shed additional light on the polar dispute, and reporters at Battle Harbour had badgered Peary's men to share everything they knew about him. Borup had obliged, up to a point, recalling that he had seen Whitney shoot an arctic hare from four hundred feet away and describing him as "a mighty genial chap." The young millionaire had taken meals with Peary's men in the ship's mess during his week aboard the *Roosevelt* and talked mostly about hunting, Borup said; never once had he mentioned Cook. Peary, for his part, refused to discuss Whitney, claiming that he was irrelevant to the polar controversy.

On September 25, three days after Cook's interview at the Waldorf Astoria, Whitney was finally heard from. He wired the press from Indian Harbour to say that he had no reason to doubt what Cook had told him, and he also sent Cook a private telegram, the message of which soon came dramatically to light: Whitney had left Cook's instruments and records at Etah.

A *Herald* correspondent who happened to be traveling on the *Jeanie* cabled the full story from Indian Harbour. According to Whitney, Peary had told him "in a very emphatic way" that he was not to bring any of Cook's property onto the *Roosevelt*. Whitney, fearing he might have no other means of returning home that summer, had obligingly removed Cook's instruments, records, and damaged sled from his trunk, boxed them up, and cached them in a pile of rocks at Etah.

Several days later, Whitney defended his decision not to return for Cook's property after leaving the *Roosevelt*, as Peary claimed he easily could have done. Though the *Jeanie* had been just a day's voyage from Etah, Whitney now explained that the ship had been having engine problems, and there was the honest fact that he'd wanted to get home as soon as possible. "No one who has not spent a winter in the Arctic can realize the feeling when starting for the good old South and civilization. I had been there then for more than a year, and I did not want any more of it," he told the *Herald*. He also claimed to have been unaware of the significance of Cook's instruments, and had therefore simply planned to buy Cook new ones when he returned.

This latest example of Peary's intransigence was widely condemned. W. T. Stead wrote what many felt—"Peary's refusal to bring back Dr. Cook's instruments and observations reveals the heart of a churl and an undeveloped brain"—and Hubbard considered the decision so inflammatory that he told Peary to let him handle questions about it whenever reporters brought it up. But Peary's consignment of his trunk to the rocks at Etah appeared to be bad news for Cook, too. The day it was learned that Whitney was coming back empty-handed, half a dozen reporters flocked to the Waldorf Astoria. They were met there by Walter Lonsdale, a dapper young Englishman whom Cook had hired to be his personal secretary in Copenhagen on the recommendation of the American diplomat Maurice Egan. When Cook came down from his suite half an hour later, he "seemed to be considerably agitated," the *Times* reported. He admitted that Whitney's message from Battle Harbour disconcerted him and that it would be impossible for scientists to fully evaluate his navigational records without also examining the sextant, compass, and artificial horizon he'd used to make them. "To be perfectly frank, it is most desirable to have the instrumental corrections," Cook granted. But he assured the reporters that all was not lost. His instruments were sealed in a watertight case and could be retrieved the following year if necessary, and he possessed duplicates or originals of "all the essential records." Earlier, Cook had claimed that he'd told Whitney the box contained important proofs, but now he conceded that he might have been mistaken on that point. He declined to comment about Peary's actions until he'd learned more from Whitney.

The interview's most awkward moment came when Cook was asked to respond to something Lonsdale had said to the reporters before Cook had joined them: that it was possible, theoretically, for a knowledgeable person to fabricate data showing he'd been to the North Pole. Lonsdale's point was not that Cook would do such a thing, but that an explorer's overall trustworthiness mattered at least as much as his scientific proofs. "Something must be taken on faith," he'd insisted. When a journalist repeated this statement to Cook, he "looked more nervous than at any time since he landed last week," *The World* reported. *The World* had no stake in the dispute and appeared to be enjoying it more than the *Times* or the *Herald*. Here is how it described Cook's exchange with its reporter:

> "Wouldn't it be perfectly possible for a scientific man who has only got within a couple of hundred miles of the Pole to put down cer-

tain scientific figures which would indicate that he had finished the trip and reached the Pole, taking observations all the way? And would not these observations be hard to refute unless he made some flagrant error in his calculations?"

"I can't answer that," replied Dr. Cook, flushing and fidgeting on his feet. "My observations will be made public in due course and what they show will then be open to everybody."

"But isn't it a fact, doctor . . . that in the last analysis something will have to be taken on faith, as Mr. Lonsdale put it, and that it is impossible to prove to an absolute certainty, from mere records of observation, that you actually reached the Pole?"

The doctor swung on one foot, then on the other, biting his moustache and fingering his watch chain and replied after a moment's thought:

"I shall have to let the scientific men who examine my data answer that question. I cannot undertake to do so."

Asked if he would prefer the scientists to take him at his word, Cook smiled and insisted that he would not. "Not on faith, but on the proofs," he said.

# CHAPTER FORTY-TWO

While Cook faced questioning in New York, Peary was hurrahed at station stops between maritime Canada and southern Maine. Perhaps these northeastern crowds saw a bit of themselves in this "rugged, honest, blunt old Yankee," as one contemporary magazine described him, or perhaps they were simply honored to be on his itinerary. Whatever the case, they stood behind him, and thousands turned out to celebrate his arrival in Portland. It was a decent crowd by local standards, albeit modest compared with the one that had engulfed Cook in New York City.

In Portland, General Thomas Hubbard met Peary on the station platform, took a sheaf of documents from him, and promptly boarded a train for Bar Harbor. Several days later, Delt Edwards of the *Herald* discovered what the two men were up to: Hubbard was busy converting Peary's bundle of notes and figures into a public statement intended to systematically dismantle Cook's polar claim. Before releasing their itemized document to the press, both men shared it with Edwards, who was quietly sympathetic to their cause, in hopes of turning Cook's most powerful print advocate against him. On September 30, the *Herald* gladly previewed and denigrated their "defective indictment" all at once.

The first point raised against Cook consisted of the testimony that

Henson had apparently collected from the explorer's Inuit companions, details of which would be forthcoming, Peary and Hubbard wrote. The laundry list of charges (which became known as Peary's "Fourteen Points") also addressed supposed deficiencies in Cook's sleds, snowshoes, and scientific instruments and sought to justify Peary's controversial refusal to take Cook's property, including the American flag he claimed to have raised at the pole, aboard the *Roosevelt* at Etah:

> Tenth—That Dr. Cook's leaving of his records at Etah was a scheme on his part by which he could claim they were lost or destroyed and so could escape being forced to produce them to substantiate his claims.
>
> Eleventh—That no man who had carried the American flag to the Pole would leave such a slight and easily transportable article in the charge of a perfect stranger.

The *Herald* was unmoved by Peary's arguments. "The only thing he proves is that he really has no proof. He has merely stated the reasons why in his opinion Dr. Cook could not have reached the pole," it concluded. Most readers agreed with this assessment, including Cook skeptics like Louis Bernacchi. "Commander Peary's indictment is not incisive," Bernacchi wrote. "It says much that might be damaging to Dr. Cook, but not more than any other person who disliked the doctor might say."

Many of Peary's objections were undermined by his all-too-evident certainty that the only credible method of reaching the pole was his own. Cook hadn't used his sleds, his system, his instruments, or his route, and therefore could not possibly have succeeded. The one thing of Peary's that Cook *had* used were "his" Inuit, and for that Peary had essentially accused him of cheating. Peary's lifelong touchiness regarding rivals, his quickness to decry honest competition as unfair, was finally laid bare. The likability gap between him and Cook widened further.

According to the *Herald*, which prided itself on its navy connections, Peary had already "distinctly injured himself in the minds of officers of the naval service." Now the normally supportive Washington press turned against him, too. "Peary, in his effort to grab it all, is in danger of winning something very much like contempt of all fair-minded people," *The Washington Times* warned. *The Washington Post* defended Cook as "a man unused to cunning and indirection." Like editors nearly everywhere, except at *The New York Times*, its editors rejected the cynical suggestion that Cook's unopened trunk was part of a "scheme" to avoid having to prove his claim. Most Americans concluded that Peary had simply destroyed his rival's evidence.

Meanwhile, Cook remained a paragon of civility and decency. In a spirit of peacekeeping, he asked fellow speakers not to mention his antagonist by name when introducing him at dinners and waved off suggestions that he sue Peary for libel or for the alleged theft of his property at Anoritoq. The so-called polar controversy was a misnomer, the *Herald* argued: "As a matter of fact it takes two to make a controversy, and Mr. Peary in this instance has the field all to himself."

The editors and Arctic experts who criticized Peary did not go so far as to challenge his polar claim. Even the *Herald* merely kept pointing out that he, like Cook, would eventually have to furnish proofs. Among the public, though, disgust with Peary led to distrust, and the more Cook was attacked, the more credible his story became. "Strange to say, more people today believe Dr. Cook reached the North Pole because Peary says that he did not, than those who believe it on the strength of Dr. Cook's own assertion," noted Stead, who'd learned much about popular sentiment as a crusading newspaper editor in London. For a moment in early September, Americans had believed both men. By month's end, though, partisan feeling had risen to the point where most could no longer credit one claim without simultaneously rejecting the other. The results of a mail-in survey conducted by a Pittsburgh newspaper in late September pointedly suggested as much: 96 percent of the seventy-six thousand respondents believed Cook had been to the pole, while 76 percent believed that Peary hadn't.

Meanwhile, the idea that neither explorer was to be believed was considered beneath discussion. *The Sun* reported in October that the Tennyson Literary Club of Nutley, New Jersey, "discussed the polar controversy and concluded that both Cook and Peary are fakers and that neither had reached the pole." Clearly intended to be humorous, the six-line news item was headlined THAT SETTLES IT.

Did the opinion of the average New Jerseyite or Pennsylvanian really matter? *The New York Times* was at pains to remind its readers that it did not, and that the dispute would ultimately be resolved by highly trained scientists. For the moment, though, there was little for these impatient authorities to do but sit tight as an initial wave of public feeling became a tsunami. Would it grow powerful enough to swamp expert judgment? Maurice Egan, observing this American spectacle from Copenhagen, worried that it might. "I never before realized," he later wrote, "how firmly my own people believed that the most important question may be settled by the vote of a majority."

# CHAPTER FORTY-THREE

Peary had vowed to accept no exploring honors until his attainment of the pole had been certified by a "competent authority." Earlier, though, he had committed the *Roosevelt* to a boat parade in downstate New York as part of the Hudson-Fulton festivities. He decided to stick to this plan, in part because the pageant's organizers had assured Bridgman that the *Roosevelt* would be awarded its top prize if he did.

Peary could hardly have chosen a worse time to appear in public. On October 1, the *Herald* reported that it had scoured the nation's editorial columns in search of a defense of his latest actions and failed to find one. Early that same morning, Robert and Josephine Peary entered New York City by train unheralded. Only the Bridgmans and a handful of reporters came to Grand Central Station to greet them. The *Herald* sniped that the poor turnout was "entirely due to Mr. Peary's own unfortunate course of conduct."

South of Manhattan, at Sandy Hook, the *Roosevelt* was not looking its finest. Animal trophies that had not yet been delivered to the American Museum of Natural History had begun to smell, and the Greenland huskies that had howled in Battle Harbour two weeks earlier now languished in the mid-Atlantic heat. Captain Bartlett grumbled to reporters that he'd had no time to whip his ship into parading form. He also strained to clean up the mess created by his story of emotional distress at the 88th parallel. The skipper's tale had been widely held up as yet another example of Peary's heartless egotism—"as though Roosevelt had left the other intrepid Rough Riders at the foot of San Juan Hill," the editors of *Life* scoffed—and he had been trying to retract it ever since. "My whole idea was to help Commander Peary in finding the pole. . . . I was only the hired man in this, and as long as he was satisfied, it was none of my affair," he now told the *Herald*.

On October 1, the *Roosevelt* led an impressive naval column up the Hudson River from midtown Manhattan. Peary stood at the bridge, waving to spectators onshore and on nearby vessels. Not all of them waved back. "Occasionally a taunt or challenge would come over from some insulting, impertinent crowd of excursionists," Bridgman recalled. Peary ordered his seething men to say nothing in reply. "It does them more harm than it does us," he assured them. They grudgingly obeyed, but years later George Borup told a Peary confidant "that never in his life had he endured such an ordeal and that for Peary it must have been absolute hell."

Most of the other parading vessels eventually overtook the sluggish *Roosevelt*. Bartlett kept two crew members busy dipping its colors to every passing man-of-war. J. P. Morgan tipped his cap as his 304-foot superyacht, the *Corsair*, sped past. Around fifteen miles south of the rendezvous point at Newburgh, the *Roosevelt*'s steering gear broke. Realizing that it would not be repaired until the parade was over, Peary went ashore in a tugboat with Jo. They took an overnight train back to Maine without lingering in New York City.

Thomas Hubbard met Peary at the Portland station, where the two men paced the platform together for nearly an hour. The explorer pulled a thick white envelope from inside his coat and handed it to Hubbard, who departed for Bar Harbor. Approached by curious reporters, Peary said that his next moves were literally in the hands of the president of the Peary Arctic Club and that for the moment he had nothing more to say. He planned to spend October relaxing at his summer home in Casco Bay, on Eagle Island, and asked the press to respect his privacy.

PEARY HAD BOUGHT EAGLE ISLAND IN 1881 FOR $500 SAVED FROM HIS earnings as a young naval engineer. Situated off the coast of Harpswell, Maine, it was a seventeen-acre refuge of high cliffs and pocket beaches, of walking trails that wound through birch and spruce trees and pointed firs. "It seems as remote from the haunts of man as a virgin wood, and is full of ferns and wildflowers, and possesses springs," Helen Bridgman wrote. But on nights when the stormy Atlantic flung itself high up over the rocks, Eagle Island was not a place for the faint of heart. That was one of the things Peary liked about it. He had built a rustic cottage there only five years previously, and called Eagle Island his "Promised Land."

Peary gave the press and some of his private correspondents the impression that Eagle Island that fall was an oasis of loving calm. "The quiet, undisturbed time which I am now having is very pleasant to me," he wrote to *National Geographic*'s editor Gilbert Grosvenor in October. "It is particularly agreeable to have this opportunity after so many years of effort, of being with my wife and children in our little island home, with no thought of the future to disturb either of us, and with the feeling of intense satisfaction and content that results from having done the thing that one has started out to do, and has put one's whole life into."

In fact, Peary was following other newspapers closely and finding plenty in them to get upset about. He'd begun collecting Cook's *Herald* articles in a scrapbook, the better to locate and hammer away at flaws in his account. Peary also read that on October 5, George B. McClellan, mayor of New York City, had signed a proposal to award Cook the freedom of the city, a civic honor that had been extended to only three individuals before: the Revolutionary War hero the Marquis de Lafayette, the author Charles Dickens, and Prince Henry of Prussia. Cook, described in the official resolution drawn up by city aldermen as "the premier explorer of the twentieth century," would now be the first American to receive it. Peary worked furiously to pull the ceremonial carpet out from under him, communicating daily with Bridgman and Hubbard about press strategy, including how best to present the testimony of Etukishuk and Ahwelah.

He was convinced that his most formidable enemy at this point was the *Herald*. After the paper had roundly dismissed his "Fourteen Points," he'd written to remind Hubbard of the powerful entity they were up against: "We are now fighting not [Cook] alone but JGB [James Gordon Bennett] with all the influence and experience that that means." In early October, he drove the same point home again, this time with more urgency. "The Cook matter through the unscrupulous and persistent work of the 'Herald' has taken a deep hold on the general public. It must be stamped out in the same thorough and persistent manner," he told Hubbard.

Meanwhile, Hubbard also worked on getting Peary's claim validated. Any number of routes could be taken here, for the race to the North Pole was unlike other international sporting contests. It had no ultimate authority for bestowing laurels or adjudicating disputes; all it had was an international constellation of scientific and geographical bodies, some of them more rigorous than others and each with slightly different priorities and spheres of influence. Polar explorers typically submitted their scientific results to the government or society to which they answered. Cook answered to no one and had thus been free to repay Danish hospitality by promising the University of Copenhagen the first look at his proofs. Peary answered to the Peary Arctic Club, which lacked the scientific standing and impartiality for its judgment to carry weight. While Peary was parading up the Hudson, Hubbard therefore asked Ira Remsen, president of the National Academy of Sciences, to intervene.

Hubbard suggested that a panel of academy experts chosen by Remsen— or "other scientists impartially selected"—be assigned to examine both Cook's and Peary's data. Peary amended this proposal five days later, specifying that he would allow his proofs to be reviewed by American scientists only. Peary and Hubbard did not negotiate terms with this learned body on their own. They had help from the leaders of the American Geographical Society, the National Geographic Society, and the American Museum of Natural History, all of which had long been on good terms with Peary—especially the museum, where Morris Jesup's successor, the paleontologist Henry Fairfield Osborn, had recently approved a $40,000 purchase of the Cape York meteorites on loan from Peary. Though it was publicly unknown at the time, Osborn and the museum's director, Hermon Bumpus, were also members of the Peary Arctic Club.

Using these loyalists as intermediaries, Hubbard, the veteran businessman and lawyer, walked a fine line that was no doubt familiar to him. Without blatantly overstepping, he used the tools at his disposal to line up "impartially selected" arbiters who were likely to rule in his party's favor. Unfortunately for him, Cook refused to play along. Asked by a representative from the American Geographical Society to submit his records to the National Academy of Sciences alongside Peary's, he demurred, citing his prior commitment to the University of Copenhagen. Remsen, in turn, declined to create a panel for the purpose of examining Peary's records only. To do so, he explained to Hubbard, would imply that the National Academy of Sciences was taking sides. Two precious weeks were lost in this failed effort to settle the polar controversy promptly.

# CHAPTER FORTY-FOUR

With scientific authorities unwilling or unable to render judgment, the North Pole controversy spun further out of control, and a national triumph became a national embarrassment. Throughout September, the public overwhelmingly favored the genial Cook over the vindictive Peary. Opinions began to shift in October, once it became clear that Cook was getting rich from a story that remained unproven.

His friends had urged him to cash in on his success, on the grounds that there was no obvious reason not to. Cook's lone financial backer, John Bradley, had lauded his "good sporting performance" and asked no more of him. Cook had furthermore learned, upon returning to New York, that he and his wife were insolvent. The bank that held their savings had failed during the panic of 1907, forcing Marie to give up their house in Brooklyn and move in with friends and relatives. By the time Cook was fully apprised of his financial plight, he stood to net $30,000 from his popular *Herald* articles. But he later explained that he felt entitled to more than this, even if striking while the iron was hot meant postponing the submission of his records to Copenhagen. "My feeling at the time was that I was under no obligation to patrons, to the Government, to any society, or anyone, and that I had a right to deliver lectures at a time when public interest was keyed up, and to prepare my detailed reports at a time when I should have more leisure," he wrote.

His lecture tour kicked off at Carnegie Hall on September 27. Cook next spoke in Boston, where he asked Harry Whitney to come meet him. Whitney stayed home in Connecticut. After nearly a week of harassment from the press, the skilled young slayer of Arctic megafauna "palpably trembled at the mention of either Cook or Peary," Barton Currie of *The World* reported from New Haven. "If only something else will turn up that will make them forget me, I will be happy," Whitney told him. "I have been dragged into this thing by the neck. If anyone will show me a quick way out of it I will take it—provided that way does not lead north again."

By October 7, the day the twelfth and last installment of his polar narrative ran in the *Herald*, Cook had addressed full houses in New York, Boston, Philadelphia, Washington, Baltimore, and Pittsburgh, and was reported to be earning up to $10,000 for each appearance. In his next stop, St. Louis, he was mobbed by a crowd of fifteen thousand upon arrival. After St. Louis, he lectured in Chicago, where it was said that the city's Coliseum had quaked with that much cheering only twice before, during the Republican Party's nominations of Presidents Roosevelt and Taft.

Cook's lecture engagements, while popular, also began to generate stirrings of disapproval. He'd claimed that he needed two months to prepare his proofs for the University of Copenhagen. Rather than busying himself with that task, he appeared to be cashing in. Scientists noted that his polar claim hinged on his astronomical observations and other field notes and that there was no need to "prepare" these; either he had them or he didn't. Cook maintained that he should be allowed to present his records in the tidiest, most comprehensible form possible. After hearing Whitney's news, he'd also indicated that he might not submit his proofs until his instruments could be retrieved from Etah—which meant next summer at the earliest. Meanwhile, as the highbrow New York *Evening Post* pointed out, he profited from the "uncritical enthusiasm of the multitude."

As a cloud of impropriety gathered around Cook that October, both American polar claimants came under heavier criticism. Contrary to what the *Herald* had argued, their feud was in fact two-sided. Cook refrained from attacking Peary publicly, but his friends and allies didn't, and nor did they mince words. C. M. Norman-Hansen wrote in a widely reprinted letter to *Politiken* that Peary's boatswain, John Murphy, had treated Whitney "like a dog" at Anoritoq. In the *Herald*, the explorer Dillon Wallace blasted former friends of Cook's who had "tried to knife him in the back" on Peary's behalf—a veiled reference to Herbert Bridgman, among others.

The fur gloves were off now. Men who'd previously feuded only indirectly, or behind closed doors, were engaged in a verbal street brawl. "'Controversy' is altogether too dignified a term to describe the miserable war of words that now rages about the Pole. The situation is deplorable," *The Nation* commented. Adolphus Greely, who'd recently retired from the army to write full time on Arctic subjects, worried about the implications for America's next generation of explorers. "Questions of private profit and personal glory are distasteful, and, when complicated with accusations and countercharges, will bring exploration into disrepute. America wants the glory with a clean record," he wrote in *Munsey's*. The record was already so sullied that many were wondering what the point of all this pole seeking had been in the first place. "It is not a service to humanity, but a sportsman's stunt, that appeals nowadays chiefly to vanity. The only thing at the North Pole that anyone wants is newspaper headlines," the editors at *Life* concluded.

The headlines had come fast and furious from the beginning, thanks to the enormity of the news itself and the willingness of the *Times* and the *Herald* to spare no expense in delivering it to expectant readers. "It is doubtful if any other achievement of man was ever so rapidly, fully, and graphically described to an entire world," the monthly *American Review of Reviews* declared that October. But then the achievement had become engulfed in argument, releasing a flurry of unexpected contingencies and emotions. The story of the discovery of the North Pole cast a strange spell on sound and unsound minds alike. One evening in late September, a thirty-seven-year-old escapee from a mental asylum was arrested in Brooklyn. "He was standing in the middle of a crowd and was telling a thrilling, though disconnected, story of how he had reached the North Pole," *The World* reported.

Nearly every American, from the most celebrated to the most obscure, had an opinion on the subject. Mark Twain's take, to cite just one example, was that both Cook and Peary were telling the truth but that it was a shame they had to share the glory. "Well, it is a pity that *two* men did it," he wrote in an autobiographical manuscript that he might or might not have wanted published. "While it was the achievement of one man it placed him alongside of Columbus, away up in the very sky—apparently to remain there forever—discoverers whose feat could never be repeated, there being no more worlds to discover, & no more poles *worth* discovering. But now that honor is divided—well, the bulk of the value is gone." Twain, seventy-three and growing senile, would die the following April. His mutterings about polar glory were among the last things he ever wrote.

Many newspapers had fun with the polar controversy. Bennett's own *Evening Telegram* got in on the joke: "A fearful disease has broken out in the land called Cook-Peary-tonitis. . . . Are you afflicted?" A cartoon in *The New York Press* depicted the two explorers facing off at a game of cards, accompanied by the caption "Who's bluffing?" Similar comic illustrations appeared in newspapers nationwide, with Uncle Sam rendered as annoyed, or amused, or relieved that at least *someone* had planted the American flag up there. *The World* took special delight in the embarrassing (if lucrative) mess that the *Times* and the *Herald* had gotten themselves into, publishing a satirical full-page "exclusive" by a fictional explorer, Richard Mountjoy Gilfeather, who announced that he had in fact reached the pole before either Cook or Peary. Gilfeather claimed that his contractual agreement with the metropolitan section had prevented him from sharing news of his discovery earlier, and that he had subsisted on a diet of ice cream and pumpkin pie all the way to the pole and back. He assured readers that he would clear up the many outstanding questions about his journey in his forthcoming book—which would be available in three years.

Often, though, the subject was treated with dead seriousness. The national quarrel got so loud that the diplomat Maurice Egan could hear it from Copenhagen. "Homes were disrupted, we were informed, and hitherto affectionate members of families parted at least temporarily by the conflict," he recalled in his memoir. Twelve years later, one New York City journalist looking back on the polar controversy likened it to a great ideological schism. "In the promotion of domestic strife in every nation, in the setting of households against each other and bringing not peace, but a sword to every breakfast table, Cook and Peary did better than Lenin and Trotsky ever dreamed of doing," he wrote.

Clearly, America was arguing over something more significant than a "sportsman's stunt." Behind the gun smoke of the polar controversy lay a hidden landscape of political and cultural divisions, and Cook and Peary, stark in their differences, occupied opposite sides of this contested terrain. What registered to some as Peary's Yankee grit and self-discipline struck others as the ruthlessness of the corporate monopolist. Cook, on the other hand, was a resourceful child of immigrants, an underdog who had dared to challenge Peary's so-called Arctic Trust. This was one reason crowds went crazy for him, especially in rural areas and in cities along the Eastern Seaboard. Even in Massachusetts, smack in the center of New England, support for Peary dwindled the farther one got from Boston.

The polar feud would conform explicitly to party lines later, when it reached the halls of Congress, but even at this early stage signs of that partisan divide were plainly discernible. Like Peary himself, most of his top allies were Republicans, from Theodore Roosevelt to Thomas Hubbard on down. Meanwhile, support for Cook, a Democrat, was strongest in many of the same quarters that embraced William Jennings Bryan's Democratic populism. Based on the results of newspaper surveys conducted that fall, Cook would have routed Peary in a general election. The Peary camp was, in effect, an elite minority. It considered Cook a sneak and an impostor and viewed his popularity as just another sign of how easy it was to pull one over on the uneducated.

The proxy war between the *Times* and the *Herald* was being fought along strikingly similar lines. The *Times* deferred to institutional authority, as it nearly always had. The *Herald*, for all its insider accounts of yacht races and high society, and its selective opposition to the "new journalism" of Hearst and Pulitzer, nevertheless possessed a populist streak, and Bennett was rumored to be personally delighted that Cook had gotten the *Times*-reading intelligentsia so bent out of shape.

Both the *Times* and the *Herald* were eager to demonstrate that they had scored big with their polar exclusives. The *Herald* called Cook's initial scoop and serial account priceless, but also bragged that for $28,000 plus cable fees it had secured the deal of the century. The *Times* revealed, with pained discretion, that "the sum realized for the Peary dispatches has been greatly in excess of the amount advanced to Commander Peary." And yet these excess profits—which went to Peary, per his agreement with Ochs— amounted to less than they might have, given how many newspapers reprinted his dispatches verbatim without paying for them. Some editors lifted them wholesale, while others tore off pieces, usually on the dubious pretext that the material had been copied from the London *Times*, whose legal rights did not extend to America, and then cabled over. *The New York Times* considered such tactics piracy and sought to curtail them by filing a restraining order against *The Sun* and *The World*. Both papers swiftly moved to have the injunction lifted. It was hoped that the federal judge assigned to the case, Learned Hand, would help publishers to understand what constituted fair use of press materials. Some argued for the proprietary rights of the *Times*, while others claimed it was absurd for a single entity to "own" news of national significance. If the *Times* won, it was noted, Bennett would be able to turn around and sue Ochs for having reprinted portions of Cook's *Herald* account. Judge Hand, citing an oversight in Peary's written contract with the *Times*, dissolved the injunction on a technicality, leaving *The Sun* and *The World* unpunished and the definition of journalistic fair use unsettled. The *Times* declared victory anyway, on the grounds that the widespread reproduction of its scoop had advertised its superiority over the competition.

*The New York Herald* also trumpeted its ownership of Cook's account, only to have its copyrighted property appear the same day in American papers whose cable correspondents had plagiarized it from that morning's *Paris Herald*. Despite this shared headache, the *Times* and the *Herald* failed to find common cause. Bennett, offended by a warning from the *Times* not to infringe on its copyright, jeered his rival's legal maneuvering. His own paper's policy, he noted airily, had "never been to treat the products of its costly news gathering service as a miser treats his hoard." The

*Times* had merely lent Peary $4,000, Bennett scoffed, and assumed virtually no risk in the venture. This point was fair enough, but Bennett went further when he asserted that the deal "makes Shylock's bond seem quite moderate in comparison. . . . Apparently, in addition to being 'fit to print,' the news must also be cheap."

It was understood and even perhaps expected that the newspapers that had invested in Cook and Peary might have directly competing interests at stake, but the openness with which these interests were discussed, to say nothing of the occasional outburst of anti-Semitism, gave critics yet one more reason to shake their heads. As Shailer Mathews, dean of the University of Chicago Divinity School, wrote in the popular magazine *The World To-Day*, "The call of the North Pole to heroism has become a quarrel by wireless telegraph, a lawsuit over copyrights, and a canny thrift that would garner wealth from lectures and syndicated interviews. . . . The matter is something more than a squabble between two rivals. It is a distinct outraging of ideals." And by mid-October, it had only just begun.

# CHAPTER FORTY-FIVE

Peary had predicted that Cook's case would collapse by the end of September. But what *The World* called his "bombardment of facts" had failed even to make it wobble. Peary's next salvo would be the potentially damning testimony of Etukishuk and Ahwelah.

In August, both young men had provided a detailed oral account of their 1907–9 journey with "Daagtikoorsuaq" (Dr. Cook) to Matthew Henson, Donald MacMillan, and George Borup. They told Peary's men that they had accompanied Cook onto the sea ice north of Cape Thomas Hubbard and that after one "sleep"—that is, less than two days of travel—they had encountered a lead of open water and a patch of rough ice. Rather than attempt to surmount these obstacles, the small party had turned west, returned to Axel Heiberg Land, and retrieved some supplies from a cache they had left there. They had been gone so short a time, the Inuit said, that their food and stove fuel barely needed replenishing.

Asked to trace their polar route on a map, Etukishuk and Ahwelah indicated that they had retreated at a point between the 81st and the 82nd parallels. The rest of their travels with Cook that year had been to points south and west, they said, and while the journey ultimately nearly killed them, it did not take them beyond sight of land. Cook's *Herald* account had, of course, told a different story, of reaching the pole and then making a "disheartening" return across the ice on severely reduced rations of tea and pemmican. He had said that dwindling food supplies prevented him from exploring Bradley Land, a previously unknown land whose long coastline he had sighted between the 83rd and the 85th parallels. Cook had written that after "a struggle of 20 days through thick fog," the skies had finally cleared, making Axel Heiberg Land visible to the east.

From this point forward, Cook's story of where he'd been mostly matched the accounts of his companions. But if Etukishuk, Ahwelah, and Henson—the only one of Peary's men who spoke Inuktitut fluently— were to be believed, Cook had fabricated the two-month portion of the journey during which he claimed to have gone to the North Pole and back. Not only had he not been there; he had barely ventured onto the Arctic Ocean.

The Peary Arctic Club released this information for publication on October 13, along with details of how it had been collected. Peary's men, presumably with Henson translating, had spoken with the two Inuit separately at Etah, and their stories had matched. As Herbert Bridgman noted in a brief preface, Peary himself had been present for only a small portion of these exchanges with Etukishuk and Ahwelah, "a fact that obviates any possible claim that they were awed by him." According to Etukishuk's father, Panikpah, the accounts of both young men aligned with what his son had told him earlier that summer.

The Peary Arctic Club distributed this copyrighted statement and a map on which Etukishuk and Ahwelah had drawn the roughly circular route they had taken around Ellesmere Island and Axel Heiberg Land. Cook's alleged polar route, rendered in a dotted line for reference purposes, spiked up from this cluster of known lands like a tall and ghostly appendage. The statements of both Inuit were presented verbatim, with additional commentary (written by Bridgman, but generated by Peary) in which it was argued that Cook lacked enough food to have made a thousand-mile journey to the pole and back. Etukishuk and Ahwelah confirmed that they had killed no game, left no caches, and eaten none of their dogs while on the polar ice. Given that they had taken only two sleds, Peary concluded, these simple facts rendered Cook's attainment of the pole "a physical and mathematical impossibility." The statement was signed by Peary, Bartlett, MacMillan, Borup, and Henson.

Asked to address these revelations in Cleveland, the latest stop on his lecture tour, Cook smiled wearily. "It is the same old story," he told reporters. He said that Etukishuk and Ahwelah were merely upholding their vow not to tell Peary where they'd been and that the whole misunderstanding would be cleared up when the two of them were brought back for questioning. The *Herald* backed him up, dismissing the Peary Arctic Club's latest pseudo-legal effort to discredit him as a "lame indictment."

The *Times* published the signed Inuit statement and map in full, alongside expert commentary vouching for the significance of both. George Melville, the surviving hero of the *Jeannette* tragedy, noted that many nineteenth-century Arctic explorers considered Inuit maps "marvels in accuracy," and the geographer Cyrus Adams praised the "special cartographic gifts of these natives." But Adams also predicted that their testimony would not alter the outcome of the polar controversy—and he was right. It was widely assumed that Peary, who bragged frequently about his authority over "Arctic Highlanders" and had become an important provider of Western goods, had simply been told the story he wanted to hear. Henson was known and respected locally as his representative, and it was pointed out that having him speak with Etukishuk and Ahwelah instead of Peary would have made little difference.

By the time the Inuit testimony went to press, even Peary appeared to be less than confident that it would turn the tide. "If the statement published today by the Peary Arctic Club is not sufficient to prove that Dr. Cook did not reach the pole, more evidence will be forthcoming," he told reporters in Portland.

WHAT THIS EVIDENCE WAS HE WOULD NOT SAY. BUT *THE NEW YORK TIMES* had the inside track, because Peary had been keeping in regular touch with William Reick. In a letter that fall to Thomas Hubbard, he described Reick as "one of the best newspaper men in New York and my personal friend." His relationship with this managing partner of the *Times* was more confiding and collaborative than anyone outside Peary's very tight inner circle realized.

Reick had been actively involved in the paper's coverage of the polar controversy from the beginning, and his recent bad blood with Bennett gave him additional reason to want Cook and the *Herald* disgraced. At first, he had treated the North Pole story like any other urgent piece of breaking news. On the evening of September 6, 1909, when Peary's telegram from Indian Harbour arrived at the *Times* offices, Reick had "erupted into the room," the *Times* reporter Walter Scott Meriwether later recalled. Reick had ordered Meriwether—one of several former *Herald* staffers he'd poached for the *Times*—to board the next overnight train to Sydney. The reporter had set out at once, bringing little more than his notepad, the clothes on his back, and an envelope full of cash.

Meriwether had cooled his heels with the other journalists in Sydney while Peary and the *Roosevelt* remained at Battle Harbour. But when the press boat *Tyrian* headed north on September 12, he wasn't on it, because Reick had ordered him to stay behind and ensure that Peary's *Times* narrative was properly relayed to New York. Reick might have wished to avoid the fate of the *Herald*, whose original scoop from Lerwick had been marred by confusing transmission errors. The decision, which forced the *Times* to acquire news of Peary's latest movements from a third party, baffled Van Anda. "Van, who was a master of sarcasm, employed some of his best in authorizing this staff writer of The Times to buy from an outside newspaper the story of an expedition The Times had financed," Meriwether recalled. From a business perspective, though, it made sense. Peary's exclusive account of his polar journey was worth far more to the *Times* than anything he or his fellow travelers might have to say at Battle Harbour; the first installment had already run on its front page on September 10, and if Meriwether left Sydney, it would be harder to ensure that the rest of it made it over the wires on time and cleanly.

Peary's account raced by undersea cable to Sydney from Labrador and from there to New York City, where it was disseminated far and wide by the *Times*. Over three nights that September, no fewer than twenty of the paper's telegraph operators relayed the three-part series thousands of miles in all directions in order to fulfill contractual obligations to the London *Times*, holder of the story's European newspaper rights, and domestic syndication partners. A total of 350,000 words were accurately transmitted, in record time. According to *Editor & Publisher*, experienced hands were calling it "the greatest feat of its kind ever performed in the history of telegraphic communication."

Peary and Reick subsequently began communicating privately about how to dismantle Cook's polar claim. On September 26, after Cook had begun speaking with the press in New York, Reick received a confidential letter from Meriwether, who'd accompanied Peary to Maine. The letter contained a list of critical points for the *Times* to raise in editorials or interviews with Cook and others. These were not Meriwether's own ideas for how the *Times* should proceed; they were Peary's. "Cook is begging the question and sparring for time. If he has any observations, [these] could be submitted to any geographical or scientific society," Meriwether wrote to Reick. "Peary gave me this material to send you." A day later, when the news broke that Peary had made Harry Whitney leave Cook's records at Etah, Meriwether contacted Reick from Maine again, this time by telegram: "Peary asks me to say that you need have no uneasiness as to the final outcome that The Times will come out on top and that he may soon call upon you for advice." Over the copy of this telegram that is preserved in the New York Times Company archives, "Mr. Ochs" is handwritten in pencil, indicating that Ochs read it.

There is no evidence that Carr Van Anda corresponded with Peary, directly or otherwise, and he might well have disapproved of Reick's close dealings with him. Ochs later recalled that Van Anda "disliked and distrusted" Reick, in part because the longtime *Herald* man favored "sensational methods." Ochs also claimed that Reick was always "held in check" in this regard—a dubious assertion, given the events of later that fall. Whereas Reick appears to have been personally invested in the polar controversy, Van Anda was merely deeply interested. Cook's sensational tale of Arctic discovery stimulated both his skepticism and his nose for news. "He sensed the volcanic controversy it would start," the *Times* columnist and historian Meyer Berger later wrote, and his news pages both covered the hoopla surrounding Cook and attempted to cut through it. On September 22, 1909, for example, the story of the explorer's return to Brooklyn ran on the front page's coveted far-right column, under a mildly accusing headline: DR. COOK HOME; NO PROOFS YET.

Surveys conducted early that fall showed more than nine in ten Americans believing Cook, but the *Times* framed the disagreement differently. It noted that "the world is divided into two camps, one of which either does not yet believe, or altogether disbelieves, Cook's story; and in this camp it appears that the chief scientific authorities of this and other countries are found." In the presumably ignorant opinions of the other "camp" the *Times* put little stock. It was more interested in hearing from people like Harold Jacoby, a professor of astronomy at Columbia University. Following one of Cook's press conferences at the Waldorf Astoria, Professor Jacoby analyzed every answer that Cook had given to questions about his instruments and observations and concluded, in a bylined commentary for the *Times*, that no significant new technical information had come to light in the two weeks since Cook had left Copenhagen: "As the matter now stands, all the voluminous interviews and newspaper correspondences amount to Dr. Cook's bare word, no more, no less."

THE SAME WAS NOW BEING SAID OF COOK'S 1906 CONQUEST OF MOUNT McKinley. Although his account of that feat had been good enough for the National Geographic Society and the Explorers Club, many Alaskans and mountaineers had remained unconvinced. Professor Herschel Parker, the Columbia physicist who'd scouted possible summit routes with Cook earlier that summer, expressed doubts about the written descriptions and photographs of his claimed ascent. "If Dr. Cook has climbed Mt. McKinley then he has made a bad case of it, as the lawyers say," Parker told the *Times* on September 9, 1909.

With the polar controversy making national headlines, Bridgman began hearing from strangers claiming to have evidence that Cook had faked the climb. The most authoritative of these sources was a glaciologist and Cornell geology professor named Ralph Tarr who had previously defended

Cook's claim. He had then spoken with climbers familiar with his purported summit route who "were absolutely confident in their assertions that it was a physical impossibility to climb the mountain in the brief period of time claimed," Tarr reported. The photograph Cook claimed to have taken at the summit "could easily have been taken almost anywhere above snow line," Tarr added, and Ed Barrill, Cook's lone companion, had subsequently "admitted to his friends that they never got up above 5,000 feet and . . . [now] jokes about the way in which the public has been fooled."

Bridgman arranged, through Reick—and without Tarr's permission—for this private letter to be printed in *The New York Times* on September 29. The fallout was immediate. Later that day, the Explorers Club's board of directors voted 5–3 to investigate Cook's McKinley claim. Already in turmoil over the polar controversy, the club was at pains to explain that it was not taking sides but simply defending the reputation of its former president. Cook, lecturing in Philadelphia, assured reporters that his proofs were safely tucked away in storage and suggested that doubters consult *To the Top of the Continent*, his book about the McKinley expedition. He also said that he would try to confer with Barrill about the matter in St. Louis.

But Barrill did not go to St. Louis. On October 14, the day after Etukishuk and Ahwelah's testimony appeared in the press, the *Times* reported that he was on his way from Montana to New York. The question of whether he was coming to support or challenge Cook—who was also en route to New York, to appear before the Explorers Club's committee—was answered later that day, when Hubbard's *Globe and Commercial Advertiser* revealed that Barrill had formally denounced him. In an affidavit signed earlier that month in Seattle, Cook's former guide now swore that they had gone barely a third of the way up the mountain in 1906, that the summit had been fourteen miles away as the crow flies when they turned back, and that the widely published summit photo was a fake. Barrill solemnly affirmed that Cook had asked him to "doctor his diary so as to make it appear therein that they had actually gone up the whole 20,390 feet of the mountain, and that the picture of the small peak was used because it looked just the same as the top of Mount McKinley as they saw it in the dim distance." Three other members of the expedition, including the lead horse packer, Fred Printz, swore that Barrill had previously discussed the hoax with them. The sensational *Globe* scoop covered almost three pages. Accompanying it were halftone reproductions of pages from Barrill's diary, showing pencil smudges where key dates and elevation figures had allegedly been falsified at Cook's instruction.

Cook was shown a copy of these explosive charges in Atlantic City, where he was speaking at a convention of the National Hardware Men's Association while on his way back to New York. He skimmed the *Globe* article twice in front of expectant reporters, then declared that he'd never once told Barrill to alter his diary, or even known that he'd kept one. Cook seemed more confused than angry about Barrill's statements. "He is a good fellow, not an educated man, but I always found him straight and I haven't the slightest idea why he should say these things," he said. "I cannot but think that undue influence of some kind must have been brought to bear on him." Barrill was unavailable for comment. Hubbard told reporters that he had met with him in New York and then turned him over to officers of the Explorers Club, who refused to reveal his whereabouts.

The *Times* joined newspapers nationwide in splashing the news of Barrill's disavowal on its front page. "It is most unfortunate for the reputation of Dr. Cook as an explorer that the men who accompanied him in the two great achievements of his life should testify against him," it noted. Barrill's motives appeared to be less than pure. He and Printz had both claimed that Cook still owed them back pay, and might therefore have had an ax to grind. But it was also suggested, in *The Sun* and elsewhere, that their desire to recoup what was owed them was the only thing that had prevented them from exposing Cook earlier. Barrill now admitted to having lied about McKinley, partly in order to ensure that Cook earned enough money from the effort to pay him his full guiding fee. As the *Times* acknowledged, if Barrill "could be induced by a reward to give false witness" once already, he could just as easily have been bribed to lie again. The *Herald* accused Peary's cronies of having done just that, in a special report from Montana in which Printz revealed that he and Barrill had been approached in Seattle several weeks earlier and that "every inducement has been offered to us to swear to something which is far from the truth." Printz declined to elaborate.

Hubbard admitted that he'd asked General James Ashton, a lawyer in Tacoma, Washington, to secure an affidavit from Barrill, but insisted that Cook's guide had not been paid to cooperate. "No money was given to him for his signature," Hubbard told the *Herald*. This denial was not as categorical as it might have seemed, for it left Hubbard room to argue, if pressed, that he had simply paid Barrill and Printz whatever they claimed to have been owed by Cook, rather than explicitly compensating them for their testimony. Records that were not public at the time show that Hubbard paid Ashton $5,000 on October 1, the same day that Ashton secured the commitment of Printz and Barrill and one day after he'd informed Hubbard by telegram of "parties increasing claims."

Barrill's affidavit, which Hubbard had asked Ashton to carry personally to New York, was dated October 4. Peary had hoped for the scoop to run on October 11, a Monday—usually a slow news day—in hopes of maximizing its impact. But Reick urged the Peary Arctic Club to wait until later in the week, because he wanted the story about Barrill's affidavit to run on the very day that Cook was to be awarded the freedom of the city. Maybe, Reick told Hubbard, the revelations would cause New York City's aldermen to rescind the honor. The *Times* urged them to do just that in an October 15 editorial, arguing that "no rightful interest would be prejudiced by deferring the proposed ceremony." The aldermen proceeded anyway.

A day later, the *Times* reprinted the contents of Barrill's semifictional diary extracts at length. Though it had, through Reick, coordinated its pro-Peary efforts with those of the smaller *Globe* to an unusual degree, the two papers framed Barrill's revelations somewhat differently. The *Globe* asserted that the "similarities between [Cook's] Mount McKinley hoax and the north pole hoax are readily discernible." The *Times*, careful as usual, made no such leap in logic. It did, however, reprint an editorial from the *Evening Post* arguing that Barrill's confession "radically alters the position in which Cook stands as regards his claim to the discovery of the north pole."

Delighted that Cook's credibility finally appeared to be cracking, Peary commended Reick for his effective use of Hubbard's investigative work. "Congratulations to you and the Times. Trust this affair may finish your yellow neighbor," he wrote from Maine. He was referring, of course, to the *Herald*, which was alluding darkly to the "large sums of money" that had been used to secure Barrill's signature and commending Cook for his recent decision to organize an expedition to retrieve the records he claimed to have left atop McKinley. Cook was saying that he would enlist allies and critics alike for the climb, and to that end had asked both the polar explorer Anthony Fiala, one of his staunchest supporters, and the skeptical Herschel Parker to accompany him to Alaska in the spring. The *Herald* considered this announcement a sure sign that Cook "wants the truth established."

The Explorers Club wanted that as well. Members of the committee it had assigned to investigate Cook's McKinley claim had interviewed Barrill several days earlier, and he had since left New York City. On October 17, the committee met with Cook at the Explorers Club's midtown Manhattan suite. He seemed warier than usual, attendees reported, and arrived in the company of a bespectacled lawyer named Henry Wellington Wack. The committee largely comprised sympathizers, including Anthony Fiala and others who'd defended Cook publicly; even Parker, who was there for observational purposes only, warmly shook the explorer's hand. The friendly atmosphere appeared to put Cook at ease. Even so, he left most of the talking to Wack and rejected the notion that he should issue an immediate and definitive statement concerning his McKinley proofs. The parties reached an agreement whereby Cook would deliver his original photographs and diary from the climb within a month, once he'd completed the rest of his western speaking engagements. Though he'd recently decided to cut short his lecture tour, Cook explained that he was contractually bound to complete six more talks. Before Cook left, Fiala and Parker both informed him that they would be unable to join his planned McKinley

expedition—Fiala because he lacked the requisite mountaineering experience, Parker because he had already committed to a separate attempt to
climb it that summer.

Cook spent the afternoon catching up on sleep at the Waldorf Astoria.
That evening, he boarded a train for Toledo, the next stop on his lecture
tour.

# CHAPTER FORTY-SIX

It was at this point, when Cook's two greatest exploring feats had been discredited by all eyewitnesses and even supporters were demanding answers, that Knud Rasmussen threw him a lifeline. It was published in the *Times*, of all places, because the celebrated Danish-Inuit explorer had insisted that his expression of "unreserved admiration for Dr. Cook" appear in the very paper that was working hardest to destroy it.

Rasmussen maintained that although "absolute proof" would be impossible to come by, the stories circulating among native communities of northern Greenland confirmed that Cook had reached the pole. He also vouched for the abundance of game along Cook's overland route, the quality of his expedition outfit, and other corroborating evidence. "No one in the world can name him as a swindler," Rasmussen wrote. At the very least, he added, the man who'd somehow endured a whole winter at Cape Sparbo "certainly deserves to have been first at the pole."

Cook was by now resorting to a different set of survival skills from those he'd used in the Arctic. He'd hired a Montana lawyer, General E. D. Weed, to procure sworn statements to the effect that Barrill had been paid to lie about their McKinley climb. The *Herald* printed second-hand reports from Montana that ran contrary to Barrill and Printz's testimony, while the *Times* asserted that the main takeaway from Weed's efforts was that "Dr. Cook has money now to fight for his reputation."

Cook's revised plan had been to return to New York City after lecturing in Minneapolis on October 25. Now he changed course again and arrived in Missoula, Montana, on October 27, after receiving rousing welcomes at Butte and other western station stops along the way. Press reports had indicated that Cook would publicly address the McKinley controversy during a free lecture in Barrill's nearby hometown of Hamilton, Montana. The evening of October 28, every seat inside Lucas Opera House was filled. Among the expectant crowd were the U.S. senator Joseph M. Dixon and the mayor of Hamilton, F. H. Drinkenberg.

Cook began by telling the tale of his polar journey, which was interrupted by regular bursts of applause. Afterward, he announced from the stage that he'd come to southwestern Montana not to seek legal retribution, as some had suggested, but "to ask for a fair deal." He'd been subjected to "bitter attacks" after his discovery of the North Pole, he said, and then worse:

> When this warfare failed, the enemy began this flank movement on the climb of Mount McKinley: men with money to burn in the flame of infamy entered the arena. Men of this community whom I had previously believed honest [that is, Barrill and Printz] fell as victims. Their statements were absolutely untrue. Still, I nurse no spirit of revenge or malice against these misguided men. My counsel, however, has been instructed to continue the investigation until we catch the guilty money givers higher up.

Unknown to Cook, Barrill and Printz were in the audience. A man claiming to be their lawyer now stood and asked that his clients be allowed to respond to Cook's charge of bribery. To nearly everyone's surprise, Cook rejected this proposal. If Barrill and Printz wished to address the audience, he said, they should book the hall for a later date. "This is not a tribunal and I am not on trial; therefore I decline to enter into any controversy over the matter. I have had my say tonight and you can have tomorrow night to say all that you please at that time. I, however, am done," he announced.

Howls of outrage followed Cook as he left the stage. But the theater lacked a rear exit, and so he remained in the wings rather than attempt to push his way through the hostile crowd. Mayor Drinkenberg and Senator Dixon both went backstage to speak with Cook, but failed to coax him out. In his absence, a local newspaper editor moved that a resolution be passed, on behalf of the state of Montana, condemning Cook and affirming the assembled crowd's faith in Printz and Barrill. Not everyone agreed to this, and an argument broke out, until Senator Dixon calmed the room and urged Barrill and Printz to stand and identify themselves. Barrill, mumbling, repeated the substance of his affidavit and gave the names of several local men he claimed to have confessed the McKinley hoax to back in 1906. More arguments ensued. An attorney in the audience, explaining that he was in town from San Francisco, volunteered to represent Cook in whatever sort of impromptu trial was about to be held. This brought a semblance of balance to the proceedings.

After nearly half an hour, Cook was persuaded to come onstage. A tense exchange between him and Barrill went nowhere, with each man essentially calling the other a liar. A call was then made for Cook to swear in writing that he had summited Mount McKinley on September 16, 1906. A pen and paper were brought out, and Cook signed a statement to that effect. "I do not care to stay any longer," he said, to more hoots and catcalls. "If it were me and my reputation was at stake, I would stay here until morning," Senator Dixon retorted. Cook stayed. Dixon and the explorer's self-appointed lawyer then conducted cross-examinations of Barrill, Printz, and Cook. Accusations and denials regarding purported bribes and the status of money owed dominated the back-and-forth. Barrill claimed that Cook had sent him $200 in cash "just the other day," with instructions to meet him in New York, and then failed to follow up. Printz denied an Associated Press report that he had offered to disavow Barrill's testimony for $350. According to some newspaper accounts of this exchange, Cook was sweating visibly and looked "the picture of dejectment" when it became clear that his accusers would have their say. But a reporter from a Helena newspaper claimed that afterward Cook "did not appear in the least downhearted or grieved over what had happened."

By the time the gathering broke up after midnight, around one-third of the original audience remained. One of the last acts of these stalwarts was to vote in favor of a resolution affirming the state of Montana's faith in Printz and Barrill. According to the *Times*, which reported on the boisterous meeting more thoroughly than many of the local papers did, the measure passed by a "large majority." Whether it would lead to anything was another matter. For all the lawyers in the audience that night, there had been no notary present, and therefore the McKinley statement that Cook had signed had no legal weight.

Cook was cheered, not heckled, during the next two days he spent touring Montana. In Helena, the capital, the local Civic Club pointedly passed its own pro-Cook resolution, affirming its "confidence in him and the results of his work." From there Cook went to New York, with the stated intention of preparing his proofs for Copenhagen.

# CHAPTER FORTY-SEVEN

Peary's allies welcomed the news of the showdown in Hamilton. "I should say that Barrill got considerably the better of Dr. Cook," Hubbard told reporters. Wack, Cook's lawyer, admitted that the trip to Montana had been a mistake. The *Herald* put more of a pro-Cook spin on the incident, emphasizing that the resolution passed inside the Lucas Opera House had stopped short of condemning him, but had nothing to say about it editorially.

Bennett's paper had by this point stopped defending Cook at every turn. Peary had noticed this apparent dip in interest, but didn't necessarily find it encouraging. Maybe the *Herald* was just lying low "while Bennett is fixing matters in Copenhagen, with the result that a favorable verdict by the Copenhagen organization will be sprung on the public unexpectedly," he wrote to Reick. Peary seemed to believe that the *Herald*'s owner was capable of anything. When Bennett had come to New York earlier that month, for the first time in two years, Peary had taken it to mean that Bennett would now "handle the Cook campaign at short range," and even when Bennett returned to Europe at the end of October, apparently having done no such thing, Peary kept worrying. He wrote to Bridgman, "Is it possible that Bennett is carrying with him the Cook manufactured observations?" He suggested to Reick that the *Times* investigate.

Peary's own data was now spoken for. Earlier that month, he'd committed his proofs to the National Geographic Society, which had offered to examine them after the National Academy of Sciences stepped aside. Though the society had grown in stature and respectability since its founding in 1888, it lacked the national academy's reputation for scientific rigor—and its impartiality. Unlike the national academy, it had enjoyed a mutually beneficial relationship with Peary for two decades. It had even contributed $1,000 to the very expedition whose results it would now be judging. And these were just the known facts. The editor of its popular monthly magazine, Gilbert Grosvenor, was secretly treating the National Geographic Society's certification of Peary's proofs as a foregone conclusion. In the same telegram, dated October 12, Grosvenor invited Peary both to submit his polar records and to select a date for his forthcoming address to the society in Washington, at which he promised the explorer "a tremendous welcome." None of Peary's evidence had been delivered to the society at this point, let alone evaluated, and the brazen impropriety of Grosvenor's gesture caught even him off guard. "Pardon inadvertence. Was under impression everything off under existing circumstances," Peary wrote back. After consulting with Hubbard, he chose November 12 as his lecture date.

The National Geographic Society's Board of Managers delegated the examination of Peary's proofs to an expert subcommittee. It consisted of three men: Henry Gannett, a veteran U.S. Geological Survey geographer; Dr. Otto H. Tittmann, superintendent of the U.S. Coast and Geodetic Survey; and Rear Admiral Colby M. Chester, an accomplished navigator and former superintendent of the U.S. Naval Observatory. These were distinguished and qualified individuals; they were also known Peary supporters. All three had been on the dinner committee for the 1906 gala at which Peary had been awarded the society's inaugural Hubbard Medal, and all three had served on the committee that approved the society's $1,000 grant to his 1908–9 expedition.

Peary sent these friendly judges his records around a week later, in the care of a Portland lawyer. Peary himself arrived in Washington on November 1—just as Cook was returning to New York from Montana—with additional written materials and a trunk containing his navigational instruments, and met with his examiners that afternoon at Admiral Chester's home in Washington. They did not formally deliver their report until two days later, but the press learned what was in it almost immediately: the committee believed that Peary had reached the pole. Finding no reason to disagree with its appointed experts, the National Geographic Society voted on November 3 to award Peary its gold medal.

Peary, declaring himself "extremely gratified" by this outcome, sold his magazine rights to *Hampton's* for $40,000 a day later and signed a lucrative book contract with the publisher Frederick Stokes shortly afterward. Having eschewed all honors and invitations until this point, he began filling his calendar with gala receptions and paid lectures, for which he charged a minimum of $1,000 apiece. On November 10, he was honored at an eighty-person dinner hosted by the Peary Arctic Club in New York City; the attendees included Adolph Ochs, who kept one of the eleven-course dinner menus as a souvenir. The next evening, the editors of *The New York Times* celebrated Peary's feat with a dinner at the Times Building at which walrus, narwhal, and "mignon de musk ox" were served. And on November 12, in Washington, Peary delivered a slideshow lecture to some fifteen hundred members of the National Geographic Society and their distinguished guests, including the British, German, French, and Austrian ambassadors.

Cook's claim to priority hung over these first-class festivities like an unmentionable odor, and his name went unsaid during the many toasts and speeches. But he could not simply be shrugged off, for as long as he withheld his evidence, he left the exploring world—and the rest of the world—in awkward limbo. The society had held off on having its gold medal for Peary struck until the exact language to be engraved on it could be determined: Was it honoring the discoverer of the pole, or merely someone who'd been there? As the *Times* pointed out, the distinction was important. "The talk of 'glory enough for two' is utter nonsense, since the glory happens to be of a kind that cannot be shared. Only one man can do anything first; to equal him afterward is an achievement, but it is not that achievement, and such glory as it confers, if any, is of a wholly different sort," it noted.

The National Geographic Society had tried to get a look at Cook's proofs once already, in mid-October, but the University of Copenhagen had refused to waive its claim to first inspection. Now that Peary's polar claim had been validated, the society tried again. Its president, Willis Moore, asked that the same subcommittee that had decided in Peary's favor be allowed to participate in the Danish review of Cook's data. The University of Copenhagen retorted by cable that it was "quite competent to undertake the examination alone." The *Times* later learned that the Danes were not necessarily against letting an American representative join the effort, but simply considered the National Geographic Society to have "no scientific standing whatsoever," as the paper's Copenhagen correspondent put it.

Following this second Danish rejection, Moore strode into the State Department with several of his National Geographic Society colleagues on November 5. A *Herald* reporter who happened to be there recognized one of Moore's companions and addressed him by name, but "the scientist promptly denied his identity and appeared annoyed at being recognized," the paper reported the next day. The society's secretive delegation met with the assistant secretary of state in hopes of using diplomatic channels to gain access to Cook's records, but got nowhere with this request. The U.S. government did not want to be involved.

The National Geographic Society formally resolved to investigate Cook's claim with or without Danish cooperation. Exactly how it would go about this was unclear, and its open-mindedness was called into question yet again when Admiral Chester, a member of the subcommittee that had decided in Peary's favor, began making it known in lectures and interviews that he considered Cook a deliberate faker who'd never been within five hundred miles of the pole. Chester, a seasoned navigator, had arrived at this conclusion after checking details of Cook's *Herald* account against astronomical data published in the *Nautical Almanac* and elsewhere. In addition, as he explained to the *Times*, some of Cook's public statements about his purported McKinley climb contradicted what the explorer himself had told Chester in 1906. Carr Van Anda put Chester's statements on the front page of the *Times*.

Cook was unavailable for comment. After two months of having the press track his every move, he had managed to disappear.

# CHAPTER FORTY-EIGHT

Henry Wellington Wack would not reveal his client's whereabouts. "He's gone out of town, into retirement, so he can finish the work on his proofs. I advised him to do it. Why, the man has been bothered to death," he told reporters.

Cook had last been seen checking out of the Waldorf Astoria on November 6. Two days later, from an undisclosed location, he issued a press statement concerning his polar proofs. He would be sending them to Copenhagen on November 25, he announced, in the care of his secretary, Walter Lonsdale. Cook did not intend to appear before the Danish panel in person and was therefore busy preparing an explanatory document that was intended to satisfy all "such questions as may arise upon the original record of my observations." The fact that his instruments were cached at Etah, he added, had made the work considerably more difficult.

Peary had learned by now to keep his opinions about Cook to himself, for anything critical he said would be dismissed as "simply a continuance of the jealous blackguard abusing a perfect gentleman," as he sarcastically complained to Bridgman. Privately, though, he railed against Cook as a "national disgrace." William Reick was one of the confidants to whom Peary vented his emotions freely. Peary wrote to his friend at the *Times* that

Cook was "morally a thief, financially a swindler, morally and physically a coward, and since his signing of the affidavit in Montana, a perjurer." Cook had, incidentally, disappeared without delivering his promised McKinley proofs to the Explorers Club, as a result of which Herschel Parker now declared his purported 1906 climb to have been a hoax.

Meanwhile, Peary continued to try to undermine Cook's polar claim and dismissed the *Herald* and its "senile expatriate" owner as a lost cause. It looked in any case as though Cook's ultimate fate would be decided in Denmark. But the testimonies of Etukishuk, Ahwelah, and Ed Barrill seemed to barely register with the Danish press, and the doubts of more educated commentators like Professor Parker hadn't caused much of a ripple, either. Peary saw this as proof that the Danish public was biased against him and that the University of Copenhagen's experts might be, too.

In late November, he and Hubbard discussed how they might get all the latest doubts about Cook to take root in Copenhagen. Hubbard noted that anyone sent abroad on behalf of the Peary Arctic Club would probably be written off as a partisan agent. "If, however, Mr. Reick, through the medium of the Times, or [some] other newspaper, can have the Copenhagen papers publish what he submits, the information would get before the public in Denmark through channels that could not well be criticized," he suggested. There was good reason to believe that Reick would be amenable. His friendship with Peary had, if anything, solidified during the polar controversy. They had been corresponding with each other at least once a week and had met several times that fall in New York City, including at least once for dinner with their wives. And of course the *Times* had already made ample use of the materials that Peary, Hubbard, and Bridgman had sent it through Reick.

On November 27, Peary sent Reick a new idea, one that was sure to get the attention of the Danish authorities if it succeeded. It involved using the editorial clout of the *Times* to pressure the State Department to take "official cognizance" of the fact that Minister Maurice Egan had acted inappropriately in September. By actively and publicly aiding Cook, Peary suggested, couldn't it be argued that the U.S. minister in Copenhagen had lent "the moral support . . . of the [U.S.] Government to what everyone now knows is an infernal fraud and imposture, and which is showing up dirtier and more contemptible with every passing day"?

Rather than push for this unlikely course of action, though, the *Times* did something that was probably more helpful to Peary's cause. It published a front-page comparison of the competing American polar claims by the American Arctic explorer Walter Wellman. In a lucidly argued five-column bylined essay, Wellman declared Peary's to be credible and his narrative "consistent in every particular." He also concluded, "with keenest regret," that Cook had intentionally set out to deceive the public. What had convinced him most of all, Wellman wrote, was Cook's failure to promptly produce his diaries "in their original condition, unedited, untouched."

Wellman stressed that no useful purpose was served by Cook's retention of his records, and compared him, unflatteringly, to a bank cashier who'd taken the company ledgers home "upon the pretext that they needed revision and preparation before being submitted" to his managers. Every day Cook's "alleged proofs" remained in the explorer's possession, Wellman argued, their value as evidence diminished. This was a point that Peary had first urged the *Times* to push two months earlier. Wellman's article emphasized just how closely Cook's submissions needed to be examined. It also served as a tacit reminder to the University of Copenhagen that if it found in Cook's favor, it would be in disagreement with a growing cohort of the American exploring establishment.

WHEN WALTER LONSDALE DEPARTED FOR COPENHAGEN ON NOVEMBER 25, it was initially reported that he had brought Cook's original data with him. Later that day, however, Henry Wellington Wack told the press that the large portfolio Cook's secretary had taken aboard the steamer *United States* was in fact a decoy.

Wack said that he and Cook had been credibly informed that a secret plot was afoot to steal the explorer's records and that as a result they had sent the *actual* originals abroad several days earlier. These precious documents were currently mid-ocean, Wack announced, in the care of a trusted courier, and Cook's enemies would be disappointed if they tried to purloin anything from Lonsdale—as he was sure they would. "I am convinced that an effort will be made to rob him of the [decoy] package which he has in his possession before the *United States* reaches the other side," Wack said. The would-be thieves, he added, would probably attempt to drug Lonsdale's champagne.

Now that Cook had not been seen or heard from in several days, anyone even remotely connected to him was asked to speculate on his whereabouts. Cook's mental state had become a subject of intense press interest, with some of his friends claiming that the strain of recent weeks had caused him to undergo a nervous breakdown. They said that he had been working nearly around the clock to prepare his proofs—at the Hotel Gramatan in Bronxville, fifteen miles north of New York City, it was now known—and sleeping poorly. The pressure of meeting his self-imposed Copenhagen deadline, combined with Admiral Chester's disparaging public comments, had purportedly put him over the edge. "The man must have quiet and rest," Wack pleaded. He also asserted that private detectives had been tailing Cook around New York City and at the Gramatan, adding to the explorer's anxieties.

The news of Cook's "nervous collapse" made him a front-page subject in the *Herald* for the first time in weeks. Its reporting was sympathetic and quoted friends who claimed to have seen the explorer looking "haggard and ten years older than when he arrived from the Arctic regions in September." The rest of the reputable New York City press approached the "dastardly anti-Cook plot," as *The Sun* called it, with heavy skepticism.

All the papers were eager to find out where the explorer was, though, and not too picky about which leads they ran with. Cook's brother, William, said that he was still in or around New York City. Others said that he was in Copenhagen, or Philadelphia, or Brooklyn. According to the *Evening Post*, he'd been spotted on Flatbush Avenue with Marie, going "to look at furniture in storage." Wack claimed that Cook had sailed for Italy, where he intended to write a book while awaiting the University of Copenhagen's verdict. Wack revised this statement hours later, after being told by John Bradley that Cook was in fact en route to Havana. The press quickly disproved that theory, though, causing Bradley to tell the Associated Press that he was "sore" at Cook for keeping him in the dark about his movements and "heartily sick of all this mystery."

It was becoming less clear by the day that Wack had any idea what he was talking about. He had also blamed Cook's reported physical decline on indigestion, on account of all the banquet food he'd been eating. The only two people Cook seemed to be actually confiding in were his wife, Marie, and his friend Charles Wake, a manager at the Equitable Life Assurance Society and fellow Arctic enthusiast. But Marie could not be found, and Wake declined to comment on Cook's whereabouts. Human imagination quickly filled the information void. The superintendent of a sanitarium in southern Maine gulled *The World* and the *Times* into printing stories that Cook was recuperating at his fine establishment. The proprietor of a similar resort in White Plains, New York, boasted that Cook was in his care. "Well, well. . . . It begins to look as if everybody was getting a little advertising out of this affair," Bradley deadpanned to the *Times*.

Only months later did a credible account of Cook's movements during late November and early December 1909 finally appear—in a travel magazine, of all places. The author of the account, his old secretary Walter Lonsdale, asserted that Cook had accompanied him from the Hotel Gramatan to New York City on November 24. Once in the city, Cook had cut his hair, shaved his mustache, donned a black slouch hat, applied "some black paste for touching up the face," and boarded a train for Toronto at Penn Station. Having made it to Canada unrecognized, Cook had then asked Marie to collect his original diaries from Charles Wake, who'd held on to them for safekeeping, and meet him in Europe.

Nearly everything Wack had said about the transport of Cook's records turned out to be wrong. Nothing had been secretly sent to Copenhagen earlier; Lonsdale brought copied materials aboard the *United States* on November 25, and Marie later brought the originals. Years later, evidence would emerge that a detective in Westchester County had in fact been hired—by whom, he would not say—to keep tabs on Cook, but not that anyone had planned to rob him.

\*

IN EARLY DECEMBER, THE *TIMES* PICKED UP AN EXPLOSIVE LEAD REGARD-
ing Cook's proofs. "I have what I consider most important development.
Where can I reach you," Reick wrote to Peary on December 3. Reick wired
Peary again three days later, this time urgently requesting a sample of
Cook's handwriting.

On December 9, a day after Walter Lonsdale arrived in Copenhagen,
the *Times* published the confidential material that Reick had been working on: FRAUDULENT OBSERVATIONS MADE FOR DR. COOK BEFORE HIS RE-
CORDS WENT TO COPENHAGEN. Two men, George Dunkle and August
Loose, had confessed that Cook had recently hired them to doctor his
astronomical data. The *Times* independently verified many of the particu-
lars of their story, but was unable to confirm whether Cook had submitted
the alleged forgeries to the University of Copenhagen. Reproductions
of the two signed affidavits occupied two full columns of the front page,
and the detailed sworn accounts of both men spilled across almost three
full inside pages. Based on the massive amount of space given over to it,
this was the biggest scoop the *Times* had scored in decades.

The story originated with George Dunkle, an insurance broker who'd
apparently come to New York from Chicago. Earlier that fall, Dunkle
told the *Times*, he had inferred from press reports that Cook's proofs were
inadequate and predicted that the explorer would be willing to pay a
"good round price" for "assistance" in preparing them. Dunkle had approached an unemployed forty-year-old sea captain named August Loose.
The Norwegian-born Loose had also deduced from Cook's *Herald* accounts
that the explorer "had claimed too much," and agreed to participate in
Dunkle's scheme.

Dunkle had secured a letter of introduction to Cook through John
Bradley, on the false pretext that he could help the explorer insure his
polar proofs against theft or loss. At their first meeting, on October 17,
Dunkle had delicately revealed the true nature of his business and told
Cook that he knew a discreet navigator who could assist him in "getting
his records off at the time he wanted." Rather than take offense, Dunkle

told the *Times*, Cook expressed guarded interest in the proposition and agreed to meet again after he returned from his western lecture tour.

When they reconvened in early November, Dunkle arranged for Loose to meet Cook alone at the Waldorf Astoria. After listening to Cook describe the data in his possession, Loose told the explorer that he did not believe his records would pass muster in Copenhagen. He informed Cook that with the right books, charts, nautical tables, and other reference texts, he could, if desired, work out "a complete log all the way to the pole, with every sort of observation in it." Intrigued, Cook asked Loose to begin working out some calculations in reverse, based on the latitude figures that had already appeared in his *Herald* series, and bring them back to him. He authorized Loose to buy whatever nautical or astronomical reference materials he deemed necessary.

Loose claimed to have been astonished by what Cook told him. "I found that he was entirely ignorant on many vital points of the method of taking observations," he told the *Times*. Just three minutes or so into their first conversation, Loose recalled, he began to suspect that Cook had not been to the pole. Not wanting to embarrass a prospective client, Loose tactfully did not ask to see Cook's data, but judged from his answers to technical questions that his documentation must be woefully incomplete. Cook had failed to record the time of day and the elevation of various stars above the horizon when taking astronomical sightings, rendering it impossible to judge their accuracy. He appeared not to understand the crucial role of a star's angle to the horizon, or azimuth, in celestial navigation. He had failed to correct his chronometer and compass after leaving the United States, and he had relied on Sverdrup and Nansen's charts whenever possible, something Loose believed no competent navigator would have done. Loose claimed that Cook couldn't, when asked, even provide the latitude and longitude of his starting point at Anoritoq, let alone the uninhabited northern tip of Axel Heiberg Land. Loose left the Waldorf Astoria convinced that his client was incapable of navigating beyond sight of land. The only way he could have reached the pole in this case was accidentally, and he would have had no way of knowing it if he did.

Pleased with Loose's initial calculations, Cook had then commissioned him to produce a complete set, including sixteen observations that could convincingly have been taken at the pole itself. Loose checked into the Gramatan on November 16, under the pseudonym Andrew H. Lewis, and spent three days working there in a room near Cook's. Dunkle had by this point smoothly exacted a promise of $4,000 from his client: $2,500 upon receipt of Loose's work, with a $1,500 bonus if Cook's proofs were accepted in Copenhagen. Both men remained intentionally vague about the exact nature of their services and told the *Times* that Cook had done the same. Dunkle claimed that while negotiating their fee, he had gotten Cook to admit only that he had "overlooked some vital things."

Cook had seemed so nervous at times, Loose told the *Times*, that he "really felt sorry for him." But he had always kept a straight face, no matter how crookedly his accomplices looked at him. Near the end of his brief residency at the Gramatan, Loose mentioned to Cook that they did not have any data for his return journey from the pole. When Cook "looked stumped for a minute," Loose winkingly suggested that he simply tell the Danish panel that he'd stashed these comparatively unimportant records in Greenland. In Loose's telling, Cook then said, "Yes, that's right. I did leave them in a cache at Etah, where my instruments are. I'm going to get them next spring if I can." Loose chuckled and replied, "Yes, if you can."

Cook had maintained that he might submit his own observations to Copenhagen after checking them against Loose's, though Loose advised him not to. Loose had never seen the data that Cook claimed to possess, and admitted to the *Times* that he did not know how—or even whether— Cook had ultimately used the manufactured figures. All that Loose could say for sure was that he had given Cook reverse-engineered observations that "might have been taken" on a trip to the pole, and that he believed his forgeries were good enough to fool the scientists in Copenhagen. Cook had then disappeared after paying him and Dunkle only $260. Both men admitted that this was the reason they had taken their story public. They had originally intended to get money out of Cook, not expose him.

The *Times* touted the scoop as "one of the most fascinating chapters in all the literature of imposture." Not since its famous 1871 exposure of the Tweed Ring had it lavished this many superlatives, subheadlines, and column inches on a news story. The fact that there was something distinctly unsavory about the two main sources, Dunkle in particular, did not invalidate the story for the *Times*. It had the signed affidavits, documentation for Loose's stay at the Gramatan during the dates that Cook had been there, and receipts for his purchases of nautical charts and reference books. It even had a note from Cook to Loose, instructing the navigator to provide "daily observations to April 23 [1908]," which Reick had authenticated using a sample of Cook's handwriting he'd obtained from Peary. The *Times* had delayed publication of the Dunkle and Loose allegations for two days while it attempted to obtain a response from Cook, but failed to locate him.

Cook later claimed that he had hired Loose to draw up observations simply for the purpose of comparing them with his own and that he had dismissed "the two nefarious conspirators" the minute they handed him a complete set of false records unsolicited. Cook also alleged that a handwriting expert later determined that the signatures of Dunkle and Loose had been rendered by the same person, making at least one of the affidavits obtained by the *Times* illegitimate. "The managing editor [of the *Times*] was shown the evidence of this forgery, admitted its force, but not a word was printed to counteract the harm done by printing false news," Cook wrote.

In the immediate wake of the story, though, he was neither seen nor heard from, and his usual defenders were helpless to discredit the allegations. Reporters went to Henry Wellington Wack, only to learn that he had severed ties with his client. The faithful Charles Wake accused Dunkle and Loose of working for parties that were "interested in discrediting Dr. Cook," but also seemed annoyed that Cook had gone missing right when an explanation from him was most needed.

The *Times* informed the University of Copenhagen that it would gladly make the affidavits, Loose's handwritten calculations, and other related materials available. The Danes warily accepted the offer.

# CHAPTER FORTY-NINE

Dunkle and Loose were widely derided as scoundrels, but the New York City press considered their allegations credible. "It would be hard to frame a more direct and circumstantial accusation of fraud," *The World* commented. It considered this latest blow against Cook "the most damaging evidence yet presented against him." The *Brooklyn Daily Eagle*, which had supported Cook throughout much of the fall, now said that he owed it to his supporters to respond immediately, or else sue the *Times* for libel. But he did neither.

The London papers positively gobbled up the story. *The Times* of London, which had been skeptical about Cook's claim from the beginning, devoted more than four columns to the "remarkable accusations" of Dunkle and Loose. The charges were being taken more seriously in America than in Europe, it noted, "chiefly because in detail they are far more formidable than a telegraphed summary can suggest." In Copenhagen, where Lonsdale delivered Cook's proofs to Professor Strömgren on the very day that the story broke, it was initially dismissed as the Peary cabal's latest attempt at character assassination. According to the *World* correspondent there, it even generated "a strong wave of sympathy in Cook's favor." But the wave subsided two days later, when Lonsdale admitted that Cook had in fact engaged Loose to "check" his observations. Most everyone

now agreed that at the very least the materials that Lonsdale had just delivered on Cook's behalf needed to be carefully compared with Loose's
work. If the two sets of figures matched, it meant that Cook had faked his
proofs, and he was done for. If they didn't, then the Danish panel would
simply take up its original task of judging Cook's work on its own merits.
The *Herald* anticipated a "thorough testing."

While they waited, newspapers speculated at length on how the six-
man committee would decide. *The New York Times* in particular scrutinized every in and out, with its correspondent in Copenhagen, Ernest
Marshall, filing almost daily updates from the Danish capital. "After
speaking with many Danes I have been forced to believe that there is a
very prevalent tendency to regard the charges made against Dr. Cook as
imputations upon Danish honor," he wrote on December 12. Whether the
panel would be influenced by such considerations was, of course, the ultimate question. Professor Strömgren was said to have privately disparaged
Peary's attacks as "so childish that they have almost proved Dr. Cook's
case," and his committee had recently given observers another reason to
believe that it would rule in Cook's favor by enlisting Knud Rasmussen,
one of Cook's staunchest defenders, as an adviser. Though the latest inves-
tigatory efforts of *The New York Times* had broken through, everyone from
King Frederick to the average Danish citizen still appeared to be rooting
for Frederick Cook. If the University of Copenhagen ruled against this
tide of public sentiment, Marshall wrote, it would constitute "a striking
example of how the scientific mind can triumph over . . . popular opinion."

While the suspense mounted in Copenhagen, the impartiality of another respected institution—*The New York Times*—came in for questioning. The sensational story of Dunkle and Loose led to a deluge of indignant
letters, and not just from Cook supporters. Readers complained not only
that the *Times* had consorted with avowed con artists but that rather than
condemn these two charlatans, it had elevated them as witnesses in its
seemingly obsessive prosecution of Frederick Cook. The whole thing
seemed beneath the *Times* to some longtime subscribers and to reek of the
very "freak journalism" it had always deplored. "Dear Sir, Cook is probably a faker," one correspondent wrote. "But how the *Times* can allow itself

to drop to gutter journalism by such rot as it publishes this morning is beyond the comprehension of this old reader."

There was, after all, plenty of non-polar news that might have claimed some of the eighteen columns the *Times* had given the Dunkle and Loose revelations. The Zelaya regime in Nicaragua was crumbling; the future of New York City's subway system was being planned. Some readers found it baffling that the typically serious-minded *Times* had apparently gone to pieces over a story of comparatively minor consequence. Wrote one, "If there is any real value to the discovery of the Pole, beyond its adaptability to the purposes of diversion and amusement, will the Times please tell us what it is, and let up on Dr. Cook for a while?"

Acknowledging that "not a few" readers felt this way, the *Times* published and responded to one of the more politely worded critiques it had received. The writer praised the *Times* for its "clean-cut style" and "safe, sane editorials," but admitted that its slanted coverage of the North Pole controversy had forced him, for the first time in years, "to buy two different papers to learn the facts." The commenter expected the claims of both explorers to be settled by "the proper tribunal" in due time and urged the *Times* to go "back to your good old plan of printing 'All the news that's fit to print' and nothing less."

The *Times* conceded nothing to these critics. "That from the very beginning we, with the rest of the world, believed Commander Peary reached the pole on the day he claimed, is true; it is also true that soon after Dr. Cook made the same claim we were assailed by doubts of his veracity, and that, as the evidence against him piled up, those doubts have strengthened and deepened until now they amount to adverse convictions," it explained. The *Times* granted that it had "an arrangement" with Peary but insisted that "there was nothing in the contract which detracted from our journalistic interest in the achievements of any other explorer." It maintained that it had "given both sides of the story."

But it was secretly collaborating with only one of them. Had readers known the extent to which Reick colluded with Hubbard and Peary in order to damage Cook, they would have had even more to complain about.

After realizing that Cook had stiffed him and Loose, George Dunkle had taken their story to William Reick in early December and asked to be paid $2,000 for it. In a confidential letter to Reick later that month, Dunkle reminded the *Times* executive of where their dealings had gone from there: "You said that you would consult another man that evening, and would tell me definitely during the next day." The man in question was Thomas Hubbard, who had then struck a deal with Dunkle. Hubbard appears to have done as much of the questioning as the *Times* did, and to have paid most of what Dunkle and Loose demanded for their testimony. The *Times* by comparison contributed a small portion. "The story was published under a 'gentleman's agreement' that we would be fairly treated and receive what the story was really worth, but I well understood that The Times was to pay only about $200—and that the balance was to be paid by another man," Dunkle told Reick. "Payment was to be made two weeks from the date of publication, but this was afterwards amended by the third person. He suggested payment to be made when the Danish Consistory had brought in its verdict."

Hubbard had apparently agreed with Cook in this respect. Both had thought it best to wait until the Copenhagen decision before assigning a fixed price to Dunkle and Loose's services.

That decision was formally announced on December 21: "Not proven."

# CHAPTER FIFTY

It turned out that Cook had made it very easy for the Danish panel to decide against him. As the *Times* was quick to learn, the long-awaited records of his polar journey contained "practically nothing that by any stretch of language could be termed proof." His submissions consisted of two typewritten documents: a sixty-one-page report, which was nearly identical to his serialized *Herald* narrative, and sixteen pages of transcribed diary entries. Cook provided no navigational observations or calculations whatsoever, only the conclusions that he claimed to have made therefrom. His proofs were deemed so inadequate that the University of Copenhagen announced its verdict—which was unanimous—a week earlier than had been expected.

The short, impersonal report of its decision must have required all the Nordic reserve its authors could muster. Outside official channels, the committee made it abundantly clear that it considered Cook's submissions an embarrassment and a disgrace. "We examined Dr. Cook's observations first and agreed unanimously that they were worthless," one of the reviewers told the press. Strömgren was rumored to have flatly said, "We have been hoaxed." Knud Rasmussen had realized the proofs were "a scandal" the minute they were presented to him. "No schoolboy could make such calculations. It is a most childish attempt at cheating," he said.

As Cook would spend the next thirty years pointing out, "not proven" is not the same as "disproven." But in the exploring world and beyond, the apparent finality of the Copenhagen verdict was resounding. Roald Amundsen, another explorer whose support had done much to solidify public faith in Cook, called it a "crushing statement." W. T. Stead wrote to Philip Gibbs, "I have lost and you have won." Fridtjof Nansen finally broke his silence to declare that Cook was "practically a dead man and ought to vanish from the consideration of the world."

It was impossible to argue that the University of Copenhagen had been biased against Cook. It was a respected scientific authority, and moreover the one Cook himself had chosen to judge his proofs. It was now revealed that in addition to the records Lonsdale had brought the committee a letter from Cook, asking it to delay deliberations until his instruments and additional observations had been retrieved from Etah. The committee had rejected this request and largely ignored Cook's assurance that his original notebooks were on their way to Copenhagen. (When they did arrive several weeks later, courtesy of Marie, the examiners found nothing in them to warrant reconsideration.)

The scientific and exploring establishment slammed its doors on Cook. The Explorers Club declared his McKinley ascent "unworthy of credence" two days after the Copenhagen verdict and expelled him. The Arctic Club of America, which had stuck with him throughout the fall, banned Cook from seeking reelection as its vice president. Former supporters like Georges Lecointe, director of the Royal Observatory in Brussels, found themselves in a difficult position. Though he had been with Cook in Antarctica and a great admirer, the question now for Lecointe was not whether his old friend had reached the pole. It was, rather, whether Cook genuinely believed that he had reached it. Perhaps he had simply been mistaken. But if Cook had knowingly failed, Lecointe said, then he had attempted "the most audacious and unpardonable imposture ever thrust upon the scientific world."

Charles Wake, one of his few remaining friends, insisted that Cook believed he'd been to the pole, but had become too crippled by nervous anxiety to make his case effectively. "There is a pronounced streak of genius in Dr. Cook, which makes him headstrong and supersensitive, perhaps. He worried greatly over the accusations made against him, and during all of the time that he was preparing the records for Copenhagen he was possessed of the idea that he was being hounded by detectives, and even that his life was in danger," Wake explained. Several days later, though, Wake declared that he, too, had been a victim of Cook's deceptions. "He has a magnetic personality, and I grew to like him so much that it is with great regret that I have been compelled to change my opinion of him," he said. He also said that Cook had assured him that the cached trunk at Etah contained "nothing material" to his polar claim.

James Gordon Bennett's true feelings were, as usual, hard to pinpoint. An anonymous source in Paris—probably a former colleague of Reick's who was still with the *Herald*—informed the *Times* that the Commodore's attitude was "to drop the matter entirely and say nothing more about it." The *Herald* pointedly noted that it had only gotten involved with Cook after he'd returned from the Arctic, reminding readers that it had not organized or otherwise lent its reputation to his expedition in advance, as it had done with Henry Stanley and George Washington De Long. Then the *Herald* turned its exploring attentions to the South Pole, for which the British explorer Robert Falcon Scott planned to depart the coming summer.

The *Times*, on the other hand, made hay of Cook's downfall for days. In a photo collage headlined DR. COOK RECEIVING HONORS HE HAD NOT WON, it recapped how countless millions had been duped, from Danish royalty to the Brooklyn masses. It scolded the city's aldermen for not immediately rescinding the municipal honors they had so hastily bestowed on Cook. The *Times* saw fit to report that an infant that had been named Frederick, in Cook's honor, was now being rechristened by its parents, and that "a bundle of odorous" Arctic skins left by Cook in the Waldorf Astoria's luggage room had begun to smell and been discovered. The *Times* squeezed every last drop of vindication and mockery out of the story that it could.

It also overstated the role it had played in Cook's unmasking. Immediately following the Copenhagen decision, the *Times* falsely claimed that he had included Loose's data in his submissions. But several weeks later, after the university announced that it had also found nothing of value in Cook's original diaries, the *Times* was forced to admit—in a short item buried on the bottom of page 5—that "contrary to expectations" neither of the committee's reports had made any reference to Loose's figures. Reick had by this time ensured that Loose and Dunkle were paid $2,250 for their cooperation anyway.

Despite this, the *Times* could credibly claim—and did—that it had been the press outlet most responsible for exposing a "monster of duplicity." It called Cook the "greatest impostor of all time" and came to the somewhat unimaginative conclusion that he had been driven by financial greed. *Times* editors calculated that between his *Herald* fees and the $92,000 he appeared to earn from his lectures—a total of $3 million in today's money—he'd grown "reasonably rich" from his polar hoax. Seeking to understand why it had taken so long for Cook to be exposed, the *Times* concluded, "The deception was kept up largely through newspaper jealousy and through a natural reluctance of men to admit that they had been so ignobly swindled."

The direction the *Times* had taken the North Pole story was the direction the North Pole story had gone. Like most *Times* readers, of course, Adolph Ochs did not know enough about celestial navigation or the other relevant technicalities to understand on what basis the Danish committee had rejected Cook's proofs—or, for that matter, on what basis the Washington committee had accepted Peary's. But he was firmly confident in the fine mind of Carr Van Anda, and thus probably believed that the story would eventually break in his paper's favor, especially as more scientists came to doubt Cook's claim. Though his response to the Copenhagen verdict is not documented, it must have been exultant. Ochs coveted few things as dearly as the respect of educated and successful men, and the *Times* collected this sweet reward in heaps as it became clearer than ever that it had backed the pole's rightful claimant all along. The conclusion of the 1909 stage of the North Pole controversy elevated the *Times* head and shoulders above its peers in a way that precious few stories had done before. Under the Ochs regime, it is fair to say that nothing compared with it up to this point.

Assessing how the paper had handled the uniquely tricky and compelling story of the year, if not the decade, the trade journal *The Fourth Estate*
bowed low and tipped its cap:

> The great victory won by The New York Times in the polar contro-
> versy which for so many weeks raged furiously through the col-
> umns of the American press is recognized by scientists the world
> over and the public generally as making more firm the reputation
> of The Times as a newspaper that does things. . . . With evident
> desire to be entirely fair, it published all the news that seemed to
> favor Cook, and all the claims of his friends in his behalf, but it
> consistently insisted upon its own view of the matter, and finally
> electrified the nations [*sic*] by printing the story of two men who
> claimed that they had under promise of pay prepared false data for
> him to submit at Copenhagen, and drove Cook into an obscurity
> from which even The [doggedly pro-Cook] Springfield Republican
> has been unable to rescue him. This "cause celebre" recalls the great
> service performed by The New York Times many years ago in the
> exposure and overthrow of the Tweed ring, and exhibits in striking
> manner the extent of its resources and the all-around capacity of
> its editorial staff.

WHAT PEARY HAD TO SAY ABOUT THE REJECTION OF COOK'S PROOFS
amounted to a perfunctory "I told you so." "Three months ago, from the
Labrador Coast, I sounded an explicit and deliberately worded warning to
the world, based upon complete and accurate information in regard to the
Cook claims," he said in a brief press statement. A victory note he'd sent
to Reick was duly republished in the *Times*: "Congratulations to *The New
York Times* for its steady, insistent, victorious stand for the truth."

There was, however, one more loop that Peary wanted closed. The
prominent Cook supporter Admiral Winfield Schley had accepted the
Danish committee's verdict but argued that it should now also examine
Peary's proofs. This proposal had in fact already been privately endorsed

by Hubbard six weeks earlier, following the National Geographic Society's acceptance of Peary's claim. Now that the situation had definitively shifted in his favor, though, Peary was in no mood to take chances. He preemptively refused to send his records to Denmark, for what he described as reasons of national pride. "It would seem entirely inappropriate that the records of an American explorer should be sent to a foreign organization, even should they ask for it," he wrote to Reick on December 24. Peary conceded that Schley's call for a reciprocal examination sounded like an "equitable proposition," and therefore worried that it would become a "popular cry." It was all the more important, Peary told Reick, that this potentially troublesome campaign be nipped in the bud. "A statement from Copenhagen, sent out by the Associated Press, to the effect that Copenhagen does not want to examine my records, would knock the last leg from under the suggestion of Schley, or others," he wrote.

The statement from Maurice Egan, the U.S. minister in Copenhagen, that was printed in the next day's papers arrived as a perfectly timed Christmas gift for Peary. According to Egan, the Danes considered his claim proven. "The university would accept the finding of the National Geographic Society with implicit faith, just as it would expect the American body to accept its verdict," he said. Whether Egan was articulating an official position or suggesting a means of restoring frayed Danish-American relations remains unclear. Either way, the University of Copenhagen never contradicted him. It never looked at Peary's records, and the National Geographic Society never looked at Cook's.

PART FIVE

# YEARNING
# TO BELIEVE

# CHAPTER FIFTY-ONE

Peary appeared to have decisively won the polar dispute, and with his disgraced rival still in seclusion his victory went unchallenged during the first two months of 1910. In February, a committee of thirty-one prominent New York City millionaires that included Andrew Carnegie, Jacob Schiff, and Henry Morgenthau organized a tribute for Peary at the Metropolitan Opera House. A note from President Taft commending him for his "great achievement" was read aloud. Governor Charles Evans Hughes, who sat next to Peary, referred to him in his speech that evening as a "great American hero" whose celebration should be "all the more hearty because, unfortunately, it has been so long delayed."

The *Times* and other allies lobbied for Peary to be tendered the official thanks of Congress and retired from the navy with the rank of rear admiral and the highest allowable pension of $6,000 a year. These measures passed in the Senate but met with unexpected resistance from the House, where the Committee on Naval Affairs refused to rubber-stamp the lionization of a figure as divisive as Robert Peary. There were technicalities of naval rank and appropriate compensation to be considered, but also a desire among some Democrats to make him answer for some of his appalling public behavior. Some of the hostile legislators also noted that no one outside the National Geographic Society had actually seen Peary's polar diary and that the exact nature of his proofs remained unclear. In order to satisfy their skepticism, two of the three National Geographic worthies who'd approved Peary's claim back in November were summoned before the congressional committee in March. What they revealed caught even some of Peary's supporters off guard.

Henry Gannett testified under oath that Peary had read aloud his diary entries from "up to the time that Bartlett left him," at around 88°N. Gannett did not know if any of the judges had read more of the diary than that; all he would say was that it had been "passed around." The National Geographic Society had been similarly incurious about the instruments Peary had brought to Washington for its perusal. Rather than check their calibrations against his recorded data, the examiners had simply peered into Peary's trunk and then closed the lid again. Gannett, who'd recently been named president of the National Geographic Society, told the congressmen that he considered a thorough check of Peary's proofs unnecessary. "Everyone who knows Peary by reputation knows he would not lie; I know him by reputation," he said. This, then, was the flimsy standard of evidence to which all scientific bodies accepting the National Geographic Society's verdict had unknowingly agreed. By contrast, the University of Copenhagen's panel had known almost at a glance that Cook's proofs were insufficient but taken more than six hours to deliberate them anyway.

The congressional subcommittee concluded that the society's review of Peary's records had been "perfunctory and hasty" and its examiners "prejudiced in his favor." But when Peary was asked to make his diaries and data publicly available, he declined, citing contractual obligations with his publishers. His request that the subcommittee go over his records privately, with either Tittmann or Gannett present, was in turn rejected. The *Times*, which had confidently predicted that the Peary bill would sail through Congress, was outraged. "Nobody with a right to an opinion doubts that Peary reached the pole. His word settled it, for one thing, but he has [an] abundance of other evidence, unquestionable in quality, to throw in for good measure, and he has presented it as fully as was necessary—as fully as he could without making it commercially worthless," the *Times* argued.

In fact, Peary's evidence for everything he had done after leaving Bartlett behind was neither abundant nor unquestionable. The *Times* ignored this fact and likened the congressmen who appeared to be troubled by it to "a community of molluscs." Representative Robert B. Macon, Democrat of Arkansas, came in for the harshest criticism. When the subcommittee reconvened ten months later, Macon would blast the "unblushing know-it-all tit-bit editors of the New York Times" from the House floor. For now, he merely declared himself "exceedingly skeptical" of Peary's claim and vowed to do everything in his power to make the explorer defend it publicly. Worried about Macon and other Democrats, the Peary Arctic Club distributed a pamphlet (which consisted mainly of his reprinted *Times* series) called *How Peary Reached the North Pole* among legislators, in hopes of moving the bill to a vote. Instead, the subcommittee dug in and postponed its investigation until after Peary's publishing agreements had expired.

Peary discovered on a speaking tour that winter that outside the friendly Northeast much of America was still against him. Citing the withholding of his proofs to Congress, the governor of Georgia, Joseph M. Brown, refused to introduce him to an Atlanta lecture audience. "If Cook has handed us a gold brick, Peary has handed us a paste diamond," Brown told the press. Peary canceled his southern tour.

Meanwhile, the National Geographic Society's fundraising campaign for a Peary-endorsed American South Pole expedition floundered. The organization's leadership blamed Cook for tarnishing the field, but many rank-and-file members considered Peary the problem. "For every letter we received containing a subscription, we received one abusing our friend Peary," Gannett reported to Thomas Hubbard. The Antarctic expedition was abandoned for lack of funds, and the South Pole was discovered on December 14, 1911, by Roald Amundsen. Robert Falcon Scott reached it five weeks later, only to discover that his rival's Norwegian flag had already been planted there. All four members of his polar party died on the journey back; their diaries, when retrieved, not only confirmed that Scott had attained the South Pole but also helped turn him, posthumously, into a paragon of British forbearance and self-sacrifice, the noblest loser of what would later be called exploration's "heroic age." Amundsen was accepted, albeit grudgingly in Great Britain, as the South Pole's discoverer.

As Scott and Amundsen prepared to sail during the spring of 1910, Peary took a victory lap in Europe. He was snubbed in Scandinavia, where he'd never been very popular, but was otherwise well received by the exploration societies of Great Britain and the Continent. The only one of these organizations to do any independent vetting of his North Pole claim, however, was the Royal Geographical Society. The London-based RGS had already awarded him a special gold medal, "for Arctic Exploration from 1886 to 1909," back in January. After examining his belatedly delivered partial proofs, its committee voted that spring by a razor-thin margin to approve them.

During the summer of 1910, a rich sportsman named Paul Rainey traveled to northern Greenland to photograph an Arctic big-game hunt. The expedition received an unusual amount of media attention because Rainey's companion was Harry Whitney, Cook's famous confidant, and the captain of their hired vessel was the former *Roosevelt* skipper Bob Bartlett. Knud Rasmussen had renounced his intention to return to Etah on Cook's behalf, and Cook was, incredibly, still missing. Once the news broke that the only two white men who knew the location of Cook's cache were headed back to Etah, the press widely assumed that they would open it. They may have done as much. But Whitney declined to comment on what had happened when he returned, and Bartlett brusquely dismissed the subject. "The only articles belonging to Dr. Cook at Etah are some clothing and such like and possibly a sextant. But as for records, you can stake your life that none are there," he told *The World*. Later that year, in an account of the trip for *Cosmopolitan*, Rainey described the cache as a "rock igloo" on an exposed stretch of coastline and reported that its top had fallen in. "I refrained from touching or opening it, on account of not wanting to be mixed up in the Peary-Cook controversy," he wrote. The next time anyone tried to visit the cache, it had washed away.

Two expeditions were launched in 1910 to settle the McKinley question. One comprised Cook partisans, the other Cook skeptics; both returned later that summer, reporting that his 1906 climb had been a hoax.

A party sent by the Explorers Club located a snowy cornice just above Ruth Glacier that was identical to the outcrop depicted in Cook's summit photograph; Herschel Parker's hypsometer placed the spot at fifty-one hundred feet, less than one-fourth of McKinley's elevation above sea level. The group, which was partly financed by Thomas Hubbard, reached Cook's "fake peak" with relative ease but failed to advance much higher. A second expedition, co-sponsored by *The New York Herald* and the *Oregonian* and launched under the auspices of Portland's Mazamas club, which had earlier credited Cook's McKinley claim, also retraced Cook's purported summit route. Its leader, the mountaineer and Cook admirer C. E. Rusk, returned convinced that his onetime idol had faked his climb, and saddened that he had "spoiled a great career" by doing so. "If he is mentally unbalanced, he is entitled to the pity of mankind," Rusk said of Cook afterward. "If he is not, there is no corner on earth where he can hide from his past."

ON OCTOBER 2, 1910, NEARLY TEN MONTHS AFTER FREDERICK COOK HAD disappeared, *The World* announced that it had found him. He had been traveling incognito around Europe and South America, both on his own and with Marie, and was now residing in an upscale hotel in the heart of London's West End theater district. His daughters were enrolled in a boarding school on the Continent. He looked tan and healthy, albeit anxious whenever he stepped out in public, and had taken to carrying a walking stick. Told by *The World*'s reporter that he hardly resembled the nervous wreck last seen fleeing New York, Cook "laughed heartily" and explained that he had begun to regain his health and equilibrium. He reaffirmed that he had reached the pole and said that he would write a book about his Arctic journey and everything that had happened afterward. The book, he stressed, would contain "an important message for the American people." William Reick and other editors put their London correspondents on his trail, but Cook disappeared again before they could find him.

Peary's book and nine-part *Hampton's* series had both come out by now and flopped. Having fulfilled his supposedly binding publishing contracts, he agreed to appear before the House Naval Affairs Committee. He'd accumulated more than a dozen prestigious exploring medals over the preceding year, as though to armor himself against attack, and he'd committed the story of his expedition to the page—and been handsomely paid for it—twice more. Before setting out in 1908, Peary had said that if Cook claimed to have reached the pole, he "should be compelled to prove it." Peary, to his credit, could prove that he'd gotten close to the North Pole and even that he'd established a new Farthest North. But as for actually reaching the pole, he still had not met the standard of evidence that had been demanded of his rival.

The world's great explorers declared their faith in Peary and assured the *Times* and other questioners that he had nothing to fear from Congress. But there was no getting around it: the hearings would be unfamiliar territory. Peary would appear in person this time around, with his polar journal. For the first time in his career, the old code of gentlemanly discretion was to be set aside. He would be asked, publicly and not necessarily amicably, to answer what one clever newspaper called the "metaphysical question" of where he'd been on the featureless, drifting landscape of the Arctic Ocean. During the three days in January 1911 during which he testified, Peary's self-regard and his nerves both took a beating. Josephine later wrote that after his "personal grilling" by Congress he was never the same man again.

Elements of Peary's original diary puzzled his examiners, beginning with its cover. He had labeled it "Roosevelt to _____ and return, February 22 to April 27," suggesting that three weeks after the day he claimed to have reached the pole, he still had not decided just how far north he'd been. His notes for the date of discovery, April 6, were similarly confusing. The sequential entry, the one that had been written on bound pages, was as uneventful as those of the previous days had been. The discovery itself—"The pole at last!!! The prize of 3 centuries, my dream and ambition for 23 years"—had been recorded separately, on a loose leaf of paper. There were no entries for April 7, when Peary also claimed to have been at the pole, or April 8.

Nor did Peary's navigational methods inspire full confidence. He admitted that he had not taken longitude readings or checked for compass variation—both standard practices—after leaving the *Roosevelt*. Between the time Bartlett left him just south of the 88th parallel and Peary's supposed arrival within five miles of the pole, he had not taken a single latitude sight. During crucial parts of the journey, in other words, his geographical position had been nearly as unfixed as the shifting terrain. As Macon aptly summarized, Peary claimed that he could advance "pell-mell over a rough, rugged, and broken ice course for a distance of 130 miles without an observation or object to guide him and go directly north to an imaginary point." Peary asked the examiners to believe that he had taken a northward beeline by means of dead reckoning—and that he had gone very, very fast. He claimed to have covered fifty miles in a single day, far more than anyone had ever logged on Arctic Ocean ice. Henson and Bartlett could surely have shed additional light on these claims, but neither was called to testify.

The most aggressive cross-examining of Peary came from Representative Macon, a trained lawyer who was known on Capitol Hill as a stickler for detail. For an Arkansan whose "'farthest north,'" as *Scientific American* mockingly pointed out, was "the semi-tropical cold of Omaha, Nebraska," Macon displayed a surprising knowledge of Arctic navigation and tested Peary with many of the questions that the National Geographic Society's starstruck experts had failed to ask. But he lacked the technical expertise to push his inquiry as far as it could have gone and, like the rest of the subcommittee, appears not to have grasped the full implications of Peary's testimony. Macon eventually grew flustered by the interruptions of his befuddled fellow congressmen, many of whom appeared to have made up their minds already, and his weakness for inflammatory speechifying did not help his cause. During final arguments on the House floor, he disparaged Peary as a "fur trader" and a "puffed-up near-hero" and flung so many insults at the "saphead" editors defending him in the daily press that the journalists in the room walked out in protest.

Peary did not get everything he wanted from the congressional vote of March 3, 1911. Though he was granted the promotion, the pension, and the thanks of Congress, he was officially recognized only for having "reached" the North Pole, not discovering it. The distinction was more symbolic than sensical, for the hearings had done nothing to reestablish Cook's discredited claim. Once this bone had been thrown to the opposition, though, the act of Congress passed resoundingly in Peary's favor, 154–34.

COOK HAD RETURNED TO NEW YORK BY NOW AND BEGUN REINGRATIATing himself with the public. The press venue he selected for his comeback tell-all was *Hampton's*, whose failed investment in Peary's narrative had put it on the verge of bankruptcy. Desperate for a blockbuster, the magazine's publisher, Benjamin Hampton, squeezed Cook's admission that he *might* not have reached the mathematical North Pole for all it was worth— and then some. Without Cook's approval, his editors inserted passages asking readers to "understand my mental condition at the time" and grow "mad with me in the glaring, burning, long and crazing Arctic day." *Hampton's* also played up the insanity angle in its promotional campaign for the series, which it disingenuously billed as COOK'S CONFESSION.

Cook was blindsided by this unauthorized twisting of his tale. "The widespread dissemination of the untrue and cruelly unfair 'confession' and 'insanity-plea' stories dazed me. I felt impotent, crushed. In my very effort to explain myself I was being irretrievably hurt. I was being made a catspaw for magazine and newspaper sensation," he wrote in *My Attainment of the Pole*, the memoir he self-published a year later. Unconstrained by editors, Cook now attacked Peary openly, for having "the heart of a hypocrite" and for conspiring with *The New York Times* in an "underhanded game of deceit" to destroy him. Cook sympathizers described his embittered account as the cri de coeur of a grievously wronged man. The *Times* offered a different explanation for his change of sentiment. "The mask is off now," it declared, and the author of a "dastardly plot" to undermine the pole's rightful discoverer was finally showing his true colors. *My Attainment of the Pole* did nothing to alter the official recognition of either explorer's claim, but it sold well, aided by music-hall lectures at which Cook railed against Peary and his "Arctic Trust."

Peary maintained a dignified silence, hoping thereby to banish the polar controversy from serious discussion. Despite his best efforts, though, it remained something more than a provincial sideshow. The Explorers Club still found the topic so "disheartening to the good fellowship and harmony among its members" in 1913 that leadership prohibited the North Pole debate from being discussed within club walls. Cook took his fight into the political arena as well, and into salacious territory, when he accused Peary in a letter to President Taft of having extramarital relations with "Arctic concubines." (Widely dismissed at the time, this sensational charge was in fact true. Both Peary and Henson had secret children by Inuit women, descendants of whom still live in Greenland today.)

Cook had more success, after several years of lobbying, in winning the U.S. representative Henry Helgesen over to his cause. After discovering that Peary's 1911 congressional testimony was mysteriously missing from many government archives, the North Dakota Republican aided future scholars by having the transcript entered into the *Appendix to the Congressional Record* in 1915. The following summer, he introduced a bill to repeal the 1911 act of Congress honoring Peary. Helgesen had also learned, among other things, that the U.S. Coast and Geodetic Survey employee who'd recomputed and vouched for Peary's observations before the subcommittee five years earlier had not analyzed the explorer's records in his official government capacity, as the congressmen had been led to believe at the time. He had, rather, been paid for his work by Peary. He'd also been recommended for the job by his boss, Otto H. Tittmann, one of the three Peary partisans from the National Geographic Society subcommittee.

Helgesen died in 1917, before his bill could be debated or voted on, and his push to dishonor Peary fizzled. The threat of renewed scrutiny might, however, have been the reason that Peary decided against running for the U.S. Senate in Maine around this time. During his retirement, Peary's exploring legacy also suffered from the removal of several of his previous contributions to the accepted Arctic map. The Danish explorer Ludwig Mylius-Erichsen had discovered in 1907 that the so-called Peary Channel of northern Greenland did not exist, and when Mylius-Erichsen's diaries were retrieved and brought back to Copenhagen in 1912, they revealed

Peary's error to have been responsible for his death. Two years later, Donald MacMillan discovered that there was no Crocker Land. Later scholars, finding no mention of this purported northern island in Peary's diaries, concluded that he'd invented it after his 1905–6 expedition for fundraising purposes.

Peary continued to advocate for American polar exploring until his death in 1920, by which point air travel had emerged as the field's most exciting new frontier. The cause of his death, at age sixty-three, was pernicious anemia, but Peary's family also blamed the polar controversy for his decline. Deep into the twentieth century, Josephine and Marie Peary closely guarded the secret that he had suffered a mental breakdown during the fall of 1909. According to Josephine, the indignity of the 1911 congressional hearings "hurt him more than all the hardships he endured in his sixteen years of research in the Arctic regions and did more toward the breaking down of his iron constitution than anything experienced in his explorations."

By the time Peary died, Cook had left New York and gone into the oil business. His ongoing bid for redemption suffered a major blow in 1923, when he was sentenced to fourteen years in federal prison for defrauding investors in a Ponzi-like promotional scheme in Texas. Cook maintained his innocence throughout; of ninety-seven men indicted, he was the only one to plead not guilty. The presiding judge in Forth Worth, well aware of Cook's prior reputation, took unseemly pleasure in punishing him. "This is one of the times when your peculiar and persuasive hypnotic personality fails you, isn't it? You have at last got to the point where you can't bunco anybody. You have come to a mountain and reached a latitude which are beyond you," the judge taunted.

Cook proved a model inmate at the federal penitentiary in Fort Leavenworth, Kansas, where he helped manage the hospital, taught classes for inmates, and edited the prison newspaper. Roald Amundsen, in America to raise funds for his second attempt to fly over the North Pole, visited Cook behind bars in 1926. Following this meeting between the world's most accomplished and its most controversial living explorers, Amundsen publicly questioned Peary's claim. The *Times* denounced his comments as "almost unforgivable" and accused him of "trying to reverse the verdict of history and of science." If Amundsen was unsure of Peary's proofs, its editors unironically advised, he need only consult Peary's book. The National Geographic Society took harsher measures against Amundsen, canceling the fundraising lecture that it had planned for him.

Amundsen managed to raise the needed money anyway and rose to fame again that spring when an international group of explorers under his command (including Umberto Nobile, his Italian pilot, and Lincoln Ellsworth, his American backer) flew over the North Pole in the airship *Norge*. Amundsen's first account of the journey was published exclusively by *The New York Times*, which had begun regularly funding aviation and exploring ventures after the great success of its Peary gamble—and which had, in fact, been so successful at it that many explorers now considered it good luck to have the paper's backing. Thanks to advances in wireless technology, and the efforts of the Norwegian correspondent that the *Times* had on board, the flight of the *Norge* produced the first North Pole dateline in the history of the press. It was a stark reminder of a shrinking world. The news of Peary's 1909 expedition had taken 153 days to reach the *Times*; news of Amundsen's took seven hours.

Amundsen's feat, though widely celebrated, was regarded at the time as a second-place finish. Three days earlier, the American aviator Richard Byrd had landed in Spitsbergen bearing the news that he and his pilot, Floyd Bennett, had circled the North Pole in their three-engine Fokker monoplane. The *Times*—which had this scoop, too—credited Byrd with "verifying Admiral Peary's observations completely," and a three-man expert subcommittee from the National Geographic Society duly accepted his proofs. But when Byrd's diary was made public seventy years later, the partially erased original sextant readings found therein strongly suggested that he'd faked success. Most impartial experts now consider the 1926 flight of the *Norge* to have been the first time anyone convincingly reached 90°N, and acknowledge Roald Amundsen as the discoverer of both poles.

# CHAPTER FIFTY-TWO

Many decades would pass before Amundsen (who died in 1928) received due credit as the first person to have reached 90°N. Long after Peary's death in 1920, it remained unthinkable within exploring circles to question his discovery of the North Pole. One reason for this was that Cook maintained until his dying day—August 5, 1940—that he had been there first. The Peary flame was vigorously kept alive because it was feared that if it weakened, Cook's would burn all the brighter.

Nevertheless, the evidence against Peary slowly piled up, thanks in part to the efforts of Charles Henshaw Ward, a noted grammarian who'd become obsessed by what struck him as an enormous cover-up. Ward corresponded with the son of a retired naval officer who'd been asked by Admiral Chester to check Peary's observations in preparation for the 1911 congressional hearings. Father and son, both of whom were expert navy navigators, had seen Peary's latitude sightings and believed that they had been fabricated. Just how Peary might have gone about this was inadvertently revealed by another one of Ward's interview subjects, Hudson Bridge Hastings, who'd been a young mathematics instructor at Bowdoin College in 1909. Hastings boasted that he had been enlisted by Peary that autumn to study Cook's public statements for evidence of navigational ignorance and fraud, but he also recalled that Peary had shown him a copy of his own polar observations and asked him to work out at which latitudes the figures he'd recorded would have placed him. Hastings blithely told Ward that he'd obliged. Moments later, realizing that this information could be construed to mean that he'd helped Peary to doctor his data, Hastings forbade Ward to repeat it. Ward then made an error of his own. By failing to understand that Peary appeared to have reverse engineered his figures *before*, not after, meeting with the National Geographic panel, Ward underrated the significance of what Hastings had told him.

Peary had delayed the congressional examination of his records for nearly a year by claiming that he'd signed them over to his publishers. But another thing Ward learned—from Lilian Kiel, former secretary to Elsa Barker, the ghostwriter of Peary's *Hampton's* series—was that Peary had withheld his most important records from the magazine as well. Kiel furnished a letter from 1910 in which Barker, working from a copy of Peary's diary, begged him for information about April 6 and 7, 1909, the days he claimed to have been at the pole. Barker had explained her dilemma to Peary extremely tactfully: "Your eyes being so tired from the observations, there are no entries in the journal." The April 6 entry that Peary later showed Congress was presented on a separate, unbound page.

Ward collected these and other findings into a book and submitted his manuscript for *The Peary Myth* to Yale University Press in 1934—then died of pneumonia. On the advice of influential Peary allies, Yale reversed course and decided not to put the book out, and Ward's widow, Florence, was dissuaded from seeking another publisher. A similar rejection occurred in 1937, when a partisan but thoroughly researched biography of Cook was turned down by Doubleday, which had commissioned it, for being too hard on Peary. A shorter version of the book, *The Case for Doctor Cook*—by a friend of Cook's named Andrew Freeman—did not see the light of day until 1961. For Cook's daughter Helen and others intent on restoring the maligned explorer's reputation, it was an important contribution to polar literature. But two flattering biographies of Peary had appeared by this time, helping to firm up his legacy, and Freeman's book did little to challenge Peary's capstone achievement.

The ground underneath Peary's North Pole claim finally began to shift in 1973, with the publication of *Peary at the North Pole: Fact or Fiction?* Its author, Dennis Rawlins, a Baltimore-based professor of physics and astronomy at Loyola College, subjected the explorer's astronomical data—all that was known of it, at least, for Peary's records were still sealed—to thorough scrutiny. He also consulted Ward's forgotten manuscript and research files, which he miraculously salvaged from the attic of the scholar's long-lived widow. Rawlins judged that Peary had missed the pole by around a hundred miles, mainly due to his failure to account for magnetic variation, and that he had then lied about getting there to Matthew Henson and every other member of the expedition. Rawlins, who found similarly compelling reasons to doubt the 1906 Farthest North that enabled Peary to raise funds for his 1908–9 attempt, came to the novel conclusion that *both* Cook and Peary were fakers. He considered Cook's navigational ineptitude to be far more obvious and his polar claim more easily discounted.

Cook was—bodily, at least—long gone at this point. He'd spent six of the last ten years of his life on parole, living modestly and losing lawsuits against authors who called him a fraud. He received a pardon from President Franklin Roosevelt just before his death in 1940 and left the rehabilitation of his reputation to a cadre of true believers. Despite the best efforts of this fervent group, most experts remained unconvinced by Cook's polar claim. Meanwhile, a new generation had begun to wonder how much the debate even mattered anymore. In a review of *Peary at the North Pole: Fact or Fiction?* for *The New York Times*, the book critic Christopher Lehmann-Haupt admitted that he "couldn't have cared less, although I'm probably a victim of now—an age when the conquest of the moon seems to have made piffle of all earthly exploration, and an age when the tremendous national pride once invested in such conquests has begun to seem a little pointless." A definitive discrediting of Peary's claim at this stage would hardly constitute a national disaster, nor would it revive the race to the pole. Amundsen (and, it was still thought, Byrd) had decidedly attained it, or at least flown over it. A four-man Russian expedition had landed at the pole in 1937 and erected a simple weather station (which had immediately begun drifting south). The U.S. Air Force had landed a C-47 aircraft there in 1952. As of 1968, there was even a properly documented overland expedition to the North Pole on the books—led by a Minnesota insurance salesman named Ralph Plaisted, using snowmobiles.

The National Geographic Society, though, remained deeply invested in the history of polar exploring. In 1985, after the airing of a television docudrama that brazenly credited Cook as the North Pole's discoverer, it commissioned the British polar explorer Wally Herbert to conduct an exhaustive study of Peary's 1908–9 journey. As someone who had himself sledged to the North Pole, Herbert understood better than most the physical and psychological challenges that Peary had faced on the ice. He also admitted to revering him. It was, perhaps, in anticipation of a positive verdict that Herbert was granted access to Peary's personal papers. But a positive verdict is not what he delivered. Instead, he concluded that Peary had taken an "astonishingly casual attitude toward the problems of navigation" and fallen short of the pole by thirty to sixty miles. For Herbert, the fact that so many subsequent expeditions, including ones using snowmobiles, had failed to replicate the fantastic speeds claimed by Peary in 1909 further discredited his story. At the very minimum, he concluded, Peary had failed to meet the burden of proof his epochal feat demanded.

It took nearly a century for the record to be corrected, and for the prevailing wisdom to be that neither of the original American polar claims was credible. As so often happens, the heat of the moment impeded the search for truth. The debate has cooled now, but it has not flamed out entirely. Cook's and Peary's claims will probably never be proven or disproven to everyone's satisfaction, and future investigations may even cloud the matter rather than clarify it. The belated reconsideration of Matthew Henson, whose contribution and authority were downplayed for decades on account of his race, is an interesting case in point. Peary's indispensable assistant was reburied with military honors at Arlington National Cemetery in 1988 and has received overdue credit in recent years. In some quarters, one form of revisionism has now supplanted the old one. The fact that Henson, as Peary's trailblazer, reached their northernmost camp some forty-five minutes in advance of Peary has inspired some to lobby for him as the pole's rightful claimant—and thereby indulge in the wishful thinking that Peary really did hit the mark after all.

Following Wally Herbert's unflattering findings, the National Geographic Society immediately commissioned another study, which determined that Peary had in fact been to the pole. But *The New York Times*, for one, had already found Herbert's argument persuasive enough to warrant an update to the record. On August 23, 1988, nearly eighty years after reporting that the North Pole had been reached by Robert Peary, its editors issued one of the most extraordinary corrections in the paper's history:

> Peary's expedition was sponsored by the National Geographic Society. The Times had exclusive global rights to the story. Thus both may have failed to scrutinize adequately what they yearned to believe. The error was doubtless committed in good faith, but most authorities today agree that no one has an untainted claim to be first—neither Cook, nor Peary, nor the two Eskimos and the American black, Matthew Henson, who accompanied Peary.

# Newspaper of Record

Histories of the American press almost never mention the polar controversy. Histories of *The New York Times* inevitably do, and hold it up as evidence of the paper's rising influence during the early twentieth century. One chronicler, assessing the impact it had on the *Times*, goes so far as to say that the polar controversy "solidified its stature as the new leader for accuracy and enterprise in the collection of the news—a role long prized by the *Herald*."

James Gordon Bennett's misguided defense of Cook further damaged the standing of his paper. Though there are signs that Bennett personally continued to believe in Cook, the *Herald* effectively threw in the towel after the Copenhagen verdict. The backslide of the *Herald* continued in the years following the North Pole controversy, and in 1917 the New York Herald Company reported the first annual loss in its history. Bennett began negotiating with Ochs about combining the *Herald* with the *Times*; according to Charles Miller's lone biographer, the two publishers struck a deal, but Bennett fell terminally ill before the papers could be signed. He died in 1918, aged seventy-seven, at his villa in Beaulieu-sur-Mer. Most of his enormous fortune had been spent, and he left no sons or daughters. He left no personal papers, either, and bequeathed no journalism schools, scholarships, or prizes.

After Bennett's death, all three of his newspapers were acquired for $4 million by the publisher Frank Munsey, who promptly merged the *Herald* with *The Sun* and then sold it, in 1924, to the new owners of the *New-York Tribune*. The *New York Herald Tribune* was a reliable and Republican-leaning source of news for several decades, before shutting down in 1966. To the delight of generations of American tourists and expats, the *International Herald Tribune* lived on. The *Times* acquired a partial stake in it in 1967 and then full ownership in 2003. When it was consolidated and renamed the International Edition of *The New York Times* in 2013, the erasure of the once-mighty *New York Herald* was complete.

THE DECADE AFTER THE POLAR CONTROVERSY OF 1909 WAS A TRANSFOR-mative one for Adolph Ochs. By 1912, he had sold both of the Philadelphia papers he'd acquired in recent years, abandoned the idea of owning a national news chain, and redoubled his efforts to refashion the *Times* into a newspaper of unprecedented authority and influence. In 1913, Ochs began publishing a quarterly—later annual—reference tome called *The New York Times Index*, which provided a far more expedient way of consulting old newspaper stories than the chronological clippings files maintained at libraries and other archives. Hailed by educators and civic organizations as a revolutionary research tool, the index made the daily news easily retrievable and imbued it with a new sense of permanence. It also inaugurated the *Times* as America's "newspaper of record."

In a speech to the National Editorial Association in 1916, Ochs named two "sensational and exceptional instances" in which the *Times* had invested grandly in a single news story. One was Peary's claimed attainment of the North Pole. (Ochs was referring not to the $4,000 expedition loan but to the far larger cost of receiving and rapidly disseminating Peary's account by cable and telegram.) The other was Van Anda's legendary coverage of the *Titanic* disaster in 1912.

World War I, which cost the *Times* as much as $750,000 a year in cable bills alone, led the paper to spend, and flourish, on a whole new scale. The *Times* had abandoned its arrangement with *The Times* of London and opened its own European bureau by the time hostilities were declared in 1914. Its coverage of the war benefited from its international orientation and the tactical genius of Carr Van Anda, who analyzed battlefield formations as adeptly as he'd read Arctic sea charts during the polar controversy. The superlative war reporting of the *Times* earned it the first ever Pulitzer Prize for Public Service, journalism's highest honor, in 1918. Its most valuable front-lines contributor was Philip Gibbs, who was given a knighthood for his service.

The *Times* distinguished itself early with its comprehensive presentation of all sides of the conflict. This policy of evenhandedness became trickier to maintain following America's entrance into the war in 1917, and when Charles Miller, in a hastily written editorial, urged the U.S. government to enter into nonbinding peace discussions with Austria, the *Times* was almost universally condemned. Rattled by the backlash, Ochs sank into a yearlong depression in 1919. The well-oiled *Times* machine rolled on without him, allowing him to avoid the unpleasant task of naming another publisher. He returned to work in 1921, in time to celebrate the twenty-fifth anniversary of his management. The *Times* was by now being hailed as the most powerful daily journal in America. The editors of year-old *Time* magazine put it this way in 1924: "If there is a national newspaper in the U.S., it is the *Times*."

A physically declining Ochs retired from active work in the early 1930s, and his depression returned as he observed the alarming rise of Adolf Hitler—and wrestled with the torturous task of appointing a successor. There was to be no question of the *Times* leaving the family. For years, the heir apparent had been Julius Ochs Adler, his dutiful and hardworking nephew. But ever since Ochs's son-in-law, Arthur Sulzberger, had arranged for the *Times* to get the aviator Charles Lindbergh's exclusive account of his record-breaking transatlantic flight in 1927, Iphigene's bright and charming husband had also been a serious contender.

Adolph Ochs died on April 8, 1935, having done more for the American press—and his family—than he'd ever dreamed of. Fearful of confrontation to the end, he avoided naming the next publisher of the *Times*, but by assigning the decision to a family trust that consisted of Iphigene and

Arthur Sulzberger and Julius Ochs Adler, he effectively anointed Arthur to lead the paper. He must have known that Iphigene would cast the deciding vote for her husband. He might have also understood that Iphigene, who had often argued with her father in favor of socialism, women's rights, and other progressive causes, found Julius "very conservative."

Ochs had himself become even more conservative in his later years, and during the topsy-turvy 1920s and early 1930s the *Times* was often criticized for its self-importance, stuffiness, and deference to established opinion. The testimonials that came flowing in when Ochs died expressed warmer sentiments, and there was a great deal of truth in these as well. According to the New York governor, Herbert Lehman, who had known Ochs as a boy, "Few men have wielded so wide an influence or used it so devotedly in the public good."

It was often said of Ochs that he treated the *Times* as a public trust, and not just as a commercial enterprise. His expectations for the future *New York Times*, as expressed in his will, encouraged this noble reading of his intentions. The *Times* would, Ochs hoped, remain free from outside influence, fair and honest in its editorials, ethical in all its business dealings, and unimpeachably evenhanded in its reporting. "I trust its news columns may continue fairly to present, without recognizing friend or foe, the news of the day—'all the news that's fit to print'—and to present it impartially, reflecting all shades of opinion," he wrote.

The will itself passed the fitness test. The *Times* published it in its entirety, across eight columns, on page 20 of the April 17, 1935, edition.

# ACKNOWLEDGMENTS

I'll admit it: even after getting to know the subject matter well, I needed help putting this book on the right track. I owe a large debt of gratitude to my agent, Farley Chase, whose early faith in my idea energized me and whose intelligent suggestions were crucial to its development. His support never wavered.

I would also like to thank Wendy Wolf, my editor at Viking. Her expert revisions improved my writing at every turn, and she guided me through the publishing process with unfailing confidence and good humor. A first-time author could hardly have asked for more. I've also benefited from the expert copy editing of Ingrid Sterner and the industrious fact-checking of Joanna Arcieri. Thanks also to Viking production editor Eric Wechter for his patience, and to Paloma Ruiz for keeping the publication machinery moving.

Researching this book opened my eyes to the wonders of the New York Public Library, whose staff helped me to take advantage of its vast holdings. Thanks to Melanie Locay and Rebecca Federman for more personalized assistance, especially with obtaining the residencies that enabled me to make sustained progress with my research. And thanks to Meredith Mann, Tal Nadan, and the rest of the Manuscripts and Archives Division. I spent many fruitful hours there, in the Brooke Russell Astor Room, seeking an intimate understanding of Adolph Ochs and his *New York Times*.

Several scholars have been very generous with their time and expertise. One is Robert Bryce, who surely knows more about the polar controversy than anyone alive. (And maybe anyone not alive, for that matter.) His readiness to discuss any and all details of this remarkable subchapter of American history was a godsend. Another is Andie Tucher of the Columbia Journalism School, an expert in the turn-of-the-century New York City press and the history of fake news, who kindly—and cheerfully—reviewed sections of my manuscript dealing with those subjects.

The list goes on. Alex S. Jones, coauthor of *The Trust*, let me interrogate him about Adolph Ochs. William Collier, managing director of G.L. Watson, helped me avoid the sort of mistakes regarding yachting that would have gotten me fired from Bennett's *Herald*. Thanks also to David Dunlap of *The New York Times*, Brian Murray of King's College London, Adrian Wisnicki of the University of Nebraska-Lincoln, Genevieve LeMoine of the Peary-MacMillan Arctic Museum at Bowdoin College, Robert Headland of the Scott Polar Research Institute at the University of Cambridge, and to the polar historians Peter Damisch and Jean de Pomereu.

Like so many other ventures over the years, the plot for this book was originally hatched at The Explorers Club, way back in the spring of 2018. The archivist there, Lacey Flint, helped me to find my way to a new and different approach to the North Pole Controversy. A pair of my fellow Explorers Club members shared their expertise as well: Martin Nweeia, who kindly answered some of my questions about Greenland and its people, and Lew Toulmin, who did the same regarding Matthew Henson. Another archivist I'd like to thank is Tom McAnear at the National Archives and Records Administration, who helped me to navigate Robert Peary's papers. John Loggins went through many of the photographs therein and made nice reproductions of them for me.

Thanks to my Catskills neighbors Carol Smith and Aldo Troiani of the Frederick Cook Society, who gave me access to archival photos. Erin Florio, my editor at *Condé Nast Traveler*, unwittingly did me a favor when she put me aboard the *Seabourn Venture*, enabling me to revise parts of the manuscript while sailing through southern Greenland right at the moment I was craving a change of scenery.

I'm lucky that many of my best friends are writers. As they have done since college, my bosom buddies Daniel Kurtz-Phelan and Reid Cherlin offered constant encouragement and good ideas. I'm grateful to the following people for their candid publishing advice and other favors: Luke Barr, Lesley Blume, David Coggins, Chris Heaney, Ben Ryder Howe, Luke Neima, Julian Sancton, Tim Sohn, and Steven Ujifusa. Thanks to Michael R. Robinson for taking a look at an early draft, and to Lucas Wittmann for offering wise counsel at many junctures. I truly appreciate the creative input I got from Jared LeBoff, Nissar Modi, and Jaed Coffin. And I owe my talented friend Peter Crosby many pints of world-class Catskills ale for his author photo. I accept responsibility for anything that is wrong with the book, except if readers decide they don't like the look of me. In that event, I blame Peter.

The deepest, most heartfelt thanks I reserve for my family, and not just for their proofreading help. This labor of love is for Mum, who taught me how to write. For Dad, who gave me a spirit of adventure. For Oliver, my brother and partner in storytelling for six important years. And for my wife, Dana, who endured a pandemic shutdown with a partner who spent many hours closed up in his writing room, muttering to himself about polar geography and keeping weird hours. Your advice and support were as crucial to the completion of this book as they are to my general well-being. Every day of our shared life, I am profoundly grateful for them both.

# A NOTE ON SOURCES

I have tried hard to let the twenty-first century creep into this narrative only at those moments when it really needed to. Nearly every quotation is something that was said during the period under discussion, if not also by someone who figured in the incident or argument in question. I used dialogue sparingly on purpose, and none of the dialogue that I did use is my creation.

One of the first things I did while researching this book was steep myself in the autobiographies of New York City journalists from the late nineteenth and early twentieth centuries. I read more of these jaunty, old-school trade memoirs than I needed to, partly because I enjoyed them so much. The beauty of—and the problem with—them is that they resemble barroom tales. The sourcing is nonexistent, and casual untruths are employed to spice up a story or cast the teller in a pluckier, more happy-go-lucky light. Biographies of James Gordon Bennett Jr. suffer from some of the same issues. They are short on dates, and the order of the many colorful yarns their authors spin can seem utterly random. Unlike Pulitzer, Ochs, Hearst, and other influential peers, Bennett left no archives. I've tried to pin the various stories about him to a particular time and place whenever possible. He was, after all, a historical figure, and not just the vaguely folkloric one he's often made out to be.

When it came to Bennett, I established a mental hierarchy of reliable sources. Near the top I put *Herald* editors and reporters writing about things they had seen firsthand. At the bottom I put information from later *Herald* chroniclers, or anything that Bennett had supposedly done at swanky private parties or aboard the *Lysistrata*—unless it was obvious that a journalist had been present. I placed Don Seitz's biography above Richard O'Connor's, in part because Seitz was an important figure at *The World* when Bennett was running the *Herald*, and would have heard contemporary tales about him, and I trusted Albert Stevens Crockett's account of working for Bennett (and his deputy, William Reick) during the first years of the twentieth century, because it was pulled straight from the author's own experience. I also put more faith in contemporary magazine profiles of Bennett by former *Herald* staffers. However, it is also evident that many of these authors trod carefully while their old boss was still alive. Partly because he published his biography after Bennett's death, Seitz's account feels less constrained—in addition to relatively well informed.

Researching Adolph S. Ochs was a very different experience. I spent more time with his personal papers, which are intermingled with older records of the New York Times Company at the New York Public Library, than with any other source or archive. His humanizing letters provided a welcome contrast to all the slightly cartoonish second- and thirdhand accounts of Bennett, and I have no reason to doubt the truth of what they contain. Ochs had a salesman's way with words, and often exaggerated his success and grandeur in the letters he wrote to family, but I don't recall finding a concrete example of his lying outright. (The flaws in some of his later recollections I attribute to failing memory.) If Ochs is the character I felt closest to, it is partly because of the many hours I spent with this trove of private correspondence.

But it is also partly because of the man himself. The letters Ochs sent to Effie during 1896 leave the reader buzzing as if from a contact high—that's how potent his energy and optimism were. Of course, this tranche of primary documents also offers a fascinating blow-by-blow account of his unlikely acquisition of *The New York Times*, a purchase that altered the trajectory of modern media. But I do not think that is the reason that Ochs bought the *Times*. Achieving personal success and respectability came first for him, however much he claimed otherwise. He was only human. Elmer Davis and even Meyer Berger—the two best early *Times* historians—cling a bit too closely to the heroic myth of Ochs, and Gerald Johnson's *Honorable Titan* is as blandly uncritical as its title implies. Harrison Salisbury dug deeper, and the all-seeing Susan Tifft and Alex Jones let Ochs get away with nothing. These nuanced later histories acknowledge the compromises, character flaws, occasional hypocrisies, and other imperfections that characterized his superlative management of the *Times*. They present a fuller portrait.

*Battle of Ink and Ice* doesn't just draw from old newspapers; it is also about them, and I was often as curious about what the papers had to say as I was about which one of them said it, and how, and what reasons it might have had for doing so. For the polar controversy of 1909 in particular, I typically relied on multiple newspaper accounts—sometimes as many as half a dozen—of the key events. When one paper's version of events didn't align with the others, I used my judgment to determine whether its story should therefore be included, discarded, or presented with a caveat. Before putting my faith in a newspaper account, I did my best to confirm that no evidence later emerged to contradict or cast significant doubt upon it. Luckily for me, many of the recent retellings of the journeys of Peary, Cook, Greely, De Long, and Stanley feature thorough and well-documented research.

One reason I decided to write this book was that I knew that so much of the correspondence between Peary, his financial backers, William Reick of the *Times*, and the American exploring and scientific establishment had been preserved. From the beginning, I've been fascinated by how Peary and his allies flexed their institutional and press influence. These archival records enabled me to study their covert campaign at close range and to see for myself that Cook's claim that he was up against an "Arctic Trust" was not all that far-fetched.

Most of the Peary camp's correspondence from the fall of 1909 is kept at the National Archives. Some of it also resides at the Explorers Club, of which I have been a member since 2014. I am not the first to consult these collections, but I do believe I am the first to consult the records of *The New York Times* in hopes of learning something new about the polar controversy—and learn something new I did. Most dramatically, I uncovered George Dunkle's confidential description of the shady three-way deal he struck with the *Times* and the Peary Arctic Club. Importantly, Dunkle went to Reick and Hubbard *after* approaching

Cook on his own initiative. Because Cook's supporters accused the Peary Arctic Club and the *Times* of employing Dunkle and August Loose to lay a trap for Cook, this archival discovery can actually be seen as exculpatory. Still, the fact remains that the *Times* violated its own ethical standards while dealing with these two schemers.

It is hard not to fall under the spell of Frederick Cook. He was a dreamer, an underdog, and a fine speaker and writer. But I approached his writings with a great deal of skepticism. Rather than try to penetrate the largely unknowable realm of Cook's mind, I relied on the observations of those around him—people like Wake, Lonsdale, Egan, Stead, and Gibbs, and various unnamed newspaper correspondents. Peary, on the other hand, left a revealing paper trail, and his correspondence from the fall of 1909 was very useful in reconstructing what he was doing and feeling at the time.

As for my own opinion regarding the polar claims of both men, I will say this. Reading the various arguments that have been made over the decades, I found myself especially drawn to those authors who had no preexisting loyalty or personal aversion to the explorer they focused on. It is notable that two of the most persuasive voices in this whole debate, Wally Herbert and Robert Bryce, reached different conclusions than they had originally expected to, displeasing the less-than-neutral organizations that had commissioned or abetted their research. Both risked going where the facts took them. I consider this a win for disinterested scholarship, and I share the increasingly uncontroversial opinion that neither Cook nor Peary reached the pole. This might seem like a disappointing place to arrive at, but I'm actually heartened by the fact that it has nearly become accepted wisdom. To me, this suggests that intellectual independence can triumph in highly polarized environments—even if the heat of opposition takes a long time to subside.

## KEY TO ABBREVIATIONS

### Newspapers/Journals

*BDE*: *Brooklyn Daily Eagle*
*E&P*: *Editor & Publisher*
*NYH*: *New York Herald*
*NYS*: *New York Sun*
*NYT*: *New York Times*
*NYTRIB*: *New York Tribune*
*NYW*: *New York World*
*TFE*: *The Fourth Estate*
*TOL*: *Times* (London)

### Organizations

NGS: National Geographic Society
PAC: Peary Arctic Club
UC: University of Copenhagen

### Archives

APAC: Archives of the Peary Arctic Club (unless otherwise stated, individual citations are from Series 15, "Claims on the North Pole")
ASOP: Adolph S. Ochs Papers, New York Times Company Records

FACP: Frederick Albert Cook Papers

JRYP: John Russell Young Papers

PFC: Peary Family Collection (unless otherwise stated, all citations are from "Letters and Telegrams Sent, 1872–1919")

### Names

ASO: Adolph S. Ochs

BLO: Bertha Levy Ochs (mother of Adolph Ochs)

CVA: Carr Van Anda

EWO: Effie Wise Ochs (wife of Adolph Ochs)

HLB: Herbert L. Bridgman (secretary of the PAC)

JGB: James Gordon Bennett Jr.

THH: Thomas H. Hubbard (president of the PAC)

For full citations, see the bibliography.

## Prologue: The Great Goal

Details of Cook's stop at Lerwick are from his *My Attainment of the Pole* and Freeman's *Case for Doctor Cook*. The telegram from JGB to Cook is in box 2, reel 2, FACP. A good summary of nineteenth-century polar exploring can be found in the first chapter of Larson's *To the Edges of the Earth*.

## PART ONE: ADVENTURES IN JOURNALISM

### One

Much of my information about Bennett Sr. comes from the biographies by Carlson, Seitz, and Fermer. Additional sources for this chapter include O'Connor's *Scandalous Mr. Bennett*; Bennett's June 2, 1872, obituary in the *NYT*; O'Brien's *Story of "The Sun"*; Parton's fifty-six-page history of the paper for the April 1866 *North American Review*; and Ford and Emery's *Highlights in the History of the American Press*. Hudson, who worked for Bennett Sr. for many years, is another good source. Hone found the *NYH* as personally offensive as its owner, writing in his private diary (*Diary of Philip Hone*) that it was "one of the penny papers which are hawked about the street by a gang of troublesome, ragged boys." The elder Bennett's exciting "new movement in civilization" was June 1, 1840. He wrote about the telegraph in *NYH*, June 4, 1844, and about the attack that sent Henrietta packing on November 10, 1850.

### Two

In sketching JGB's early years, I have drawn primarily upon the biographies by O'Connor and Seitz, the latter of which I consider more reliable. Additional information comes from JGB's childhood acquaintance (and *Herald* subordinate) Thomas B. Connery, who collected his memories for the *Fordham College Monthly* in 1901; thanks to Vivian Shen and Jennie Hoag at Fordham University's Walsh Library for tracking this article down. The *NYT* commented on JGB's cheating incident on June 28, 1858. My rendition of the transatlantic yacht race is drawn from contemporary accounts in the *NYT* and *NYH*, Fiske's 1900 account for *The Smart Set*, and Rousmaniere's history of the New York Yacht Club (*New York Yacht Club*, 57–62). Details of Bennett Sr.'s later life are taken primarily from Seitz and Crouthamel. The quotation about his overcoming so much "active opposition" is from Parton ("*New York Herald*," 381). Twain's description of his *Herald* gig is in volume 2 of *Mark Twain's Letters* (167). According to the biographer Tim Jeal, it was not until 1872 that the self-inventing Stanley settled on "Morton" as a middle name.

## Three

I've relied on Jeal's *Stanley* for much of this chapter, and to a lesser extent on the earlier Stanley biographies of McLynn and Anstruther. Chapter 7 of Moore's *Journalism's Roving Eye* discusses the origins and consequences of the Stanley-Livingstone scoop, and is one of several sources to question whether Stanley's purported Paris meeting with JGB ever happened. Jeal notes (*Stanley*, 94) that both Stanley and JGB exaggerated the expense of the relief expedition; while it was commonly said to have cost $20,000, the actual figure was probably closer to $4,000.

JGB's gag order was later discussed by John Le Sage, the *Telegraph* reporter who secured the unauthorized early interview with Stanley in Marseilles, in Ridout's 1923 article in *E&P* and in Le Sage's January 2, 1926, obituary in *The Telegraph*. Bennett's displeasure with T. P. O'Connor is mentioned in Hamilton Fyfe's biography (*T. P. O'Connor*, 49). Clarke's recollections of Stanley are taken from his memoir, *My Life and Memories*. Both Jeal and John Russell Young (box 28, JRYP) make a compelling case that Stanley worked hard to ensure that JGB received due credit for the Livingstone scoop. Any examination of the initial doubts surrounding Stanley's discovery must consider the Victorian British disdain for the American press. In a seminal essay, "Civilization in the United States," the Victorian poet and critic Matthew Arnold wrote that the "absence of truth and soberness in [American newspapers], the poverty of serious interest, the personality and sensation-mongering, are beyond belief." Arnold died in 1888, shortly before Alfred Harmsworth reinvented the British press along more American lines.

## Four

Philip Gibbs published two memoirs—one in 1923, the other in 1946—in which he relates his experience with Cook in Copenhagen. I have relied more on the earlier one, *Adventures in Journalism*. It's certainly possible that Gibbs exaggerated some of Cook's behavior aboard the *Hans Egede* after the fact, but I believe that he was earnestly puzzled by Cook's story from the get-go, and have found no evidence that he had an ax to grind, as some Cook supporters have suggested. Gibbs had been sued in London for libel once before, and so would have been aware of that threat, and yet he persisted.

## Five

Cook's tumultuous week in Copenhagen is documented by W. T. Stead in the October 1909 *Review of Reviews*. Stead probably observed Cook more during that week than any other journalist did all year, and probably spent more hours with him in Copenhagen than anyone save Egan, who published his version of events in *The Century Magazine* in 1910. In his

1924 memoir, *Recollections of a Happy Life*, Egan described Cook as "a grave, rather silent and dependable man" (268). Cook himself later recorded this short, frenzied chapter of his exploring career in *My Attainment of the Pole*. My main source for the September 4, 1909, press conference at the Hotel Phoenix was a write-up in that month's *Collier's* by H. M. Lyon, one of the few American reporters in Copenhagen—and a young fiction writer whose work had caught the eye of Theodore Dreiser. Cook's press conference was, of course, also described by dozens of daily newspapers at the time. Bernacchi's objections are taken from the *TOL*, September 6, 1909. Shackleton's contrasting descriptions are from the *Daily Mail*, March 24, 1909. The telegram JGB sent Cook, noting the London press's attempts to "disparage your triumph," is in box 2, reel 2, FACP. The account of Peary's telegram being delivered to Cook in Copenhagen is from *NYT*, September 7, 1909. Speaker Cannon's quotation is from *NYH*, September 6, 1909.

## PART TWO: BONES IN THE WHITE NORTH

### Six

Kane's descriptions are from his *Adrift in the Arctic Ice Pack*. My descriptions of Hall and the *Polaris* are taken from the superb *Weird and Tragic Shores*, by Chauncey Loomis, who arranged for Hall's corpse to be examined. Details of the Franklin, McClure, and McClintock expeditions are taken from *The Arctic Grail*, Pierre Berton's excellent survey of North Pole and Northwest Passage exploring history. Fun fact: among the many readers entranced by McClintock's account of his search for Franklin, *The Voyage of the Fox*, was a ten-year-old Joseph Conrad, who later wrote (in *Last Essays* [London: J. M. Dent & Sons, 1926], 16–17) that the tale "sent me off on the romantic explorations of my inner self." (For a modern take on how polar exploring affected the inner selves of so many other nineteenth-century readers, see Kathryn Schulz's "Literature's Arctic Obsession," *New Yorker*, April 17, 2017.) The assertion about public interest in the North Pole is from Maury's 1870 article for *The Atlantic Monthly*. Maher's article about De Long leading men through "immense fields of ice" is from *NYH*, September 11, 1873. The silence of the *Polaris* survivors was noted in *NYH*, October 5, 1873. The *NYH* editorial about the "magic circle" of the North Pole ran on October 8, 1873. All of Bennett's lesser-known exploring ventures, including this one, are nicely summarized and analyzed by Riffenburgh.

### Seven

Most of my material about the early *NYT* is from Davis and Berger, and from Francis Brown's 1951 biography of Henry Jarvis Raymond. Additional sources for this chapter include O'Connor, Connery, Seitz, Laney, and Jeal.

Fermer (*James Gordon Bennett and the "New York Herald,"* 36) quotes the *New York Standard*, May 31, 1872, on how the early *NYT* fit in among the more popular *NYTRIB* and *NYH*: "Greeley spoke to the school house and the lyceum, Bennett to the masses of hurried men, and Raymond to the family." The promise to exclude "all objectionable news and advertisements" is from a promotional handbill that was included in a 1996 exhibition about the *NYT* at the Morgan Library & Museum; many thanks to María Isabel Molestina for furnishing the exhibition list. The Tweed Ring episode is recounted in every history of the *NYT*. I also drew on the paper's own contemporary coverage and Mark D. Hirsch's 1945 article "More Light on Boss Tweed." Paul H. Weaver and James L. Aucoin are two of the scholars who trace the origins of modern investigative journalism to this episode. The 1870s newspaper figures are from Mott (*American Journalism*, 404–5) and James Melvin Lee's *History of American Journalism*. A 1929 essay by the former *NYH* reporter Francis McCullagh sheds additional light on the elder Bennett's success and legacy. *The Press Gang*, by Mark Summers, is another excellent study of Gilded Age New York City newspapers. The "Zoo Hoax" appeared in *NYH*, November 9, 1874. Moore (*Journalism's Roving Eye*, 46) is the source of the "every nook and cranny" quotation. The "reporter of today" is described in *NYTRIB*, February 11, 1873. For more on George Smith's archaeological work for *The Telegraph*, see Damrosch's *Buried Book*.

### Eight

De Long's November 10, 1874, letter to JGB is in box 9, JRYP. JGB's planning with De Long is described in Emma De Long's *Explorer's Wife*. His planning with MacGahan is described in Walker's biography of the latter, including the letter in which JGB suggested that MacGahan would "eclipse Stanley" (*Januarius MacGahan*, 164). The figure for JGB's *Pandora* expedition contribution comes from Janice Cavell's 2013 article in *Book History*. MacGahan's descriptions are from *NYH*, October 31, 1875. The voyage of the *Pandora* is discussed in Allen Young's *Cruise of the* Pandora. The Nares expedition is summarized in Berton (*Arctic Grail*, 414).

### Nine

JGB's misbehavior is colorfully related by Seitz, who mentions his sensitivity to alcohol (*James Gordon Bennetts*, 243), and O'Connor, who discusses his arrangement with Abe Hummel (*Scandalous Mr. Bennett*, 133–34). For more on Hummel, see Cait Murphy's *Scoundrels in Law*. The story about JGB's previous broken engagements is from the *Boston Post*, February 22, 1876. The quotation about "watchful glances" at the Union Club is from *NYS*, January 4, 1877, and the quotation about JGB's "bitter wrath" is from *NYTRIB*, January 8, 1877. JGB's thrashing was covered by all the New York City papers, and the subsequent duel with Fred May also received wide press coverage, including in the *NYT*, which headlined its one-column January 10, 1877, account A FARCE IN THREE SHOTS. Sides also recounts both incidents with cinematic attention to detail.

### Ten

Here and elsewhere, I have leaned on the exemplary work of Tifft and Jones for details of ASO's life. His boyhood delivery job is described in Julius Ochs's unpublished memoir (box 18, folder 13, ASOP). The *Knoxville Chronicle* editor's quotation is from James Melvin Lee's profile of Ochs in *E&P*, September 18, 1926. In the February 20, 1907, article in *Printers' Ink*, author R. E. Raymond praised ASO's business acumen but insisted that he was "not a creative spirit in journalism." When the *NYT* business manager Louis Wiley and the *Chattanooga Times* editor Lapsley Walker disputed this assessment, Raymond responded that because ASO neither wrote nor commented upon the news of the day, he could not properly be considered a journalist—as Greeley, Raymond, Bennett Sr., and Pulitzer could (box 51, folder 11, ASOP). The *Boston Globe* quip about JGB is from January 8, 1877.

## Eleven

The *Jeannette* preparations are discussed in the books of Newcomb (the expedition's naturalist) and Emma De Long, and the thoroughly researched accounts of Guttridge and Sides. The *NYT* decried the "mirage" of the open polar sea on November 8, 1874. Petermann's prediction of an inhabited polar region and his defense of Stanley appeared in *NYH*, July 15, 1876. Stanley's legacy in Africa is discussed in Norman R. Bennett's introduction to *Stanley's Despatches to the "New York Herald."* Riffenburgh (*Myth of the Explorer*, 76–77) discusses JGB's desire to replicate the Stanley-Livingstone scoop and concludes that "Bennett's last great attempt to create exclusive news in the Arctic was also the press's most obvious and disastrous meddling in polar exploration." For an example of JGB's playing up the dangers facing Nordenskiöld, see *NYH*, February 2, 1879. The prediction that the *Jeannette* was "safe at anchor" appeared in *NYH*, January 30, 1880.

## Twelve

Schwatka's expedition is summarized in Riffenburgh, who also comments on the significance of Gilder's writing. Gilder's descriptions are from *NYH*, September 24, 26, and 27, 1880. News of "the poor fellows" in Siberia was reported in *NYH*, December 21, 1881. Jack Cole's confusion is recorded in *NYH*, April 26, 1882. Danenhower's version of the disaster appears in Jackson's *NYH* dispatches of May 2 and 3, 1882; he recounted his interviews in Irkutsk during the congressional inquiry. Jackson's account of the sleigh journey to Irkutsk appears in *NYH*, April 17, 1882. Gilder's story, and the excerpts from De Long's diary that he read in Siberia, are from *Ice-Pack and Tundra*. Melville's criticism of Gilder is from *In the Lena Delta* (368), in which Melville also took Jackson to task for his "desecration" of the cairn-tomb (370). Guttridge describes the movements of both *NYH* correspondents in *Icebound* (285–90), as well as the navy inquiry and funeral ceremonies (298–312). Emma De Long's letter to JGB about her "intense suffering" is taken from his account. The "mistake" of mixing civilians with navy men is discussed in *NYT*, April 16, 1884. Chandler's "martyrs in the cause of science" quotation is from Sides (*Kingdom of Ice*, 406). As mentioned in chapter 19, the discovery of *Jeannette* relics in Greenland also helped later explorers to understand Arctic currents. The *NYT* plea for the "noble dead" appeared on March 22, 1884. The $340,000 figure comes from Berger (*Story of "The New York Times,"* 168). The *Jeannette* disaster was called JGB's "greatest disappointment" by the former *Herald* reporter Leo Redding, in a 1914 profile of his old boss for *Everybody's Magazine*.

## Thirteen

The story of the transatlantic cable is told by both Gordon and Standage, who is also the source (*Victorian Internet*, 153) of the "distant kitchen" quotation. Klein's biography of Jay Gould narrates the cable war from the financier's perspective; Crouch tells the story from Mackay Bennett's point of view. Crouch also reveals (*Bonanza King*, 11) that long before Mackay spent time with JGB in France, he had idolized Bennett Sr. and hawked the *Herald* as a New York City newsboy in the 1840s. Gould's doubling of rates was reported in *NYT*, May 16, 1882. The *NYT* called him the would-be "autocrat of America" on February 23, 1881, and described Mackay-Bennett's state-of-the-art cables on May 4, 1884. The passages about the *NYH* are drawn primarily from Mott, Seitz, and Connery. The limitations of the Fourth

Amendment are discussed in Starr (*Creation of the Media*, 187–88). Strictly speaking, the 25-cents-a-word cable rate that was eventually settled on was not "universal." As noted in *NYH*, December 5, 1889, it remained as high as $2 a word in far-flung places like Brazil and Zanzibar.

### Fourteen

I've drawn most details of Pulitzer's life from the biographies of Morris and Juergens, who quotes the "spicy, pithy, pictorial" slogan in *Joseph Pulitzer and His World*, 29. Daly's *Covering America* enumerates some of the ways in which Pulitzer revolutionized journalism. I relied on Seitz's biography of him as well, but more for those sections dealing with the mid-1890s to the early twentieth century—the period during which he worked for Pulitzer. Additional material about the *NYW* comes from McKerns. JGB grudgingly acknowledged Pulitzer's success in *NYH*, October 17, 1890.

### Fifteen

Riffenburgh's *Myth of the Explorer* provides an excellent in-depth analysis of press sensationalism and polar exploring, and is one of the studies that first got me interested in this subject. The critique of "slang-whang" journalism comes from an 1887 article in *The Westminster Review*. Worth noting: while Pulitzer was destroying privacy norms, JGB was still refusing to print interviews without the subject's "personal knowledge and consent," as John Russell Young informed James Creelman on February 21, 1890 (box 19, JRYP). *The Journalist*'s concerns about "trial by newspaper" are quoted in Lee's *Daily Newspaper in America* (633). The tale of the Lady Franklin Bay expedition is from Guttridge's *Ghosts of Cape Sabine*. Some details of this ill-fated venture come from Berton, who also notes (*Arctic Grail*, 442) that its participants survived the coldest winter on record. Greely's gratitude to the press is related in Robinson's *Coldest Crucible* (94). The premature verdict of *Harper's Weekly* ran in the August 16, 1884, edition. The story behind the *NYT*'s cannibalism scoop, including the quotation about journalists who "thrive on calamity," is briefly told in Seitz's *Training for the Newspaper Trade*, 70. The results of the corpse examination in Rochester are related in *NYT*, August 15, 1884. The *NYT* called for "an end to this folly" even before the cannibalism rumors emerged, on July 18, 1884. President Arthur on the unacceptable "loss of human life" is from Berton (*Arctic Grail*, 485). Regarding the Greely expedition's legacy, Michael Robinson writes, "Billed as the most ambitious research mission ever sent into the Arctic, it marked instead the end of serious collaboration between scientists and Arctic explorers in the nineteenth century" (*Coldest Crucible*, 85). Schwatka called for the government to get out of polar exploring in *NYT*, August 17, 1884. Details of his life are from Riffenburgh, and from Nuttall's *Encyclopedia of the Arctic*. For more on Schwatka's Yellowstone expedition, see the Winter 1983 edition of *Montana: The Magazine of Western History*. The *NYT* quotation about the pointlessness of pole hunting appeared on February 19, 1885. The *NYT* had similar things to say on November 8, 1874, regarding the pursuit of the pole and the Northwest Passage: "All this 'derring-do' has a charm for the fancy or curiosity of men, especially the men of science; for men of mere business are never greatly deluded by the *fata morgana* of the North Pole, and have little expectation that the 'short cut' from the Atlantic to the Pacific can ever be made available for any purposes of commerce or intercourse."

## Sixteen

Most details of Peary's life are taken from Herbert's *Noose of Laurels*, which draws on earlier sources—especially Weems, the first Peary biographer to consult the explorer's personal archives. Unlike his predecessors, Herbert had both access to Peary's papers and the courage to draw many unflattering conclusions from them. Peary called Nansen's success "a serious blow" in the introduction to *Northward over the Great Ice* (xxxvii), and in that same volume saluted Cook's "professional skill" (423) and Henson's usefulness (424). Given the questionable accuracy of Henson's ghostwritten 1912 memoir and Bradley Robinson's 1947 biography of Henson, *Dark Companion*, I have relied sparingly on these sources. Josephine Peary's *NYH* articles ran between September 13 and 16, 1892. Berton (*Arctic Grail*, 511–30) also deals with the early phase of Peary's exploring career, including the "low ebb" the explorer found himself at in 1902.

## Seventeen

Information about ASO in Chattanooga and New York City, and about the *NYT* at the turn of the century, comes from Davis, Berger, and Tifft and Jones. In later years, ASO often claimed that the *NYT* had been losing $1,000 a day when he acquired it; he said the same in an August 24, 1901, letter to Henry Stix (box 38, folder 7, ASOP). The "picturesque ruin" quotation is from Tifft and Jones (*Trust*, 31), as is ASO's vision of "living in luxury" (18). Box 101 of the ASOP contains much correspondence and documentation relating to ASO's efforts to secure the *NYT* in 1896.

## Eighteen

Tifft and Jones provide a thorough account of ASO's bid to buy the *NYT*. I also consulted Berger, Davis, and the ASOP, including box 26, which contains ASO's letters to EWO. He provided her with regular updates during this tense period, on everything from his intention to ask Grover Cleveland for a letter of endorsement (March 27, 1896) to his bicycle ride through Central Park (June 14) and his surprisingly seamless meeting with J. P. Morgan (June 16). The editor Edward Cary expressed his fears of Times Company stock becoming "perverted" in a letter to Flint on April 28, 1896 (box 1, Charles R. Flint Papers). The factoid about the U.S. Rubber Company is from Quentin Skrabec's *Rubber: An American Industrial History* (Jefferson, N.C.: McFarland, 2014), 37. Harry Adler's congratulatory letter to ASO is from ASOP (box 1, folder 4). ASO's famous vow to "give the news impartially, without fear or favor," appeared in *NYT*, August 19, 1896.

## PART THREE: FIT TO PRINT

## Nineteen

I drew on Berton and Fleming for my account of Nansen's polar journey, as well as the explorer's own 1897 book, *Farthest North*. Nansen discusses the *Jeannette* in his introduction, but he had of course also explained his theory of polar drift before sailing; see, for example, his article in the Royal Geographical Society's *Geographical Journal* of January 1893. Greely's "illogical scheme" is from Fleming (*Ninety Degrees North*, 241). Riffenburgh mentions the interpersonal formality maintained by the Norwegians; attuned as usual to the press angle, he also explains why Nansen was "ideal for his role as media hero" (*Myth of the Explorer*, 140). Jackson recounted his famous meeting with the Norwegian in *A Thousand Days in the Arctic*, vol. 2. The excellent condition of Nansen and his returning team was widely noted at the time, with the *NYT* remarking on September 13, 1896, that "Sverdrup's men appear to have enjoyed a three years' holiday." Nansen recounts his "strange dream" in *Farthest North* (333). My account of the middle phase of Peary's exploring career is drawn mostly from Berton and Herbert, who quotes the explorer on his supposed beneficence to the Cape York Inuit: "As a result of my various sojourns among them, the entire tribe has been raised from the most abject destitution to a condition of relative affluence" (*Noose of Laurels*, 192). The true weight of the largest Cape York meteorite (named Ahnighito) was not accurately determined until later, and is given on the American Museum of Natural History's website. The full, sad story of Minik Wallace, as he was known in the United States, is told in Kenn Harper's *Minik: The New York Eskimo* (Hanover, N.H.: Steerforth Press, 2017). Roosevelt's praise of Peary is from *NYT*, December 16, 1906. Peary's "Ferdinand of Spain" quotation is from Berton (*Arctic Grail*, 523). Peary's daughter, Marie, recalled her father's disappointment with the "four lost years" in *Discoverer of the North Pole* (169). Herbert discusses Peary's missed mapping opportunities (*Noose of Laurels*, 147–48). The description of Cook's meeting with Peary at Cape Sabine is also from Herbert (139–40), who took it from an unpublished autobiographical sketch by Cook. The meeting itself is not disputed, but there is reason to disbelieve Cook's later claim that he conducted a medical exam and detected an irregular pulse, discolored skin, and bloated stomach—all signs of pernicious anemia, of which Peary died in 1920. This appealing tale has often been retold, but Robert M. Bryce, who has studied Cook's record as critically and thoroughly as anyone, believes the examination never happened (see *Cook & Peary*, 787–88.). I have, therefore, taken the somewhat unusual step of not including it.

## Twenty

My description of turn-of-the-century New York City and its daily press comes primarily from Wallace, Campbell, Pomerantz, Alfred M. Lee, James M. Lee, and others cited below. Starr (*Creation of the Media*, 252) is the source of the 94 percent figure. The quotation about "women and children" is cited by James M. Lee (*History of American Journalism*, 323). The *NYT* ran its pictorial coverage of Queen Victoria's Diamond Jubilee, funnily enough, on July 4, 1897; according to *NYT*, August 18, 1921, pulling it off cost a hefty $5,000. The period's newspaper promotional schemes were detailed in *Scribner's* in 1897 by Lincoln Steffens. JGB's "Gift Enterprise" quip is reported in *The Journalist*, January 28, 1888. Wilcox explains the counterintuitive cost discrepancy between blank newsprint and finished newspapers, and how "as advertisements flow in at increased rates, the price of the paper can be further reduced and its attractions multiplied" ("American Newspaper," 91). Kaplan ("From Partisanship to Professionalism," 123) makes the point about poorer readers spending more time absorbing these attractions than their middle-class counterparts. Stead compared fat Sunday newspapers to "the family bible" in *Americanization of the World* (291). Pulitzer boasted of his church-beating audience in *NYW*, March 15, 1897. THE SUICIDE OF A HORSE and other dubious headlines are from Mott (*American Journalism*, 525) and Nasaw's excellent biography of Hearst (*Chief*, 103). The "economy of attention" point is from the third installment of Will Irwin's 1911 *Collier's* series. Most details of Hearst's early life and career (including his dead-fish handshake) are from Nasaw; the grizzly-bear scheme is taken from Daly. The "toy flute" quip is from Cobb (*Exit Laughing*, 123–24). The "dollar-matching contest" quotation is from Seitz (*Joseph Pulitzer*, 212). The "lead pipe" quotation is from Mott (*American Journalism*, 525).

### Twenty-One

My main sources for ASO's first years at the *NYT* are Tifft and Jones and Berger. Though his internally commissioned 1921 history of the paper paints a rosier picture, Davis is also useful. ASO's observation that "every mistake" had been made already is from a November 21, 1896, letter to the Chicago banker John R. Walsh (box 101, folder 4, ASOP). He mentioned the number of unsold issues in a twenty-fifth anniversary speech in 1921 (box 50, folder 15, ASOP). The inimitable Gay Talese did not say much about the early Ochs era at the *NYT* that had not been said before—or was not later said more comprehensively by Tifft and Jones. I did, however, take the story of ASO's adding telephones from him. Campbell (*Year That Defined American Journalism*, 15) notes the objections to typewriters. The *TOL* was publishing reader views contrary to its own before the *NYT* did; ASO privately told a correspondent that the *NYT* "has frequently published letters which are a direct attack upon the policy of the paper itself. It does what the London Times does: offers its columns freely for such letters" (ASO to Charles Lamb, June 19, 1899, box 42, folder 2, ASOP). The *NYT*'s case for "the usefulness of Bryan" appeared on October 25, 1896. Its case against "freak journalism" was made on December 25, 1896, and again on March 4, 1897. ASO cautioned against crusading in a November 24, 1896, letter to Stephen Trask (box 96, folder 30, ASOP). Mott (*American Journalism*, 604) calls the 1897 crusade against the yellows the largest effort of its kind since the 1840s pressure campaign directed at the *NYH*, but the role of the *NYT* should not be overstated. Don Seitz credits the *NYS* and the *Evening Post* with having launched the boycotts (*Joseph Pulitzer*, 229).

### Twenty-Two

Like the conflict itself, the yellow press's role in the Spanish-American War is heavily documented. It has also been exaggerated, as in the story of the famous telegram that Hearst reportedly sent to the *Journal* illustrator Frederic Remington in Cuba: "You furnish the pictures, and I'll furnish the war." No primary record of this telegram exists, and Nasaw (*Chief*, 127–28) concludes that it was probably invented by James Creelman. One of the other famous legends of this period was, of course, the notion that the Spanish had blown up the *Maine*. Compelling evidence to the contrary can be found in Hyman George Rickover's *How the Battleship* Maine *Was Destroyed* (Annapolis, Md.: Naval Institute Press, 1976). Traxel, Campbell, Kinzer, Nasaw, and Seitz's *Joseph Pulitzer* were my main book sources for this chapter. Charles Brown's *Correspondents' War* is a delightful informal study of the wartime press. Leech tells the story of Stickney on the *Olympia* (*In the Days of McKinley*, 207–8). The expense and methods of war coverage are covered in detail in a pair of September 1896 magazine articles: one by Arthur Brisbane, for Hearst's *Cosmopolitan*, and the other by Ray Stannard Baker, for *McClure's*. Brisbane's belief in "the stupidity of the public" is from Carlson's biography of him (*Brisbane*, 294), and his assertion that "people must have" sensationalism is from Alfred M. Lee (*Daily Newspaper in America*, 650). Though hoaxing and "faking" were established phenomena, Pulitzer was one of the first authorities, if not the first, to use the term "fake news." His quotation is from Ireland (*Adventure with a Genius*, 110–11), who, as Pulitzer's diary-keeping secretary, can be trusted, in my opinion, to have documented his employer's statements accurately.

## Twenty-Three

Tucher's *Not Exactly Lying* expertly narrates the history of fake news, and examines the important cultural question that arose at the end of the nineteenth century: Should readers expect only some of what they read in the newspapers to be true, as they had always done before? Or all of it? Famously, cards affixed to the wall of the *NYW* city room urged its reporters to stick to the basics: "Accuracy! Accuracy! Accuracy! Who? What? Where? When? How? The Facts—The Color—The Facts!" Dreiser insisted in *A Book About Myself* that a "flair for the ridiculous" also mattered (485). Hearst's quotation about the "modern editor" is from Brendon (*Life and Death of the Press Barons*, 134). For more on the "Great Moon Hoax," see Matthew Goodman's *"The Sun" and the Moon*. Edison's complaint is quoted by Pomerantz ("Press of Greater New York," 61–62). The "Fake Extra!" report is from *TFE*, April 14, 1898. The tales of flaming snakes and exploding coffee are cited in Milton's *Yellow Kids*. Brown's *Correspondents' War* is the source of the quotations about a "shameless bit of faking" (200) and "so much faking" (131). The Stephen Crane quotation is from "This Majestic Lie," a short story based on his experiences in Cuba. The "running" of *The World* and the *Journal*, and the "exciting emotions" it generated, were noted in *NYT*, February 16, 1897. The term itself I found in Wilcox ("American Newspaper," 88), who defined yellow journalism as "journalism that stimulates man's social senses merely for the sake of the pleasure and excitement attendant upon the stimulation" (76). Brisbane's innovations are described in Brown (*Correspondents' War*, 132) and Baker, and his observations about the accelerating pace of the news are from his 1898 *Cosmopolitan* article ("Modern Newspaper in War Time," 543–44).

## Twenty-Four

For this chapter I relied primarily on ASOP, Tifft and Jones, and Berger. ASO recalled the paper's annual deficits in a 1921 speech (box 50, folder 15, ASOP). *Printers' Ink* noted on August 12, 1896, that it was "common . . . for those connected with newspapers to claim as the circulation the entire number printed." Tifft and Jones were the first to reveal the role that Woolnough appears to have played in the famous price cut. I agree that the vengeful ex-clerk put ASO under additional pressure to boost circulation fast, but it was also true that ASO had previously expressed a desire to sell a "quality" newspaper for one cent, and circumstances might have simply forced him to take this leap earlier than anticipated. ASO claimed in 1902 that the Equitable's main representative at the *NYT*, Marcellus Hartley, had backed his decision, and even personally offered to cover the short-term losses it was sure to generate (box 15, folder 23, ASOP). But according to Hartley's grandson, Marcellus Hartley Dodge, Hartley advised ASO to wait until the paper was on sounder financial footing (box 15, folder 24, ASOP). Trask's query about the price cut is from a letter to ASO on October 11, 1898 (box 42, folder 1, ASOP). ASO noted that the presses were "taxed to their utmost" in an October 13, 1898, letter to Charles P. Bates (box 72, folder 5, ASOP), and that "everyone is happy" to BLO on November 20, 1898 (box 29, folder 9, ASOP). The frustrated auditors included the *American Newspaper Directory* publisher, George P. Rowell; ASO suggested that Rowell interview Upper West Side newsdealers on December 24, 1898 (box 72, folder 5, ASOP). ASO's dubious "almost guarantee" was made to the advertising executive Robert Ogden on August 25, 1899 (box 119, folder 6, ASOP). Miller's meeting with JGB in Paris is recounted in Bond (*Mr. Miller of the "Times,"* 94–95). Rowell (*Forty Years an Advertising Agent*, 433) skips this episode, but confirms the story that the *Evening Telegram* quickly got back on its feet after JGB agreed to reveal its circulation figures to prospective advertisers.

### Twenty-Five

JGB's exploration ventures are chronicled in Riffenburgh; Villard's *Blue Ribbon of the Air* describes his later interest in aviation, automobiles, and other sports. "Mr. Bennett's liberality" is from an April 11, 1899, letter from an unnamed *NYH* news editor to HLB (APAC Series 7, file 80). The $27,000 figure is from Villard's *Blue Ribbon* (13). Cook wrote about the *Belgica* in *NYH*, July 2, 1899. His medical discoveries are discussed in Sancton (*Madhouse at the End of the Earth*, 313–15). Seitz recalled that the attainment of the pole "seemed chimerical" to Pulitzer in "Portrait of an Editor" (295), a claim supported by a March 25, 1900, *NYW* headline: THE COLOSSAL FOLLY OF THE CENTURY: THE USELESS SEARCH FOR THE NORTH POLE.

### Twenty-Six

Most of the material about JGB's life and work comes from the newsmen Seitz, O'Connor, and Crockett, and the wealth experts Beebe and Vanderbilt. *TFE* called the *NYH* the most profitable newspaper on May 19, 1898. The $625,000 figure comes from JGB's obituary in *NYT*, May 15, 1918. *Motoring and Boating* called his new yacht a "floating palace" on June 8, 1904. Vanderbilt, among others, tells the story of the surprise cruise toward Egypt (*The Glitter and the Gold*, 63–64). JGB's quip about "my own medicine" is mentioned in *TFE*, December 12, 1903; the "most picturesque" quotation is from Redding, "Bennett of the *Herald*." The *NYH* described its new headquarters on July 8, 1894, in an article immodestly headlined THEY GAZE WITH WONDER, but the best description of the building that I found was in Hennessy's 1895 article for *Metropolitan*, "How the 'Herald' Is Made." Roosevelt's quip about JGB appears in his *Realizable Ideals*, 145. "Paris toy" is quoted in McCullagh ("Gordon Bennetts and American Journalism," 408). Fun fact: JGB's Newport Casino is now home to the International Tennis Hall of Fame.

### Twenty-Seven

Tifft and Jones (*Trust*, 66–68) discuss the 1900 Paris project in more detail than other *NYT* chroniclers. ASO boasted about *NYT* advertising revenue in a December 30, 1900, letter to BLO (box 29, folder 9, ASOP), and knew he'd been gaining on Pulitzer in this area because his business manager, John Norris, had recently worked at the *NYW*. The "taken over a ship" quotation is from a 1949 letter to *NYT* editors from Marcellus Hartley Dodge (box 15, folder 24, ASOP). Pomerantz ("Press of Greater New York," 62) notes the paper's avoidance of illustrations. ASO discussed competing with the *NYH* on January 22, 1899 (box 29, folder 2, ASOP). Frederic's obituary appeared in *NYT*, October 20, 1898. George Ochs reported to ASO from Paris on February 29, 1900 (box 102, folder 3, ASOP). Contextual descriptions of the Paris Expo are from Fenby, Mandell, and *NYT*, March 26, 1900. The impact of Linotype is discussed in *Newspaperdom*, January 25, 1900, and in "Recent Changes in the Press," a 1901 lecture by Whitelaw Reid that appears in his *American and English Studies*. The *NYT* boasted of "fuller American cable news" on June 1, 1900, quoted *L'Écho* on June 2, and described the Paris edition's production and distribution on June 17. ASO said that he was "seriously contemplating" continuing it on August 24, 1900 (box 88, folder 7, ASOP). The line about ASO's thinking "beyond the boundaries of his own country" is from Johnson's *Honorable Titan*.

### Twenty-Eight

The "Peary system" is explained by Herbert and by Berton, who also enumerates which elements were borrowed from Peary's predecessors (*Arctic Grail*, 553–54). Peary's claim to have seen "snow-clad summits" is from Herbert (*Noose of Laurels*, 196–97). The description of "the poor old *Roosevelt*" is from Bartlett (*Log of "Bob" Bartlett*, 178). Steffens claimed that "Dunn simply could not lie" in his *Autobiography* (326). All of Dunn's passages are quoted from his *Outing* series, except for the one about Cook's "bovine face," which is from *World Alive* (99). Additional details of Cook's 1906 McKinley expedition, including the no-show hunting client, Henry Disston, are from Bryce's *Cook & Peary*. Cook's statement about "hellish conditions" is from his May 1907 *Harper's* article, "Conquest of Mount McKinley," 821.

### Twenty-Nine

Kluger identified the city's "most vital running story" (*Paper*, 165). Pulitzer's attempts to reform the *NYW* in absentia are described by Seitz and others, including Irvin Cobb, who wrote that by around 1900 the publisher was "over the yellow fever but still had the yellow jaundice" (*Exit Laughing*, 30). I am tempted to agree with Mott, who considers it "probable that the *Times*' object lesson influenced Pulitzer to withdraw from competition in the yellow methods" (*American Journalism*, 549). After all, Pulitzer read and respected the *NYT*. On May 26, 1908, he wrote to ASO, "You may not know that I have the Times sent to me abroad when the World is forbidden & that most of my news I really receive from your paper. You have a very, very able editorial page" (box 29, folder 32, ASOP). ASO's comment about "old journalism" is taken from Rogers (*Newspaper Building*, 58). Godkin's concerns regarding "sensible and high-minded men" are quoted in Davis (*History of "The New York Times,"* 78). ASO calculated his total *NYT* earnings on August 24, 1900 (box 88, folder 7, ASOP). Stern's "something more than money" comment is from ASO to BLO, November 4, 1900 (box 29, folder 9, ASOP). ASO's daily routine and status within the family are discussed in the Faber and Dryfoos versions of Iphigene Ochs Sulzberger's memoir. "Wellington after Waterloo" is quoted in Tifft and Jones (*Trust*, 40). ASO wrote to BLO of his "great satisfaction" on February 3, 1901 (box 29, folder 10, ASOP). The 1901 European tour is related in Faber, "*New York Times* Girlhood," chap. 5; the letters ASO wrote to BLO while abroad are preserved in ASOP (box 115, folder 7).

### Thirty

My sketch of CVA is drawn from Berger, Talese, and Fine. The story about riding the delivery trucks is from his *NYT* obituary on January 29, 1945. Stewart and Tebbel (*Makers of Modern Journalism*, 133) are two of many chroniclers who called him the best in the business. "Telephone mania" is quoted in Campbell (*Year That Defined American Journalism*, 33–34). ASO demanded credit for having created "a free atmosphere and environment" for CVA in an October 17, 1932, letter to Wiley (box 42, folder 16, ASOP). The emergence of a new, facts-based ideal of early twentieth-century journalism is described by Forde and Foss, who cite the growing emphasis on what Daston and Galison call "trained judgment" in their study of the notion of scientific objectivity. Garrett's diary entry is from Cornuelle ("Remembrance of the *Times*," 432). Cary saluted ASO as a "representative American" in a June 12, 1915, statement for publication (box 51, folder 11, ASOP). Eleven years later, Stolberg made a similar point in *The Atlantic*: "It is because Mr. Ochs in his own person represents the median of our national culture that he is by all odds the best judge on his staff as to what news is 'fit to print'" ("Man Behind the 'Times,'" 724). For more on Pulitzer's educational legacy, see James R. Boylan's *Pulitzer's School: Columbia University's School of Journalism, 1903–2003* (New York: Columbia University Press, 2003). Rogers (*Newspaper Building*, 59) records ASO's claim that he never reduced a salary; he also praised the "machine-like regularity" of the paper's growth (47). *E&P* complained of vanishing editorial pages on October 4, 1902. Hearst's *Evening Journal* was typically nasty in its assessment of ASO: "It happens that Mr. Ochs is an uneducated gentleman, and he does not write." My account of the Times Tower is mostly drawn from Davis, Edward H. Edwards, and the fulsome self-coverage of the *NYT* on January 1, 1905. For more on the historical relationship between Times Square and the New York subway system, see Clifton Hood's *722 Miles: The Building of the Subways and How They Transformed New York* (New York: Simon & Schuster, 1993).

Thirty-One

My account of the Equitable scandal is taken mainly from Buley, with some details from Beard. The tale of ASO, the Times Tower, and the Equitable scandal is told by Salisbury (*Without Fear or Favor*, 102–7). The *Evening Journal* attacked ASO on April 7, 1904. Tifft and Jones (*Trust*, 75) accuse ASO of giving James Hazen Hyde special treatment in the *NYT*, and also counted the 115 front-page stories. The "widespread injury" quotation is from *NYT*, March 16, 1905. The *NYT* fretted that the scandal had become "a menace to the peace and good order of the financial district" on June 11, 1905. Roosevelt's "crooked and objectionable" quotation is from *NYT*, June 22, 1905. Wiley's defense of ASO was printed in *Collier's*, May 13, 1911. Years earlier, after picking up where the Tweed-whacking *NYT* had left off by exposing the Crédit Mobilier scandal, the *NYS* lamented its rival's withdrawal from investigative work: "The mistake of the *Times* was in lapsing into the dullness of respectable conservatism after its Ring fight. It should have kept on and made a crusade against frauds of all sorts" (*NYS*, September 3, 1875). My brief account of muckraking is taken mostly from Regier. For a contemporary critique of the "literature of exposure," see Alger's August 1905 essay in *The Atlantic*. Pulitzer's "money or the mob" quotation is from "The College of Journalism" (679). The most persistent criticism of the *NYT* under ASO came from the left: Oswald Garrison Villard, owner of *The Nation*, blasted ASO for his "unending devotion to the God of things as they are" (*Some Newspapers and Newspaper-Men*, 10), and the socialist crusader Upton Sinclair accused him of spiking an article about New York City's social and financial elite for self-interested reasons. ASO simply would not risk offending the "sacred divinities of New York," Sinclair claimed—even if it meant overriding CVA, and despite the fact that the *NYT* had treated Sinclair's earlier exposures of the Chicago meatpacking industry as important news (*Brass Check*, 76–77).

## Thirty-Two

My account of Hearst's early politicking, including the controversy surrounding McKinley's assassination, is taken mostly from Nasaw. Stead put Hearst atop America's "government by journalism" in *The Americanization of the World* (296). The *NYH* condemned "organized hatred" on November 6, 1906. JGB's disgust with Hearst's Cuba coverage is from Kluger (*Paper*, 183). Hearst's belittling nicknames were recorded in *NYT*, October 9, 1906. The "dog-catcher" quotation is from O'Connor (*Scandalous Mr. Bennett*, 271). The "personals" examples are taken from the various JGB biographies; the *NYH*, November 1, 1898; and the *New York American*, July 8, 1906. There are many outtakes. My favorite (from Stewart and Tebbel, *Makers of Modern Journalism*, 57) is this one, delightful in its coquettish understatement: "A handsome young girl desires copying or some other profitable work." JGB's "I shall never forget you" is from Winkler (*W. R. Hearst*, 220), who presents it as a quotation, whereas *NYT*, October 9, 1906, quotes Hearst's response only. Roosevelt (*Realizable Ideals*, 148) claimed that JGB secretly used "every species of pressure and influence" to try to avoid the court appearance, which was documented in *NYT*, April 11, 1907. The judge's description of the *NYH* as a "directory of local harlots" is quoted in Godfrey Hodgson's *Colonel: The Life and Wars of Henry Stimson, 1867–1950* (New York: Knopf, 1990). Redding quotes JGB issuing the following orders to his newsroom after the personals scandal: "If Hearst dies, goes to jail, or is elected president of the United States, I want no mention of him in the *Herald*" ("Bennett of the *Herald*," 855). *Life* complained about the lack of accountability on June 13, 1907, 815. My account of journalism's evolving ethical standards is drawn mostly from James Melvin Lee's *History of American Journalism* and Irwin's 1911 *Collier's* series, part 10.

## Thirty-Three

The story of JGB's later reign is taken from the books of Crockett, Seitz, O'Connor, and Laney, and from the contemporary articles of Nathan, Hennessy, and Fish, as well as the memoirs and magazine pieces cited below. *TFE* reported that JGB "absolutely dominated" the *NYH* on December 19, 1903, and that he held 994 of the Herald Company's 1,000 shares on January 6, 1900. Creelman's observations about JGB's "nose for news" and self-imposed loneliness are from his 1894 (as opposed to his 1902) profile for *Cosmopolitan*, and JGB's editorial peccadilloes are listed in O'Connor (*Scandalous Mr. Bennett*, 170). In *News Hunting*, Chambers characterized his acrimonious departure from the *NYH* as "typical," but also described JGB as "the most brilliant editorial chief I have ever served" (307–9). Bonsal's "up like a rocket" analogy is from *Heyday in a Vanished World* (421). Reick's complaint about JGB's favored clubmen is quoted in Seitz's *James Gordon Bennetts* (218). *TFE* reported the circumstances surrounding Howland's death on May 16, 1903, and JGB's talk of a "headless republic" on December 19, 1903. The first version of JGB's Herald Building quip is from Seitz (*James Gordon Bennetts*, 360); the second is from O'Connor (*Scandalous Mr. Bennett*, 223). JGB's "bigness as well as littleness" was identified by McCullagh ("Gordon Bennetts and American Journalism," 412), and his "swift, severe" punishments were noted by Redding

("Bennett of the *Herald*," 852). Paine attests to the near-universal dread of being assigned a yachting story in *Roads of Adventure* (385).

### Thirty-Four

Descriptions of the December 15, 1906, NGS dinner are from the *NYH*, December 16, 1906. Extracts from the speeches are taken from transcriptions in the January 1907 *National Geographic*. Cook's note that he had "hit upon a new route" was reported in *NYT*, October 5, 1907. Peary's preemptive protest to Brussels is quoted by Freeman (*Case for Doctor Cook*, 101); Georges Lecointe, director of Belgium's Royal Observatory, confirmed to the *NYH* on October 22, 1909, that he had received Peary's letter, but declined to discuss its contents.

### Thirty-Five

Some details of Reick's early career are taken from various contemporary profiles. Others come from his December 8, 1924, *NYT* obituary, which described the career opportunity he had seized at the *NYH* in amusingly polite terms: "There were many competent men on its staff, but few who cared to take responsibility in view of the personal peculiarities of its proprietor." O'Connor (*Scandalous Mr. Bennett*, 220) mentions JGB's gift of Manhattan real estate, and Reick's delight upon learning that it would lie along the city's first subway line, vastly increasing its value. Reick's 1903 discussions with ASO are documented in ASOP (box 33, folder 1). Crockett, who worked for Reick during this period, offers the most detailed account of his humiliation by JGB in France and claimed that Reick thereafter "aimed at revenge" (*When James Gordon Bennett Was Caliph of Baghdad*, 306). Laney records the judgment of JGB's private secretary, Alfred Jaurett (*"Paris Herald,"* 46).

### Thirty-Six

Peary's fundraising efforts were documented by the *NYTRIB* and other New York City newspapers of May 17–24, 1908. The *NYT* declared that "Dr. Cook knows his business" on October 4, 1907. Peary's complaint about Cook to the *NYT*, dated May 1908, was finally published there on September 9, 1909. My account of Peary's rejection by the *NYH* is taken from Davis, Berger, and O'Connor. To me, Marie Peary's later claim that her father promised the scoop to Reick and therefore went straight to the *NYT* (and consequently never suffered the embarrassment of a rejection by the *NYH*) smacks of face-saving revisionism. Bartlett's version of the story—that Reick personally lent Peary the $4,000, then brought the story to the *NYT* after quitting the *NYH*—is laughably inaccurate, as Freeman (*Case for Doctor Cook*, 278–79) points out. Peary's contract with the *NYT* was signed on July 6, 1908, according to *NYT*, September 11, 1909. The *NYH* derided the deal's supposedly lopsided terms on September 15, 1909.

### PART FOUR: ANTIHEROES

Note: Any newspaper source for part 4 for which the year is not given is from 1909.

## Thirty-Seven

ASO wrote of his "stupendous scoop" to EWO on September 8 (box 27, ASOP). Davis writes of the "disappointment" among *NYT* management upon hearing Cook's news (*History of "The New York Times*," 291). "Almost inconceivable" is from *NYT*, September 3. Gibbs's account is from the *NYT* stories he filed in early September and his (somewhat redundant) later autobiographies, *Adventures in Journalism* and *The Pageant of the Years*. Freuchen was not known for his fidelity to the facts, and so I've drawn sparingly from his account in *Arctic Adventure*. Egan's description of Gibbs is from his 1910 article for *Century*. The *NYH* slammed ignorant reporters on September 11. Amundsen's defense of Cook as "upright" is quoted in Bryce (*Cook & Peary*, 206). The *TOL* acknowledged the "profound impression" Cook made upon the Copenhagen press corps on September 6. Stead's assessment of Cook's lecture is from his "Character Sketch." Cook's exchange with Rector Torp at the diploma presentation is given by Morris, in *Finding the North Pole*. "I show you my hands!" is from *NYH*, September 10.

## Thirty-Eight

Grand Central Station, as it was called at the time, would become Grand Central Terminal in 1913. The press comments that HLB gave there appeared in *NYT*, September 7. Adams predicted that no "vital human interest" would be affected by the pole's discovery in *The American Review of Reviews*, October 1909, 420. The *NYT* downplayed the "sentimental attractions" of the pole on September 6; The Cornell physicist John S. Shearer went further, referring to Peary's and Cook's work as "vaudeville science" in *NYT*, September 8. The government official's comment about "a sportsman's job" is from *NYH*, September 12. The *NYW* sports editor was quoted in *E&P*, September 11; "a sort of athletic enterprise" is from *NYW*, September 20. Cook's "feat of brain and muscle" is from *My Attainment of the Pole* (74). It later emerged that Marvin did not drown. In 1926, one of Peary's longest-serving drivers, Kudlooktoo, confessed that he had shot and killed him during an argument in which Marvin threatened to abandon Kudlooktoo's cousin on the ice. The *NYT* reported that there was no wireless aboard the *Roosevelt* on July 4, 1908. Peary's fateful telegrams appeared in *NYH*, September 11, 1909. Andrews recalled Peary's confession in the January 1953 issue of *True* magazine, a clipping of which is in the APAC at the Explorers Club, and again in his book *Beyond Adventure: The Lives of Three Explorers* (New York: Duell, Sloan & Pearce, 1954), 7. The *NYH* compared the initial accounts of Cook and Peary on September 12, and quoted Dellenbaugh on September 14. Markham's comment is from *The Paris Herald*, October 1. The *NYH* quoted the French paper's quip on September 10 and published Franke's story on September 13. The "miserable creature" letter from Josephine to Robert Peary is dated September 12, and preserved in "Scrapbook One" of her papers at the University of New England.

## Thirty-Nine

My account of Peary at Battle Harbour is taken from D. M. Edwards—both his *NYH* dispatches of September 15, 20, and 26, 1909, and his recollection for *E&P* in 1959. Currie's descriptions, some of the best writing of that fall's newspaper coverage, are from *NYW*, September 20, 1909. Additional details are taken from *NYT*, September 16–19.

### Forty

An undated obituary of THH (probably May 20, 1915) in the *Portland Evening Express*, a clipping of which I found in the Hubbard Family Papers at Bowdoin College, described him as Bowdoin's biggest donor. The bond of the two "Bowdoin men" was noted in *NYTRIB*, May 20, 1915. THH's quotation about "government property" is from *BDE*, September 7, 1909. Peary sought THH's help crafting the "most destructive" strategy on September 13 (box 12, PFC). The news from Sydney appeared in various New York City papers on September 22; I've taken Bartlett's revelations from that day's *NYH*, Henson's from the *NYW*, and Peary's announcement that he would skip events from the *NYT*.

### Forty-One

Cook's arrival in New York City is drawn from the September 22, 1909, editions of the *NYT, NYW, BDE, NYS,* and *NYH*. Additional details come from Bryce (*Cook & Peary*, 386–93), who leaves no stone unturned. Even Cook's supporters understood that the Danish "virtual guarantee" was contingent upon his provision of further evidence. As Stead wrote in *The American Review of Reviews* that November, "Dr. Cook was accepted at Copenhagen upon the face of his statements, with the distinct understanding that he could and would justify the unstinted kindness and honor conferred upon him by submitting to the University of Copenhagen, and the scientific men associated with it, all the data that would be needed to satisfy them of the truth of his claims." For an overview of the Hudson-Fulton celebrations, I consulted *NYH*, September 26. Cook's first press interview at the Waldorf Astoria is taken from the September 23 *NYT, NYH,* and *NYW*. The illegibility of his notebooks to the naked eye is attested to by Charles Wake in *NYT*, December 27, and by Norman-Hansen, who'd seen them in Greenland and wrote, "All [Cook's] notebooks and greasy and soiled record books, which have been so closely written up, he kept and carried with him. To me, who understands only a very little astronomy, the records written down so closely, and in all directions, were very hard to read" (*NYT*, September 13). Borup called Whitney a "mighty genial chap" in *NYW*, September 27. The press interview that Cook gave after learning that his trunk had been left at Etah is taken from the September 27 *NYT, NYH,* and *NYW*. Whitney's excuses for leaving Cook's trunk are from *NYH*, September 30. Peary's "undeveloped brain" was diagnosed by Stead in his "Character Sketch" of Cook (339). Lonsdale seems to have been a real clotheshorse: the *BDE* reported that he was "attired in a tweed suit, a green necktie, and a horizontal scarfpin two inches broad" at the Waldorf and that he had come to New York with "six trunks full of clothes" (September 23). Cook had previously claimed that his trunk at Etah both did and did not contain essential documents. Upon arriving in New York, he'd told reporters, "I have all the proofs in my possession. I have them here, now" (*BDE*, September 22, 1909).

### Forty-Two

Much of this chapter is drawn from contemporary newspaper accounts, in particular *NYH*, September 28 and 30. The "honest, blunt old Yankee" quotation is from Winchester ("Dr. Cook, Faker," 253). Bernacchi's conclusion is from *The Paris Herald*, October 1. The *NYH* noted that Peary had "distinctly injured himself" among naval colleagues on September 12 and that "it takes two to make a controversy" on October 2. It quoted *The Washington Times* on September 28 and *The Washington Post* on September 29, and cited *The Pittsburgh Press* on September 30. Rawlins (*Peary at the North Pole*, 166–67) emphasizes an element of this popular survey that was overlooked at the time but would take on significance decades later: "No one—of more than 75,000 readers voting—indicated a belief that both claimants could be phonies." Stead's "strange to say" comment is from his "Character Sketch" (339). The verdict of the Tennyson Literary Club appeared in the *NYS*, October 16. Egan's epiphany regarding "the vote of a majority" is from his *Recollections* (271).

### Forty-Three

The *NYH* claimed that it could find no Peary defenders in the national press—and also interviewed Bartlett in Sandy Hook—on October 1. It reported Peary's arrival in New York on October 2. The San Juan Hill analogy is from *Life*, September 30, 430. Bridgman recalled the taunting in "Peary" (8); "absolute hell" is from Andrews in *True* (January 1953, 88). Helen Bartlett Bridgman's description of Eagle Island is from her book *Within My Horizon* (Boston: Small, Maynard, 1920), 181. Peary's October 28, 1909, letter to Grosvenor is quoted in Rawlins (*Peary at the North Pole*, 177). Peary mentioned his scrapbook of Cook press clippings in a November 22, 1909, letter to HLB (box 6, folder 188, APAC). For the full text of the city's official recognition of Cook, see *Ordinances, Resolutions, Etc. Passed by the Board of Aldermen of the City of New York and Approved by the Mayor, 1909* (New York: Martin B. Brown, 1909), 12:531. Peary told THH that "we are now fighting . . . JGB" on September 30 (box 12, PFC). He wrote to THH of the *NYH*'s "unscrupulous and persistent work" on October 7 (folder 188, APAC). THH's "other scientists impartially selected" is quoted in Rawlins (*Peary at the North Pole*, 170). Bumpus and Osborn's membership in the PAC is asserted by Eames (*Winner Lose All*, 179–80). Not-so-fun fact: Osborn would go on to co-found the American Eugenics Society in 1922. Rawlins (*Peary at the North Pole*, 170) accuses THH of "jury tampering," based on the lawyer's instructions to Osborn on September 29: "Please defer final arrangements of Committee until you see Peary. Give Peary acceptance, and declination of other party, to Associated Press." THH is probably referring not to the "acceptance" of Peary's proofs but to Peary's acceptance of the terms of the National Academy's examination thereof.

### Forty-Four

Charles Wake admitted in *NYT*, December 27, that he'd urged Cook to profit from his discovery shortly after the explorer arrived in New York. Bradley told the *NYH* on September 19, "I call it a good sporting performance—the greatest ever." Whitney's interview is from *NYW*, October 4. Cook suggested waiting nearly a whole year before submitting his proofs in *NYW*, October 3. Eight decades later, Herbert agreed that Cook had no valid reason to withhold them: "Data of this nature, if genuine, does not need time for preparation. If the observations and diary are genuine it is because they are made in the field. If Cook had been to the Pole as he claimed, he could have handed over the relevant data then" (*Noose of Laurels*, 304). The *Evening Post* editorial was reprinted in *NYT*, October 12. Dillon Wallace's tirade against anti-Cook forces—"men without conscience or any sense of right, who would blast a life and rob a man of a well and hard earned reward as readily as they would flip the ashes from a cigar"—is from *NYH*, September 16. *The Nation* addressed the "deplorable" polar controversy in its lead editorial that same day. Greely's plea for a "clean record" appeared in *Munsey's*, November 1909, 295. The story of the insane polar claimant appeared in *NYW*, September 28. Twain's musings are from *The Autobiography of Mark Twain*, vol. 3, edited by Harriet E. Smith et al. (Oakland: University of California Press, 2015). The *NYW*'s satirical polar claim ran on September 26. The assertion that "homes were disrupted" is from Egan's *Recollections* (273); Davis (*History of "The New York Times,"* 293) compared Cook and Peary to Lenin and Trotsky. The *NYH* said of Cook's narrative on September 29: "The money value of such a story cannot be estimated. It is worth any sum the explorer and writer might decide to ask." The comment about ASO the "miser" is from the same editorial. The *NYT* referred to "the sum realized for the Peary dispatches" on September 11; according to Berger (*Story of "The New York Times,"* 176), Peary came out $12,000 on top, which would mean that the *NYT* earned $16,000 in syndication profits. ASO's agreement was compared to "Shylock's bond" in *NYH*, September 15. I am confident that this commentary was penned by JGB; he rarely let others speak so freely on behalf of the *Herald* and had indulged in anti-Semitic editorializing during previous disagreements, including one with the impresario Oscar Hammerstein. Matthews lamented the "quarrel by wireless telegraph" in a short essay, cited in Larson, that was titled "Cheapening Heroism" and appeared in *World Today*, November 1909, 1117–18.

## Forty-Five

Etukishuk and Ahwelah's testimony and related materials are from *NYT*, October 13. "A struggle of 20 days" is from *NYH*, October 7. Peary's "more evidence will be forthcoming" is from *NYT*, October 14. Peary's endorsement of Reick is quoted in Bryce (*Cook & Peary*, 430). Indian Harbour and Battle Harbour's only telecommunication link with the outside world was via Marconi wireless, by which Peary's news from both places was transmitted to Cape Ray, Newfoundland. From there it went to Glace Bay, Nova Scotia, and onward to New York City via cable and landline (Berger, *Story of "The New York Times,"* 172–73). Meriwether's recollection of Reick's orders (and CVA's sarcastic response) appeared in his 1949 *Times Talk* article. *E&P* saluted the *NYT*'s feat of rapid transmission on September 18. Stead agreed: "Seldom has the efficiency of the cable, telegraph, and Marconi lines been so strikingly demonstrated," he wrote in the October *American Review of Reviews* (390). Meriwether's confidential September 26 and 27 messages to Reick are in ASOP (box 77, folder 1). ASO mentioned CVA's distrust of Reick in a letter to Wiley on October 17, 1932 (box 42, folder 16, ASOP). The *NYT* noted that "the world is divided into two camps" on September 29, the same day it published Tarr's letter. The astronomer Jacoby's editorial appeared on September 23. *The Globe and Commercial Advertiser* ("New York's Oldest Newspaper") printed the Mount McKinley bombshell on the afternoon of October 14. The extracts from Barrill's affidavit are from *NYT*, October 15; Cook's response is from *NYW*, October 15. Bryce reveals Hubbard's dealings with Ashton and Reick's role in delaying the McKinley scoop (*Cook & Peary*, 429–30). Peary wrote to Reick about the newsman's "yellow neighbor" on October 16 (box 13, PFC), the same day that the *NYH* reported on "large sums of money" and Cook's plan to return to McKinley. Cook's meeting with the Explorers Club is taken from Bryce (*Cook & Peary*, 438).

## Forty-Six

Rasmussen's defense of Cook appeared in *NYT*, October 21. "Dr. Cook has money now to fight" is from *NYT*, October 24. Events leading up to Cook's showdown in Hamilton, and details of the confrontation itself, are taken from Bryce (*Cook & Peary*, 442–47), Hunt ("Confrontation in Montana," 53–54), and the October 29 *NYT* and *NYH*.

## Forty-Seven

Peary wrote to Reick about "Bennett fixing matters" on October 26 (box 13, PFC), and confessed similar fears to HLB on October 30 (folder 188, APAC). His exchange of telegrams with Grosvenor occurred on October 12 and 13 (folder 188, APAC). The NGS had made an unprecedented investment in Peary; according to Poole, its $1,000 grant was the first time it had ever contributed to an expedition (*Explorers House*, 85). Herbert (*Noose of Laurels*, 300) talks about the support the NGS judges had previously shown Peary. The explorer declared himself "extremely gratified" with their verdict in *NYT*, November 4. Both Herbert (*Noose of Laurels*, 323) and Rawlins (*Peary at the North Pole*, 183) discuss the deals that Peary cut once his proofs had been accepted. The *NYH* exposed Moore's "secret mission" on November 6. The dinner menus are preserved in ASOP (box 77, folder 5). The *NYT* rejected "glory enough for two" on November 8. UC's insistence that it was "quite competent" to proceed without the help of NGS is from *The American Review of Reviews*, December 1909, 660. "No scientific standing whatsoever" is from *NYT*, December 12. Admiral Chester's anti-Cook statements appeared in *NYT*, November 8.

## Forty-Eight

Cook's announcement regarding the delivery of his proofs, and Wack's comment that his client had been "bothered to death," are both taken from *NYT*, November 9. Peary sarcastically described himself to HLB as a "jealous blackguard" on October 26 and called Cook a "national disgrace" on October 30 (both in folder 188, APAC). He called his rival "a thief" in a November 21 letter to Reick (box 13, PFC), and referred to JGB as a "senile expatriate" in a November 5 letter to HLB (folder 188, APAC). THH suggested to Peary that Reick try to sway the Danish press—starting with *Politiken*—on November 22 (folder 161, APAC). Peary mentioned dinner with their respective wives to Reick on November 6, and the government's possible complicity in "an infernal fraud and imposture" on November 27 (both box 13, PFC). Wellman's analysis appeared in *NYT*, November 29. The search for Cook, and discussion of the supposed plot against him, are from November 26–29 editions of the *NYH, NYT, NYW, NYS*, and *BDE*. Bradley's comment about "a little advertising" is from *NYT*, December 2. The *NYT* reprinted the item about Cook's having been spotted on Flatbush Avenue on December 10. Lonsdale described Cook's flight from New York in part 1 of his 1910 account for *The Travel Magazine* (427). Wake more or less corroborated this version of events in *NYH*, December 27, 1909. In *My Attainment of the Pole*, Cook claimed to have fled the country in order "to resolve my case in quietude and secrecy" (564). Reick's "important development" telegram is from December 3 (box 13, PFC). Dunkle and Loose's stories are taken entirely from *NYT*, December 9. Like Wellman, Loose found it suspicious that Cook had recorded his latitude observations down to the second, "when every navigator knows that seconds are not usually considered." The *NYT* said that it had delayed publication of the scoop for "several days" while it sought a response from Cook; Wack later recalled that the paper had given him forty-eight hours to procure one (*NYS*, December 22). Cook finally broke his silence regarding Dunkle and Loose in *My Attainment of the Pole*, in which he described them as "men who offered to sell me fake figures—most likely to betray me had I been dishonest enough to buy them—and who, failing, perjured themselves" (564). He insinuated that they had been put up to the scheme by Peary's allies.

### Forty-Nine

The *TOL* confirmed that the *NYT* scoop was significant on December 11, after Lonsdale admitted that Cook had hired Loose, and accorded the story full consideration on December 15. The angry letters from readers (to which the *NYT* responded on December 13) are in ASOP (box 77, folder 1). Dunkle's December 27, 1909, letter to Reick, in which he describes the agreement he'd reached with the *NYT* and THH, and his confirmation of receipt of payment for testimony, are both preserved in ASOP (box 77, folder 4). In the December 27 letter, Dunkle also alludes to THH's role in the "grilling."

### Fifty

The press statements of Wake, Lecointe, and the UC judges are all taken from the *NYS* and *NYH* of December 22. Nansen's assertion that Cook was "a dead man" is from *NYH*, December 23. Stead's concession to Gibbs is from *Adventures in Journalism* (51). JGB's intention to "drop the matter" was reported in *NYT*, December 22. The *NYT* items about baby Frederick and the odorous animal skins appeared on December 28, 1909, and February 9, 1910, respectively. The *NYT* called Cook "the greatest impostor of all time" on December 22, 1909, and falsely claimed that he had submitted some of Loose's figures to UC that same day. It quietly admitted its error on January 21, 1910. *TFE*'s comment on the "great victory" of the *NYT* was reprinted in *NYT*, January 18, 1910. THH suggested that Peary send his proofs to UC in a November 15, 1909, letter to HLB (folder 161, APAC). Peary refused to do so in a December 24 letter to Reick (box 13, PFC). Egan declared that UC had "implicit faith" in the verdict of NGS in *NYT*, December 25.

### PART FIVE: YEARNING TO BELIEVE

### Fifty-One

Hughes's comments were recorded in *NYT*, February 10, 1910. The $6,000 figure is from *NYT*, March 29, 1911. The 1909 NGS examination, and the 1910 congressional hearings that showed just how cursory that process had been, are described by Rawlins (*Peary at the North Pole*, 176–242) and Herbert (*Noose of Laurels*, 324–29). The *NYT* argued that Peary's "word settled it" on March 9, 1910, and likened congressional doubters to "molluscs" on March 6, 1910. Macon's tirade against the "tit-bit editors" of the *NYT* appeared in *NYT*, February 17, 1911. The congressman's "exceeding" skepticism was reported in the *Jonesboro* (Ark.) *Evening Sun*, March 10, 1910. "From every letter" is taken from Weems (*Peary*, 283). The description of Peary's RGS medal is from Herbert (*Noose of Laurels*, 327), as is Bartlett's assertion that there were "no records" of Cook's at Etah in 1910 (313). Rainey described the wrecked cache in his *Cosmopolitan* article ("Bagging Arctic Monsters with Rope, Gun, and Camera," 97). Bryce (*Cook & Peary*, 908–11) believes that the cache was in fact opened but that nothing important was found inside. Etukishuk was later found to have Cook's sextant. My brief account of the two 1910 McKinley expeditions is drawn primarily from Bryce (*Cook & Peary*, 489–96); Rusk's quotations are taken directly from the concluding article of his three-part 1910–11 series for *Pacific Monthly* (62). Bryce describes the mysterious gaps in Peary's diary in his introduction to the 2001 reprinting of *The North Pole* (xii). Herbert highlights the navigational issues raised during Peary's congressional testimony, and helpfully includes an edited transcript of the hearings in the appendix of *Noose of Laurels* (339–53). Rawlins quotes both Macon's doubts about Peary's claim (*Peary at the North Pole*, 240) and *Scientific American*'s doubts about Macon's credentials (223). Macon's attack on "saphead" editors is from *NYT*, February 17, 1911. Behind-the-scenes details of Cook's and Peary's *Hampton's* articles were revealed by a stenographer for the magazine, Lilian Kiel, in sworn testimony that is preserved in the 1915 *Congressional Record* (Appendix: "Statement of Miss Lilian Eleanor Kiel," 675–77). Bryce shows that Peary and the *Hampton's* publisher, Benjamin Hampton, actively discussed how publishing Cook's "Confession" would serve both their interests (*Cook & Peary*, 475). The following quotations are from Cook's *My Attainment of the Pole*: "I felt impotent, crushed" (555), "heart of a hypocrite" (517), "underhanded game of deceit" (482), and "Arctic concubines" (601). "The mask is off now" is from *NYT*, December 31, 1911. The Explorers Club's gag order is cited in Rawlins (*Peary at the North Pole*, 291). Like Peary's Crocker Land, Cook's Bradley Land was later shown not to exist. Josephine Peary's views of her husband's decline are quoted in Herbert (*Noose of Laurels*, 328–29). Judge John M. Killits is quoted in Bryce (*Cook & Peary*, 671). Amundsen's comments about Peary, and the *NYT*'s furious response, are from *NYT*, January 24 and 25, 1926. From Berger, I took my summary of the post-1909 exploring ventures of the *NYT* (*Story of "The New York Times*,*"* 170), the paper's claim about Amundsen "verifying Admiral Peary's observations" (283), and the point about the comparative speed with which Peary's and Amundsen's news were delivered (286).

### Fifty-Two

The first comprehensive attempt to debunk Peary's claim was in fact Thomas F. Hall's *Has the North Pole Been Discovered?* Published in 1917, Hall's analysis presented compelling evidence that Peary had in fact perpetrated a deliberate hoax, and also mounted the first challenge to the explorer's claimed 1906 Farthest North. Though the self-published volume—which Hall wrote with help from Cook's paid lobbyist, Ernest Rost—never found an audience (Bryce, *Cook & Peary*, 606–8), it would aid later, more successful Peary skeptics, including Rawlins. Barker's 1910 request for additional details from Peary, and other discoveries of Charles Henshaw Ward, are described by Rawlins in his appendix (*Peary at the North Pole*, 281–90); Peary's employment of Hastings is confirmed in a letter he wrote to HLB on October 29, 1909, in which the explorer mentioned that he was working with a "bright young Professor of mathematics" (folder 188, APAC). Note: throughout much of her adult life, Helen Cook went by the name Helene Cook Vetter. Lehmann-Haupt declared his indifference to the question of polar priority in *NYT*, July 31, 1973. Herbert noted in his *National Geographic* article ("Commander Robert E. Peary," 412–13) that Peary had failed to account for longitude, magnetic variation, or the degree to which "strong easterly and northeasterly winds might have blown him off course to the west." The mere fact that Peary's chronometer had been ten minutes fast, Herbert added, "could have put him west of the Pole by 18 miles." Struggling to explain how an explorer as experienced as Peary had overlooked these crucial details, Herbert theorized that "during those last five marches northward Peary was being driven not by the rational mind but by a conviction that the Pole was his and that he had the divine right to discover it and return to proclaim his achievement" (413). In 1993,

Bryce discovered a long-forgotten photostatic copy of Cook's polar notebook in Copenhagen. (For a transcribed and annotated reproduction of the notebook, see Bryce, *The Lost Polar Notebook of Dr. Frederick A. Cook*.) After examining the various deletions and handwritten insertions therein, and comparing Cook's notes from 1908–9 with the known geography of the regions he claimed to have visited, Bryce concluded that the explorer had faked his discovery of the pole and survived the winter of 1908–9 in far easier conditions than he had claimed. He also concluded that Cook had initially intended to make "an honest attempt" to get to the pole, realized even before reaching land's end that it would be impossible, ventured onto the frozen sea ice anyway, and then turned back after advancing some hundred miles in six days—that he had, in other words, gone considerably farther than Ahwelah, Etukishuk, and Peary's supporters gave him credit for, if only to make his false claim more convincing (974–75). Henson's overlooked contributions, and the existence of his and Peary's mixed-race offspring in Greenland, gained widespread attention with the publication of S. Allen Counter's 1991 book, *North Pole Legacy*. Henson's headstone at Arlington dubiously describes him as the "co-discoverer of the North Pole" (*NYT*, April 7, 1988). The *NYT* characterized its failure to scrutinize Peary's claim as an "error" on August 23, 1988.

### Epilogue: Newspaper of Record

The conclusion that the *NYT* "solidified its stature" with the polar controversy is from Kluger (*Paper*, 184). Several sources attest to JGB's ongoing belief in Cook: O'Connor claimed that he "refused to accept [UC's] findings or concede that Peary had won the race to the Pole" (*Scandalous Mr. Bennett*, 286). Meriwether said (in *Times Talk*) that JGB proudly kept a photo, purportedly of the North Pole, that Cook had given him. And Crockett, whom I trust more than either of these sources, writes of JGB's "insistence upon Cook's veracity after the imposture had been proclaimed" and treats this attitude as evidence that JGB's judgment had "begun to be impaired" (*When James Gordon Bennett Was Caliph of Baghdad*, 400). The *NYH*'s slide into the red in 1917 is taken from Seitz (*James Gordon Bennetts*, 377–78) and confirmed by documents in box 20, folder 95, ASOP. The story of the deal-that-almost-was between JGB and ASO is from Bond (*Mr. Miller of the "Times,"* 45–46). Details of JGB's estate are from *E&P*, June 17, 1922. The $4 million figure paid by Munsey was reported in *NYT*, January 21, 1928. Davis discusses the creation of the *Times Index* (*History of "The New York Times,"* 328); Tifft and Jones explicitly link it to the establishment of a "newspaper of record" (*Trust*, 64). ASO's 1916 speech is quoted in Rogers (*Newspaper Building*, 61). World War I's boost to the paper's prestige and fortunes is discussed in all the book-length histories of the *NYT*; Tifft and Jones (*Trust*, 118–19) also examine its financial and psychological toll. Stolberg claimed in 1926 that the *NYT* earned around $4 million in annual profits, "of which almost ninety-seven per cent are ploughed back into the business" ("Man Behind the 'Times,'" 730). Lehman's testimonial appeared in *NYT*, April 9, 1935. Tifft and Jones describe ASO's succession plan (*Trust*, 166–68). "At the time of Adolph's death," they write, "*The New York Times* was considered the best newspaper in the country, if not the world."

# BIBLIOGRAPHY

## ARCHIVES

Cook, Frederick Albert. Papers. Manuscript Division. Library of Congress, Washington, D.C.

Flint, Charles R. Papers. Manuscripts and Archives Division. New York Public Library.

Hubbard Family. Papers. George J. Mitchell Department of Special Collections & Archives. Bowdoin College Library, Brunswick, Maine.

Ochs, Adolph S. Papers. New York Times Company Records. Manuscripts and Archives Division. New York Public Library.

Peary, Josephine Diebitsch. Papers. Maine Women Writers Collection. University of New England, Portland, Maine.

Peary, Robert E. Family Collection (Record Group XP). National Archives and Records Administration, College Park, Md.

Peary Arctic Club. Archives. Explorers Club, New York.

Salisbury, Harrison E. Papers. Rare Book & Manuscript Library, Columbia University, New York.

Young, John Russell. Papers. Manuscript Division. Library of Congress, Washington, D.C.


## SELECTED BOOKS

Anstruther, Ian. *I Presume: Stanley's Triumph and Disaster.* London: G. Bles, 1956.

Aucoin, James L. *The Evolution of Investigative Journalism.* Columbia: University of Missouri Press, 2005.

Bartlett, Robert A. *The Log of "Bob" Bartlett.* New York: G. P. Putnam's Sons, 1928.

Beard, Patricia. *After the Ball: Gilded Age Secrets, Boardroom Betrayals, and the Party That Ignited the Great Wall Street Scandal of 1905.* New York: HarperCollins, 2003.

Beebe, Lucius. *The Big Spenders.* Garden City, N.Y.: Doubleday, 1966.

Bennett, Norman R., ed. *Stanley's Despatches to the "New York Herald," 1871–1872, 1874–1877*. Boston: Boston University Press, 1970.

Berger, Meyer. *The Story of "The New York Times," 1851–1951*. New York: Simon & Schuster, 1951.

Berton, Pierre. *The Arctic Grail: The Quest for the North West Passage and the North Pole, 1818–1909*. New York: Penguin, 1988.

Blumenfeld, Ralph. *The Press in My Time*. London: Rich & Cowan, 1933.

Bond, F. Fraser. *Mr. Miller of "The Times": The Story of an Editor*. New York: Charles Scribner's Sons, 1931.

Bonsal, Stephen. *Heyday in a Vanished World*. New York: W. W. Norton, 1937.

Brendon, Piers. *The Life and Death of the Press Barons*. New York: Atheneum, 1983.

Brown, Charles H. *The Correspondents' War: Journalists in the Spanish-American War*. New York: Charles Scribner's Sons, 1967.

Brown, Francis. *Raymond of the "Times."* New York: W. W. Norton, 1951.

Bryce, Robert M. *Cook & Peary: The Polar Controversy, Resolved*. Mechanicsburg, Pa.: Stackpole Books, 1997.

———, ed. *The Lost Polar Notebook of Dr. Frederick A. Cook*. Monrovia, Md.: Openlead Books, 2018.

Buley, R. Carlyle. *The Equitable Life Assurance Society of the United States, 1859–1964*. New York: Appleton-Century-Crofts, 1967.

Campbell, Joseph W. *The Year That Defined American Journalism: 1897 and the Clash of Paradigms*. New York: Routledge, 2006.

Carlson, Oliver. *Brisbane: A Candid Biography*. Westport, Conn.: Greenwood Press, 1970.

———. *The Man Who Made News: James Gordon Bennett*. New York: Duell, Sloan and Pearce, 1942.

Chambers, Julius. *News Hunting on Three Continents*. New York: M. Kennerley, 1921.

Churchill, Allen. *Park Row*. New York: Rinehart, 1958.

Clarke, Joseph I. C. *My Life and Memories*. New York: Dodd, Mead, 1925.

Cobb, Irvin S. *Exit Laughing*. Indianapolis: Bobbs-Merrill, 1941.

Cook, Frederick A. *My Attainment of the Pole: Being the Record of the Expedition That First Reached the Boreal Center, 1907–1909*. New York: M. Kennerley, 1913.

Counter, S. Allen. *North Pole Legacy: Black, White & Eskimo*. Amherst: University of Massachusetts Press, 1991.

Crockett, Albert Stevens. *When James Gordon Bennett Was Caliph of Baghdad*. New York: Funk & Wagnalls, 1926.

Crouch, Gregory. *The Bonanza King: John Mackay and the Battle over the Greatest Riches in the American West*. New York: Scribner, 2018.

Crouthamel, James L. *Bennett's "New York Herald" and the Rise of the Popular Press*. New York: Syracuse University Press, 1989.

Daly, Christopher B. *Covering America: A Narrative History of a Nation's Journalism*. Amherst: University of Massachusetts Press, 2012.

Damrosch, David. *The Buried Book: The Loss and Rediscovery of the Great Epic of Gilgamesh*. New York: Henry Holt, 2007.

Daston, Lorraine, and Peter Galison. *Objectivity*. Cambridge, Mass.: MIT Press, 2007.

Davis, Elmer. *History of "The New York Times," 1851–1921*. New York: New York Times Company, 1921.

De Long, Emma Wotton. *Explorer's Wife*. New York: Dodd, Mead, 1938.

Desmond, Robert W. *The Information Process: World News Reporting to the Twentieth Century.* Iowa City: University of Iowa Press, 1977.

Dippel, John H. V. *To the Ends of the Earth: The Truth Behind the Glory of Polar Exploration.* Amherst, N.Y.: Prometheus, 2018.

Douglas, George H. *The Golden Age of the Newspaper.* Westport, Conn.: Greenwood Press, 1999.

Dreiser, Theodore. *A Book About Myself.* New York: Boni & Liveright, 1922.

Dryfoos, Susan. *Iphigene: Memoirs of Iphigene Ochs Sulzberger of the "New York Times" Family, as Told to Her Granddaughter, Susan W. Dryfoos.* New York: Dodd & Mead, 1981.

Dunn, Robert. *World Alive: A Personal Story.* New York: Crown, 1956.

Eames, Hugh. *Winner Lose All: Dr. Cook and the Theft of the North Pole.* Boston: Little, Brown, 1973.

Egan, Maurice Francis. *Recollections of a Happy Life.* New York: George H. Doran, 1924.

Fenby, Jonathan. *The History of Modern France: From the Revolution to the Present Day.* New York: Simon & Schuster, 2015.

Fermer, Douglas. *James Gordon Bennett and the "New York Herald": A Study of Editorial Opinion in the Civil War Era.* New York: St. Martin's Press, 1986.

Fine, Barnett. *A Giant of the Press.* New York: *Editor & Publisher*, 1933.

Fiske, Stephen. *Off-Hand Portraits of Prominent New Yorkers.* New York: G. R. Lockwood & Son, 1884.

Fleming, Fergus. *Ninety Degrees North: The Quest for the North Pole.* New York: Grove Press, 2001.

Ford, Edwin H., and Edwin Emery. *Highlights in the History of the American Press.* Minneapolis: University of Minnesota Press, 1954.

Freeman, Andrew. *The Case for Doctor Cook.* New York: Coward-McCann, 1961.

Freuchen, Peter. *Arctic Adventure: My Life in the Frozen North.* New York: Farrar & Rinehart, 1935.

Fyfe, Hamilton. *T. P. O'Connor.* London: Allen & Unwin, 1934.

Gibbs, Philip. *Adventures in Journalism.* London: W. Heinemann, 1923.

———. *The Pageant of the Years: An Autobiography.* London: W. Heinemann, 1946.

Gilder, William H. *Ice-Pack and Tundra.* London: Sampson Low, Marston, Searle, & Rivington, 1883.

Goodman, Matthew. *"The Sun" and the Moon: The Remarkable True Account of Hoaxers, Showmen, Dueling Journalists, and Lunar Man-Bats in Nineteenth-Century New York.* New York: Basic Books, 2008.

Gordon, John Steele. *A Thread Across the Ocean: The Heroic Story of the Transatlantic Cable.* New York: Walker, 2002.

Guttridge, Leonard F. *Ghosts of Cape Sabine: The Harrowing True Story of the Greely Expedition.* New York: G. P. Putnam's Sons, 2000.

———. *Icebound: The* Jeannette *Expedition's Quest for the North Pole.* Annapolis, Md.: Naval Institute Press, 1986.

Henderson, Bruce. *True North: Cook, Peary, and the Race to the Pole.* New York: W. W. Norton, 2005.

Henson, Matthew A. *A Negro Explorer at the North Pole.* New York: Frederick A. Stokes, 1912.

Herbert, Wally. *The Noose of Laurels: Robert E. Peary and the Race to the North Pole.* New York: Atheneum, 1989.

Hobbs, William Herbert. *Peary*. New York: Macmillan, 1936.

Hone, Philip. *The Diary of Philip Hone*. Carlisle, Mass.: Applewood Books, 2009.

Hudson, Frederic. *Journalism in the United States, from 1690 to 1872*. New York: Haskell House, 1968.

Ireland, Alleyne. *An Adventure with a Genius: Recollections of Joseph Pulitzer*. New York: E. P. Dutton, 1921.

Jackson, Frederick G. *A Thousand Days in the Arctic*. London: Harper & Brothers, 1899.

Jeal, Tim. *Stanley: The Impossible Life of Africa's Greatest Explorer*. London: Faber & Faber, 2007.

Jefferson, Sam. *Gordon Bennett and the First Yacht Race Across the Atlantic*. New York: Bloomsbury, 2016.

Johnson, Gerald W. *An Honorable Titan: A Biographical Study of Adolph S. Ochs*. New York: Harper & Brothers, 1946.

Juergens, George. *Joseph Pulitzer and His World*. New York: Vanguard Press, 1966.

Kane, Elisha Kent. *Adrift in the Arctic Ice Pack: From the History of the First U.S. Grinnell Expedition in Search of Sir John Franklin*. Oyster Bay, N.Y.: Nelson Doubleday, 1915.

Kinzer, Stephen. *True Flag: Theodore Roosevelt, Mark Twain, and the Birth of American Empire*. New York: Henry Holt, 2017.

Klein, Maury. *The Life and Legend of Jay Gould*. Baltimore: Johns Hopkins University Press, 1986.

Kluger, Richard. *The Paper: The Life and Death of the "New York Herald Tribune."* New York: Random House, 1986.

Laney, Al. *"Paris Herald": The Incredible Newspaper*. Westport, Conn.: Greenwood Press, 1968.

Larson, Edward J. *To the Edges of the Earth: 1909, the Race for the Three Poles, and the Climax of the Age of Exploration*. New York: William Morrow, 2018.

Lee, Alfred M. *The Daily Newspaper in America: The Evolution of a Social Instrument*. New York: Macmillan, 1937.

Lee, James Melvin. *History of American Journalism*. Boston: Houghton Mifflin, 1917.

Leech, Margaret. *In the Days of McKinley*. New York: Harper & Brothers, 1959.

Loomis, Chauncey. *Weird and Tragic Shores: The Story of Charles Francis Hall, Explorer*. New York: Modern Library, 2000.

Mandell, Richard D. *Paris 1900: The Great World's Fair*. Toronto: University of Toronto Press, 1967.

McKerns, Joseph P., ed. *Biographical Dictionary of American Journalism*. Westport, Conn.: Greenwood Press, 1989.

McLynn, Frank. *Stanley: The Making of an African Explorer*. London: Constable, 1989.

Melville, George. *In the Lena Delta*. Boston: Houghton Mifflin, 1884.

Milton, Joyce. *Yellow Kids: Foreign Correspondents in the Heyday of Yellow Journalism*. New York: Harper & Row, 1989.

Moore, Leonard N. *Journalism's Roving Eye: A History of American Foreign Reporting*. Baton Rouge: Louisiana State University Press, 2010.

Morris, Charles, ed. *Finding the North Pole*. Philadelphia: W. E. Scull, 1909.

Morris, James McGrath. *Pulitzer: A Life in Politics, Print, and Power*. New York: Harper, 2010.

Mott, Frank Luther. *American Journalism: A History, 1609–1960*. 3rd ed. New York: Macmillan, 1962.

Murphy, Cait. *Scoundrels in Law: The Trials of Howe & Hummel, Lawyers to the Gangsters, Cops, Starlets, and Rakes Who Made the Gilded Age.* New York: HarperCollins, 2010.

Nansen, Fridtjof. *Farthest North.* London: Archibald Constable, 1897.

Nasaw, David. *The Chief: The Life of William Randolph Hearst.* New York: Houghton Mifflin, 2000.

Newcomb, Raymond Lee. *Our Lost Explorers: The Narrative of the* Jeannette *Arctic Expedition as Related by the Survivors, and in the Records and Lost Journals of Lieutenant De Long.* Hartford: American Publishing, 1882.

Nuttall, Mark, ed. *Encyclopedia of the Arctic.* New York: Routledge, 2005.

O'Brien, Frank. *The Story of "The Sun": New York, 1833–1918.* New York: George H. Doran, 1918.

O'Connor, Richard. *The Scandalous Mr. Bennett.* Garden City, NY: Doubleday, 1962.

Paine, Ralph D. *Roads of Adventure.* Boston: Houghton Mifflin, 1922.

Peary, Robert E. *The North Pole: Its Discovery in 1909 Under the Auspices of the Peary Arctic Club.* New York: Frederick A. Stokes, 1910.

———. *The North Pole: Its Discovery in 1909 Under the Auspices of the Peary Arctic Club.* With an introduction by Robert M. Bryce. New York: Cooper Square Press, 2001.

———. *Northward over the "Great Ice": A Narrative of Life and Work Along the Shores and upon the Interior Ice-Cap of Northern Greenland in the Years 1886 and 1891–1897.* New York: Frederick A. Stokes, 1898.

Poole, Robert M. *Explorers House: "National Geographic" and the World It Made.* New York: Penguin Press, 2004.

Rawlins, Dennis. *Peary at the North Pole: Fact or Fiction?* Washington, D.C.: Robert B. Luce, 1973.

Regier, C. C. *The Era of the Muckrakers.* Gloucester, Mass.: Peter Smith, 1957.

Reid, Whitelaw. *American and English Studies.* Vol. 2, *Biography, History, and Journalism.* New York: Charles Scribner's Sons, 1913.

Riffenburgh, Beau. *The Myth of the Explorer: The Press, Sensationalism, and Geographical Discovery.* London: Belhaven Press, 1993.

Robinson, Bradley. *Dark Companion.* New York: K. M. McBride, 1947.

Robinson, Michael F. *The Coldest Crucible: Arctic Exploration and American Culture.* Chicago: University of Chicago Press, 2006.

Rogers, Jason. *Newspaper Building: Application of Efficiency to Editing, to Mechanical Production, to Circulation and Advertising, with Cost Finding Methods, Office Forms, and Systems.* New York: Harper & Brothers, 1918.

Roosevelt, Theodore. *Realizable Ideals: Earl Lectures of Pacific Theological Seminary Delivered at Berkeley, California, in 1911.* San Francisco: Whitaker & Ray-Wiggin, 1912.

Ross, Ishbel. *Ladies of the Press: The Story of Women in Journalism by an Insider.* New York: Harper & Brothers, 1936.

Rousmaniere, John. *The New York Yacht Club: A History, 1844–2008.* Brooklin, Maine: Seapoint Books, 2008.

Rowell, George P. *Forty Years an Advertising Agent, 1865–1905.* New York: Printers' Ink, 1906.

Salisbury, Harrison E. *Without Fear or Favor: "The New York Times" and Its Times.* New York: Times Books, 1980.

Sancton, Julian. *Madhouse at the End of the Earth: The* Belgica's *Journey into the Dark Antarctic Night.* New York: Crown, 2021.

Schudson, Michael. *Discovering the News: A Social History of American Newspapers*. New York: Basic Books, 1978.

Seitz, Don C. *The James Gordon Bennetts, Father and Son: Proprietors of the "New York Herald."* Indianapolis: Bobbs-Merrill, 1928.

———. *Joseph Pulitzer, His Life & Letters*. New York: Simon & Schuster, 1924.

———. *Training for the Newspaper Trade*. Philadelphia: J. B. Lippincott, 1916.

Sides, Hampton. *In the Kingdom of Ice: The Grand and Terrible Polar Voyage of the USS* Jeannette. New York: Doubleday, 2014.

Sinclair, Upton. *The Brass Check: A Study of American Journalism*. Pasadena, Calif.: published by the author, 1919.

Stafford, Marie Peary. *Discoverer of the North Pole: The Story of Robert E. Peary*. New York: William Morrow, 1959.

Standage, Tom. *The Victorian Internet: The Remarkable Story of the Telegraph and the Nineteenth Century's Online Pioneers*. New York: Berkley Books, 1999.

Starr, Paul. *The Creation of the Media: Political Origins of Modern Communications*. New York: Basic Books, 2004.

Stead, W. T. *The Americanization of the World; or, The Trend of the Twentieth Century*. New York: Horace Markley, 1902.

Steffens, Lincoln. *The Autobiography of Lincoln Steffens*. New York: Harcourt, Brace, 1931.

Stewart, Kenneth N., and John Tebbel. *Makers of Modern Journalism*. New York: Prentice-Hall, 1952.

Summers, Mark Wahlgren. *The Press Gang: Newspapers and Politics, 1865–1878*. Chapel Hill: University of North Carolina Press, 1994.

Talese, Gay. *The Kingdom and the Power*. New York: World, 1969.

Tifft, Susan E., and Alex S. Jones. *The Trust: The Private and Powerful Family Behind "The New York Times."* Boston: Little, Brown, 1999.

Traxel, David. *1898: The Birth of the American Century*. New York: Random House, 1998.

Tucher, Andie. *Not Exactly Lying: Fake News and Fake Journalism in American History*. New York: Columbia University Press, 2022.

Twain, Mark. *Mark Twain's Letters*. Vol. 2. Edited by Edgar Marquess Branch, Michael B. Frank, Kenneth M. Sanderson, Harriet Elinor Smith, Lin Salamo, and Richard Bucci. Berkeley: University of California Press, 1988.

Vanderbilt, Consuelo. *The Glitter and the Gold*. New York: Harper, 1952.

Villard, Henry Serrano. *Blue Ribbon of the Air: The Gordon Bennett Races*. Washington, D.C.: Smithsonian Institution Press, 1987.

Villard, Oswald Garrison. *Some Newspapers and Newspaper-Men*. New York: Knopf, 1923.

Walker, Dale. *Januarius MacGahan: The Life and Campaigns of an American War Correspondent*. Athens: Ohio University Press, 1988.

Wallace, Mike. *Greater Gotham: A History of New York City from 1898 to 1919*. New York: Oxford University Press, 2017.

Weems, John Edward. *Peary: The Explorer and the Man*. Boston: Houghton Mifflin, 1967.

Whyte, Kenneth. *The Uncrowned King: The Sensational Rise of William Randolph Hearst*. Berkeley, Calif.: Publishers Group West, 2009.

Winkler, John K. *W. R. Hearst: An American Phenomenon*. New York: Simon & Schuster, 1928.

Young, Allen. *Cruise of the Pandora: From the Private Journal Kept by Allen Young*. London: W. Clowes, 1876.

## SELECTED ESSAYS AND ARTICLES

Alger, George W. "The Literature of Exposure." *Atlantic Monthly*, August 1905, 210–13.

Arnold, Matthew. "Civilization in the United States." *Nineteenth Century and After: A Monthly Review* 23, no. 134 (April 1888): 481–96.

Baker, Ray Stannard. "How the News of the War Is Reported." *McClure's*, September 1898, 491–95.

Bridgman, Herbert L. "Peary." *Natural History* 20, no. 1 (January–February 1920): 5–11.

Brisbane, Arthur. "The Modern Newspaper in War Time." *Cosmopolitan*, September 1898, 541–57.

Cavell, Janice. "Publishing Sir John Franklin's Fate." *Book History* 16 (2013): 155–84.

Connery, Thomas B. "College Recollections: Fordham in the Fifties." *Fordham College Monthly* 20 (1901): 301–19.

Cook, Frederick A. "The Conquest of Mount McKinley." *Harper's Monthly Magazine*, May 1907, 821–37.

———. "Dr. Cook's Own Story, Part One." *Hampton's Magazine*, January 1911, 51–66.

Cornuelle, R. C. "Remembrance of the *Times*: From the Papers of Garet Garrett." *American Scholar* 36, no. 3 (Summer 1967).

Creelman, James. "Captains of Industry: James Gordon Bennett." *Cosmopolitan*, May 1902, 44–47.

———. "The Chiefs of the American Press." *Cosmopolitan*, November 1894, 81–90.

Dunn, Robert. "Across the Forbidden Tundra." *Outing*, January 1904, 459–70.

———. "Highest on Mt. McKinley." *Outing*, April 1904, 27–35.

———. "Home by Ice and by Swimming from Mt. McKinley." *Outing*, May 1904, 214–19.

———. "Into the Mists of Mt. McKinley." *Outing*, February 1904, 536–45.

———. "Storm-Wrapped on Mt. McKinley." *Outing*, March 1904, 697–706.

Edwards, D. M. "Go Find Peary! Wild Race for Truth." *Editor & Publisher*, December 26, 1959, 46–47.

Egan, Maurice Francis. "Dr. Cook in Copenhagen: A Foot-Note to History." *Century Magazine*, September 1910, 759–63.

Fish, Henry. "James Gordon Bennett." *Munsey's Magazine*, August 1895, 452–54.

Fiske, Stephen. "The First Ocean Yacht Race." *Smart Set*, July 1900, 59–65.

Forde, Kathy Roberts, and Katharine A. Foss. "'The Facts—the Color!—the Facts': The Idea of a Report in American Print Culture, 1885–1910." *Book History* 15 (2012): 123–51.

Gorbach, Julien. "Not Your Grandpa's Hoax: A Comparative History of Fake News." *American Journalism* 35, no. 2 (April 2018): 236–49.

Greely, Adolphus. "The Discoverers of the North Pole." *Munsey's*, November 1909, 290–96.

Hennessy, Roland Burke. "How the 'Herald' Is Made." *Metropolitan Magazine*, September 1895, 107–21.

Herbert, Wally. "Commander Robert E. Peary: Did He Reach the Pole?" *National Geographic*, September 1988, 386–413.

Hirsch, Mark D. "More Light on Boss Tweed." *Political Science Quarterly* 60, no. 2 (June 1945): 267–78.

Hunt, William R. "Confrontation in Montana: Frederick A. Cook and the Mount McKinley Controversy." *Montana: The Magazine of Western History* 34, no. 1 (Winter 1984): 46–56.

Irwin, Will. "The American Newspaper: A Study of Journalism in Its Relation to the Public. Part 3: The Fourth Current." *Collier's*, February 18, 1911, 14.

———. "The American Newspaper: A Study of Journalism in Its Relation to the Public. Part 6: The Editor and the News." *Collier's*, April 1, 1911, 18.

———. "The American Newspaper: A Study of Journalism in Its Relation to the Public. Part 10: The Unhealthy Alliance." *Collier's*, June 3, 1911, 17.

Kaplan, Richard L. "From Partisanship to Professionalism: The Transformation of the Daily Press." In *Print in Motion: The Expansion of Publishing and Reading in the United States, 1880–1940*, edited by Carl F. Kaestle and Janice A. Radway. Vol. 4 of *A History of the Book in America*. Chapel Hill: University of North Carolina Press, 2009.

Kimball, Arthur Reed. "The Invasion of Journalism." *Atlantic Monthly*, July 1900, 119–24.

Lang, William L. "'At the Greatest Personal Peril to the Photographer': The Schwatka-Haynes Winter Expedition in Yellowstone, 1887." *Montana: The Magazine of Western History* 33, no. 1 (Winter 1983): 14–29.

Lee, James Melvin. "Ochs' Career from Printer's Devil to Famous Publisher." *Editor & Publisher*, September 18, 1926, 5–7.

Lonsdale, Walter. "The Real Story of Dr. Cook and the North Pole, Part One." *Travel Magazine*, May 1910, 373–404.

———. "The Real Story of Dr. Cook and the North Pole, Part Two." *Travel Magazine*, June 1910, 425–53.

Lyon, H. M. "When Cook Came to Copenhagen: The Brooklyn Explorer Gets the Third Degree from British and Danish Reporters." *Collier's*, September 25, 1909, 22.

Maury, T. B. "The Eastern Portal to the Pole." *Putnam's Magazine*, April 1870, 437–45.

———. "The New American Polar Expedition and Its Hopes." *Atlantic Monthly*, October 1870, 492–504.

McCullagh, Francis. "The Gordon Bennetts and American Journalism." *Studies: An Irish Quarterly Review* 18, no. 71 (September 1929): 397–412.

Meriwether, Walter Scott. "Polar Echo from Warm South." *Times Talk* 3, no. 1 (September 1949): 12.

Nansen, Fridtjof. "How Can the North Polar Region Be Crossed?" *Geographical Journal* 1, no. 1 (January 1893): 1–22.

Nathan, George Jean. "James Gordon Bennett: The Monte Cristo of Modern Journalism." *Outing Magazine*, March 1909, 690–96.

*National Geographic*. "Honors to Peary." January 1907, 49–60.

Parton, James. "The *New York Herald*." *North American Review* 102, no. 2 (April 1866): 363–419.

Pomerantz, Sidney I. "The Press of Greater New York, 1898–1900." *New York History* 39, no. 1 (January 1958): 50–66.

Pulitzer, Joseph. "The College of Journalism." *North American Review* 178, no. 570 (May 1904): 641–80.

Rainey, Paul J. "Bagging Arctic Monsters with Rope, Gun, and Camera." *Cosmopolitan*, December 1910, 91–103.

Raymond, R. E. "Who's Who and Wherefore: Adolph S. Ochs." *Printers' Ink*, February 20, 1907, 9–11.

Redding, Leo. "Bennett of the *Herald*." *Everybody's Magazine*, June 1914, 846–58.

Ridout, Herbert C. "Sir John Le Sage Recalls Dramas During 60 Years in Fleet Street." *Editor & Publisher*, September 8, 1923, 16.

Roseboro, Viola. "Down-Town New York." *Cosmopolitan*, June 1886, 217–23.

Rusk, C. E. "On the Trail of Cook, Part Three." *Pacific Monthly*, January 1911, 48–62.

Saalberg, Harvey. "Bennett and Greeley, Professional Rivals, Had Much in Common." *Journalism Quarterly* 49, no. 3 (September 1972): 538–49.

Seitz, Don C. "The Portrait of an Editor." *Atlantic Monthly*, September 1924, 290–300.

Stead, W. T. "Character Sketch and Interview: Dr. F. A. Cook." *Review of Reviews*, October 1909, 322–39.

Steffens, Lincoln. "The Business of a Newspaper." *Scribner's*, October 1897, 447–67.

Stolberg, Benjamin. "The Man Behind the 'Times': Portrait of a Publisher." *Atlantic Monthly*, December 1926, 721–31.

*Time*. "Papers and Politics." September 1, 1924, 20–22.

Villard, Oswald Garrison. "Adolph S. Ochs and His *Times*." *Nation*, August 31, 1921, 221–22.

Weaver, Paul H. "The New Journalism and the Old—Thoughts After Watergate." *Public Interest* 35 (Spring 1974): 67–88.

White, Z. L. "A Decade of American Journalism." *Westminster Review*, October 1887, 850–62.

Wilcox, Delos F. "The American Newspaper: A Study in Social Psychology." *Annals of the American Academy of Political and Social Science* 16 (July 1900): 56–92.

Winchester, J. W. "Dr. Cook, Faker." *Pacific Monthly*, March 1911, 251–56.

## OFFICIAL DOCUMENTS, PAMPHLETS, UNPUBLISHED MANUSCRIPTS, AND SUCH

*Congressional Record: The Proceedings and Debates of the 63rd Congress, Third Session*. Vol. 52. Washington, D.C.: Government Printing Office, 1915.

Edwards, Edward H. "Adolph S. Ochs: Practical Idealist." Unpublished manuscript, possibly from 1928. Box 10, folders 2–5, Adolph S. Ochs Papers. New York Public Library.

Faber, Doris. "A *New York Times* Girlhood." With Iphigene Ochs Sulzberger. Unpublished autobiographical manuscript. Box 163, folder 53, Harrison E. Salisbury Papers. Columbia University, New York.

"*Jeannette* Inquiry: Before the Committee on Naval Affairs of the United States House of Representatives, Forty-Eighth Congress." Washington, D.C.: Government Printing Office, 1884.

Nelson, Christine. "Documenting the *Times*: Adolph S. Ochs and the Early Years of the *New York Times*, Checklist of the Exhibition at the Pierpont Morgan Library, June 26–September 15, 1996." Photocopy provided to the author by the Morgan Library & Museum.

"Travelers' Official Guide of the Railway and Steam Navigation Lines in the United States and Canada." New York: National Railway Publication Company, October 1881.

# IMAGE CREDITS

Insert Page 1: (*top*) Frederick A. Cook Society; (*bottom*) *New York Herald*, September 2, 1909

Page 2: (*top left*) Library of Congress, George Grantham Bain Collection. [LC-DIG-ggbain-04200]; (*top right*) Library of Congress, Frederick A. Cook Collection [LC-USZ62-120542]; (*bottom*) Royal Danish Library and Frederick A. Cook Society

Page 3: (*top*) Library of Congress, Prints & Photographs Division. [LC-USZ62-109995]; (*bottom*) Library of Congress, Prints & Photographs Division [LC-DIG-cwpb-06532]

Page 4: U.S. Naval Institute

Page 5: (*top left*) Wellcome Collection; (*center right*) U.S. Naval Academy Museum; (*bottom left*) Library of Congress, Prints & Photographs Division [LC-USZ62-22445]

Page 6: (*top right*) Rear Admiral Robert E. Peary Family Collection (National Archives and Records Administration); (*center left*) Bibliothèque Nationale de France / Société de Géographie; (*bottom right*) Rear Admiral Robert E. Peary Family Collection (National Archives and Records Administration)

Page 7: (*top*) Rear Admiral Robert E. Peary Family Collection (National Archives and Records Administration); (*bottom left*) Library of Congress, George Grantham Bain Collection [LC-DIG-ggbain-03377]; (*bottom right*) Library of Congress, Prints & Photographs Division [LC-USZ62-105333]

Page 8: (*top*) New York Times Company Records, Manuscripts and Archives Division, The New York Public Library; (*center left*) New York Times Company Records, Manuscripts and Archives Division, The New York Public Library; (*bottom left*) New York Times Company Records, Manuscripts and Archives Division, The New York Public Library; (*bottom right*) Library of Congress, Prints & Photographs Division. Copyright Keppler & Schwarzmann, 1898 [LC-DIG-ppmsca-28685]

Page 9: (*top*) Library of Congress, Detroit Publishing Company Photograph Collection [LC-DIG-det-4a10784]; (*bottom*) Library of Congress, George Grantham Bain Collection [LC-USZ62-68875]

Page 10: (*top*) Courtesy of Mystic Seaport Museum, Rosenfeld Collection, James Burton Photographer; (*bottom left*) GL Stock Photo / Alamy; (*bottom right*) Library of Congress, Prints & Photographs Division [LC-USZ62-53967]

Page 11: (*top*) National Portrait Gallery, London; (*bottom left*) Courtesy of Robert M. Bryce; (*bottom right*) Frederick A. Cook Society

Page 12: (*top left*) Courtesy of The Peary-MacMillan Arctic Museum, Bowdoin College; (*top right*) Rear Admiral Robert E. Peary Family Collection; (*bottom*) Rear Admiral Robert E. Peary Family Collection

Page 13: (*top*) Rear Admiral Robert E. Peary Family Collection; (*center*) Rear Admiral Robert E. Peary Family Collection; (*bottom*) Library of Congress, New York World-Telegram and the Sun Newspaper Photograph Collection [LC-USZ62-120192]

Page 14: (*top*) Library of Congress, Prints & Photographs Division [LC-DIG-ggbain-12778]; (*bottom left*) Courtesy of the George J. Mitchell Department of Special Collections & Archives, Bowdoin College Library, Brunswick, Maine; (*bottom right*) Library of Congress, Prints & Photographs Division [LC-USZ62-42993]

Page 15: (*top left*) Library of Congress, Frederick A. Cook Collection [LC-USZ62-103160]; (*top right*) Library of Congress, Prints & Photographs Division. Copyright Keppler & Schwarzmann, 1909 [LC-DIG-ppmsca-26413]; (*bottom*) Byrd Polar and Climate Research Center Archival Program, Frederick A. Cook Society Records, including Papers of Dr. Frederick Albert Cook

Page 16: (*top left*) Courtesy of Robert M. Bryce; (*top right*) Library of Congress, Prints & Photographs Division [LC-DIG-npcc-19844]; (*bottom*) Library of Congress, Prints & Photographs Division [LC-USZ62-120176]

# INDEX

Adams, Cyrus, 228, 270
Adler, Henry, 114
Adler, Julius Ochs (nephew), 327, 328
*The Adventures of Captain Hatteras*
    (Verne), 72
advertisements, newspaper
    campaign, 194
    classified, 165
    competition for, 4
    department at *NYH*, 201
    *NYT*, 105, 149–52, 197
    objectionable, 53
    with oversight, 196–97
    personals, 194–96, 210
    sales, 105, 127
Africa, 5, 23–28, 30, 56, 59, 73, 120
Agassiz, Louis, 98
Ahwelah (Inuit guide)
    on expedition with Cook, Frederick, 38,
        223, 226, 229, 242–43, 248,
        268–69
    on expedition with Peary, Robert, 243
    testimony of, 223, 258, 268–70, 274, 289
Air Force, U.S., 322
airships, 215, 319
Alaska, 47, 48, 82. *See also* McKinley
    expedition, Cook, Frederick
    *NYT* and Schwatka expedition,
        97–98, 155
    purchase of, 50

Alexandrine (Crown Princess of Denmark),
    225–26
Alexei (Inuit hunter), 82
*Alliance*, USS, 77–78
American Geographical Society, 101, 123,
    232, 259, 260
American Museum of Natural History
    Cape York meteorite and, 122, 259–60
    Inuit people as specimens at, 122
    with trophies from Peary, Robert, 122,
        123, 256
*American Review of Reviews* (magazine), 263
the *American* (newspaper), 195. *See also*
    *New York Journal*
Amundsen, Roald, 222, 302, 311, 312, 318
    as discoverer of North Pole, 319, 320, 322
    Farthest North and, 121
Andrée, Salomon August, 155
Andrews, Roy Chapman, 231
Antarctica, 40, 155, 302
anti-Semitism, 69, 150, 178, 185, 189
*Appendix to the Congressional Record*, 317
Arctic Club of America, 245, 247, 302
Arctic exploration, 4, 215, 312. *See also*
    North Pole expeditions
    Canadian, 76–77, 81, 100
    evolution of, 96–97, 155–56
    Franklin, John, with, 3, 48, 49, 50,
        76, 170
    government funding, 53, 97

*Arctic Explorations* (Kane), 50, 101
Arlington National Cemetery, 323
army
  Confederate, 19
  Union, 90
Army, U.S., 24, 76, 94
Arthur, Chester, 96
Ashton, James (General), 276
Associated Press, 87, 111, 281, 292, 306
  creation of, 15
  *Douglas Thomas* and, 236
Assyria, 58–59
*The Atlanta Constitution* (newspaper), 111
*The Atlantic Monthly* (magazine), 50, 191
Austro-Hungary, 50
automobiles, 5, 32, 154, 182, 196, 199,
    212–13, 246
aviation, 5, 154, 182, 199, 212, 213, 222
  Amundsen and North Pole, 319, 322
  Byrd with North Pole hoax, 319
  Lindbergh, 327
  U.S. Air Force, 322
Axel Heiberg Land, 37–38, 171, 207, 223,
    229, 268–69, 294

balloons
  hot-air, 72, 144, 154, 215
  hydrogen, 155, 215
Barker, Elsa, 234, 321
Barrill, Ed, 174–75, 274–83, 289
Bartlett, Robert (Captain), 232, 238–39,
    242–43, 256–57, 270, 310, 311,
    312, 315
*Belgica* expedition (1897–99), 155, 172
Bell, Alexander Graham, 205
Belmont, August, 105, 113, 183, 188, 189
Bennett, Floyd, 319
Bennett, Henrietta (Crean) (mother), 14,
    15–16
Bennett, James Gordon, Jr.
  alcohol-fueled antics of, 63–64, 65, 162
  childhood, 11, 15–16
  Commercial Cable Company and,
    88–89, 212
  conflict with May, Fred, 65–66, 67
  Cook, Frederick, and, 1, 2, 7, 40,
    42, 303
  criticism of, 83
  death and legacy, 325, 326
  as employer and leader, 198–204,
    209–12, 271
  with exploration, 5

family and, 14, 15–16, 21, 66
  Hearst, William Randolph, and, 194–96,
    202, 203, 209
  independent press and, 86
  *Lysistrata* and, 157–59, 160
  move to France, 66
  as *NYH* editor and publisher, 4–5, 7, 16,
    21–22, 56–58, 60–62, 71–75, 77–79,
    83–84, 86, 127, 140, 154–56,
    194–97, 266–67, 283, 325
  Ochs, Adolph, and, 5, 67, 152, 168, 178,
    185, 187, 211, 266, 325
  as *The Paris Herald* publisher, 162–63, 167,
    179, 202, 211, 228, 266
  Peary, Robert, and, 259
  Pulitzer and, 91–92, 194, 202, 204,
    265, 266
  Roosevelt, Theodore, on, 162
  scandal and, 62, 63–66
  with staff reporters, 23–30, 58, 60,
    61–62
  youth, 16–18, 20
Bennett, James Gordon, Sr. (father)
  death and legacy, 55, 56
  family and, 14, 15–16, 19, 21, 66
  Greeley on, 13, 55
  independent press and, 11, 55
  as innovator, 11–15
  as *NYH* editor and publisher, 11–21, 144
  personal attacks on, 12
  physical attacks on, 13, 15, 18
  rival publishers and, 12, 13, 14
Bennett, Jeannette (sister), 15, 65, 72
Berger, Meyer, 272–73
Bernacchi, Louis, 40, 41, 221, 253
the Bible, 58, 128
"Black Stream" (Kuroshio Current), 71
Blaine, James G., 104
Blumenfeld, Ralph, 203
Board of Aldermen, New York City, 135
boats. *See also specific ships*
  shipbuilding technology, 48
  transatlantic steamship service, 13
bombs, 18
Bonsal, Stephen, 202, 203
Borup, George, 228, 229, 243, 248–49, 257,
    268, 270
*The Boston Globe* (newspaper), 67
Bradley, John, 207, 233, 261, 291–92, 293
Brainard, David (Sergeant), 94
bribes, 27, 54, 68, 127, 275, 280, 281
Bridgman, Helen (wife), 227, 256, 258

Bridgman, Herbert, 154, 174, 207
  with McKinley expedition, 273, 274
  Peary, Robert, and, 227–28, 231, 234, 241,
    243, 256–58, 263, 283, 288
  Peary Arctic Club and, 124–25, 170,
    227, 269
Brisbane, Arthur, 131, 138, 140, 141, 147
British National Antarctic Expedition
    (1901–4), 40
*British Quarterly Review*, 56
*Brooklyn Daily Eagle* (newspaper), 297
Bryan, William Jennings, 134–35, 265
Bryant, William Cullen, 21
Bulgaria, 61
Bumpus, Hermon, 260
Burton, Richard Francis, 23
business managers
  *Evening Telegram*, 152
  *Knoxville Tribune*, 69
  *NYH*, 14, 203
  *NYT*, 184–85, 191–92
  *NYW*, 130, 141, 155, 204, 209
  *Standard-Union*, 227
bylines, *NYT*, 183, 273, 290
Byrd, Richard, 319

Cagni, Umberto, 121, 125, 171
Canada, Arctic exploration, 76–77, 81, 100
cannibalism rumors, 95–96
Cannon, Henry, 123
Cannon, Joseph, 44
Cape Morris Jesup expedition (1898–1902),
    123–25
Cape York Inuit, 103, 122, 125
Carlos (King of Portugal), 159
Carnegie, Andrew, 309
cartoonists, 54–55, 133, 264
Carvalho, S. S., 130
Cary, Edward, 112, 185
*The Case for Doctor Cook* (Freeman), 321
Chamberlain, Samuel, 202
Chambers, Julius, 202
Chandler, William, 83
Chase National Bank, 123
*Chattanooga Daily Dispatch* (newspaper), 69
*Chattanooga Daily Times* (newspaper), 69,
    106, 107, 108, 110, 111
Chester, Colby M. (Rear Admiral), 284–85,
    286–87, 291, 320
*Chicago Daily News* (newspaper), 145–46
*Chicago Record-Herald* (newspaper), 155–56
*The Chicago Times-Herald* (newspaper), 111

Chipp, Charles (Lieutenant), 74, 80, 81, 82
Christian (Crown Prince of Denmark), 35,
    36, 220, 224, 225–26
*Chronicle*, San Francisco (newspaper), 129
Churchill, Winston, 63
circulation
  New York City and daily, 56
  *New York Journal*, 139, 152
  *NYH*, 4, 12, 19, 56, 58, 149, 152, 157
  *NYS*, 149
  *NYT*, 55, 104, 149–52
  *NYTRIB*, 149, 152
  *NYW*, 128–29, 152
circulation managers, 14, 150, 184
Cisneros, Evangelina, 137
city editors
  *New York Journal*, 202
  *NYH*, 199, 201, 203, 209, 215–16
  *NYT*, 58, 210, 212, 216
  *NYW*, 143, 216
Civil War, U.S., 18–19, 56, 67, 90
Clarke, Joseph, 29–30
Clemens, Samuel (Mark Twain), 22, 57, 264
Cleveland, Grover, 104, 105, 110
Coast and Geodetic Survey, U.S., 229, 317
Cobb, Irvin, 129
Cole, Jack, 79
*Collier's* (magazine), 128–29
Collins, Jerome, 74, 82–84
Collins, Wilkie, 48
color illustrations, 211
color ink, 128, 131, 163
Columbia University, journalism school, 186
columnists, 272–73
comic illustrations, 55, 264
comic strips, 126, 128, 131, 211
Commercial Cable Company (Mackay-
    Bennett), 88–89, 212
complaint departments, newspapers, 196
Confederate army, 19
Congress, U.S., 84, 265, 309–11, 314–18,
    320–21
congressional hearings (1911), 314–18, 320, 321
Cook, Frederick. *See also* McKinley
    expedition, Cook, Frederick; North
    Pole expedition, Cook, Frederick
  *Belgica* expedition and, 155, 172
  Bennett, James Gordon, Jr., and, 1, 2, 7,
    40, 42, 303
  childhood, 101
  with comeback attempt, 316
  with exploration award, 41, 172, 224

Cook, Frederick (*cont.*)
  Explorers Club and, 205, 207
  in federal prison for Ponzi-like scheme, 318
  finances, 261, 262, 304
  "Great Interview" and, 37–39, 40, 223
  on Greenland expedition in 1891, with
      Peary, Robert, 101–2
  on Greenland expedition in 1901, with
      Peary, Robert, 124–25
  honors conferred on, 41–42
  lecture circuit, 261–62, 277–78, 280–82
  legacy, 322
  National Geographic Society and,
      205–6, 286
  "nervous collapse" of, 291–92
  on North Pole hunting, 229
  *NYW* and, 313
  Peary, Robert, and, 43–44, 101–2,
      124–25, 148, 172, 205–8, 215,
      227–34, 237–42, 244, 248–50,
      252–55, 258–61, 263–65, 283,
      288–89, 298, 305, 311, 314,
      316–18, 320, 322
  with presidential pardon, 322
Cook, Helen (daughter), 245, 321
Cook, Marie (wife), 1, 245, 247, 261, 291,
      292, 313
Cook, Ruth (daughter), 245
Cook, William (brother), 291
copyboys, 19, 185
copy editors, 200
corrections, in newspapers, 146, 324
corruption, 190–91
*Cosmopolitan* (magazine), 42, 312
*Courier-Journal*, Louisville (newspaper), 68
Crane, Stephen, 146
Crane, Zenas, 214
Crean, Henrietta. *See* Bennett, Henrietta
Creelman, James, 199, 202
Crocker, George, 171
Crocker Land, 171, 318
Crockett, Albert Stevens, 210–11
Cuba, 137, 139–42, 145–46
culture
  Arctic exploration in popular, 50
  newspapers and national, 19, 55–56, 91,
      126–27, 128
Cunard, transatlantic steamship
      service, 13
Currie, Barton, 236–38, 262
Custer, George (General), 57
Cuyler, Theodore, 135–36

*Daily Chronicle*, London (newspaper)
  editor, 221, 225
  Polar controversy and, 40
  reporters, 31–34, 39, 183, 220–26, 234
*Daily Mail*, London (newspaper), 41, 120
*Daily News*, London (newspaper), 25, 38,
      61, 72
*Daily Telegraph*, London (newspaper), 26,
      27–28, 58–59
Dana, Charles Anderson, 21, 53
Danenhower, John (Lieutenant), 79, 80
Danish Greenland Company, 32
Dedrick, Thomas, 124
Dellenbaugh, Frederick, 232
De Long, Emma (wife), 73, 83, 84
De Long, George Washington
  diary, 81, 82
  North Pole expedition and, 60, 61–62,
      71–75, 78–84, 94, 303
De Long, Sylvie (daughter), 73
De Long Archipelago, 83
Democratic Party, 54, 105, 134, 193,
      265, 309
Dewey, George (Admiral), 140, 145, 246
diaries
  Barrill, 274–75, 276
  Byrd, 319
  Collins, Jerome, 82–83
  Cook, Frederick, from 1891 Greenland
      expedition, 102
  Cook, Frederick, in North Pole, 33, 39, 41,
      102, 220, 248, 290, 292, 304
  Cook, Frederick, on Mount McKinley, 277
  De Long, George Washington, 81, 82
  Dunn, 173
  Mylius-Erichsen, 317–18
  Nansen, 121
  Peary, Robert, 310, 314, 318, 321
Dickens, Charles, 48, 258
Dickson, Alexander (Captain), 235,
      236, 238
Diebitsch, Josephine. *See* Peary, Josephine
dirigible, 156
Discovery expedition, 40
distribution, newspapers, 13, 54, 129,
      149–50, 166, 186
Dixon, Joseph M., 280, 281
Dodge, Marcellus, 190
dogs, Inuit people with
  on Cook, Frederick, expedition, 2, 32,
      37, 269
  on Nansen expedition, 118, 119

on Peary, Robert, expeditions, 124,
169–70, 230, 239, 256
on Schwatka expedition, 76–77, 100
with search for *Jeannette*, 80
*Douglas Thomas* (tugboat), 236
Dreiser, Theodore, 143
Drinkenberg, F. H., 280, 281
Duncan, Isadora, 166
Dunkle, George, 293–300, 304
Dunn, Robert, 172–73
Dupuy de Lôme, Enrique, 139
Edison, Thomas, 144

editorials
discontinuing of, 186
*NYH*, 17, 18, 29, 194
*NYT*, 53, 54, 134–35, 190, 327
*Editor & Publisher* (magazine), 186, 272
editors
city, 58, 143, 199, 201–3, 209–10, 212,
215–16
copy, 200
*Daily Chronicle*, London, 221, 225
*Evening Journal*, New York, 138, 140,
141, 147
managing, 106, 111, 133, 145–46, 181–85,
190, 202, 296
*NYH*, 12, 21, 28, 200, 201, 202
*NYT*, 54, 104–5, 112, 133, 152, 165, 181,
184, 185, 254, 285, 311, 327
*NYW*, 128–29, 131, 143
Park Row, 21
Edwards, Delt, 235, 242, 252
Egan, Maurice
with Cook, Frederick, 35–37, 42, 250
Polar controversy and, 221, 255, 264–65,
289–90, 306
Egingwah (Inuit guide), 232
entrepreneur-explorers, 3, 97, 155–56
Equitable Life Assurance Society,
189, 190
*Erebus* (ship), 48
Esquimau. *See* Inuit people
Etukishuk (Inuit guide)
on expedition with Cook, Frederick, 38,
223, 226, 229, 242–43, 248, 268–69
on expedition with Peary, Robert, 243
testimony of, 223, 258, 268–70, 274, 289
Europe
foreign news from, 21–22
*NYT* and popularity in, 179–80
Peary, Robert, with victory lap in, 312

*Evening Journal*, New York (newspaper),
138–41, 147, 189
*Evening Post*, New York (newspaper), 21, 177,
262, 276, 291
*Evening Star*, Washington (newspaper), 155–56
*Evening Telegram*, New York (newspaper), 21,
152, 264
*The Evening World* (newspaper), 138. *See also*
*New York World*
*Examiner*, San Francisco (newspaper), 129
exclusive rights, 4, 6, 42, 102, 216, 219
expeditions. *See also* Greenland expeditions,
Peary, Robert; McKinley expedition,
Cook, Frederick; North Pole
expeditions
*Belgica*, 155, 172
British National Antarctic, 40
with crew problems, 50–51, 52, 83, 96, 102
of Franklin, John, 3, 48, 49, 50, 76, 170
to Franz Josef Land, 119
funding, 3, 5, 24, 29, 53, 84, 97, 101, 123,
130, 154–56, 170–71, 174, 207,
213–16, 231–34, 241, 311, 318–19
Hall and *Polaris*, 50–51, 52, 60, 72
hoaxes, 312–13, 317–19
Lady Franklin Bay, 94–96, 117, 118, 237
Nansen, 100–101, 117–21
Nares, 60, 61, 72, 77
relief, 24–26, 48, 124
Schwatka and Canadian Arctic, 76–77,
81, 100
Schwatka and *NYT* Alaska, 97–98, 155
Shackleton with Discovery, 40
exploration. *See also* Arctic exploration
awards, 28, 41, 123, 172, 205, 206, 224,
285–86, 312
deaths, 49, 51, 76, 81, 82, 83, 84, 94, 230,
237, 311–12, 318
Livingstone and Stanley, 28–29
Nile River source, 23, 26, 28
Northeast Passage, 75
Northwest Passage, 3, 5, 47–49, 60–61, 222
reasons for, 3–4
explorers. *See also specific explorers*
code among, 227, 265
entrepreneur-, 3, 97, 155–56
exposé on, 172–73
with profits, 263
satire and fictional, 264
scientists and, 96–97, 100–101, 120,
228–29, 232, 245–46, 259, 262
women, 101, 102, 124, 125

Explorers Club, 231
    Cook, Frederick, and, 205, 207
    with McKinley expedition, 273–75, 277,
        289, 302, 313
    with North Pole as topic, 317

fair use practices, 266
fake news, 57–58, 142–46
Farthest North
    Amundsen, 121
    Cagni, 125
    Greely expedition, 94
    Johansen, 118, 120
    Nansen, 117, 118, 120
    Nares and, 61, 72
    Peary, Robert and, 5, 43, 171, 205,
        314, 322
Fiala, Anthony, 277–78
Field, Cyrus, 89
financial coverage, in *NYT*, 133–34, 176–77
Fiske, Stephen, 20
Fleet Street, London, 7, 180, 221
Flint, Charles R., 110, 112, 152
foreign
    correspondents, 13, 165, 211
    news, 5, 13, 15, 21–22, 57, 85–86, 126,
        165, 211
Fourth Amendment, 87
*The Fourth Estate* (trade journal), 144, 147,
    199, 305
*Fram* (ship), 117–18, 120, 121, 166
Franke, Rudolph, 207, 229, 233
Franklin, Benjamin, 19
Franklin, Jane (Lady), 49
Franklin, John (Sir), 3, 48, 49, 50, 76, 170
Franz Josef Land, 119, 121
Frederic, Harold, 165
Frederick VIII (King of Denmark), 37, 41,
    222, 225, 298
Freeman, Andrew, 321
"free silver" movement, 105, 111
Freuchen, Peter, 32, 221, 225
frostbite, 81, 124, 125, 169, 232
"fudge box," 147
Fulton, Robert, 245

Gannett, Henry, 284, 310, 311
Garfield, James A., 77
Garrett, Garet, 185, 186
George (Prince of Greece and Denmark),
    225–26
Germany, 50, 179, 327

Gibbs, Philip
    Cook, Frederick, and, 31–34, 39, 220–26,
        234, 302
    as *Daily Chronicle* reporter, 31–34, 39, 183,
        220–26, 234
    with knighthood, 327
    *NYT* and, 183, 220, 327
Gide, André, 166
Gilded Age, 57, 66, 91
Gilder, William Henry, 76, 77, 80–81,
    82, 86
*Globe and Commercial Advertiser*, New York
    (newspaper), 241, 274–75, 276
Goddard, Morrill, 128–29, 131
Godkin, E. L., 177
gold rush, 14, 98
Gould, Jay, 86–90, 194, 201, 202
Great Britain, 3, 47–50, 55, 60–62, 135,
    221, 312
"Great Moon Hoax" (1835), 144
Great Plains tribes, 24
Greeley, Horace, 12–13, 21, 54–56, 68
Greely, Adolphus, 94–96, 117, 118, 124,
    205, 263
Greely (Lady Franklin Bay) expedition,
    94–96, 117, 118, 237
Greenland, 2, 3, 6, 48
    Danish Greenland Company, 32
    Nansen and first crossing of, 100–101
    Paris Expo and, 166
Greenland expeditions, Peary, Robert
    in 1886, 99–100
    in 1891, 101–2, 121
    in 1893, 102
    in 1894–95, 102–3
    in 1896–97, 121–22
    in 1898–1902, Cape Morris Jesup, 123–25
Grosvenor, Gilbert, 258, 284

Hall, Charles Francis, 50–51, 52, 60,
    72, 77
Hampton, Benjamin, 316
*Hampton's Magazine*, 42, 234, 285, 313–14,
    316, 321
Hand, Learned, 266
*Hans Egede* (ship), 1, 2, 6, 31, 32, 33, 35,
    220, 221
Hansen, Oscar, 223, 225
Harmsworth, Alfred, 119, 120, 123, 169
*Harper's Weekly* (magazine), 55, 95, 175
Hartley, Marcellus, 189, 190
Hastings, Hudson Bridge, 320–21

Hay, John, 141
Hayes, Isaac Israel, 72
Hearst, George (father), 129
Hearst, Phoebe (mother), 129, 130
Hearst, William Randolph, 42, 114, 171,
    192, 193, 201
  with anti-Semitism, 189
  Bennett, James Gordon, Jr., and, 194–96,
    202, 203, 209
  as New York *Evening Journal* publisher,
    138–41, 147, 189
  as *New York Journal* publisher, 129–31,
    137, 139, 155
  Ochs, Adolph, and, 189, 190, 194
  Pulitzer and, 4–5, 130–31, 137–38, 140,
    141–45, 157
  as San Francisco *Examiner* publisher, 129
Hearst news service, 35, 42
Helgesen, Henry, 317
*Henrietta* (sailboat), 18, 20
Henry (Prince of Prussia), 258
Henson, Matthew
  on Cook, Frederick, 242–43, 248, 253
  on expeditions with Peary, Robert, 100,
    101, 124–25, 171, 230, 232, 237, 239,
    322, 323
  on Greenland expeditions, 101, 124, 125
  as Inuit-language speaker, 125, 270
  on Nicaraguan canal survey, 100
  at North Pole, 323, 324
  with Peary, Robert, and racism, 239, 323
  on *Roosevelt* with press corps, 237
  with testimony of Etukishuk and Ahwelah,
    268, 269, 270
Herald Building, 18, 92, 160–62, 198,
    204, 215
the *Herald*. See New York Herald
Herbert, Wally, 323, 324
Hewitt, Abram, 111
Hill, James J., 123
Hitler, Adolf, 327
hoaxes. *See also* McKinley expedition, Cook,
    Frederick; North Pole expedition,
    Cook, Frederick
  Byrd with North Pole expedition, 319
  Crocker Land as, 171, 318
  "Great Moon," 144
  *NYS* hot-air balloon, 144
  Peary Channel discovery as, 317–18
  "Zoo," 57–58, 144
Hone, Philip, 14
House Naval Affairs Committee, 314

House of Representatives, U.S., 44, 54, 193,
    309, 314
Hovgaard, Andreas, 222
Howe & Hummel, 64
Howland, Gardiner, 203, 210
Hubbard, Thomas (General), 242, 243,
    249–50, 252–53
  with Dunkle and Loose, 300
  with *Globe and Commercial Advertiser*, 241,
    274–75, 276
  McKinley expedition and, 274–77, 283, 313
  Peary, Robert, and, 258, 259, 265, 270,
    284, 299, 311
  Peary Arctic Club and, 241, 257, 259, 260,
    276, 289
Hudson-Fulton Celebration, 244–45, 256, 257
Hudson's Bay Company, 78
Hughes, Charles Evans, 193, 194, 309
Hummel, Abe, 64
Hyde, Henry B., 113, 114, 189
Hyde, James Hazen (son), 190

ice, ships trapped in, 48–49, 75, 78, 79,
    117–18
independent press, 11, 54, 55, 58, 86, 180, 192
influenza epidemic (1918), 122
*International Herald Tribune* (newspaper), 326
International Polar Commission, 1, 208
International Polar Conference, 96
interview, Jewett murder and first, 13
Inuit (Esquimau) people, 71. *See also* dogs,
    Inuit people with
  Cape York, 103, 122, 125
  diet, 77
  on expeditions with Peary, Robert, 124,
    170, 229–30, 232, 239, 242–43,
    258, 269
  on Hall expedition, 50, 51
  language, 50, 81, 125, 270
  maps of, 270
  meteorite and, 103, 121–22
  as museum specimens, 122
  on North Pole expedition, with Cook,
    Frederick, 2, 38, 207, 223, 226, 229,
    242–43, 248, 268–69
  on *NYH* North Pole expedition with De
    Long, 82
  Peary, Robert, and treatment of, 103, 122
  with racism, 232
  on Schwatka expedition, 76–77, 100
  survival skills, 50
  testimony of, 223, 258, 268–70, 274, 289

investigative journalism, 55, 191, 192
*Investigator* (ship), 48–49
Italy, 5, 50, 121, 125

Jackson, Frederick, 119–20
Jackson, John P., 79, 80, 82–83, 84
Jacoby, Harold, 273
Japan, 141, 182
*Jeanie* (schooner), 238, 248, 249
*Jeannette* (ship), 73–75, 77–82, 84, 94, 117,
    154, 270
Jennings, Louis, 54
Jerome, Jennie, 63
Jerome, Larry, 20
Jesup, Maria (wife), 241
Jesup, Morris, 123, 170–71, 214, 241, 259
Jewett, Helen, 13
Johansen, Hjalmar, 118–19, 120
Jones, George, 54, 98, 104, 133
journalism
   awards, 186, 327
   investigative, 55, 191, 192
   politics and, 54, 56, 134–35, 171, 192,
     193–94
   school, 186
   yellow, 131, 144
journalists. *See* reporters
*The Journalist* (newspaper), 93
the *Journal*. *See* New York Journal

Kane, Elisha Kent, 50, 72, 101
Kiel, Lilian, 321
Kislingbury, Frederick (Second Lieutenant),
    95, 237
*Knoxville Chronicle* (newspaper), 68, 69
*Knoxville Tribune* (newspaper), 68–69
Kohlsaat, H. H., 111
Kuroshio Current ("Black Stream"), 71

Lady Franklin Bay (Greely) expedition, 117,
    118, 237
   cannibalism rumors, 95–96
   disaster and rescue, 94–95
Lafayette, Marquis de, 258
Lawson, Victor, 145–46
Lecointe, Georges, 302
Lehman, Herbert, 328
Lehmann-Haupt, Christopher, 322
Leopold (King of Belgium), 159
Levy-Lawson, Edward, 59
libel laws, 146, 196
*Life* (magazine), 196, 257, 263

Lincoln, Abraham, 19
Lincoln, Charles, 216
Lindbergh, Charles, 327
Linotype machine, 166–67
Livingstone, David, 5, 23–29, 56, 59, 126
Lockwood, James (Lieutenant), 94
Loewenthal, Henry, 133, 181
London
   *Daily Chronicle*, 31–34, 39, 40, 183,
    220–26, 234
   *Daily Mail*, 41, 120
   *Daily News*, 25, 38, 61, 72
   *Daily Telegraph*, 26, 27–28, 58–59
   newspapers, 4, 7, 20
   *TOL*, 26, 28, 37, 40, 86, 135, 180, 182,
    212, 223, 266, 271–72, 297, 326
Long, John Davis, 139
Lonsdale, Walter, 250, 251, 288, 290–93,
    297–98, 302
Loose, August, 293–300, 303–4
Louis XIV (King of France), 159
Luks, George, 131
*Lysistrata* (yacht), 157–59, 160

MacGahan, Januarius, 60–61
Mackay, J. W., 88–89
Mackay, Louise (wife), 88
Mackay-Bennett (Commercial Cable
    Company), 88–89, 212
MacMillan, Donald, 228–29, 232, 237, 243,
    268, 270, 318
Macon, Robert B., 311, 315
Maher, Martin, 51–52
*Maine* (cruiser), 139, 140, 149
managing editors, 106, 111, 133, 145–46,
    181–85, 190, 202, 296
maps, of Inuit people, 270
Marconi, Guglielmo, 148, 211–12
Marconi wireless, 148, 211, 212
Marie (Princess of Greece and Denmark),
    225–26
Markham, Clements (Sir), 28, 232
Marshall, Ernest, 211, 298
Marvin, Ross, 230, 238
Mathews, Shailer, 267
*Le Matin* (newspaper), 224
May, Caroline, 65
May, Fred (brother), 65–66, 67
May, William (brother), 66
Mazamas club, Portland, 313
McClellan, George B., 258
McClintock, Francis Leopold, 49, 170

McClure, Robert (Captain), 48–49
*McClure's* (magazine), 192
McKinley, William, 134, 135, 139, 141,
    145, 194
McKinley expedition, Cook, Frederick, 205
    Barrill and, 174–75, 274–83, 289
    controversy, 273–83, 287, 302
    diary of Cook, Frederick, 277
    first attempt, 172–73
    as hoax, 312–13
    photographic "proof," 175, 274–75, 277,
        289, 313
media. *See also* newspapers; press
    radio, 4, 128, 182, 212
    television, 4, 128, 323
Melville, George, 74, 78–84, 270
*Mercury*, New York (newspaper), 105,
    107, 129
Meriwether, Walter Scott, 140, 271, 272
meteorite, Cape York, 103, 121–22, 259–60
Metropolitan Opera House, 309
Mexican-American War, 14
Miller, Charles, 325
    as *NYT* chief executive, 105, 109–13
    as *NYT* editor, 104–5, 133, 152, 165,
        184–85, 327
Miller, Frances (wife), 109
Minik (Inuit boy), 122
Moore, Willis, 206, 286
Morgan, J. P., 105, 113, 257
Morgenthau, Henry, 309
muckraking, 191
Munsey, Frank, 326
*Munsey's* (magazine), 192, 263
murder, 13, 51, 52, 91
"murder squads," 155
Murphy, John, 233, 237, 263
*My Arctic Journal* (Peary, J.), 102
*My Attainment of the Pole* (Cook, F.), 316
Mylius-Erichsen, Ludwig, 317–18

Nansen, Fridtjof, 100–101, 117–21, 166,
    294, 302
Nares, George (Captain), 60, 61, 72, 77, 221
Nast, Thomas, 55
National Academy of Sciences, 259, 260, 284
*National Geographic* (magazine), 100, 101, 258
National Geographic Society, 100, 172,
    219–20, 259
    annual dinner, 205–7
    with Byrd and North Pole hoax
        expedition, 319

Cook, Frederick, and, 205–6, 286
    fundraising for Peary, Robert, 311
    with Herbert and study of Peary, Robert,
        expedition, 323, 324
    with McKinley expedition, 273
    Peary, Robert, with claim accepted by,
        284–86, 306, 309, 315, 317
    Peary, Robert, with doctored data for, 321
*The Nation* (magazine), 263
Native Americans, 24. *See also* Inuit people
navy, Great Britain, 3, 47–50, 60–62
Navy, U.S., 51, 60, 73, 74, 80, 81, 83–84
    Peary, Robert, in, 5, 99–100, 103, 123,
        169, 253, 309
    Spanish-American War, 139–41
*Nearest the Pole* (Peary, R.), 171
*New Haven Courier* (newspaper), 26
newsboys, 141, 144
*Newspaperdom* (trade journal), 127
newspapers. *See also* advertisements,
        newspaper; readership, newspapers;
        *specific newspapers*
    complaint departments, 196
    corrections in, 146, 324
    distribution, 13, 54, 129, 140–50,
        166, 186
    London, 4, 7, 20
    national culture and, 19, 55–56, 91,
        126–27, 128
    in New York City, 4, 19, 126
*The New York Times Index*, 326
*The New York Times Magazine*, 134
New York City
    newspapers in, 4, 19, 126
    subway, 188, 299
    total daily circulation, 56
New York Harbor, 13, 245
*New York Herald* (*NYH*, the *Herald*)
        (newspaper). *See also* North Pole
        expedition, *NYH*
    advertising department, 201
    with Associated Press, 15
    Bartlett in, 257
    Bennett, James Gordon, Jr., and, 4–5, 7,
        16, 21–22, 56–58, 60–62, 71–75,
        77–79, 83–84, 86, 127, 140, 154–56,
        194–97, 266–67, 283, 325
    Bennett, James Gordon, Sr., and,
        11–21, 144
    business manager, 14, 203
    circulation, 4, 12, 19, 56, 58, 149, 152, 157
    circulation manager, 14

*New York Herald (cont.)*
  city editor, 199, 201, 203, 209, 215–16
  copy editors, 200
  Cuba and, 137, 139
  *Daily Telegraph* and, 58–59
  distribution, 13
  editorials, 17, 18, 29, 194
  editors, 12, 21, 28, 200, 201, 202
  foreign news, 5, 13, 21–22, 57, 85–86,
    165, 211
  fraud accusations against, 28–29, 30, 57
  Hall expedition in, 51–52
  Herald Building, 18, 92, 160–62, 198,
    204, 215
  with Livingstone, 23–29, 56
  McKinley expedition and, 275–76,
    279–80, 283, 313
  with North Pole and Cook, Frederick, 1–3,
    6–7, 37–42, 155, 222, 244, 245, 246,
    258, 261–63, 266, 268–70, 286, 289,
    291, 293, 294, 298, 325
  North Pole hunting in, 229
  *NYS* and, 192, 326
  *NYT* and, 5, 6, 17–18, 53, 58, 78, 83, 187,
    210–12, 216, 265–67, 277, 303, 325
  *NYTRIB* and, 85, 326
  *NYW* and, 92
  Peary, Josephine, and, 102
  Peary, Robert, and, 5, 100, 215–16,
    230, 231, 233, 240, 252–53, 254,
    256, 259
  Peary Arctic Club and, 154
  personal ads in, 194–96, 210
  polar exploration funding and, 84, 154–56
  printing press, 161
  readership, 11–12, 56, 57, 196, 263
  reporters, 5, 13, 14, 18, 21–30, 51–52, 58,
    60, 61–62, 71–84, 86, 96, 140, 145,
    155, 159, 161, 165, 199, 200–203,
    210–11, 235, 242, 249, 252–53, 271
  revenue, 4, 19, 165, 325
  scoops, 6–7, 14–15, 18–19, 24, 27, 56, 57,
    86, 200, 271
  Spanish-American War and, 140, 141
  staff exodus from, 211, 216
  story budget, 21–22, 24, 25, 29, 57, 58, 59,
    60, 86
  with telegraph system, 1, 2, 5, 6, 14–15, 87
  transatlantic cables and, 86, 199
  with Tweed Ring and anticorruption, 55
  with "untouchables" list, 202–3
  U.S. Civil War in, 18–19, 56

  weather bureau, 57, 74
  "Zoo Hoax" in, 57–58, 144
New York Herald Corporation, 196, 199,
    203, 210–11, 325
*New York Journal* (the *Journal*) (newspaper),
    136, 146, 151, 192, 209
  as the *American*, 195
  circulation, 139, 152
  city and managing editors, 202
  Hearst, William Randolph, and, 129–31,
    137, 139, 155
  with "murder squads," 155
  as *New York Morning Journal*, 129
  reporters, 130, 145, 195
  Spanish-American War and, 138, 139,
    140, 141, 147
  "Yellow Kid" comic strip in, 131
*New York Mirror* (newspaper), 54
*New York Morning Journal* (newspaper), 129.
    *See also New York Journal*
*New York Press* (newspaper), 131, 264
New York Stock Exchange, 88
*New York Sun* (*NYS*, *The Sun*) (newspaper),
    66, 92, 105, 183
  with Associated Press, 15
  balloon hoax in, 144
  carrier pigeons and, 15
  circulation, 149
  Dana and, 21
  decline, 155
  "Great Moon Hoax" in, 144
  lawsuit payout by, 11
  McKinley expedition and, 275
  *NYH* and, 192, 326
  *NYT* and, 266
  with Peary, Robert, and 1891 Greenland
    expedition, 101
  personal attacks by, 12, 29, 30
  Polar controversy in, 247, 254–55, 291
  reporters, 145
  Van Anda and, 181, 182
*New York Times* (*NYT*) (newspaper)
  advertisements, 105, 149–52, 197
  business manager, 184–85, 191–92
  bylines, 183, 273, 290
  circulation, 55, 104, 149–52
  circulation manager, 150, 184
  city editor, 58, 210, 212, 216
  columnists, 272–73
  on Cook, Frederick, and North Pole
    expedition, 220, 250
  corrections in, 324

Cuba and, 137, 140
*Daily Chronicle* in London and, 220, 223
Dana on, 53
decline, 104–6, 107–8
distribution, 54, 149–50, 166
editorials, 53, 54, 134–35, 190, 327
editors, 54, 104–5, 112, 133, 152, 165,
    181, 184, 185, 254, 285, 311, 327
Europe and popularity of, 179–80
with expedition funding, 5, 155, 216,
    231–34
financial coverage in, 133–34, 176–77
Gibbs and, 183, 220, 327
Jones and, 54, 98, 104, 133
Lady Franklin Bay expedition in, 95–96
Loewenthal and, 133, 181
McKinley expedition and, 273–74, 275,
    276, 280
Miller, Charles, and, 104–5, 109–13, 133,
    152, 165, 184–85, 327
with newsroom and business firewall,
    135, 183
on North Pole hunting, 228–29
*NYH* and, 5, 6, 17–18, 53, 58, 78, 83, 187,
    210–12, 216, 265–67, 277, 303, 325
*NYS and*, 266
*NYTRIB* and, 182
*NYW* and, 191, 266
Ochs, Adolph, and, 4–5, 114, 127,
    132–36, 148–53, 164–68, 176–92,
    210–12, 272, 304, 326–28
Ochs, Adolph, with purchase of, 107–14
on open polar sea, 72
at Paris Expo, 165–67, 179
Peary, Robert, and, 100, 208, 214, 215,
    230–31, 241, 255, 266, 285, 299,
    309–11, 316, 318–19, 326
Polar controversy in, 270–72, 274,
    276–77, 279, 286–87, 290, 292–96,
    298–99, 303–4, 325
politics and, 134–35
price reduction, 150–51, 152
promotional schemes, 212–13
with Pulitzer Prize, 327
Raymond and, 21, 53, 54
readership, 53–54, 139, 146, 149, 151, 152,
    183, 185, 196, 263, 298–99
Reick at, 211–12, 216, 270–72, 274, 276,
    277, 283, 288–89, 293–96, 299, 300,
    304, 305–6, 313
reporters, 97–98, 155, 165, 183, 211, 212,
    271, 272, 298

restoring, 132–36, 164–65
revenue, 150, 153, 164
Saturday book review, 134
with Schwatka and Alaska expedition,
    97–98, 155
scoops, 182, 219, 293–96, 319
slogan, 136, 267, 299, 328
story budget, 326
Sunday supplement, 134, 151
Times Tower, 187–90, 212
*TOL* and, 180, 182, 212, 271–72, 326
with Tweed Ring and anticorruption,
    54–55, 104, 192, 295, 305
Van Anda and, 181–85, 190, 210, 212,
    216, 271, 272, 287, 304, 326, 327
with wireless news service, 212
World War I and, 183–84, 185,
    326–27
New York Times Company
    Miller, Charles, and, 105, 109–13
    Ochs, Adolph, and, 148, 152–53, 165, 177,
        189, 210, 272
    reorganization committee, 106, 110–13
    shareholders, 110–12, 133, 135, 152–53,
        177, 185, 189
    stock, 113, 165, 177
*New-York Tribune* (*NYTRIB*, the *Tribune*)
    (newspaper), 18, 66, 137, 140, 167
    with Associated Press, 15
    circulation, 149, 152
    Greeley and, 12, 21, 56
    *NYH* and, 85, 326
    *NYS* and, 326
    *NYT* and, 182
    Peary, Robert, and, 214, 241
    polar exploration, funding and, 155
    Reid and decline of, 56
*New York World* (*NYW*, *The World*)
    (newspaper), 151, 229, 263,
    292, 312
    business manager, 130, 141, 155, 204, 209
    circulation, 128–29, 152
    city editor, 143, 216
    Cook, Frederick, and, 313
    on corruption, 190
    Cuba and, 137, 145
    editors, 128–29, 131, 143
    *The Evening World*, 138
    with North Pole and Cook, Frederick,
        246–48, 249, 250–51, 297
    *NYH* and, 92
    *NYT* and, 191, 266

*New York World (cont.)*
  Peary, Robert, and, 122, 268
  polar exploration, funding and, 155
  Pulitzer and, 4, 89–92, 127–28, 141–42,
    192, 200
  readership, 90–91, 92, 128, 136
  reporters, 91, 93, 129, 130, 143, 146, 181,
    182, 183, 236–38, 250–51, 262
  revenue, 130, 164
  satire and fictional explorers in, 264
  with Schwatka and Yellowstone National
    Park, 98
  "sob stories" in, 91, 128
  Spanish-American War and, 139, 140,
    141, 147
  *Sunday World*, 128–29
  World Building, 92, 160
  "Yellow Kid" comic strip in, 128, 131
New York Yacht Club, 17, 20, 56, 203
Nicaraguan canal survey, 99–100
Nile River, 23, 26, 28, 158
Nindemann, William, 80, 81
Nordenskiöld, Nils Adolf Erik, 74–75, 78,
  83, 222
*Norge* (airship), 319
Norman-Hansen, C. M., 224, 233, 263
Noros, Louis, 80, 81
*North American Review* (magazine), 19
Northeast Passage, 75
North Pole, 38, 44, 47, 50, 52, 72. *See also*
  Farthest North
  Amundsen as discoverer of, 319, 320, 322
  Explorers Club and topic of, 317
  Henson at, 323, 324
  *My Attainment of the Pole*, 316
  *Nearest the Pole*, 171
  opinions on merits of reaching, 228–30,
    263, 267, 299
  *Peary at the North Pole*, 322
  Plaisted with snowmobiles at, 323
  *To the Top of the Continent*, 274
North Pole expedition (1879), *NYH*, 60,
  61–62
  De Long, George Washington, and,
    71–75, 78–84, 94, 303
  disaster, 77–84
  funding costs, 84
  Inuit guide on, 82
North Pole expedition (1907), Cook,
  Frederick
  account of, 2–3, 33–34, 37–39, 40–41,
    229–33, 268–69, 280

cache, 249, 268, 288, 295, 303, 312
*The Case for Doctor Cook*, 321
with claim denied by University of
  Copenhagen, 300–302, 303, 310
diary, 33, 39, 41, 102, 220, 248, 290,
  292, 304
documentation, 38, 39
with documentation forged, 293–98, 305
dogs on, 2, 32, 37, 269
doubts and controversy about, 6, 33–34,
  37–38, 40–41, 219–26, 228, 230–31,
  242–43, 245–55, 258–60, 262–74,
  276–77, 279, 285–306, 325
evidence against success of, 322
homecoming, 244–51
instruments used, 33, 38, 39
Inuit guides on, 2, 38, 207, 223, 226, 229,
  242–43, 248, 268–69
*My Attainment of the Pole*, 316
*NYH* with, 1–3, 6–7, 37–42, 155, 222,
  244, 245, 246, 258, 261–63, 266,
  268–70, 286, 289, 291, 293, 294,
  298, 325
*NYS* with, 247, 254–55, 291
*NYT* on, 220, 250
*NYW* with, 246–48, 249, 250–51
Peary, Robert, with criticism of, 208, 215,
  230–31
telegram, 1, 2, 5, 6
with testimony of Inuit guides, 223, 258,
  268–70, 274, 289
*To the Top of the Continent*, 274
University of Copenhagen and, 42
validation and support for, 38, 41
welcome at Copenhagen, 33–37
North Pole expedition (1908–09), Peary,
  Robert, 6
  accounts, 228–33, 242
  claim accepted by National Geographic
    Society, 284–86, 306, 309, 315, 317
  claim accepted by RGS, 312
  claim accepted by University of
    Copenhagen, 306
  diary, 310, 314, 318, 321
  evidence against success of, 320–22, 323
  funding for, 5, 213–16, 231–34, 241
  National Geographic Society, Herbert and
    study of, 323, 324
  navigational methods, 315
  news of success, 43–44
  *Peary at the North Pole*, 322
  with press corp on *Roosevelt*, 236–39

North Pole expeditions
    Byrd with hoax, 319
    Lady Franklin Bay, 94–96, 117, 118, 237
    *Norge* (airship), 319
    Peary, Robert, in 1905–06, 169–71
Northwest Passage, 3, 5, 47–49,
        60–61, 222
*NYH. See New York Herald*
*NYS. See New York Sun*
*NYT. See New York Times*
*NYTRIB. See New-York Tribune*
*NYW. See New York World*

Ochs, Adolph, 231, 285
    automobile race and, 212–13
    Bennett, James Gordon, Jr., and, 5, 67,
        152, 168, 178, 185, 187, 211,
        266, 325
    as *Chattanooga Daily Times* publisher,
        69, 106, 107, 108, 110, 111
    death, 327–28
    early life, 67–68
    family, 106–7, 113–14, 177–79
    Hearst, William Randolph, and, 189,
        190, 194
    legacy, 187–88, 327–28
    with managing editors, 181–84
    newspaper experience, 68–70, 129
    *The New York Times Index* and, 326
    as *NYT* publisher, 4–5, 114, 127, 132–36,
        148–53, 164–68, 176–92, 210–12,
        272, 304, 326–28
    with *NYT* purchase, 107–14
    personal attacks on, 189, 194
    Reick and, 210–12, 216
Ochs, Bertha (mother), 68, 178–79
Ochs, Effie (Wise) (wife), 107, 108, 113–14,
        132, 178, 179, 219
Ochs, George (brother), 68, 106, 153, 166,
        167, 168, 178
Ochs, Iphigene (daughter), 107, 177, 178,
        179, 327–28
Ochs, Julius (father), 67–68, 106, 107
Ochs, Milton (brother), 68, 106
Ochs Building, 107
O'Connor, T. P., 28
*Olympia* (cruiser), 140
Ooqueah (Inuit guide), 232
Ootah (Inuit guide), 232
open polar sea, 71, 72, 83
*Oregonian* (newspaper), 313
Osborn, Henry Fairfield, 259–60

*Oscar II* (ship), 234, 244, 245
Outcault, Richard F., 131
*Outing* magazine, 172

Paine, Ralph, 200, 203
Pancoast, George, 131
*Pandora* (ship), 60–61, 72–73, 76
Panikpah (Inuit guide), 269
paper, cheap, 55, 127
Paris Expo (1900), 164, 165–67, 179
*The Paris Herald* (newspaper), 162–63, 167,
        179, 202, 211, 228, 266
Parker, Herschel, 174, 273, 277–78, 289, 313
Park Row, New York City, 19, 21, 29, 104,
        114, 130, 177, 187–88
Pavy, Octave, 96
Peary, Josephine (Diebitsch) (wife), 100, 230,
        234, 239, 314
    on Greenland expeditions, 101, 102,
        124, 125
    with homecoming of Peary, Robert, 240,
        256, 257
    on mental breakdown of Peary, Robert, 318
    with Minik returning home, 122
Peary, Marie (daughter), 99, 102, 124, 234,
        240, 318
Peary, Mary (mother), 99, 100, 102
Peary, Robert. *See also* Greenland
        expeditions, Peary, Robert; North
        Pole expedition, Peary
    Bennett, James Gordon, Jr., and, 259
    with book and nine-part *Hampton's* series,
        313–14
    Bridgman, Herbert, and, 227–28, 231,
        234, 241, 243, 256–58, 263, 283, 288
    childhood, 99
    congressional hearings of 1911 and,
        314–18, 320, 321
    controversy, 230–31, 233, 239, 242,
        249–50, 253, 272, 318
    Cook, Frederick, and, 43–44, 101–2,
        124–25, 148, 172, 205–8, 215, 227–34,
        237–42, 244, 248–50, 252–55,
        258–61, 263–65, 283, 288–89, 298,
        305, 311, 314, 316–18, 320, 322
    death of, 318
    drive and ambition, 43, 100, 101, 124
    with exploration awards, 123, 172, 205,
        206, 285–86, 312
    family, 100, 102, 124, 125, 243, 258
    Farthest North and, 5, 43, 171, 205,
        314, 322

Peary, Robert (*cont.*)
  finances, 314
  with frostbitten feet, 124, 125, 169
  with funding, 5, 123, 154, 170–71,
      213–16, 231–34, 241, 311, 318
  Henson and, 100, 101, 124–25, 171, 230,
      232, 237, 239, 322, 323
  homecoming, 240, 242, 243, 252, 256–58
  Hubbard and, 258, 259, 265, 270, 284,
      299, 311
  hypercompetitiveness of, 101, 124
  Inuit people and treatment by, 103, 122
  legacy, 98, 315–16, 317, 320–22
  mental breakdown, 318
  Nansen and, 100–101, 120
  at National Geographic Society annual
      dinner, 205–7
  Nicaraguan canal survey and, 99–100
  with North Pole expedition in 1905–06,
      169–71
  *NYH* and, 5, 100, 215–16, 230, 231, 233,
      240, 252–53, 254, 256, 259
  *NYT* and, 100, 208, 214, 215, 230–31,
      241, 255, 285, 299, 309–11, 316,
      318–19, 326
  *NYTRIB* and, 214, 241
  *NYW* and, 122, 268
  with Peary Channel discovery as hoax,
      317–18
  with racism, 232, 239, 323
  with Reick at *NYT*, 270–72, 276, 277,
      283, 288–89, 293, 299, 305–6
  Roosevelt, Theodore, and, 169, 205,
      206–7, 214, 257, 265
  speaking tour, 285, 311
  Sverdrup and, 123, 124
  tribute at Metropolitan Opera House, 309
  in U.S. Navy, 5, 99–100, 103, 123, 169,
      253, 309
  victory lap in Europe, 312
Peary, Robert, Jr. (son), 234, 240
Peary Arctic Club, 233
  Bridgman, Herbert, and, 124–25, 170,
      227, 269
  honorary dinner, 285
  Hubbard and, 241, 257, 259, 260, 276,
      284, 289
  Jesup, Morris, with funding, 170–71
  *NYH* and, 154
  with testimony of Etukishuk and Ahwelah,
      269, 270
*Peary at the North Pole* (Rawlins), 322

Peary Channel, 317–18
Perris, E. A., 221, 225
personal ads, in *NYH*, 194–96, 210
Petermann, August, 71, 72, 73
Philadelphia Academy of Natural Sciences,
      101, 103
photographers, 35, 140, 228, 236
Picasso, Pablo, 166
pigeons, carrier, 15
Plaisted, Ralph, 323
Poe, Edgar Allan, 144
"polar anaemia" ("winter-over syndrome"), 155
*Polaris*, Hall expedition and, 50–51, 52, 60, 72
police, 15, 32, 36, 57–58, 137, 246
politics, journalism and, 54, 56, 134–35,
      171, 192, 193–94
*Politiken* (newspaper), 2, 42, 233, 263
postage rates, 191
Postal Telegraph Company, 88
press corps, 13, 37–39, 42, 235–39, 245–47
presses, printing, 132, 141
  with color ink, 128, 131, 163
  Hoe, 131
  *NYH*, 161
  Paris Expo exhibit, 166–67
  steam-run, 56
printers, 68
*Printers' Ink* (trade magazine), 70, 187
Printz, Fred, 174, 275–76, 279–82
Pritchard, Billy, 237–38, 240
Proctor, Redfield, 145
promotional schemes, 127, 136, 212–13, 318
Pulitzer, Joseph
  Bennett, James Gordon, Jr., and, 91–92,
      194, 202, 204, 265, 266
  Hearst, William Randolph, and, 4–5,
      130–31, 137–38, 140, 141–45, 157
  with journalism school at Columbia
      University, 186
  as *NYW* publisher, 4, 89–92, 127–28,
      141–42, 192, 200
  personal attacks on, 91
  as *St. Louis Post-Dispatch* owner, 90
  in U.S. Civil War, 90
Pulitzer Prizes, 186, 327
*Putnam's Magazine*, 71

Qisuk (Inuit tribal leader), 122

racism, 69, 150, 178, 185, 189, 232, 239, 323
radio, 4, 128, 182, 212
Rainey, Paul, 312

Rasmussen, Dagmar (wife), 32, 223, 224, 225
Rasmussen, Knud, 32, 38, 223–24, 226, 279, 298, 301, 312
Rawlins, Dennis, 322
Raymond, Henry Jarvis, 21, 53, 54
Rea, George Bronson, 203
readership, newspapers
  competition for, 4, 5, 147–48
  *New York Journal*, 136
  *NYH*, 11–12, 56, 57, 196, 263
  *NYT*, 53–54, 139, 146, 149, 151, 152, 183, 185, 196, 263, 298–99
  *NYW*, 90–91, 92, 128, 136
  reporters and, 144–45
real estate, 57, 107, 133, 189, 204, 209
*The Recorder* (newspaper), 105, 112, 114
Reick, William C.
  as New York Herald Corporation president, 210–11
  as *NYH* city editor, 199, 201, 203, 209, 215
  at *NYT*, 211–12, 216, 270–72, 274, 276, 277, 283, 288–89, 293–96, 299, 300, 304, 305–6, 313
  Ochs, Adolph, and, 210–12, 216
Reid, Whitelaw, 56, 134
relief expeditions, 24–26, 48, 124
Remsen, Ira, 259, 260
reporters (journalists)
  the *American*, 195
  crime, 201
  *Daily Chronicle*, London, 31–34, 39, 183, 220–26, 234
  death of, 81, 82, 83, 84, 165
  foreign correspondents, 13, 165, 211
  as globe-trotting swashbucklers, 58
  investigative, 55, 191, 192
  *New York Journal*, 130, 145, 195
  *NYH*, 5, 13, 14, 18, 21–30, 51–52, 58, 60, 61–62, 71–84, 86, 96, 140, 145, 155, 159, 161, 165, 199, 200–203, 210–11, 235, 242, 249, 252–53, 271
  *NYS*, 145
  *NYT*, 97–98, 155, 165, 183, 211, 212, 271, 272, 298
  *NYTRIB*, 58
  *NYW*, 91, 93, 129, 130, 143, 146, 181, 182, 183, 236–38, 250–51, 262
  readership and, 144–45
  *TOL*, 37, 223
Republican Party, 54, 104, 134, 265, 317

rescues
  Lady Franklin Bay expedition, 94–95
  *Polaris* crew, 51, 52
RGS (Royal Geographical Society), 25, 28, 78, 119, 123, 232, 312
*Rodgers*, USS, 78, 80
Rodin, Auguste, 166
Rood, Henry, 234
*Roosevelt* (icebreaker), 43, 207, 228, 230, 231, 233, 234, 249
  with Hudson-Fulton Celebration, 256, 257
  looting of, 243
  Peary Arctic Club and funds for, 170–71
  on Peary expedition, 242, 253
  press corp and Peary, Robert, on, 236–39
Roosevelt, Franklin Delano, 322
Roosevelt, Theodore, 5, 123, 140, 262
  on Bennett, James Gordon, Jr., 162
  on corruption, 190–91
  Hearst, W. R. and, 193, 194
  Peary, Robert, and, 169, 205, 206–7, 214, 257, 265
Royal Danish Geographical Society, 35, 41, 222, 224, 246
Royal Geographical Society (RGS), 25, 28, 78, 119, 123, 232, 312
Royal Navy (Great Britain), 3, 47–50, 60–62
Rusk, C. E., 313
Russia, 50, 79, 166, 182, 322
Russo-Turkish War, 61

Sadayakko (Madame), 166
St. Elias mountain range, 97, 98
*St. Louis Post-Dispatch* (newspaper), 90
Samuels, Sam (Captain), 20
Schiff, Jacob, 105, 113, 190, 309
Schley, Winfield (Admiral), 94, 95, 96, 305–6
Schwatka, Frederick (Lieutenant)
  Alaska expedition for *NYT*, 97–98, 155
  Canadian Arctic expedition and, 76–77, 81, 100
  with native travel methods, 76–77, 100, 170
*Scientific American* (magazine), 315
scientists, explorers and, 96–97, 100–101, 120, 228–29, 232, 245–46, 259, 262
scoops
  *Globe and Commercial Advertiser*, 275
  *NYH*, 6–7, 14–15, 18–19, 24, 27, 56, 57, 86, 200, 271
  *NYT*, 182, 219, 293–96, 319
  strategies for securing, 24, 27
Scott, Robert Falcon, 303, 311–12

*Scribner's* (magazine), 146–47
scurvy, 49, 61, 77, 233
Seeglo (Inuit guide), 232
Seilhamer, George, 30
Seitz, Don, 130, 141, 155, 204, 209
Senate, U.S., 145, 309, 317
sensationalism, 13, 138
sex, 13, 14, 53, 64, 130, 195, 317
Shackleton, Ernest, 38, 40
Siemens, 88
slavery, 17–18, 24
Smith, George, 58–59
"sob sisters," 129
"sob stories," 91, 128, 129
society column, 12
South Pole, 38, 40, 311–12, 319
Spain, U.S. and, 137–41, 147, 148, 165, 209
Speke, John Hanning, 23
*Standard-Union*, Brooklyn (newspaper), 227
Stanley, Henry Morton, 98, 303
   Livingstone and, 5, 23–29, 56, 59, 126
   as *NYH* reporter, 5, 22, 23–30, 86
   with violence against African porters, 73
starvation, 39, 49, 80–81, 94–96, 137, 145,
   170, 237
State Department, U.S., 286, 289–90, 306
Stead, W. T.
   Cook, Frederick, and, 35–37, 43, 221,
     224–25, 302
   on Hearst, William Randolph, 193
   on Peary, Robert, 249, 254
   on Sunday editions, 128
Steffens, Lincoln, 6, 146–47, 172–73
Stern, Louis, 177
Stickney, Joseph, 140
Stokes, Frederick, 285
Stone, Melville, 111, 134
Straus, Nathan, 183
Strömgren, Elis, 41, 222, 223, 224, 225, 297,
   298, 301
subway, New York City, 188, 299
Sulzberger, Arthur, 151, 327, 328
Sunday supplement, *NYT*, 134, 151
*Sunday World* (newspaper), 128–29. *See also*
   *New York World*
*The Sun. See New York Sun*
Sverdrup, Otto (Captain), 38, 118, 123–24,
   222, 294

Taft, William Howard, 262, 309, 317
Tammany Hall, 15, 54, 135
Tarr, Ralph, 273–74

technology, 22, 48, 148, 166–67, 211, 319.
   *See also* telegraph system
telegraph system
   *NYH* with, 1, 2, 5, 6, 14–15, 87
   Postal Telegraph Company, 88
   rates, 15, 57, 86–89, 140, 326
   scoop strategies and, 24, 27
   transatlantic cable, 57, 85–88, 148, 199,
     271–72
   Western Union and, 87
*The Telegraph*, London. *See Daily Telegraph*
television, 4, 128, 323
temperance, 12, 177
*Le Temps* (journal), 39
Tennyson, Alfred, 49
*Terror* (ship), 48
timber, paper and, 55, 127
Times Building, 285
Times Square, 187–88, 212
*The Times*, London (*TOL*) (newspaper), 26,
   28, 40, 86, 135, 266
   *NYT* and, 180, 182, 212, 271–72, 326
   Polar controversy and, 297
   reporters, 37, 223
Times Tower, 187–90, 212
*Titanic* (ship), 182, 326
Tittmann, Otto H., 284, 310, 317
Tlingit people, 97
*TOL. See The Times*, London
Torp, Carl, 41, 226
Torrence, Joseph, 114
*To the Top of the Continent* (Cook, F.), 274
Trans-Siberian Railway, 166
Trask, Spencer, 110, 114, 151, 153, 168
the *Tribune. See New-York Tribune*
Twain, Mark (Samuel Clemens),
   22, 57, 264
Tweed, William "Boss," 54–55, 104, 192,
   295, 305
*Tyrian* (cable ship), 235–36, 238, 271

Union army, 90
United Press (wire service), 235
United States (U.S.)
   Air Force, 322
   with Alaska purchase, 50
   with Arctic problem, 3
   Army, 24, 76, 94
   Civil War, 18–19, 56, 67, 90
   Coast and Geodetic Survey, 229, 317
   Congress, 84, 265, 309–11, 314–18,
     320–21

House of Representatives, 44, 54, 193, 309, 314

Navy, 5, 51, 60, 73, 74, 80, 81, 83–84, 99–100, 103, 123, 139–41, 169, 253, 309

Senate, 145, 309, 317

Spain and, 137–41, 147, 148, 165, 209

State Department, 286, 289–90, 306

University of Copenhagen, 42, 222, 224, 225–26, 246, 259, 260, 261, 262, 286

Cook, Frederick, with claim denied, 300–302, 303, 310

Cook, Frederick, with forged proofs for, 293–98, 305

on diary of Cook, Frederick, 304

Peary, Robert, with claim accepted by, 306

Polar controversy and pressure on, 289–90

Untermyer, Samuel, 183

U.S. *See* United States

Usaakassak (Inuit boy), 122

Valdemar (Prince of Denmark), 37

Van Anda, Carr
as *NYT* city editor, 210, 212, 216
as *NYT* managing editor, 181–85, 190
with objectivity, 184
with Polar controversy for *NYT*, 271, 272, 287, 304
*Titanic* coverage for *NYT* and, 182, 326
World War I coverage for *NYT* and, 327

*Vega* (ship), 75, 78, 222

Verhoeff, John, 102

Verne, Jules, 72

Victoria (Queen of England), 13, 20, 28, 127

Wack, Henry Wellington, 277, 283, 288, 290–92, 296

Wake, Charles, 292, 296, 302–3

Wallace, Dillon, 263

Wall Street, 11, 12, 180, 189, 190

*The Wall Street Journal* (newspaper), 134

Ward, Charles Henshaw, 320, 321, 322

Ward, Florence (wife), 321

*The Washington Post* (newspaper), 254

*Washington Times* (newspaper), 254

Watterson, Henry, 68

weather bureau, *NYH*, 57, 74

Weed, E. D., 279, 280

Wellman, Walter, 156, 290

Western Union, 87

White, Stanford, 160, 161

Whitney, Harry, 237–38, 239, 248–50, 262, 263, 272, 312

Wiley, Louis, 150, 184–85, 191–92

Williams, James, 203

*Windward* (relief ship), 119, 120, 123–24, 169

"winter-over syndrome" ("polar anaemia"), 155

wireless news service, 212

Wise, Effie. *See* Ochs, Effie

women
with breach-of-promise suits, 64
explorers, 101, 102, 124, 125
"sob sisters," 129

Woolnough, W. L., 150–52

World Building, 92, 160

*The World. See New York World*

*The World Today* (magazine), 267

World War I, 183–84, 185, 326–27

Wright, Wilbur, 213

Yale University Press, 321

yellow journalism, 131, 144

yellow journals, 4, 134, 136–37, 138, 139, 141, 145, 191

"Yellow Kid" (comic strip), 128, 131

Yellowstone National Park, 98

Young, Allen (Captain), 60, 61, 72, 76

"Zoo Hoax," in *NYH*, 57–58, 144